Michael Grant is a distinguished historian and populariser of the ancient world. He has held many academic posts, including those of Fellow of Trinity College, Cambridge, Professor of Humanity at Edinburgh University and Vice Chancellor of the Queen's University, Belfast. He now lives and writes in Italy

MYTHS
OF THE GREEKS
& ROMANS

Michael Grant

A PHOENIX GIANT PAPERBACK

First published in Great Britain
by Weidenfeld and Nicolson in 1962
Revised paperback edition published in 1989
This paperback published in 1994
by Phoenix, a division of Orion Books Ltd,
Orion House, 5 Upper St Martin's Lane,
London WC2H 9EA

Reissued 1998

Printed and bound in Great Britain by
Butler & Tanner Ltd, Frome and London

ISBN 1 85799 121 4

CONTENTS

CONTENTS

CONTENTS

PART VI: HEROIC SEARCHERS

PART VII: THE THOUSAND FACES OF LOVE

CONTENTS

GENEALOGICAL TABLES

FOREWORD

THE MYTHS told by the Greeks and Romans are as important as history for our understanding of what those peoples, ancestors of our own civilization, believed and thought and felt, and expressed in writing and in visual art. For their mythologies were inextricably interwoven, to an extent far beyond anything in our own experience, with the whole fabric of their public and private lives.

And then without these myths we should be hard put to it to understand the arts and literature and ways of thinking of the west, and of many other parts of the world as well, during the centuries that have passed since the classical world came to an end. Time after time these products of ancient imagination have been used to inspire fresh creative efforts, which amount to a substantial part of our whole cultural inheritance. Such renewals and adaptations have often seemed far removed, in character and spirit, from the original tradition; yet they stem directly from it, and are unimaginable without it.

> The intelligible forms of ancient poets,
> The fair humanities of old religion,
> The Power, the Beauty, and the Majesty,
> That had their haunts in dale, or piny mountain,
> Or forest by slow stream, or pebbly spring,
> Or chasms and watery depths: all these have vanished.
> They live no longer in the faith of reason!
> But still the heart doth need a language, still
> Doth the old instinct bring back the old names. . .

And so even communities professing that quite different code of beliefs which is Christianity have, after various struggles, found it impracticable to dispense with the classical stories. Today new political systems have fabricated their own myths which Coleridge, writing those lines under the Graeco-Roman spell, had never imagined. Yet twentieth-century writers, from tragic theatre to comic strip, have continued to employ the archetypes with renewed vigour. These dramatic, concrete, individual, insistently probing ancient myths still supplement the deductions of science as clues to much in the world that does not alter.

The atmosphere to which they translate us is life-enhancing; for it gives us fresh strength by providing a route of escape. The escape is from day-to-day reality, of which, as we know, it is not possible to endure very much. Yet this is not escapism of any ordinary kind, for the road leads to another sort of reality, a more imposing sort, than the reality which dominates our ordinary lives. At times, in receptive conditions, these myths generate and throw off potent, almost violent, flashes of inextinguishable, universal truths. Those are not of course, as far as we are concerned, the religious truths which (among much else) the Greeks and Romans saw in their mythology. However they are truths that still impinge, sometimes with ungovernable force, upon the mind and feelings, and illuminate aspects of our human condition.

This particular brand of enlightenment is difficult or impossible to grasp by more logical and rational means, and would elude non-mythical presentation. Yet it would be wrong to say that myths seem modern or topical; they are as relevant to our time as to any other, no more no less. That is to say, they are not specifically antique either. They are ostensibly lodged, it is true, within a certain framework of the remote past, but that does not impede their perpetual compulsive tenacity. Indeed, their relevance to life's basic, continuing situations is sharpened into high relief by this setting which, though ancient in origin and form, remains unaffected by temporal circumstances.

For the images of myth, once they have stirred our perceptions, precipitate them into a new, unforeseen dimension outside time.

The Greeks and Romans, although in different epochs they saw mythology in different lights, were by training and inclination ready to enter this exciting, unearthly dimension of timelessness, this

> Dark, illimitable ocean, without bound,
> Without dimension, where length and breadth and height,
> And time and place, are lost.

Heavy with unplumbed meaning is this ocean—beckoning, inviting immersion and obsession. Perhaps after so long a time we can only reach its shallows; yet we shall be losing an irreplaceable experience if we do not go as deep as we can. But we need, for this enterprise, a more detailed preparation than the ancients needed.

Each myth means something different to everybody who reads and studies it. The stories are hard to forget; feelings about them come unpredictably. Their underlying qualities do not readily yield to definition or classification—still less to weird searches for mystic hidden meanings and anachronistic allegories. Above all, as I hope will become clear, they are varied. *No single theory*, however valuably suggestive, will suffice to explain the whole range of Greek and Roman mythology, or even a major proportion of its content. Indeed, such all-embracing theories (of which there are many), whether put forward by anthropologists or classicists or psychoanalysts or scholars of religion, present the most dangerous hazard which students of this strange subject will encounter. And in this field we are exceptionally vulnerable to hazards, since we almost all come to it after an education in which the myths are neglected or, to the accompaniment of gutless illustrations, reduced to whimsical travesty.

So the only safe hope would seem to be the Horatian maxim:

> Ask not, to what Doctors I apply;
> Sworn to no Master, of no Sect am I.

Or, better, go to as many of the doctors as one can, and sit at their feet, and from all of them accept something—though (since they contradict one another) obviously not everything. For each of these different kinds of scholar that I mentioned has during the present century, in spite of these all too comprehensive theories, added to our realization that mythology is something far more serious than the primitive, unreflecting, childish precursor of science or of developed religion that it was formerly believed to be. Indeed, the revitalizing of the classical myths can be claimed as the most significant of all the impacts that the Graeco-Roman world has made upon modern thought.

I have included in this book not only purely fictional stories which everyone would classify as myths, and the folk-tales and fairy-tales which are their younger sisters, but also some of those sagas and legends which build imaginatively upon at least a minimum of historical basis. However, there are thousands of these various tales, and rather than attempt a dictionary I have wanted to say something about each one that I include. So I am selecting those which seem to me, for one reason or another, the most important and necessary; though, once you leave agreed territory such as Homer and the *Agamemnon*, this is a subjective process in which everyone would provide a different list.

Before discussing each theme, I shall tell the story which it comprises: since the actual course of 'events' often tends to be forgotten—eclipsed by other, high-lighted elements—when the myths are currently discussed. I was also encouraged by reading a remark by C. S. Lewis that the significant something, the something of great power and moment, which each of the basic myths seems to suggest, is communicable not only when a good ancient author tells them but even in the most atrocious modern summary.

Nevertheless, it would be misleading to ignore the principal ancient literary expressions of these stories—the sparks which they ignited in writers of genius. I have, therefore, made my summaries of each myth follow the version (probably one of many different versions) in which it was told by its most remarkable narrator; and I have included passages from among the best modern translators that I could find. These Greek and Latin authors are taken in chronological order so as to give a general survey of the changes in the ancient world's ideas about myths. That is to say, the love-hate connection between myth and literature having, in the course of time, become very intimate, I have tried to sum up that relationship by seizing upon the outstanding encounters between the two. This will not satisfy a person who wants to look at the myths in a more primitive form than they assume even in the earliest Greek literature. Yet it was only in the hands of great writers that the power of the stories achieved its full realization, and was communicated to the world. However, the origins of a myth, although (especially in the classical field) they are seldom fully understood, need to be thought about as well: and in the discussions which in each chapter follow the narrative sections, I say something not only about the ancient author whose treatment of the theme I have chosen to describe, but about these earlier stages too. I also refer to aftermaths and repercussions, in the ancient world and in later Europe and elsewhere up to the present day.

Inevitably my debts to other writers are enormous. I also particularly want to thank Miss Jill Weldon, for choosing and collecting photographs and for much other invaluable assistance, and Mr H. M. Luther for advice on modern art. In connection with the illustrations, I wish to thank, too, those private collectors who have permitted the reproduction of works of art in their collections, as well as the representatives of museums and galleries from which objects and pictures illustrated in this book have come, and the agencies and photographers who have helped to make them available. In addition I want to record my appreciation, for help of various kinds, to Miss Martine Franck, Miss Veronica Lemmon, Professor Joseph Campbell; Dr R. A. Higgins and Dr J. P. C. Kent of the British Museum; and officials of the London Library and the Hellenic and Roman Societies.

I am grateful to the following for quotations from copyright works: E. V. Rieu and Penguin Books for *Homer: Iliad, Homer: Odyssey* and *Apollonius Rhodius: Argonautica*, Robert Graves and Penguin Books for *Apuleius: Golden Ass*, Philip Vellacott and Penguin Books for *Aeschylus: Oresteia*, W. F. Jackson Knight and Penguin Books for *Virgil: Aeneid*, A. de Selincourt and Penguin Books for *Livy: Early History of Rome*, E. F. Watling and Penguin Books for *Sophocles: Theban Plays*, F. Wood and University of

FOREWORD

Minnesota Press for *Rainer Maria Rilke: The Ring of Forms*, D. Grene, R. Lattimore, W. Arrowsmith, E. T. Vermeule, E. Wyckoff, J. Moore, M. Jameson and University of Chicago Press for *Complete Greek Tragedies*, R. Lattimore and University of Chicago Press for *Homer: The Iliad, Odes of Pindar, Greek Lyrics, Greek Tragedies*, R. Lattimore and University of Michigan Press for *Hesiod: Works and Days and Theogony*, A. E. Watts and University of California Press for *Ovid: Metamorphoses*, J. B. Pritchard and Princeton University Press and Oxford University Press for *Ancient Near Eastern Texts*, D. Fitts and R. Fitzgerald and Oxford University Press for *Sophocles: Antigone*, D. Fitts and R. Fitzgerald and Dial Press for *Greek Plays in Modern Translation*, D. Fitts and R. Fitzgerald and Messrs. Faber and Faber for *Oedipus at Colonus* and *Euripides: Alcestis*, Messrs. Faber and Faber for *Collected Poems 1931–1958* by Edwin Muir, L. P. Wilkinson and Cambridge University Press for *Ovid Recalled*, H. G. Evelyn-White and Loeb Classical Library for *Homeric Hymns*, F. L. Lucas and Messrs. J. M. Dent for *Greek Poetry for Everyman*, M. Balkwill, Sir Maurice Bowra, T. F. Higham, Gilbert Highet, G. Allen, J. Sterling and Clarendon Press for *Oxford Book of Greek Verse in Translation*, Sir F. Fletcher and Clarendon Press for *Virgil: Aeneid VI*, J. B. Leishman and Hogarth Press for translations of R. M. Rilke, J. Mavrogordato and the Hogarth Press for *Cavafy: Poems Translated with Notes*, Rae Dalven, Harcourt Brace & World, and the Hogarth Press for *Complete Poems of Cavafy*, P. Green and Messrs. John Murray for *Essays in Antiquity*, R. Fitzgerald and Messrs. Wm. Heinemann and Doubleday for *Homer: The Odyssey*, Rolfe Humphries and Messrs. Scribner for *The Aeneid of Virgil*, A. R. Burn and Messrs. Edward Arnold for *The Lyric Age of Greece*, L. MacNeice and Messrs. Faber and Faber for *Aeschylus: Agamemnon*, R. Payne and Messrs. Heinemann for *The Wanton Nymph*, C. Day Lewis and Messrs. Jonathan Cape for *The Georgics of Virgil*, C. Day Lewis and the Hogarth Press for *Virgil: The Aeneid*, the late Professor T. A. Sinclair and Messrs. Routledge and Kegan Paul for *History of Greek Political Thought*, O. Kiefer, G. Highet and Messrs. Routledge for *Sexual Life in Ancient Rome*, R. Warner and

The Bodley Head for *Poems of George Seferis*, R. Warner, S. O'Sheed and The Bodley Head for L. R. Lind's *Ten Greek Plays in Contemporary Translation*, Mrs Yeats and Messrs. A. P. Watt and Messrs. Macmillan for *Sophocles' King Oedipus* translated by W. B. Yeats, Richard Aldington and Messrs. Chatto and Windus for *Euripides: Alcestis*, H. T. Wade-Gery, Sir Maurice Bowra and the Nonesuch Press for *The Odes of Pindar*, Graham Hough and Messrs. Duckworth for *Legends and Pastorals*. Professor George Thomson and Cambridge University Press for *Aeschylus: The Oresteia*, Messrs. Thornton Butterworth for a translation in Gilbert Murray's *Euripides and His Age*.

I am also grateful for certain passages to my fellow-author of *Greeks* and *Romans*, Mr Don Pottinger, and to the publisher Messrs. Thomas Nelson and Sons, Ltd.

I want also to thank Miss Jocelyn Burton for seeing this edition through the press.

MICHAEL GRANT

Note. See two headings in the Index (methods, theories; myth, divisions of) for some of the various ways in which the subject can be approached.

PART I

THE HEROES OF HOMER

CHAPTER 1

THE WRATH OF ACHILLES

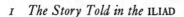

1   The Story Told in the ILIAD

THE POET begins his story, in the tenth year of Troy's siege by the Greeks, with an invocation to the Muse.

> Sing through me
> That anger which most ruinously
> Inflamed Achilles, Peleus' son,
> And which before the tale was done
> Had glutted hell with champions bold,
> Stern spirits by the thousandfold;
> Ravens and dogs their corpses ate.
> For thus did Zeus, who watched their fate,
> See his resolve, first taken when
> Proud Agamemnon king of men
> An insult on Achilles cast,
> Achieve accomplishment at last.[1]

The flowing rhythm of the *Iliad* was given this more abrupt, ballad-like shape by Robert Graves.

While attacking Chryse not far from Troy, Agamemnon, commander-in-chief of the invaders, had taken as his share of the plunder Chryseis, daughter of Chryses priest of Apollo. Before the assembled Greek army, her father appealed to Agamemnon to release her, but his plea was refused and the old man was dismissed from the camp. Chryses prayed to Apollo to punish the invaders, and Apollo, hearing his prayer, came down from Olympus, afflicting the Greeks with a plague. 'As he set out, the arrows clanged on the shoulder of the angry god; and his descent was like nightfall. He sat down opposite the ships and shot an arrow, with a dreadful twang, from his silver bow. He attacked the mules first and the nimble dogs, and then he aimed his sharp arrows at the men, and struck again and again. Day and night, innumerable fires consumed the dead. For nine days the god's arrows rained on the camp.'[2]

On the tenth day Achilles called for a council of war. The prophet Calchas declared that Chryseis must be given back to her father. Agamemnon angrily agreed but seized, instead of her, the girl Briseis, who had been allotted to Achilles. And so Achilles withdrew from the war, appealing to his immortal mother Thetis, who persuaded Zeus to right the wrongs of her son. Accordingly, the king of the gods sent Agamemnon a deceptive dream assuring him that he can now capture Troy. Agamemnon tested his army by suggesting that they should all return home. They took him too seriously and rushed for the ships, but the goddess Hera dispatched Athene to stop the retreat. Odysseus summoned a council of war, at which, after beating the ugly demagogue Thersites into silence, he induced the soldiers to fight. There follows a list marshalling the Greek and Trojan forces.

The Trojan prince Paris, who had brought about the war by abducting Helen from Sparta, challenged her husband Menelaus to a duel on which the result of the war was to depend. The father of Paris, King Priam, came to the city walls, where Helen pointed out to him the Greek chieftains. Though defeated by Menelaus, Paris was spirited from the battle-field by Aphrodite. There was no pact because, while Hera was implacably opposed to Troy, her husband Zeus had promised satisfaction to Achilles: so Athene, in disguise, tempted Troy's Asian ally Pandarus to shoot an arrow at Menelaus. He was slightly wounded, and the fighting broke out again.

In the battles that followed, the Greek hero Diomede performed glorious exploits, 'like a winter torrent that comes tearing down and flattens out the dykes'. The gods and goddesses entered the battle, and Diomede's spear scratched Aphrodite's wrist as she rescued from him Anchises' son Aeneas. On the Trojan side, Hector was supported by the war-god Ares himself, but even Ares received a wounding blow from Diomede. Returning to Troy to bid his mother Hecabe sacrifice to Athene, Hector spoke with Helen and Paris and then with his wife Andromache, who had their little son Astyanax with her.

Hector stepped out into no man's land, and addressed the armies with a challenge. The gods, too, were present; for Athene and Apollo were enjoying the scene, in the form of vultures perching upon a tall oak. Ajax responded to Hector's offer of a duel, which turned out slightly to the advantage of the Greek. But on the advice of the aged Nestor, the Greeks began to fortify their camp. Zeus forbade the gods to intervene and heartened the Trojans.

'Thus all night long they sat, across the corridors of battle, thinking great thoughts and keeping their many fires alight. There are nights when the upper air is windless and the stars in heaven stand out in their full splendour round the bright moon; when every mountain-top and headland and ravine starts into sight, as the infinite depths of the sky are torn open to the very firmament; when every star is seen, and the shepherd rejoices. Such and so many were the Trojans' fires, twinkling in front of Troy midway between the ships and the streams of Xanthus. There were a thousand fires burning on the plain, and round each one sat fifty men in the light of its blaze, while the horses stood beside their chariots, munching white barley and rye, and waiting for Dawn to take her golden throne.'[3]

Agamemnon, discouraged, was now willing to make the fullest amends to Achilles, and dispatched Ajax, Odysseus and Phoenix to his tent. They were to seek a reconciliation, so that the greatest of the Greeks could return to the battle. But Achilles in tragic pride rejected their proposals. He would only come back, he said, if Hector actually threatened the ships of his own men, the Myrmidons. Odysseus and Diomede raided the Trojan positions and killed the Thracian King Rhesus, capturing his horses. But next day both these Greek leaders, and Agamemnon too, were wounded, and their army fell back to its fortified camp.

There is an interlude while Nestor, returning to his hut with a casualty, Machaon, has a meal prepared for them by a maidservant, captured from Tenedos. 'She began by moving up to them a handsome polished table with enamelled legs. On this she put a bronze dish with an onion to flavour the drink, some yellow honey, and sacred barley-meal, and beside these a magnificent beaker adorned with golden studs, which the old man had brought from home. It had four handles. Each was supported by two legs; and on top of each, facing one another, a pair of golden doves were feeding. Anyone else would have found it difficult to shift the beaker from the table when it was full, but Nestor, old as he was, could lift it without trouble. In this cup their comely attendant mixed them the pottage with Pramnian wine, and after making it ready by grating into it some goat's milk cheese with a bronze grater and sprinkling white barley on top, she invited them to drink.'[4] And then Patroclus, sent by Achilles to ask who had been hurt, appeared in the doorway of the hut, 'like a god'.

Now, however, desperate fighting broke out again, and the Trojans, led by Hector, stormed the Greek battlements. Yet Hera planned to rescue the Greeks. Obtaining from Aphrodite (although they were on different sides) a charm which would make herself irresistibly attractive, she enticed Zeus into her arms. He made love to her, and then fell asleep. Posidon, who had intervened on the Greek side, drove back the Trojans, and Hector was stunned by a stone. But Zeus woke up, and ordered Posidon to leave the battle, and Apollo to revive Hector. The Greeks were driven right back to the ships.

In this emergency, Patroclus persuaded Achilles to allow him to intervene. And so Patroclus fought Hector, and was killed; and Hector transferred the immortal armour of Achilles from the dead man's body to his own. As a violent battle raged round the corpse, Achilles, maddened by revengeful grief, demanded new armour from his mother, and the god Hephaestus made it. Though forewarned that he would not live long after Hector, Achilles was now determined to go into battle at once. After a formal reconciliation, he received Briseis back from Agamemnon.

Led by Achilles, the Greek troops rushed from the ships. On either side the gods ranged themselves. With the Greeks were Hera, Athene, Posidon, Hephaestus and Hermes. On the Trojan side stood Ares, Apollo, Artemis, Leto, Aphrodite and the river god Xanthus who was also called Scamander. Before the terrifying advance of Achilles, the Trojans gave ground. Divine intervention saved Aeneas and Hector, but many others met their end at his hands. As even god fought with god in this greatest of battles, Achilles raged with his spear 'like a driving wind that whirls the flames this way and that, when a conflagration rages in the gullies on a sun-baked mountain-side, and the high forest is consumed. He chased his victims with the fury of a fiend, and the earth was dark with blood. At their imperious master's will the horses of Achilles with their massive hooves trampled dead men and shields alike with no more ado than when a farmer has yoked a pair of broad-browed cattle to trample the white barley on a threshing-floor, and his lowing bulls tread out the grain. The axle-tree under his chariot, and the rails that ran round it, were sprayed with the blood thrown up by the horses' hooves and by the tyres. And the son of Peleus pressed on in search of glory, be-spattering his unconquerable hands with gore.'[5]

When the resisting river was choked with corpses until its waters rose and nearly engulfed him, he moved towards the walls of Troy itself. Outside the city gates, Hector was waiting alone for him. But as Achilles leapt forward, Hector's courage failed him and he ran before his enemy three times round the walls. Then, however, Athene tricked him into making his fatal stand. As he fell, his throat pierced by Achilles' lance, he called with his dying breath upon the knees and life and parents of the slayer, begging that his own father and mother should be allowed to ransom his body. 'You cur,' replied Achilles, 'don't talk to me of knees or name my parents in your prayers. I only wish that I could summon up the appetite to carve and eat you raw myself, for what you have done to me.' And in full view of the walls, and of Andromache looking out from them, he dragged Hector's corpse back to the camp behind his chariot.

Visited at night by the ghost of Patroclus demanding burial, Achilles arranged for him a splendid funeral, sacrificing twelve captured Trojans on the pyre; and the funeral was followed by athletic sports. But Hector was still unburied. For eleven days his body, kept whole by Apollo, was dragged each day round the tomb of Patroclus by his killer. But compassion now came upon the gods, and Zeus intervened. Instructing Thetis to bid her son accept ransom for the corpse, he ordered Priam, through his divine messenger Iris, to take the ransom by night to the camp of the Greeks. Led by Hermes, Priam passed through the Greek lines. With his own aged father Peleus in mind, Achilles received the old king with courtesy and granted his plea for the body of Hector, calling upon the ghost of Patroclus not to resent the restoration of his enemy's corpse.

Priam slept in the forecourt and left before dawn. There was a truce of eleven days for Hector's funeral. Then the battle began again.

2 Troy and Homer

More than five thousand years ago, Greece was inhabited by people who ground and polished their stone tools, made painted pottery, and scraped a living in villages near the scarce arable land where there was a river or a spring. About 3000 BC their dwellings were destroyed by invaders, possibly from Asia Minor. These were people, probably of non-Indo-European tongue, whose bronze tools made their lives rather easier; though civilization was much further advanced in more fertile countries such as Egypt, Sumeria and Crete. That island, with its good soil and climate, produced ship's timber and a surplus of wine and oil. Its non-Greek inhabitants (again perhaps from Asia Minor) united in about 2000 BC into a single kingdom, based on sea-power, with its capital at Cnossus. These prosperous Cretans developed an imaginative, lively civilization and a flowing, curving, naturalistic art very different from the hieratic style of their teachers the Egyptians.

Meanwhile on the Greek mainland, people speaking a language somewhat resembling Greek, and perhaps originating from the South Russian steppes, began to arrive during the first centuries of the second millennium BC. Intermingling with other racial strains, they developed a culture partly indebted to Crete—and revealing common ground with the Hittites of inland Asia Minor (page 34)—but partly novel. This reached its climax in the royal fortresses of southern Greece, such as Mycenae, Tiryns and Pylos. The monarchs of those places, whose luxury caused a sensation when the German archaeologist Schliemann disclosed the royal Mycenaean graves in 1876, possessed powerful new armaments—bronze rapiers, shields and chariots. By 1500 BC the Mycenaeans were influencing Cretan civilization in their turn, and ruled the whole island for about fifty years. Thousands of clay writing tablets found at Cnossus, dating apparently (though this is contested) from *c.* 1400 BC—and others of *c.* 1200, still strangely similar, at the mainland centres —are written in a script known as 'Linear B', which has been shown to be an early form of the Greek language.

Mycenaean Cnossus seems to have fallen in *c.* 1400, but during the next two hundred years the cities of the mainland, and especially Mycenae, were at their height as powerful land empires and Mediterranean trading centres. The thirteenth century was a time of great upheavals throughout the near east; Mycenaean exports to Egypt and the Levant ceased abruptly, and in about 1250 BC, as archaeology confirms, invaders (of whom there were many at this time, in Asia Minor and in Egypt) besieged and burnt the key-city of Troy near the Hellespont (Dardanelles). Then in the twelfth century not only did great hordes of invaders again inflict terrible destruction upon Syria and Egypt but the holocaust, of whatever origin (page 35), spread to Greece itself. For excavation shows that the palaces of Pylos, Mycenae and Tiryns came to grief in their turn.

Almost all the principal Greek myths are connected with centres of this Mycenaean civilization, which provided many a subject and hero. However mythical their exploits, the names of the *Iliad*'s great warriors are likely enough to be the real names of men who lived in Mycenaean Greece—and fought the Trojans; another 'Hector' appears on a Linear B tablet. Moreover, the catalogue of contingents in the *Iliad* seems to go back to an historically true Order of Battle of that period. There may well be some historical truth (though coloured by his own time, page 39) in the picture the poet gives of the Greek besiegers as a loose confederacy, under their overlord Agamemnon, of proud, recalcitrant, meat-fed chiefs, jealous of their reputations. Possibly, too, the invading army already believed in the Olympian gods as a similar loose confederacy under Zeus—who may conceivably appear with his scales of destiny upon a Mycenaean amphora. At any rate, Homer's knowledge of Mycenaean objects came from a po : dition going back to those days. The huge shield of Ajax like a tower, Hector's bronze helmet, the cup of Nestor, the silver-studded swords, and the only reference to writing,[6] are traceable to the Mycenaean age.

One of its last and culminating efforts must have been the siege of the horse-rearing, textile-fabricating city of Troy, in its strategic position on the Hellespont. That city, where there had been at least six earlier successive settlements, was already at this epoch, as archaeologists have shown, somewhat beyond its prime ('Troy VIIa'); Homer's tales of its grandeur rather fit the immediately preceding fourteenth century BC ('Troy VI'), in which there had been a great rise in the importance of the town. Excavators have also proved that 'Troy VIIa' fell to a violent fire, probably by human agency. There was nothing new about sieges in the ancient world, nor were they new to near eastern story-tellers. From the Hittites, for example, who had ruled until the thirteenth century on the Anatolian plateau and display resemblances to the peoples across the Aegean (page 93), we have a tolerably preserved account of the siege of Urshu (somewhere in northern Syria) by their army; while the epics of Ugarit, in the same area, tell of a siege of Udum (page 50).

'And so,' says the geographer Strabo (himself from Asia Minor) in the days of Augustus, 'Homer took the Trojan War, an historical fact, and decked it out with his fanciful stories.'[7] According to one convenient definition of terms, this makes his story a legend (that is to say a story based, however remotely, on historical fact), as opposed to a myth which has no basis of fact at all. At any rate the Greeks, who felt their lack of ancient records such as those of Egypt and Asia, took the whole thing as history, and based a great part of their entire cultural tradition upon this acceptance. The heroes and their doings were believed to have been authentic—a supposition which Homer had encouraged by the careful orderliness with which he circumscribes them all within two or three generations. Some of the leading figures, it has been suggested, may really have been personifications of warring tribes, whose varying fortunes during the migrations are reflected in the victories or deaths of this or that hero. Be that as it may, the poem, though its subject is the Wrath of Achilles and not the war as a whole—of which we do not see the end —is made to look like a chronicle.

Since people like having remote ancestors to venerate, the stories were perpetuated and elaborated as each family or city attached a glorious pedigree to itself. Down to Roman times, there were tombs and relics attributed to the heroes to be seen everywhere in Greece, and they were accorded a specific kind of worship of their own (page 235). Similar remains are also found in Homer's native country, western Asia Minor. Myths and legends of Greece had been transplanted there when the country was colonized (amid raids and migrations such as those which had earlier given birth to epics) at the end of the first millennium BC*; and so we find 'tombs' of Achilles, Idomeneus and Calchas on those coasts. The island of Lesbos retained stronger links: for across the gulf of time which separated the Trojan War from the Greek city-states, the royal house and the constitution survived and remained the same. At Cyme in Aeolis, too, there was a king Agamemnon who claimed descent from the Homeric hero.

The destroyers of Mycenae may (though this cannot be said for certain) have been no less Greek than their victims—backward relations, the last stream of Greek invaders. That is to say, they may have been the Dorians, who passed through the Balkans into northern Greece (c. 1150–1100), pushing before them earlier Greek arrivals (Aeolians and Ionians) who thus became the migrants to Asia Minor to whom reference has just been made. Of the first four centuries after these events we have little knowledge, and we call it a 'Dark Age'. At least material prosperity was smaller, and communications were fewer; though the break may not have been so complete as was

---

* Pottery of the eleventh century BC has now been discovered at Smyrna, of which the traditional foundation-date is 1104 BC.

supposed. How dark was the 'Dark Age'? Or is it only our knowledge that is dark? That is a question that archaeologists are trying to answer. But at any rate the age was one of great changes. There was, for example, a marked artistic break. Writing, which had existed so abundantly on Cretan and Mycenaean 'Linear B' tablets, vanished or almost vanished for four hundred years; the fine arts of fresco, metal-work and ivory-carving came to an end; and the designs of the characteristic Geometric pottery, made at Athens* and other centres during these 'dark' centuries, were schematic and linear, so far removed from Minoan and Mycenaean curves that a direct line of artistic descent (other, perhaps, than in the actual shapes of the vases) is hard to imagine.

Towards 750 or even 700 BC, the Homeric poems took something like their final shape. During the intermediate period, the bards had been illiterate or at any rate did not commit their poems to writing. In these intervening centuries the epic poems, with their stock formulas (themes, word-groups, and phrases) as mnemonic guides for impromptu singing, had been orally transmitted from bard to bard like the Norse and German sagas, or the stories still to be found in western Ireland. In the 28,000 lines of the *Iliad* and *Odyssey* there are 25,000 repeated phrases, large and small, and for each of thirty-seven leading characters in the two poems there is a stock descriptive phrase of the same length. Handed down by such means through the generations, the *Iliad* brings us not only the distant events and stories of the siege of Troy, but many accretions of subject matter as well as varying dialects (Aeolic, Arcadian, Ionic, Attic) from the centuries between—and from the time of the genius who, perhaps in the eighth century, cast the poem into its superb and timeless form. By a unique paradox, Greek literature *begins*, for us, with poems of unsurpassable beauty.

Whether this poet of the *Iliad* himself transformed into a single epic the multitudinous, relatively short lays (concerned with religion, history, folk-lore, ritual and fancy) that he inherited, or whether this amalgamation had already, in whole or part, been gradually evolved by many composers over a long period, is and may well remain

* There is already excellent 'Proto-Geometric' pottery at Athens in *c.* 1025–900 BC.

unknown. 'The nearest thing to a fact,' as Sir Denys Page once observed, 'is the name of Homer, the man who, by his skill as master poet, absorbed the finest products of the poetic past into a balanced and harmonious unity.' Probably he accompanied his own recitation of the poem with the lyre used by a bard in the *Odyssey*[8]—unless he employed a baton, attributed to him by Pindar (518–438 BC), and directed the performances of others. Whether the poems were composed for this specific purpose or not, their recitation is likely to have taken place at a great festival; we do not know which, but perhaps it was the Pan-Ionian festival at Mount Mycale, the promontory between Ephesus and Miletus in western Asia Minor.

There had long been festivals, but during the eighth century (in which the Olympic games too were founded) they became larger and grander. The *Iliad* could be recited in fifteen two-hour sessions, that is to say in three days, or two if the audience had enough stamina; no doubt the bards worked in relays. This was about the time when, as inscriptions show, the Phoenician alphabet was coming to the Greeks. That meant that the poem was copied down—not necessarily by Homer, though not long after his day. The *Iliad* and *Odyssey*, when composed, became the property of a guild or clan, the Homeridae, who 'published' them by recitation.[10] Perhaps King Pisistratus of Athens (560–527 BC) arranged for them to be given their final form; and then, for another four hundred years, editors continued to leave their mark on the text. The present division into twenty-four books may date from the third century BC.

There were in the Trojan Cycle, in addition to the *Iliad* and *Odyssey*, six other poems of uncertain authorship but attributed to Homer: the *Cypria* (from the Judgment of Paris, page 441, to the War); *Aethiopis* (about Achilles' slaying of Penthesilea the Amazon, Thersites and the Ethiopian Memnon, followed by his own death); the *Little Iliad*; *Sack of Troy*; *Returns* (*Nostoi*) of the heroes; and *Telegony* (about Telegonus, Odysseus' son by Circe). The *Iliad* itself, about the Wrath of Achilles, was one of a cycle of poems about Wraths. A very long period indeed, full of convulsions and vicissitudes, and lacking in records other than this constantly growing oral tradition, had elapsed between the Mycenaean age and the welding together of the Homeric poems. The situation might almost be compared to the Mexican village of Santiago where, according to John Steinbeck, 'they set out a battle between peoples they did not know in a land they had never heard of in a time that was forgotten'. So far distant from the events, the *Iliad*'s points of contact with Mycenae are sometimes tenuous. For example, the 'Linear B' tablets now show the Mycenaeans to have possessed a highly organized, bureaucratic society of inventories, land tenures, labour specialization, and much writing—endless counting and classifying and assessing—far closer to the Hittites and the peoples of north Syria than to the simpler picture by Homer.

And then again, with an eye on later times, the poet perhaps overestimates the West-East aspect of the original siege of Troy. Trojan culture had looked westwards (as archaeological remains make clear) rather than to its mainland Hittite neighbours, and its population was of somewhat similar cultural background to the Greek invaders. So Homer may only be reflecting a later awareness of difference between Greece and the East (which was to culminate in the Persian War) when he stresses the oriental cosmopolitanism of the Trojan ranks. 'They were like the sheep that stand in their thousands in a rich farmer's yard yielding their white milk and bleating incessantly because they hear their lambs. Such was the babel that went up from the great Trojan army, which hailed from many parts, and being without a common language used many different cries and calls.'[11] The significance of the war as origin of the strife between Greece and the East, much stressed by historians such as Herodotus, may only have become apparent after Ionian and Aeolian Greek settlers on the coast of Asia Minor—ancestors of Homer himself—had clashed, perhaps in the ninth century, with Asian peoples such as the Phrygians.

Indeed, even if the Greek conception of the heroic age began on the mainland after the fall of Mycenae, its survival may have been largely due to the Ionian forerunners of Homer preserving across the Aegean, with the retentiveness of a 'colonial' outlook, their ties with their original homes in Greece itself. While the *Iliad*'s predominantly war-like tone belongs to a strain which was to reach its climax in Sparta, the quite different tradition represented by its sensitivity of touch, its candid individualism and its flowing narrative seems Ionian. And then again, the iron axes, knives and arrow-heads mentioned in the *Iliad* likewise date from not earlier than the turn of the first millennium, when the Iron Age came to the Aegean; and, incidentally, even many of the blows attributed to bronze weapons in the poem could only have been struck by iron. Cremation, too, in the Geometric urns which this later age produced (page 36), is the universal Homeric practice, whereas the normal Mycenaean custom had been inhumation. The poet of the *Iliad* lived in these new times, and his poem shows much more of its poet's Geometric age than of his subject's Mycenaean epoch. Back across the centuries, from his own supposedly inferior 'dark' age, looks Homer with nostalgic approval at an earlier time of golden bellicosities, feudal homes, baronial mansions and loyal retainers. Perhaps this picture was flattering and comforting to the squireens or princelings of his own day; at any rate they must have applauded the rapid discomfiture of the only political malcontent of the *Iliad*, Thersites.

Is there any relation between the Homeric *Iliad* and contemporary visual art? If so our knowledge of each would be enriched. It is certainly possible to trace on the Geometric pottery, made at Athens and also at Smyrna (one of the contestants for Homer's birthplace) and other centres across the Aegean, a gradual development—alongside purely linear motif—of scene and figure-painting. By the middle of the eighth century, when the first Greek temple with architectural pretensions, Hera's temple at Samos, was erected, there were big funeral vases, some showing designs of races and processions, and many with battle scenes. Among these scenes, incidents from the *Iliad* and other epic poems have been identified; but without certainty. Figure sculpture was still highly formal, and a new way of depicting human beings and human life was being worked out step by step. It is hard to say which figure is meant to represent a god or a hero, or if so who this is, until writing and personal attributes appear on vases during the seventh century. Then incidents from the *Iliad* are soon found in Boeotia, Sparta, Corinth, eastern Greece and the islands. Did the poets inspire the painters, or was it the other way round? The visual artists have been credited with hitting upon a way of representing the human body, and setting up a chain reaction which transformed the narrations of the poets. But Homer with his consummate artistry and eyewitness technique is so much more advanced than the Geometric painters that this seems unlikely; and the interactions between poet and visual artist, such as occur in later western art, are hard to trace.

Yet Homer possessed the abnormally strong and imaginative visual sense which earned him Voltaire's description as a 'sublime painter'. The colour and vivid tenderness of his similes, drawn from a wide range of nature and human life, present a marked contrast to the simplicity and rarity of such figures in the *Song of Roland* or *Beowulf*. If Dante's similes make us see the scene more definitely, Homer's make us feel one particular feature of it; and they are the very essence of his intuition. Often two pictures follow rapidly upon one another, to emphasize different aspects, or a contrast or change.

> As obliterating fire lights up a vast forest
> along the crests of a mountain, and the flare shows
> > far off,
> so, as they marched, from the magnificent bronze the
> > gleam went
> dazzling all about through the upper air to the heaven.
> These, as the multitudinous nations of birds winged,
> of geese, and of cranes, and of swans long-throated,
> in the Asian meadow beside the Caystrian waters
> this way and that way make their flights in the pride
> > of their wings, then
> settle in clashing swarms and the whole meadow echoes
> > with them,
> so of these the multitudinous tribes from the ships and
> shelters poured to the plain of Scamander, and the
> > earth beneath their
> feet and under the feet of their horses thundered
> > horribly.

They took position in the blossoming meadow of
   Scamander,
thousands of them, as leaves and flowers appear in their
   season.
  Like the multitudinous nations of swarming insects
who drive hither and thither about the stalls of the
   sheepfold
in the season of spring when the milk splashes in the
   milk pails:
in such numbers the flowing-haired Achaeans stood up
through the plain against the Trojans, hearts burning
   to break them.[12]

Homer conveys the pictorial and emotional appeal not only of a
great battle but of humble, natural scenes and doings. This is one
aspect of his unique descriptive powers, of his simple, natural,
picturesque, imaginative style, suited perfectly to its theme.

3   Achilles: Helen

Each person in the Homeric myths is a strongly differentiated individual. The greatest warrior among them is Achilles. He is, at times,
savage; this may be intended to reflect his origins from Greece's
Thessalian periphery. But he is also the most beautiful, eloquent,
courteous, generous and wise among the heroes. He obeyed his
father's orders 'always to be the best and to surpass others'.[13] There
are few signs, naturally enough, of the Christian chivalry of Roland,
Lancelot or Beowulf. Yet he is a man of taste and artistic skill,
'singing of famous men, accompanying himself on a tuneful lyre',
and a great gentleman—not at all the spoilt, boastful boy, dreading a
scene, into whom Euripides was to make him (page 261)[14]

Iliad concentrates interest upon this formidable personality.
With his lust for undying fame, his prowess in battle and his
sensitivity to insults, he is the most nearly perfect practitioner of the
Homeric code. He has a good deal in common with Shakespeare's
Hotspur—youth, prowess, passion for honour and a personal wrong

to resent. Yet Achilles is not only more ferocious, but also more tragic. Though there is not, until the Roman poet Statius, any mention of that all too mortal heel which limits the invulnerability conferred on him by his mother Thetis, and he is no more vulnerable or invulnerable than anyone else, he knows he is foredoomed.[15] Like the Sumerian hero Gilgamesh, and Keret of Syrian Ugarit (page 50), he is partly of divine extraction, and yet he, again like them, is fated to die. This is the classic tragedy of man's futile quest to overcome death, a theme on which many Greek myths were to brood.

Achilles embodies the qualities which most men would like to have. He possesses in extreme degree all the virtues and faults of the hero, and these are the cause of all that happens. He resents being flouted by Agamemnon because this denies due honour to his outstanding heroic qualities.[16] Yet Achilles, in his turn, is put in the wrong by his refusal to accept Agamemnon's terms: this is disregard both of his commander and of his companions—one of whom, Odysseus, suggests that he should give way now so as to receive payment as part of the apology due.[17] Later, half-maddened with grief and passion after the death of Patroclus, Achilles is no longer interested in honour or propriety. But then, in the last book, comes his unforgettable vindication—the deeply moving encounter with Priam, a purification and a surprise; yet no surprise, for we ought to have expected it of him. Though fierce emotions still burn below the surface,[18] the hand he reaches out to the old man repairs the failure in his character (page 57).

Before this, we have seen all his complexity vanish in the rage of the supreme warrior, whose appearance is as terrifying as his ferocity.

> A clash went from the grinding of his teeth, and his
>   eyes glowed
> as if they were the stare of a fire, and the heart
>   inside him
> was entered with sorrow beyond endurance. Raging at
>   the Trojans
> he put on the gifts of the god, that Hephaestus wrought
>   him with much toil.

First he placed along his legs the fair greaves
    linked with
silver fastenings to hold the greaves at the ankles.
Afterwards he girt on about his chest the corselet,
and across his shoulders slung the sword with the
    nails of silver,
a bronze sword, and caught up the great shield, huge
    and heavy
next, and from it the light glimmered far, as from the
    moon.
And as when from across water a light shines to mariners
from a blazing fire, when the fire is burning
    high in the mountains
in a desolate steading, as the mariners are carried
    unwilling
by storm winds over the fish-swarming sea, far away from
    their loved ones;
so the light from the fair elaborate shield of Achilles
shot into the high air. And lifting the helm he set it
massive upon his head, and the helmet crested with
    horse-hair
shone like a star, the golden fringes were shaken about it
which Hephaestus had driven close along the horn
    of the helmet.
And brilliant Achilles tried himself in his armour, to see
if it fitted close, and how his glorious limbs
    ran within it,
and the armour became as wings and upheld the shepherd
    of the people.
Next he pulled out from its standing place the spear
    of his father,
huge, heavy, thick, which no one else of all the Achaeans
could handle, but Achilles alone knew how to wield it,
the Pelian ash spear which Chiron had brought
    to his father
from high on Pelion, to be death for fighters in battle.[19]

As the glitter of bronze rippled like laughter over the plain, and the glory of arms lit up the sky, he gnashed his teeth in an intolerable fury, and his eyes blazed with a fire which burned down the centuries in the heart of every Greek.

> Even in death, songs did not leave him,
> but, standing beside his pyre and his grave, the maidens
> of Helicon let fall upon him their abundant dirge.
> Even the immortals were pleased
> to bestow on a brave man, though perished, the song of
> goddesses.[20]

It is Achilles who gives the *Iliad* its architectural unity. The poem is a great bridge with five massive piers—his quarrel with his supreme commander; his refusal to forgive; the resulting death of Patroclus; the vengeance on Hector; and the final scene of mercy to Priam.

Hector, too, is a glorious fighter. 'In front of him he holds his rounded shield, with its close layers of hide and its ample sheath of beaten bronze; and his burnished helmet sways upon his temples.[21] But he is less whole-hearted than Achilles, and perhaps a better leader than warrior. He is not, as some have called him, weak and valueless, nor is he a proud warrior madly leading his city to ruin. He is a good man in whom the warlike and elegiac moods meet, a good son, husband, father and champion. But he, too, is fated to die.

> Out of the bright sky Zeus himself was working to
> help him
> and among men so numerous he honoured this one man
> and glorified him, since Hector was to have only a
> short life,
> and already the day of his death was being driven
> upon him
> by Pallas Athene through the strength of Achilles.[22]

Hector himself, like Achilles, is not hopeful about his fate; and knows that Troy will fall.[23] But although he and his city cannot escape, he will win glory if he dies bravely.

THE WRATH OF ACHILLES

TABLE 1

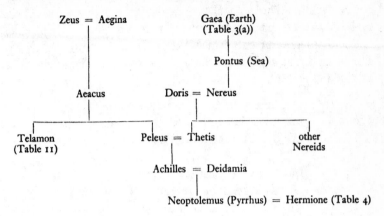

Zeus = Aegina   Gaea (Earth)
(Table 3(a))

Pontus (Sea)

Aeacus   Doris = Nereus

Telamon
(Table 11)   Peleus = Thetis   other
Nereids

Achilles = Deidamia

Neoptolemus (Pyrrhus) = Hermione (Table 4)

TABLE 2

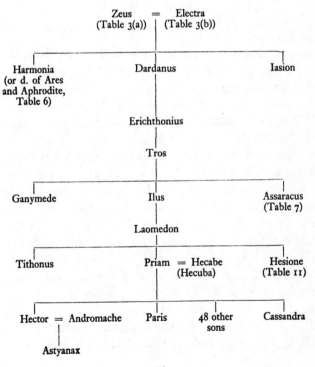

Zeus = Electra
(Table 3(a)) (Table 3(b))

Harmonia
(or d. of Ares
and Aphrodite,
Table 6)   Dardanus   Iasion

Erichthonius

Tros

Ganymede   Ilus   Assaracus
(Table 7)

Laomedon

Tithonus   Priam = Hecabe
(Hecuba)   Hesione
(Table 11)

Hector = Andromache   Paris   48 other
sons   Cassandra

Astyanax

45

It is a terrible moment when this mighty man quails and runs before Achilles. The moment has caught the attention of that dryly realistic yet compassionate, much more Hellenistic than epic, Alexandrian poet of our own century, Cavafy: writing, as E. M. Forster said, 'at a slight angle to the universe' about the interactions of past and present.

> Our efforts are like those of the Trojans.
> We think that with resolution and daring
> We will alter the downdrag of destiny.

> But when the great crisis comes,
> Our daring and our resolution vanish
> And we run all around the walls
> Seeking to save ourselves in flight.

> However, our fall is certain. Above
> On the walls, the dirge has already begun.

But until that desperate time, Hector is the leader and hope of Troy.

He is critical of his brother Paris, who had caused the war by taking Helen, and earlier (as Homer does not tell) by the Judgment through which he preferred Aphrodite to Hera and Athene (page 441). ' "Sir," said Hector of the glittering helmet, "no reasonable man could make light of your achievements in battle: you have plenty of courage. But you are too ready to give up when it suits you, and refuse to fight. And I find it mortifying to hear you abused by the Trojans, whom you yourself have brought to this pass." '[24]

The most interesting of the other heroes are all Greeks. The supreme commander Agamemnon is physically brave, but lacking in moral courage and resolution. Worried, truculent, greedy, untruthful, violent and boastful, he says and does the wrong thing, veering between pigheadedness and generosity, confidence and despair. Homer's careful delineation of his faults seems to reflect the hatred of feudal princes for the necessity of accepting a temporary overlord. Agamemnon's brother Menelaus, unfortunate to be cuckolded, is brave but lacks glamour, has bad luck in not winning his duel with Paris, and is no leader. ' "Sir," remarks King Agamemnon to Nestor, "there are times when I should indeed be glad to see you take Menelaus to task. He is often inclined to do nothing and let things slide, not through laziness or any lack of brains, but because he looks to me and depends on my initiative." '25

Odysseus, on the other hand, is the complete man of action, unromantically but lovingly drawn. Vigorous (on one day he eats three dinners) and extremely intelligent, he is nevertheless everybody's friend because of his good sense—or nearly everybody's, for the beefy, dull-witted Ajax (whom he cheats at wrestling) suffered from his cleverness.26 Nestor is a long-winded Polonius whose advice is sound; though at the games he elaborately advises his son how to cheat. And he is good at urging men who, unlike himself, are still fit for fighting not to hang back—even the mightiest of the warriors, such as Diomede. 'The prince Diomedes was asleep, with the hide of a farm-yard ox beneath him, and a glossy rug drawn under his head. Nestor the Gerenian charioteer went up to him, woke him with a touch of his foot, and flung a taunt at him to rouse him further. "Wake up," he said. "Why should you sleep in comfort all night long? Has it escaped your notice that the Trojans are sitting on the plain above us, barely a stone's throw from the ships?" Diomedes, who had woken and leapt up in a trice, replied with some feeling: "You are a hard old man, sir, and you never take a moment's rest. Are there not younger men in the army to go the rounds and call up all the kings? There is no holding you down, my venerable lord." '27

There are real women, also, in the *Iliad*. It is true that they are not in the midst of public affairs, as in the Icelandic sagas, and when they are slaves they are baubles to be traded and exchanged—not always at a flatteringly high price. 'Losing no time, the son of Peleus brought out and displayed fresh prizes for the third event, the all-in wrestling. For the winner there was a big three-legged cauldron to go on the fire—it was worth a dozen oxen by Achaean reckoning—and for the loser he brought forward a woman thoroughly trained in domestic work, who was valued at four oxen in the camp.'28 Yet the wives of the heroes play their part with dignity, like Gudrun and Brynhild, and they have sensitivity, poise, responsibility and good

47

taste. Helen and Andromache are as seriously depicted as Achilles—though in this masculine world love sometimes seems below the dignity of the fighting man; we are not among the lovers of a troubadour. But Hector and Andromache are a loving couple, there are even signs of an attachment between Achilles and Briseis, and it is because of Paris' fatal love for Helen that the whole war was fought.

An unhappy woman, doomed by Zeus (as she knows) to be a subject for poets, to the Greeks Helen was a desperate, beautiful, tragic curse (page 190). But such was her beauty that the Trojan elders of the *Iliad* had only to see her to understand how it had all happened—though they would prefer that she was not with them.

> These were seated by the Scaean gates, elders of
>   the people.
> Now through old age these fought no longer, yet
>   were they excellent
> speakers still, and clear, as cicadas who through
>   the forest
> settle on trees, to issue their delicate voice of
>   singing.
> Such were they who sat on the tower, chief men of
>   the Trojans.
> And these, as they saw Helen along the tower
>   approaching,
> murmuring softly to each other uttered their winged
>   words:
> 'Surely there is no blame on Trojans and strong-
>   greaved Achaeans
> If for long time they suffer hardship for a woman
>   like this one.
> Terrible is the likeness of her face to immortal
>   goddesses.
> Still, though she be such, let her go away in
>   the ships, lest
> she be left behind, a grief to us and our children.[29]

Helen's name is pre-Greek; perhaps she began her history and cult as a tree-goddess. The stories about her are conflicting. It is said that the poet Stesichorus, perhaps living in the sixth century BC, was struck blind for blaming Helen, and wrote a 'palinode' denying that she had ever been at Troy—it was only a phantom had been there, and she got no farther than Egypt; and the story is told again in Euripides' *Helen*.[30] This tradition has been perpetuated in our own day by his compatriot George Seferis:

> She was there, at the desert's edge. I touched her.
>   She spoke to me.
> 'It is not true, it is not true,' she cried.
> 'I never went aboard that coloured ship;
> I never trod the ground of manly Troy' . . .
>
> She was there, on the banks of a Delta.
>   And at Troy?
> Nothing.   At Troy a phantom.
> So the gods willed it.
> And Paris lay with a shadow as though it were
>   solid flesh:
> And we were slaughtered for Helen ten long years.

The alternative and more famous version, telling of Helen's abduction to Troy, may well have been no part of the original Trojan legend. The poets seem to have borrowed it from some source dependent upon an epic of Ugarit, on the Syrian coast. Ugarit, now Ras Shamra near Latakia, was a flourishing kingdom between the eighteenth and thirteenth centuries BC, and the town included what was perhaps the world's first great international port. The Ugarit poems, mainly of fourteenth-century date, belong to the north-western branch of the Semitic languages, and are written in Canaanite alphabetic cuneiform, foreshadowing the Phoenician alphabet which was to come to Greece in the eighth century BC (page 37). The Ugaritic poems have strong links not only with the Old Testament but also with the Homeric cycle. For there are very many detailed echoes of these poems in the *Iliad*[31] and *Odyssey*[32]—

for example, the *Odyssey* likes dogs [33](page 88) which are popular at Ugarit but nowhere else in the Semitic world; and there are foreshadowings of the story of Helen. In the epic *Keret*, the prince of that name mourns the departure of his wife, but the god El—called 'father of men' like Zeus—tells him to besiege Udum and demand the king's daughter Hurriya 'whose eye-balls are gems of sapphires, whose eyelids alabaster cups'. Keret does so, and the besieged city surrenders her.

These correspondences raise a question which is important to our historical knowledge of the transmission of mythology. Are the similarities due, ultimately, to the connections between the Minoans and Ugarit in the seventeenth and sixteenth centuries BC?—for Cretan pottery was imported to Ugarit, and there was probably a Minoan settlement there. But then, in the fourteenth and thirteenth centuries, this colony was superseded by a Mycenaean settlement. Did that play a part in the transmission? Or does the link between Homeric and Ugaritic poems instead indicate a literary association in the *eighth* century, between Homer and the Phoenicians who had taken over Ugarit traditions? There was by then a Greek colony—in the closest relation with the great Phoenician cities of Byblus, Tyre and Sidon—at Al Mina not far from the mouth of the Orontes. Moreover, that was the time when the Greeks borrowed, first, the Phoenician alphabet, and then (and increasingly in the next century) the many 'orientalizing' artistic features, fantastic monsters and the like, for which Phoenicia was the natural intermediary between Greek lands and the near or middle east—Babylon and Assyria, with their roots in the Sumerian past (page 94). The answers to these problems are not with us yet; but the researches of the next few years may provide them.

At any rate Helen might never have got to Troy if it had not been for Levantine *Keret*. But the alternative rendering—that she did not—reflects the existence of a second version unaffected by *Keret*.

4   *The Qualities of a Hero*

One of the *Iliad*'s outstanding contributions to human civilization, for good and for evil, is its concept of the hero. The Greeks of the eighth century BC, and for ever afterwards,[34] saw something splendid and superhuman about what they supposed to be their lost past. This seemed to them filled with superb figures living for renown, and pursuing it with competitive vigour. The hero must use his superior qualities at all times to excel and win applause, for that is the reward and demonstration of his manhood. He makes honour his paramount code, and glory the driving force and aim of his existence. Birth, wealth and prowess confirm a hero's title; his ideals are courage, endurance, strength and beauty. Enthusiastically confident in what he achieves and possesses, he relies upon his own ability to make the fullest use of his powers.

Yet, although he is no god, there is something about him which brings him not too far from heaven: Hesiod thought of the heroes as half-way between gods and men (page 126).[35] Their mighty achievements inspired poets to suggest that human nature, far though it is from divinity, can yet come within reach of it—a conclusion which the greater claims of the supernatural had made impossible for Egypt or Babylonia. For the Greeks, too, there were many reserves and qualifications; yet man could still aspire. In the words of Pindar the Boeotian:

> We can in greatness of mind
> Or of body be like the Immortals,
> Though we know not to what goal
> By day or in the nights
> Fate has written that we shall run.[36]

Glory—favourable public opinion—was the quality by which the individual could become like the gods. It was a glory of military and athletic prowess, hereditary arrogance and aristocratic class privilege. The only demagogue in the *Iliad*, Thersites, receives contemptuous punishment. Heroic aspiration is the keynote; denial of due honour was a catastrophe for Achilles (page 42). The hero's whole career was an unremitting struggle, undertaken with all his manly endurance (*tlemosyne*),[37] for the first prize among his peers. In a period of rapid transition Homer, like Dante and Shakespeare after him, is upholding a traditional nostalgic system of values.

No remote serenity was attributed to these legendary figures. They were violently emotional, and of erratic temperamental stability. When Patroclus is killed, there is no question of the greatest of the heroes, Achilles, keeping a stiff upper lip. 'He picked up the dark dust in both his hands and poured it on his head. He soiled his comely face with it, and filthy ashes settled on his scented tunic. He cast himself down on the earth and lay there like a fallen giant, fouling his hair and tearing it out with his own hands. The maid-servants whom he and Patroclus had captured caught the alarm and all ran screaming out of doors. They beat their breasts with their hands and sank to the ground beside their royal master. On the other side, Antilochus shedding tears of misery held the hands of Achilles as he sobbed out his noble heart, for fear that he might take a knife and cut his throat.'[38]

Yet in weakness and strength alike the Hero has transformed our ways of thinking. The heroic outlook shook off primitive super-stitions and taboos by showing that man can do amazing things by his own effort and by his own nature, indeed that he can almost rise *above* his own nature into strengths scarcely known or under-stood. As early as the Homeric poems themselves the great stories are held up as educational examples.[39] This continued throughout antiquity, and then again in the schools of the Renaissance upon which the *élite* institutions of today, not least in Britain and America, are still based. When we read the *Iliad*, we feel larger than life, freed from the compulsion of present realities. The epic heroes carry us with them in their struggles and their sufferings; they are not as we are, yet we follow after them. And so when they suffer or exult, so do we.

Herder in 1773 attacked all rococo attempts to prettify the heroes. His admirer Goethe saw in the Greeks a people that had understood better than any other how to give form to life on a grand scale—they knew how to strike out and, while keeping within bounds, savour life to the limit. The Greeks, with their heroes, were the most vivid experience of Goethe's life—though a disillusioning one in the end, because he, a modern northerner, came to despair of reviving them from the dead. To Hölderlin, before his mind failed, the heroes were a ruling passion. 'Greece was my first love, and shall I say that she will be my last? . . . Who can endure it? Whom does the terrifying glory of antiquity not uproot, as the hurricane uproots young woods when it seizes them, as it seized me? . . . I loved my heroes as a moth loves the light.'

Yet much of the militancy of the western tradition, as well as its humanity, can also be traced back to the personages of the *Iliad*; for instance, the spirit of Thomas Carlyle, writing *On Heroes and Hero Worship*. He feels a 'heart-felt prostrate admiration, submission, burning, boundless, for a noblest god-like Form of Man'. Quoting Novalis on the Body of Man as the one, holy Temple in the Universe, Carlyle claims to link the hero-cult with Christianity—'the greatest of Heroes is one'—but it is a Christian ideal far from the humility of the New Testament.

For the Homeric hero loved battle, and fighting was his life. The society to which he is said to belong devotes peculiar, maximum attention to war, like the heroic ages in Russia, India, among the south Slavs, and also (we are learning) in Africa. A hero's activity is narrower than a god's because it is concentrated on the most testing kind of action, war—hateful perhaps and with miserable moments, but an unequalled field for achievement and glory. Large stretches of the *Iliad* have been described as a bath of blood, gloriously described. The fighting can occasionally be broken off for a conference (*Iliad* II, III). But, although there are subordinate traces of a more peaceful ethic embodying ideas of justice, the heroic pursuit of glory leaves no room for chivalry or the sporting spirit, because lack of suitably emphasized vengeance would mean an inadequate satisfaction of honour. It was, usually, futile to plead with a hero's sense of injury. 'Patroclus picked up a jagged, sparkling stone —his hand just covered it—and standing in no awe of Hector threw it with all his force. He did not make an idle cast, for the sharp stone caught Hector's driver Cebriones, King Priam's bastard son, on the forehead, with the horses' reins in his hands. It shattered both his eyebrows, crushing in the bone; and his eyes fell out and rolled in the dust at his feet. He dropped from the well-built chariot like a diver and yielded up his life. The knight Patroclus jeered at him:

"Ha! Quite an acrobat, I see, judging by that graceful dive! The man who takes so neat a header from a chariot on land could dive for oysters from a ship at sea in any weather and fetch up plenty for a feast. I did not know that the Trojans had such divers." '[40]

The gloating reaches its culmination when Achilles and Hector meet in the duel that is fatal to Hector.

> Clean through the soft part of the neck the spear-
> point was driven.
> Yet the ash spear heavy with bronze did not sever the
> windpipe,
> so that Hector could still make exchange of words
> spoken.
> But he dropped in the dust, and brilliant Achilles
> vaunted above him:
> 'Hector, surely you thought as you killed Patroclus
> you would be
> safe, and since I was far away you thought nothing of
> me,
> o fool, for an avenger was left, far greater than
> he was,
> behind him and away by the hollow ships. And it
> was I;
> and I have broken your strength; on you the dogs
> and the vultures
> shall feed and foully rip you; the Achaeans will
> bury Patroclus.'[41]

And Achilles, each day, dragged the corpse in the dust behind his chariot, three times round the tomb of Patroclus.[42] Already at the funeral of Patroclus, Achilles in his grief had gone beyond the Homeric norm—by human sacrifice. He had 'done an evil thing: he put a dozen brave men, the sons of noble Trojans, to the sword, and set the pyre alight so that pitiless flames might feed on them'.[43] Genocide, too, already thousands of years old, had been the stated aim of the Trojan War as Homer described it. 'No, we are not going to leave a single one of them alive, down to the babies in their mothers' wombs—not even they must live. The whole people must be wiped out of existence, and none be left to think of them and shed a tear.'[44]

Such barbarities apart, an atmosphere of tragedy surrounds the Hero. There is pathos in his struggle against his fellows and against fate; he fulfils himself in death, the last and most searching ordeal, the true test of worth. The death of the old in battle, thought Homer and after him the Spartan poet Tyrtaeus, was even more to be deplored than the death of the young, for the old man's corpse looks less noble. But the death of a hero, too, was seen as utterly hateful. 'To Homer above all,' remarked Louise Matthaei, 'we owe that amazed and stricken sense of the utterly unjustifiable oppression of death, which has dogged us ever since.' To Simone Weil it seemed that when a great hero of the *Iliad* fell, 'the bitterness of this scene, we savour it whole, alleviated by no comforting fiction, no consoling immortality, no faint halo of patriotic glory'. Heroism leads to misery and death, honour to slaughter: the poet knows much about human suffering. Such a myth, to psychoanalysts like Geza Roheim, reflects human nature's tragic ambivalence, of which there is no termination but death.

The epic bards of all nations inherited a tradition of sorrow and defeat. And above all the deaths of Hector and Patroclus, for all the bragging over them, are too pitiful for savage exultation to prevail. There is pity for the shortness of heroes' lives and the waste caused by their anger and pride, and pity is heightened by the contrast between their passionate delight in living and our knowledge (which they sometimes share) of what lies in store for them. Yet this is not the melancholy of Edda and Beowulf and *Ecclesiastes*, but a conviction based less on pessimism than on the belief that life is important because there is little beyond the grave (page 94). The pathos and war weariness of the *Iliad* are subordinate to the main clash of arms; nevertheless, at times, the sadness is clearly heard. It is a tragic conception, already sounded in the first five verses, that a quarrel should bring so much death and disaster.

On the Trojan side, there is impending catastrophe in Hector's meeting with his baby boy Astyanax.

'But may I be dead and the piled earth hide me
  under before I
hear you crying and know by this that they drag
  you captive.'
    So speaking glorious Hector held out his
    arms to his baby,
who shrank back to his fair-girdled nurse's
    bosom
screaming, and frightened at the aspect of his own
    father,
terrified as he saw the bronze and the crest with
  its horsehair,
nodding dreadfully, as he thought, from the peak
  of the helmet.
Then his beloved father laughed out, and his
  honoured mother,
and at once glorious Hector lifted from his head
  the helmet
and laid it in all its shining upon the ground. Then
  taking
up his dear son he tossed him about in his arms, and
  kissed him,
and lifted his voice in prayer to Zeus and the other
  immortals:
'Zeus, and you other immortals, grant that this boy,
  who is my son,
may be as I am, pre-eminent among the
    Trojans,
great in strength, as am I, and rule strongly over
    Ilion;
and some day let them say of him: "He is better by
  far than his father,"
as he comes in from the fighting; and let him kill
  his enemy
and bring home the blooded spoils, and delight the
  heart of his mother.'[45]

The chain of events that had begun with the old father of Chryseis hounded from the Greek camp ends with Hector's old father being sent home, by the most ferocious of heroes, with mercy (page 42). That meeting of Achilles, at the end of the poem, with the bereaved father of his enemy is in profound contrast to slaughter and human sacrifice; it is like the Reversal or Recoil which was later to be the hallmark of many an Athenian tragedy (page 224). The ostensibly simple description of this scene is all the more pathetic because the dominant note of the whole poem still remains, not pathos, but the roar and exultation of battle. Out of the degradation and misery comes compassion.

Such compassionate chords make up the profound humanity of the *Iliad*. Though scarcely pointing any moral, the poem (with a magical blend of simplicity and grandeur) justifies the ways of men and women at their finest and best. These myths did much to launch the Greeks upon their abiding concern with human dignity. The view is impersonal and disengaged, yet interpretation of thoughts and motives is both lively and understanding, tolerant but never indifferent, passionate but balanced. Far above the level of saga, the *Iliad* combines the unfaltering vision of Dante with Shakespeare's boundless sympathy. Men are unscrupulous, hot-tempered, irresolute and domineering, but they are also noble, self-sacrificing, impelled by deep emotions, and devoted to an exacting code.

Already in the Homeric poems themselves its stories are held up as educational models and sagas for the attention of posterity (page 52); and part of the significance of the Trojan myth lies in the variety of responses that it has evoked from creative imaginations throughout the ages. Achilles and the rest have been needed, at many epochs, to invigorate men's perceptions of their own surroundings. To this day they provide, as Myres expressed it, 'an enlargement, disentanglement and articulation of our own experience.'

In classical times the Trojan story was everywhere. Homer had his commentators as early as Theagenes of Rhegium in the sixth century BC. The most famous of all painters, Polygnotus, depicted Troy's fall at Delphi, on behalf of the people of Cnidus. One-fifth of all Aeschylus and Euripides comes from the Trojan cycle, two-fifths of Sophocles. 'My father,' said a friend of Xenophon, 'eager to have me become a good man, compelled me to commit to memory all the poetry of Homer, and thus it happens that even now I can repeat from memory all the *Iliad* and *Odyssey*.'[46] Alexander the Great made Achilles his pattern, and carried the *Iliad* about with him in a jewelled casket. For one thousand years of antiquity this poem was the greatest unifying, civilizing factor in Greek and Graeco-Roman history, exercising influence in a thousand ways upon literary, educational, political and moral thought.

Prose versions in Latin, of uncertain authorship but known by the name of 'Dares' and 'Dictys' who were the alleged writers of their Greek originals, reintroduced the story to the medieval world; until the sixteenth century, these epitomes were accepted as more 'reliable' than Homer. But men's imaginations, for five hundred years, were also caught by a discursive epic romance likewise derived from the *Iliad*, the *Roman de Troie* of Benoit de Ste Maure (*c.* AD 1160–5). And for the same length of time reigned Geoffrey of Monmouth's story that Britain's origin was Trojan.

The reinterpretations of Homer have been innumerable. Titian, Tintoretto and Veronese imposed their own Venetian stamp upon many a legend of Troy (page 90); Marlowe wrote memorably of Helen (page 48), and Shakespeare's *Troilus and Cressida* (Chryseis), based on a medieval offshoot of the *Iliad* elaborated by Chaucer, adds a brutal, cynical slant. In the great age of French tragedy, Racine's first important play was his *Andromaque* (1667). He was particularly at home in this world (page 197)—though criticized in his day for recasting Achilles as a courtly lover. Goethe, on the other hand, in his unfinished *Achilleis* (1797–9), makes the hero a life-weary Hamlet, mirroring the deadly ennui which Goethe himself knew. Goethe also paid repeated tributes to Helen, from the time of his *Iphigenie* (1779) to the publication of his *Helena* (1827), twenty-seven years after its inception.

> Whom Helena has paralysed,
> His reason hardly shall regain.

A plethora of Homeric operas and operettas had now come to an end, and the nineteenth century was adding its specific quota of sentiment, philosophical idealism and romance. Chapman's translation (1596–1611) had been unpopular in the time of Pope, but Keats hailed it as the discovery of a new imaginative world. Matthew Arnold wrote *On Translating Homer*, and his *Palladium* (1867) is perhaps the most firmly rounded of the poems in which he touches morality with emotion.

> We shall renew the battle in the plain
> Tomorrow: red with blood will Xanthus be;
> Hector and Ajax will be there again,
> Helen will come upon the wall to see.

Countless French writers of the same time contemplated her; and so did Edgar Allan Poe.

> Helen, thy beauty is to me
> Like those Nicaean barks of yore,
> That gently, o'er a perfumed sea,
> The weary, wayworn wanderer bore
> To his own native shore.

Walt Whitman, however, had had enough of all this.

> Come Muse, migrate from Greece and Ionia,
> Cross out please those immensely overpaid accounts,
> That matter of Troy and Achilles' wrath, and Aeneas',
>   Odysseus' wanderings;
> Placard 'Removed' and 'To let' on the rocks of your
>   snowy Parnassus.

Yet still in our own century Edwin Muir was a poet absorbed in the Sack of Troy, which is the archetype, in a group of his poems, of the fallen town or citadel, betrayed and ruined by time and time's human agents.

Giraudoux, blending tragedy and burlesque in his often-performed play *The Trojan War Shall Not Take Place* (1935), is obsessed by this as the symbol of all wars, which flatter human instincts and are the crudest of egalitarian devices. The dramatist sharpens our reasoning power and sensitivity without proposing a clear conclusion, as Hector, feeling the modern conflict in his soul, veers suddenly to renunciation: 'the spear clashing on his shield has suddenly rung false'. To Giraudoux, living in our world, destiny weighs desperately heavy. Yet, even so, it is only a last-minute failure of diplomacy which unleashes hostilities and disaster.

5   A Hero and His Gods

The gods of Greek myth are almost beyond our emotional reach, because they are many instead of one. But the anthropologists have, at least, made it impossible for us to generalize from the Old Testament that polytheism, *everywhere*, is the more elementary stage of religion, and monotheism the more advanced stage. For, although the earliest object of worship was very often an undifferentiated power, Andrew Lang pointed out in 1898 that even very primitive peoples, such as Australian aborigines, have a remote, transcendent High God. Evans-Pritchard has subsequently shown that Kwoth, worshipped by the Sudanese Nuer, is in the same category. Sometimes, indeed, the high god of an earlier stage fades when a polytheistic array of spirits is invented at a later epoch. Or, in other religions, the two conceptions continue simultaneously. Among the Dakota Indians, what the ordinary man regards as eight distinct deities the priest takes to be aspects of one and the same.

In Egypt, the revolutionary reign of Akhenaten in the fourteenth century BC introduced some sort of a monotheism or universal, cosmic idea of a divinity, addressed in the singular. Yet the gods of the *Iliad* remain firmly distinct one from another, and indeed the products of 'Linear B' decipherment (page 33) suggest that there had already been considerable individuation of these beings as early as the thirteenth century. It may be that in Greece an earlier, general sense of divinity was gradually fragmented, and that (in the case of female deities) the use of the word 'Potnia' (lady) with dependent genitive or epithet marks an intermediate stage in this process. The differentiation was probably due in part to an increasing idea of divided functions: Zeus rules the sky, Posidon the sea, and so on. But it is likely also that when, in the second millennium BC, the ancestors of the Greeks gradually infiltrated the country that was to belong to them, their religious ideas incorporated, one after another, the local deities of the various, more or less isolated, communities which they encountered (page 146). Indeed, the favoured treatment accorded to one hero or another by Homeric gods could go back to specific regional links of this kind, reflecting the ancient near-eastern tradition of petty states and parochial beliefs. And the inhabitants had their local favourites, too, among the gods, just as a peasant of Chios to this day will say, in a scarcely monotheistic spirit, that the Virgin of his village church is superior to those in the valleys round about.

Yet the creation of the Olympians, as Greece knew them, is to a very great extent due not directly to religious thought (or, as some believe, to ritual, page 157) but to the epic poets. The gods, it is true, came down from the past, but their vividness is a result of the poetic tradition which imagined them in the radiant colouring of the Homeric myths. It was the achievement of the epic tradition to weld this heterogeneous collection of deities into a single family of clear-cut individuals, displaying the firm outlines and consistency of a classical masterpiece; the poets not only inherited myth but created it. And above all, it was from the poet of the *Iliad* that the gods took shape, with whatever assistance he may have received from his forerunners (page 36). This religion and this mythology are the outcome of poetic and artistic genius, conveying an euphoric vision, aesthetic not moral in its origin, of a dazzling, awe-inspiringly vital Olympian world.

This world, no less than its heroic counterpart on earth, fascinated the German romantic poets. Schiller's hypnotic poem *The Gods of Greece* (1788) struck chords of sorrow and desolation for deities who had become faded and precious. In Heine, answering him, the nostalgia is sharper. The gods are helpless, because being mere 'holiday-gods', unloving and unloved, they have been conquered by young deities. 'So feasted they all day', he wrote in a letter (1828) translated by E. M. Butler, 'till the setting of the sun . . . Then suddenly there came panting in a pale Jew, dripping with blood, a crown of thorn upon his head and a great wooden cross upon his shoulders; and he threw down the cross on to the high table of the gods, so that the golden bowls trembled, and the gods fell silent, and grew pale, and became ever paler until they finally dissolved away altogether in mist.'

Yet for all its literary origins and repercussions, the Homeric picture of divinity was to acquire a strong religious aspect, which the Greeks came to take very seriously; their imaginative thinkers set a decisive stamp upon the history of the race. From our modern viewpoint, Greek religion may be explained negatively—by a description of all that we *cannot* share with it. For, as W. Kranz observed, '*we* have no trust in oracles, mysteries, soothsayings and dreams; we do not pray at sunrise and sunset, before we drink, at departure and home-coming. We make no libation of bread and wine, no sacrifice to the souls of our dead; we do not give the god his share at each success in battle, in the games, in the theatre, in the work of our hands.' Conversely, we expect a religion to have a creed or a general code or a system of morality. The Greeks did not. Nor did they, in Homer's time, have prophets or priests, revelations or sacred books, doctrines of redemption and salvation. Yet, for all that, their unflinching faith in the reality of the unseen, and the guise in which they embodied this faith, represent an important stage in the history of human belief.

This is chiefly because they believed that their gods were in the shape of human beings. In itself that was nothing new, since man has always transferred to the objects of his worship the qualities he recognizes in himself; all ancient societies—including at times the Jews[47]—were sure that Nature was governed by man-like forces: God made man in his own image. Indeed, most believers in God today still see Him, in their mind's eye, in human shape. But the Greek gods were the most thoroughly human and anthropomorphic that the world has ever seen. It is true that the *Iliad* retains faint traces of animal-shaped gods—cow-eyed Hera, owl-eyed Athene, and the like—but these are far removed from the grotesque animal epiphanies of Asia in the second millennium BC, or of Polynesia, or of the Montana Crow Indians with their sun-coyote. For the Greeks took it for granted that man is the crown of creation, and so, since heaven is seen in terms of earth, the gods have his shape; they felt themselves unlike orientals in 'believing the gods to have the same nature as man'.[48] Indeed, such was their confidence in humanity and its range and possibilities that they could feel man to be closest to divinity when he was most completely himself. So this transformation of the gods into human shape was a prodigious influence towards emancipation—or spiritual pride.

Homer and Hesiod, said Herodotus, 'taught the Greeks the descent of the gods and assigned to them their names and honours and arts, and described their appearance.'[49] But the way in which the gods were characterized conflicts with our ideas of divinity. They were not perfect; they were not even good. They fought, feasted, misgoverned and seduced just like the conquering chieftains and buccaneers on earth. Indeed, the Trojan royal house behaved a good deal better than the gods did. But the gods were everlasting, and they were immeasurably beautiful, strong and impressive. To an art-loving people, they were an inspiration for centuries.

Yet it was by no means impossible to mock them. Peoples more primitive than this, ancestral to Homeric ideas, had already been accustomed to regard their gods under a ludicrous, buffoon aspect as well as seriously. Besides, as Sir Maurice Bowra observed, a heroic age like Homer's has so high a sense of the dignity of man that it can afford to make fun of the gods; as in Cervantes and Shakespeare, even tragedy may be strongly salted with humour, satire and ridicule. Thus Zeus himself, the ruler of all (page 184), is a petulant, sensual, hen-pecked figure, who can change sides twice a day. 'My father,' observes his daughter Athene, 'is in a wicked mood, obstinate old sinner that he is, always meddling with my plans.'[50] Nor does the poet intend us to take too seriously the vivid terms in which he asserts his undoubted supremacy over the other Olympians.

> Whenever I might strongly be minded to pull you,
> I could drag you up, earth and all and sea and all
>   with you,

> then fetch the golden rope about the horn of Olympus
> and make it fast, so that all once more should dangle
>   in mid air.
> So much stronger am I than the gods, and stronger than
>   mortals.[51]

His wife Hera, venerated by Bronze Age communities (at first quite separately from him) at Argos, Mycenae, Sparta and Samos, appears as a cruel, sly termagant who farcically tricks him into wasting time in bed with her—in a story which may reflect a rite of divine marriage and seasonal renewal (page 112). But Zeus retaliates reminding her of a humiliating punishment she had experienced before. 'Have you forgotten the time when I strung you aloft with a couple of anvils hanging from your feet and your hands lashed together with a golden chain you could not break? There you dangled, up in the air and in among the clouds; and the gods on high Olympus, though they rallied round you in their indignation, found it impossible to set you free.'[52]

Posidon, a native Greek god—though not originally of the sea— is more prominent at Pylos even than Zeus; in the epic poems he escaped most indignities. In his maritime aspect he inspired Leonardo da Vinci—his was the first of many Renaissance interpretations of this deity (1504), paralleled by Milton's invocation in *Comus*. But Ares, the god of war (originally a foreign divinity, with Thracian associations), is blustering, brutal and even cowardly.

> Ares is blind, and with unseeing eyes
> Set in a swine's face stirs up all to evil.[53]

The most sordid scene of all, however, occurs when Athene, at Hera's instigation, clouts Aphrodite the partisan of Troy, and there is a thoroughly unseemly scuffle (which some try to excise from the poem):

> Athene caught up with her and drove a blow at her
>   breasts with her ponderous
> hand, so that her knees went slack and the heart
>   inside her.
> Those two both lay sprawled on the generous earth.[54]

A Greek would enjoy this scrapping between the two radiant, terrific beauties, and he would not worship them less reverently because of such a brawl.

Their intervention in his life seemed to him formidable but sporadic. There was something contradictory about making the participants in these unedifying Olympian scenes the arbiters of human behaviour. Yet man is, it seemed, inextricably connected with the gods, for the poet does not quite regard human beings as responsible for their own decisions; there is less tragic affirmation of personal freedom than in the heroic poetry of the Teutons. So the Olympians are seen in two ways. They live apart—yet on, or not too far from, the earth. Their home is the enormous massif of Mount Olympus, between Thessaly and Macedonia, with its splendid displays of light and cloud. The Olympian family would have been too separate if each had been allowed to stay in his own village or valley; and mountain-tops had long been the home of the sky-god Zeus. So the mythographers concentrated the gods upon Olympus. Yet there was a feeling that they retained a strong interest in the world. Not only did some of them supervise the operation of the earth's natural elements, but they protected cities and peoples and, when they chose to, exercised a fierce power to hurt individuals or to help them.

When we say 'by an effort of will', the Greek might say 'by the help of some god'. Life at its intensest moments seemed lit with a sudden brightness and brilliance from some non-human source; the existence of divinity meant that, in critical and climactic times, human life could touch a new dimension. This was particularly needful in that greatest of occupations, fighting. Many millennia before the Angels of Mons, the need was felt for guardian angels in battle. The heroes, as they fought, were accompanied by their gods—perhaps they were 'possessed', as in Haitian Voodoo.

> Hector stood up close to Ajax and hacked at
>   the ash spear
> with his great sword, striking behind the socket of
>   the spearhead,
> and slashed it clean away, so that Telamonian Ajax

> shook there in his hand a lopped spear, while far
>   away from him
> the bronze spearhead fell echoing to the ground; and
>   Ajax
> knew in his blameless heart, and shivered for knowing
>   it, how this
> was god's work, how Zeus high-thundering cut across
>   the intention
> in all his battle, how he planned that the Trojans
>   should conquer.[55]

Later writers gave a more sophisticated twist to these happenings. Not long after the *Iliad*, Stasinus of Cyprus[56] ascribed the Trojan war to a wise and pitying Zeus, on the Malthusian assumption that he 'decided to relieve the all-nurturing earth of men'. And then Euripides, in his *Trojan Women*, emphasized the destructiveness of the gods in this war (page 68).

What could be done to be preserved from their violence? There was always prayer. That was an entreaty, without confession of short-comings or promise of improvement; a matter of contracts, bargains and mutual assistance. But it was still very important, for to most men religion meant forms of worship. Yet the amount of divine intervention, good or bad, to be expected was not too great. The *Iliad* has its miracles, and a good many of them; and the gods inspire the main doings of a hero, but they leave him room to display his own vigorous capacity for action. They are extraneous, and when they intervene, they throw into relief a contrast between the grandeur of human life and its imperfection. They are useful as narrative, but they do not change human nature, except to remind it of fallibility or, conversely, to fortify its self-esteem—for instance, by reconciling it to the greatest of Homeric terrors, death. For the rest, there was freedom of choice, and the supremacy of the gods was acknowledged without sacrificing the dignity and independence of man.

It is, therefore, too simple to label the gods as 'coaches, substitutes, referees, spectators and spongers'. But the question does arise whether their interventions were regarded as backing right against wrong. When Gladstone saw in the Homeric gods a sense of duty and a consciousness of moral responsibility, he exaggerated. Even if we leave their personal irregularities aside, the most that can be said is that the Homeric poems contain casual, but inconsistent, references to the punishment of the wicked. Zeus tended to protect the stranger and the oppressed, and perhaps fear of the gods might lead a man into moderation; but they lacked true affection for mortals. There was something devastatingly arbitrary about their fitful decisions and *actes de présence*. It warranted the pessimism—greater than Homer's—of the lyric poet Archilochus, who probably lived not long after him.

> To the gods all things are easy. Many times from
>   circumstance
> of disaster they set upright those who have been
>   sprawled at length
> on the ground, but often again when men stand
>   planted on firm feet
> these same gods will knock them on their backs, and
>   then the evils come,
> so that a man wanders homeless, destitute, at his
>   wit's end.[57]

Yet, for all the inadequacies of the gods in guidance and support, the epic poems simultaneously show another sanction working strongly upon the heroes. This is not metaphysical but psychological. Catastrophes were often brought about, among these warriors bursting with heroic energy, by pride (*hubris*). By excess of this quality the hero was lost to *aidos*, which is shame or decency or the restraining force of public opinion. This loss meant a fatal hardening of character (*atasthalie*), and also signified in the shame-culture of Homer—an earlier stage than our own (declining) guilt-culture (page 183)—that he had forfeited the good repute for which men so greatly strove; for the characteristic of a shame-culture is tension between the individual impulse and the pressure of social conformity. And so the hero, for all his brilliant ferocity, succumbs to the terrible power of blind folly, which (like Strife, Death and Rumour)

is half personified (page 187): as *ate*, 'the eldest daughter of Zeus'.[58]
Then his lot is *nemesis*, the retribution which falls on the justly
disapproved.[59]

That is how disaster came upon both Agamemnon and Achilles.
Their arrogant grandeur (Agamemnon admits it) had made them
forgetful of the common cause; just as later the downfall of rich
Croesus of Lydia was a by-word for the results of *hubris* (page 188).
There was something of all this inherent in the whole story of the
Fall of Troy, as Euripides, in a more reflective age, was to state more
explicitly:

> That mortal who sacks fallen cities is a fool;
> Who gives the temples and the tombs, the hallowed
>   places
> Of the dead to desolation. His own turn must come.[60]

Most men believe, even now, *both* in fate *and* in freedom of will, at
the same time—and the Homeric poems are equally contradictory.
That is why Michael Tippett used the story of *King Priam* for his
opera (1962) centred upon the mysterious nature of human choice.
At the outset of the *Iliad* we are told of the fulfilling of Zeus' purpose
(page 27); yet it is more often thwarted and diverted. Normally
Fate, a fixed order rather than a fully personified power, is the
instrument of Zeus, or his partner,[61] or even synonymous with him:
both Zeus and Fate stand for the causes of events which man is
powerless to alter. So there can be no conflict with Zeus. Yet, three
times, Fate decides which way his balance shall dip. Perhaps this
dramatic emphasis seemed to the poets the proper compensation for
a certain lack of omnipotence in the gods. They have their failings;
they are not the creators of the universe (page 109); and Zeus cannot
avert the death of his own protégé Sarpedon. He can, however,
postpone it. But for others the day is fixed and cannot be delayed.
The *Iliad* dates from before the time when fate is separate from the
gods, or above them, or when it symbolizes the unaccountable in
human experience (in the *Odyssey*), or is linked with Chance.[62]

Yet fate is never far away from the *Iliad*, which like all great epics
and myths has important things to say about human destiny. It

frankly admits the stubborn, mysterious inconsistencies of life. At the end, Achilles' words to Priam are bleak: 'We men are wretched things, and the gods, who have no cares themselves, have woven sorrow into the very pattern of our lives. You know that Zeus the thunderer has two jars standing on the floor of his palace in which he keeps his gifts, the evils in one and the blessings in the other. People who receive from him a mixture of the two have varying fortunes, sometimes good and sometimes bad; though when Zeus serves a man from the jar of evil only, he makes him an outcast, who is chased by the gadfly of despair over the face of the earth and goes his way damned by gods and men alike.'[63] This is a stark realism, bordering on hopelessness, in which the hero needed all the enduring self-reliance that he could muster. With its aid, he faced the world boldly and proudly, accepting whatever fate might bring.

CHAPTER 2

ODYSSEUS

———————

1 The Story Told in the ODYSSEY

THE ILIAD had ended with the death of Hector, and Troy was to fall soon afterwards. Then the heroes had to find their way home again. The *Odyssey* describes the adventures of one of them. Just as the *Iliad* told of the tenth year of the Trojan War, so the *Odyssey* begins in the tenth year of the wanderings of Odysseus.

The gods, in the absence of Odysseus' enemy Posidon, met in council upon Mount Olympus. His protector Athene asked that he should be rescued from the island of Ogygia—on which he had spent seven wasted years as the guest and prisoner of Calypso— and allowed to return to his home on the isle of Ithaca. Zeus agreed; and Athene departed for Ithaca. Disguised as Mentes, a friend of Odysseus, she appeared to the hero's son Telemachus, and urged him to assert himself by dismissing from the palace the one hundred and twelve importunate suitors who were courting his mother Penelope. He must also try to find out news of his father.

Telemachus summoned an assembly, and ordered the suitors to go. They refused, but Athene appeared again—this time as another fellow-citizen, Mentor. She provided Telemachus with a ship and crew, and they sailed together for Nestor's home at Pylos. He had no news of Odysseus, but sent Telemachus on to Sparta, supplying him with a chariot and with his own son Pisistratus as an escort. At

Sparta they found King Menelaus, the last of the Greeks, so far, to come home; he had brought back his wife Helen, whose abduction had caused the war. Menelaus revealed to Telemachus what he had heard, while becalmed at the Egyptian island of Pharos, from Proteus the shepherd of the ocean. Describing the fortunes of the other Greeks, Proteus had disclosed that Odysseus was not dead but a prisoner of the nymph Calypso on her island.

At Ithaca, meanwhile, the suitors plotted to ambush and slay Telemachus on his way home. But Athene comforted Penelope in a dream, and Zeus sent Hermes to Ogygia with orders for Calypso. Hermes found her in the great cavern which was her home.

> Upon her hearthstone a great fire blazing
> Scented the farthest shores with cedar smoke
> And smoke of thyme; and singing high and low
> In her sweet voice, before her loom a-weaving,
> She passed her golden shuttle to and fro.
> A deep wood grew outside, with summer leaves
> Of alder and black poplar, pungent cypress.
> Ornate birds here rested their stretched wings—
> Horned owls, falcons, cormorants—long-tongued
> Beach-combing birds, and followers of the sea.
> Around the smooth-walled cave a crooking vine
> Held purple clusters under ply of green;
> And four springs, bubbling up near one another
> Shallow and clear, took channels here and there
> Through beds of violets and tender parsley.
> Even a god who found this place
> Would gaze, and feel his heart beat with delight:
> So Hermes did . . .[1]

Hermes told Calypso the will of Zeus, which was that Odysseus should leave her. Sadly and reluctantly she accepted this decision, as she must, and sought out Odysseus. 'She found him sitting on the shore. His eyes were wet with weeping, as they always were. Life with its sweetness was ebbing away in the tears he shed for his lost home. For the nymph had long since ceased to please. At nights, it is true, he had to sleep with her under the roof of the cavern, cold lover with an ardent dame. But the days found him sitting on the rocks or sands, torturing himself with tears and groans and heart-ache, and looking out with streaming eyes across the watery wilderness.'

Calypso, though asserting that she was by no means inferior to Penelope in looks and figure, gave Odysseus the material to build a boat; and he sailed away. Navigating by the stars, in the early morning light of the eighteenth day he saw the mountainous Phaeacian coast ahead. But Posidon caught sight of him and wrecked his ship, and he was narrowly saved from death by the sea-nymph Ino-Leucothea, sent to rescue him by Athene. After battling against the storm for two days and two nights, he staggered ashore exhausted upon the isle of Scheria, land of the Phaeacians. Sinking down in a bed of dry leaves, he fell asleep.

Nausicaa, daughter of the Phaeacian King Alcinous, had been prompted by Athene in a dream to bring her family linen to the river-mouth to be washed.

> Her mother, for their luncheon, packed a hamper
> With picnic fare and filled a skin of wine,
> And, when the princess had been handed up,
> Gave her a golden bottle of olive oil
> For softening girls' bodies, after bathing.

When they arrived,

> The girls unhitched the mules, and sent them down
> Along the eddying stream to crop sweet grass.
> Then sliding out the cart's tailboard, they took
> Armloads of clothing to the dusky water,
> And trod them in the pits, making a race of it.
> All being drubbed, all blemish rinsed away,
> They spread them, piece by piece, along the beach
> Whose pebbles had been laundered by the sea;
> Then took a dip themselves, and, all anointed
> With golden oil, ate lunch beside the river

While the bright burning sun dried out their linen.
Princess and maids delighted in that feast;
Then, putting off their veils,
They ran and passed a ball to a rhythmic beat,
Nausicaa flashing first with her white arms . . .
                                        It happened
When the king's daughter threw her ball off line
And missed, and put it in the whirling stream—
At which they all gave such a shout, Odysseus
Awoke and sat up . . .
He pushed aside the bushes, breaking off
With his great hand a single branch of olive,
Whose leaves might shield him in his nakedness;
So came out rustling, like a mountain lion,
Rain-drenched, wind-buffeted, but in his might at ease,
With burning eyes—who prowls among the herds
Or flocks, or after game, his hungry belly
Taking him near stout homesteads for his prey.
Odysseus had this look, in his rough skin
Advancing on the girls with pretty braids;
And he was driven on by hunger, too.
Streaked with brine, and swollen, he terrified them,
So that they fled, this way and that. Only
Alcinous' daughter stood her ground, being given
A bold heart by Athene, and steady knees.'[2]

Nausicaa fed and clothed him, and showed the way to her father's
magnificent palace. Though well received by the king and by Arete
his queen, Odysseus showed annoyance at a slur on his sportsman-
ship from the young Euryalus, whom he had refused to join in a game.
'That, sir,' the hero told him, 'was an ugly speech and you must be a
fool to have made it . . . You yourself, sir, present a most distinguished exterior to the world—the gods themselves could not improve
it—but you have the brains of a dolt.' Put on his mettle, Odysseus
attracted interest by an enormous discus-throw. 'But the things,' the
king pointed out, 'in which we take a perennial delight are the feast,

the lyre, the dance, clean linen in plenty, a hot bath and our beds.' After a dance, the blind minstrel Demodocus sang of how Hephaestus had ensnared under a net his wife Aphrodite, when he caught her in the arms of her lover Ares. Then there was a banquet, and Odysseus, disclosing his name, told this tale of his adventures.

After leaving captured Troy, he had raided the territory of the Cicones in Thrace; but they had driven the raider off. In the lands of the Lotus-Eaters, to which a storm had next brought him, some of his men had nearly succumbed to the forgetfulness induced by eating the plant. Then they had arrived at a little island off the coast of the Cyclopes, and on crossing to the mainland he and some of his followers were captured by the one-eyed giant Polyphemus. After Polyphemus had eaten four of them, the rest, when he was drunk, blinded him with a pointed stake, and escaped from his cave under the bellies of his sheep. Polyphemus, hurling rocks at the departing Greeks, knew that his blinding was the fulfilment of a prophecy— 'but I always expected some big and handsome fellow of tremendous strength to come along. And now a puny, good-for-nothing little runt fuddles me with wine and then puts out my eye.' This was the deed which had made Posidon angry with Odysseus; for Polyphemus was Posidon's son.

Odysseus next told the Phaeacians how he had landed at the island of Aeolus the wind-god. On leaving that island, and already within sight of Ithaca, his men had untied the winds from a bag given them by the wind-god, and were driven off course to the land of the Laestrygonians, giants who ate them all except Odysseus and the crew of his own ship. From there he had gone on to Aeaea, where the goddess Circe turned half his crew into pigs. The magic herb moly, given him by Hermes, enabled him to make her restore their human shape, and he lived with her for a year.

She told him that before going home he must visit Hades, to consult the spirit of the Theban prophet Tiresias. And so Odysseus went on to describe to the Phaeacians how he had come to the place beyond the ocean indicated by Circe. After digging a trench, he had poured out sacrifices of honey, milk, wine, water and white barley meal, and had slaughtered a ram and black sheep. He conjured up many shades of the dead including Tiresias, who drank the blood of the sacrifices and promised him return to his home and vengeance, though many troubles too. Next his mother came up, and other noble women, and heroes; and then Odysseus saw Minos, king and judge of Hades, and those who were in torment there, and the phantom of Heracles.

Odysseus told how he had then gone back to his ship, and how, after returning briefly to Aeaea, he had safely overcome the successive dangers of the Sirens—in passing them he had had himself lashed to the mast—and of the monster Scylla and the whirlpool Charybdis. Next he had arrived at the island Thrinacia, the home of the cattle of the Sun. Unknown to him, his men killed some of these cattle, and for this sacrilege they were destroyed by a storm, only Odysseus escaping. So he had come to Calypso and thence to Scheria where he was now being entertained.

Accepting a proposal of their king, who promised to reimburse them by a general tax 'since it would be hard on us singly', the Phaeacians gave Odysseus rich gifts and a ship to take him on his way; and its crew landed him and his treasure upon the coast of Ithaca itself, beside a sacred cavern. But on their return journey they and their ship were turned to stone by Posidon and sent to the bottom of the sea, and Alcinous, propitiating the god by sacrifice, bewailed the evils that had come from hospitality.

Odysseus was asleep when they landed him on the shores of Ithaca, and, when he awoke, he did not recognize the island. But Athene appeared to him in human form and told him where he was; and they hid his possessions in a cave. Disguised as an old beggar, and recounting one of a whole series of fictitious tales of adventure, he was well received at the home of his own swineherd Eumaeus. Meanwhile Athene appeared in a dream to Telemachus at Sparta, and warned him to avoid the ambush of Penelope's suitors on the way home. Telemachus returned and met Odysseus, and they planned how to overcome the suitors. Telemachus went to the palace, where a prophet who had joined him on his journey, Theoclymenus of Argos, told Penelope that her husband would soon be returning. Odysseus, again in the guise of a beggar, made his way to the palace, encountering on the way his goat-herd Melanthius who abused and struck him. In the palace court he found his old decrepit dog Argus, who recognized him after twenty years, and died.

Eumaeus led Odysseus into the banqueting hall, where he was insulted by Antinous, the most shameless of the suitors, who threw a footstool at him. A sturdy beggar, Irus, tried to chase Odysseus from the palace, but a fight between them, prompted by Antinous, ended with the breaking of Irus' jaw. The suitors showered bridal gifts on Penelope—who still had no intention of making a choice between them—and dispersed for the night.

Odysseus and Telemachus now took down the helmets, shields and lances which were hung on the walls of the banqueting hall, and collected them together in the store-room. Odysseus visited Penelope and narrated an elaborate fiction about his identity; but his old nurse Eurycleia, washing his feet, recognized him from a scar. Without Penelope seeing, Odysseus stopped the nurse from revealing who he was.

Penelope, after recounting a dream in which an eagle had killed twenty geese—but adding that dreams are obscure, and not always fulfilled—told him that she had decided to marry whichever of the suitors could string the great bow of Odysseus and shoot an arrow through the holes in twelve axes placed one in front of another. Next day the contest took place, but the suitors could not string the bow, and decided to postpone the trial. Odysseus, however, asked if he might be allowed to try his hand at shooting the arrow through the axes; and as Telemachus entered with sword and spear, his father threw off his rags, took his bow, and shot Antinous in the throat. Then he and his son and two faithful herdsmen slaughtered every one of the suitors. Their supporter Melanthius, who had armed them, was trussed up and his nose, ears, hands, feet and genitals cut off. Only Medon the herald and Phemius the bard were spared. The maids who had slept with the suitors were summoned and, after they had been made to clean the hall of blood, were all hanged in a row.

Penelope was finally convinced of Odysseus' identity when he disclosed a secret in the construction of their marriage bed. 'What happiness for the few swimmers that have fought their way through the white surf to the shore, when, caked with brine but safe and sound, they tread on solid earth!' Odysseus and Penelope spent the night in each other's company and spoke of all they had experienced and suffered; and Odysseus told her, on the authority of the seer Tiresias, that there were more travels ahead of him, but that then an easy old age would be his, in which death would come gently to him out of the sea.

Meanwhile the souls of the dead were escorted by Hermes across the ocean to Hades, where they met the phantoms of the Greek heroes who had lost their lives in the Trojan War. On the next day, Odysseus left the town to visit his old father Laertes, whom he found weeding his garden. As they talked there, Eupithes, the father of Antinous, organized an attack upon them. But, at the instigation of Athene, Eupithes was killed; and Zeus, by hurling a thunderbolt between the contestants, made peace.

2 *Odysseus*

Odysseus resembles the typical hero of the *Iliad* in his unconquerable, enduring great heart. By this he survives fantastic obstacles.

> I am like those men
> Who suffer the worst trials that you know,
> And miseries greater yet.[3]

He overcomes them by the sheer force of his character, amazingly resourceful, yet recklessly ferocious. He is the type, for all time, of a man who has battled with the varied storms of life and won. Miraculous though his adventures are, yet they illuminate his character and confirm his violent belief, like Ivan Karamazov's, in his own powers. 'Still is my strength unbroken', and the magic of the poem, as of Shakespeare's *Tempest*, is bound up with that strength.

Yet there is one exceptional feature about this heavy-jawed, beetle-browed hero. He is tremendously clever, far more clever than any hero of the *Iliad*. In his heroic character an unexpectedly prominent, indeed pre-eminent, part is played by intelligence, assuming multifarious forms from strategic and tactical sageness to the weaving of an endless web of lies and fancies. He has been called the supreme 'homo mediterraneus', the image of the scorched sea coasts of the south.

Early Greek artists were not very interested in him; a Geometric (page 39) vase at Munich shows a shipwreck which may or may not be his, and a seventh-century jug from Aegina depicts him with a ram. The classical fifth century usually, though not always, regarded Odysseus as an evil product of overcleverness: cruel, corrupt, sophistical and deceitful, a hardboiled confidence man. 'May I never,' said the old-fashioned, aristocratic Pindar, 'have a character like that, but walk in straightforward ways.' To Sophocles, Odysseus is a magnanimous hero in the *Ajax*, but a cold blooded schemer in the *Philoctetes*. So he is in several plays of Euripides, written in the age of the Peloponnesian War, when many people thought that cleverness was ruining Athens (page 263):

> ———that vile, that slippery man,
> Right's enemy, brute murderous beast,
> That mouth of lies and treachery, that makes void
> Faith in things promised
> And that which was beloved turns to hate.[4]

The first recorded Roman poet-dramatist Livius Andronicus, in South Italy full of memories of Odysseus (page 91), found a public for his *Odyssia Latina*. But in general the Romans found this hero a good deal too tricky; although those of them brought up on Stoic ideals admired his perseverance. Allegorizing Christian fathers read into his adventures a spiritual aspiration curiously contrasting with the villainy others saw in the same events.

His first great vernacular portrayal was in Dante's *Inferno* (XXVI), where he is presented in a new and quite unmedieval way. Crafty and greedy to learn, as the city of Florence in Dante's day was greedy to gain, he is nevertheless highly respected by the poet, uttering proverbial lines taken for Dante's own voice. Gower in his *Confessio Amantis* (1390) looked on Odysseus as a sorcerer, and Calderon allegorized and Christianized his enchantments; Spanish Counter-Reformation gallants made him their pattern—but so did Protestants; and Fénélon commended to politicians his flexible attitude to truth. Odysseus was a sympathetic figure to the Renaissance, which no longer found it difficult to blend warrior-knight and learned clerk.

When Goethe began to study Greek—before coming to find the Gothic sorceries of Faust more congenial—he fell deeply under the spell of the *Odyssey*. This, together with a Sicilian journey, led him to assert, in his *Nausikaa*, that the Greeks were ideal men living in ideal places. Werther, too, unable to harness his abnormal sensitivity to anything solid, was fascinated by Odysseus' steadfastness in the face of every convulsion. Tennyson's *Ulysses*, one of what Swinburne calls his 'magnificent hashes and stews of old and new', shows that poet's brave swing and strength at their best. Written after the death of his friend Hallam, the *Ulysses*, though un-Greek in its elegiac, reflective sensibility, reflects Tennyson's need to go forward and brave the struggle:

> To follow knowledge, like a sinking star,
> Beyond the utmost bound of human thought.

James Joyce, in his *Ulysses* (1922), uses the myth (as T. S. Eliot observed) not for imitation, but 'simply as a way of controlling, of ordering, of giving a shape and significance to the immense panorama of futility and anarchy which is contemporary history'. Bloom, bourgeois everyman, only wanders over one square mile at Dublin; but he is cosmic in the wanderings of his imagination, not mock-heroic like Tom Jones and not anti-heroic, but cast with compassionate humanism into the Homeric pattern. The basic motifs of the *Ulysses* are organized round an elaborate system of correspondences with the *Odyssey*, even if Ezra Pound was perhaps over-optimistic in saying that 'any blockhead can trace them'. The Homeric parallels (of which many more are found in Joyce's notes than in the text) are primarily structural and controlling devices, scaffoldings for the reader and even more for the author, 'fixed ports of call' as he described them himself. Stephen Daedalus, whose name comes from another myth (page 385), is Bloom's Telemachus (and more), and his suspicions and frustrations are the Suitors. There is a Circe episode in the brothel scene of Night Town—in which men are turned into swine—and the visit to Hades is Paddy Dignam's funeral in a rat-haunted cemetery.

Kazantzakis is another who takes the Odysseus story and uses it as a symbol of rebellion from the tradition into which he himself has cast his poem: he ends up by defying God, in a profoundly nihilistic reshaping of the close of Homer's *Odyssey*, in which his Odysseus leaves the island for ever. This modern *Odyssey* (1938) challenged the view that it is now impossible to compose a long narrative poem based on myth. 33,333 lines long, the work is heavy with symbols of contemporary aspirations and perplexities. The hero shoulders all western civilization's burdens, profoundly conscious of living in a transitional, anti-classical era of ethical tension, in which the moulds are broken. Kazantzakis, with his 'Cretan glance' of a third inner eye—between those of Hellas (Apollo) and the orient (Dionysus)—finds that it is in such ages which come between two cultures, 'when one myth dissolves and another struggles to be born, that epic poems are created. Our great-grandchildren will know whether the search can reach its goal.'

His Alexandrian compatriot Cavafy (page 46), on the other hand, had warned ourselves, and Odysseus, that we can benefit from the quest without worrying about the goal (1911).

> Setting out on the voyage to Ithaca
> You must pray that the way be long . . .
> Many be the summer mornings
> When with what pleasure, with what delight
> You enter harbours never seen before.
>
> Do not hurry the journey at all.
> Better that it should last many years;
> Be quite old when you anchor at the island,
> Rich with all you have gained on the way,
> Not expecting Ithaca to give you riches.
> Ithaca has given you your lovely journey—
> Without Ithaca you would not have set out.

Ithaca has no more to give you now.
Poor though you find it, Ithaca has not cheated you.
Wise as you have become, with all your experience,
You will have understood the meaning of an Ithaca.

Another Greek, George Seferis (page 49), again saw Odysseus as one whose storm-tossed exile is never quite over, his past and present co-existing in our thoughts (1931). Earlier, there had been the pessimistic, anarchistic Odysseus of Pascoli's *Ultimo Viaggio* (1904), and D'Annunzio's self-willed Nietzschean explorer. There was also the nervous and ageing liar of Jean Giono's *Naissance de l'Odyssée* (1938); the lucidly rounded figure of Giraudoux (page 59); Eyvind Johnson's lust-shattered ruin of a warrior. The fishermen of Ithaca say that Odysseus still turns up from time to time.

3 Ever-repeated Tales

The *Odyssey* is a collection of folk-tales and fairy-tales: fictitious stories, less sophisticated half-sisters of myth—'backyard mythology', because they seem to have been handed down for entertainment rather than with the more solemn and purposeful motives or overtones which have given many other myths their power. The *Iliad* was a legend with a basis, however tenuous, of fact; in the *Odyssey*, though it describes the adventurous saga of a person believed historical (and linked to the Trojan War), we find the products not of memory, still less of reason, but of imagination— neither factual nor explanatory. In the words of Strabo of Amaseia, geographer of the Roman empire: 'If a man were to tell of the wanderings of Odysseus or Menelaus or Jason, he would not seem to make any contribution to knowledge, which is the aim of the practical man.'[5]

For the human being of earlier days, as Sir James Frazer remarked, 'was not for ever pondering the enigmas of the universe; he, like ourselves, had doubtless often need to relax the strain and to vary the monotony of ordinary life by excursions into the realm of fancy'. In other words, he wanted something to amuse him and occupy his leisure—or rather, Mediterranean man did, for among the North American Indians, for example, comparable tales were to a greater extent articles of belief. But among the Greeks such loosely strung stories, full of wishful thinking, supernatural interventions and mighty deeds, were rather intended to provide an escape 'from the dull routine of a peasant's life, the drabness of a winter night, the tedium of the road'.

The brothers Grimm (d. 1859, 1863) collected many of these stories in the hope of gathering the nucleus of an Indo-European mythology. The formulas and motifs that compose such narratives appear in large numbers in the *Odyssey*. As will be suggested in connection with the fairy-tale of Cupid and Psyche (page 408), such motifs are found all over the world in astonishingly similar form, though with diverse local colourings. It was the merit of J. W. E. Mannhardt (1831–80), and then at the turn of the century of Andrew Lang, to emphasize this. But, since their day, many actual *transmissions* of such tales, often between distant regions of the world, have been convincingly traced. Numerous African stories, for example, are borrowed from Arabs and Indians, and Red Indian stories can be traced back to Scandinavia. Celtic motifs came from migrants, and Bantu themes from Europeans; Siberian and Tibetan *shamans* owe some of their lore ultimately to Greece and Rome. Frobenius and Jensen have plausibly argued in favour of a common source for Polynesian-Melanesian and Graeco-Roman stories—and it has been asked whether close resemblances between myths (and artifacts) on either side of the Pacific should not be accounted for in the same way. There are great 'trade-routes'—as well as local transmissions from village to village—and this applies to folk-tales as well as to proverbs and spells. Some anthropologists today believe that the common origin of all these narratives may be traced back to *c.* 7500–5500 BC, and probably to the near east; although (among many other theories) there are also those who would suggest a more easterly base, in Malaya or Polynesia.

This is the sort of evidence against which we must nowadays consider, and reconsider, C. G. Jung's attribution of all such resemblances to a 'collective unconscious' (page 151). The mind delights in imagery for its own sake, and its imagery assumes such surprisingly similar forms that the world's folk-tales (as well as many myths) look like dialects of a single language. People's imaginations being limited, they prefer to use old stocks of imaginative happenings. Now the student of this lore, it is true, must not 'invade the garden of romance and with a sweep of his scythe lay the flowers of fancy in the dust'. Nevertheless, such correspondences in different parts of the world are significant to the psychologist and psychoanalyst (page 229). For example, these stories often contain the fear-element of dreams, from which, indeed, some of them are derived (page 398); and their supernatural achievements provide imaginary triumphs in overcoming the frustrations and limitations of earthly existence. For folk-tales have happy endings more often than the 'higher' kind of myth proper. 'In the folk-tale', supposes Geza Roheim, 'we relate how we overcame the anxiety connected with the "bad parents" and grew up, in myth we confess that only death can end the tragic ambivalence of human nature.' The nearest equivalent to the folk-tale in un-selfconscious western life today is the comic strip of the daily newspapers, in which the 'return of the repressed' makes itself manifest in characters close to the ancient archetypes.

The folk-tale world is one of astuteness, violence and cruelty. Such components, and the strange and irrational actions which accompany them, have been held by some to point to an origin from remote, primitive societies, of whose thoughts and customs these folk-tales are fossil survivals—the unwritten literature and anthropological detritus of distant ages. Others, however, prefer to see the folk-tale as a comparatively late *reaction* against the myth proper: the teller is turning against myth's grimly symbolized reality of human existence and its limitations, he is an anti-tragedian denying the tragedy of myth. Such questions of relative dating are likely to remain insoluble, but to the latter view it must be objected that much of the subject-matter of—for example—the *Odyssey* seems to go back to an unfathomable antiquity. Its folk-tales exhibit types of variation that are uniform with others of this genre and in accordance with the dream-like associations of ideas by which it is characterized. The reader's mind is continually switched, by bizarre transitions, to new yet not unfamiliar tracks. It comes to cross-roads at which any one of three or four paths can be followed. Often in the end we have followed each of them, and yet they have all converged upon the same place. But definitions are elusive, for we are dealing with a region of the human spirit which does not lend itself readily to classification.

The *Odyssey* is cast in the form of an epic. But its basis is a widespread folk-tale: that of the man so long absent that he is given up for dead, yet finally, after he has successfully sought and found his home again, reunited with his faithful wife. One good story, however, attracts another—often by reciprocal action between popular and literary composition—and the main tale has drawn to it many others that are romances or deep-sea yarns, containing monsters and witches in unknown lands. The principal stories of the *Odyssey* have been classified by W. J. Woodhouse under the following familiar and all but universal headings: Woman's Wit, or Playing for Time; Penelope and her Web (undoing by night what is done by day is a common folk-lore theme); the Husband Returned or the Acid Test; the Sign of the Scar, Bow, Bed; the Grass Widow or the Nick of Time; Virtue Triumphs; the Stolen Prince or Blood will Tell; the Dark Horse or Winning a Wife (the Nausicaa story, necessarily cut off in the *Odyssey* before its usual happy ending is reached). To these must be added such further narratives of various origins as the Quest of Telemachus; the Slaying of the three hundred and fifty Cattle of the Sun (for an explanation see page 122); the scenes of storm and shipwreck; travellers' tales such as the Isle of Aeolus and the Clashing Rocks; the monster Scylla and the Sirens; the witches Circe and Calypso (two variant versions, perhaps, of the same basic fairy-story); and the Cyclops Polyphemus. This is an early subject of Greek illustration—the burning of his eye appears on Argive and Attic vases of the seventh century BC, the orientalizing age which created visual mythology (page 39). The tale of Polyphemus in the *Odyssey* is a fantastic combination of many versions. The basic story is expanded by incidents from numerous other variants—and numerous they are, for 125 versions were collected (in 1904); they range as far afield as Lapland (perhaps all stemming from a common source), and the scene of the giant's chase of Odysseus is akin to the third voyage of Sinbad the Sailor.

The *Odyssey* contains contradictions and inconsistencies, but these indicate reliance on a variety of sources, not necessarily collective authorship for the poem as we have it. The result is a group of folk-tales ingeniously converted into the most exciting and readable of stories, for the author of the *Odyssey*, in addition to adding elements of his own, has stamped his mark upon the whole. His Odysseus is the Sly Boots or Wily Lad of many a folk-tale, the Jack the Giant Killer or David who conquered the Giant or Valiant Tailor, but he is also the product of unequalled narrative genius. The poet knows he belongs to a noble calling, and ensures that its importance—and so his own contribution—should not be forgotten. At Alcinous' palace, 'an equerry came in leading their beloved bard Demodocus, the people's favourite. He seated him in the centre of the company with his back against one of the high columns, and at once the thoughtful Odysseus, carving a portion from the chine of a white-tusked boar (which was so large that more than half was left), with plenty of rich fat on either side, called to a serving-man and said: "Here, my man, take this helping to Demodocus and let him eat it, with kindly wishes from my unhappy self. No one on earth can help honouring and respecting the bards." '[6] Moreover, one of the few people spared from the final holocaust at Ithaca is another of the same profession, named Phemius.

Finding what is lost, the *Odyssey*'s basic subject, is a powerful theme of the world's great writers, and one which is very prominent in Greek and Roman mythology (pages 287 ff.). It is the core of Shakespeare's later plays, *Cymbeline*, *The Winter's Tale*, *The Tempest* and *Pericles*. Royalty is what is lost there, and it serves as a symbol of the deeper spiritual search. The power-quest also dominates the mythologies, for example, of North American Indians. It is stimulating, but conjectural, to see its origin in the primitive community's rites to ensure the annual return of the fertility of the earth; to hear an echo of the primitive initiations of hunting epochs, in which the young men were (and are) segregated to tread labyrinthine paths in darkness, imitating the wanderings of ancestral divinities and totemic animals in their representation of the annual loss and recovery of the soil's procreative power (page 148). At any rate the Quest was imprinted very early in our human minds and hearts —and the *Odyssey* is its supreme manifestation.

After centuries of voluminous and embittered controversy, we cannot prove that the ancients were wrong in supposing that the poet of the *Odyssey* was the same as the poet of the *Iliad*. The Augustan critic Dionysius of Halicarnassus believed the *Iliad* the work of Homer's youth, and the *Odyssey* the work of his age. We equally cannot demonstrate that those who believed the two poems to be the work of one man were right. But what we can say is that the spirit of the two poems is different—there is no evidence that the poet of one had read the other—and that the *Odyssey* seems the later of the two. Perhaps it is the later work by something like a generation, and was written towards the end of the eighth century BC, just before the recent arrival of the alphabet (page 37) created a mass of literary and historical records. The *Odyssey*, like the *Iliad*, is a display of courage, endurance and resourcefulness. But it is much more complex in structure—an epic changing into a novel. That vivid ancient critic whom we know as Longinus[7] compared its poet to the sinking sun, not less great but less intense, or to an ebbing ocean, uncovering strange monsters as its tide turns home. There has been a move away from bitter and joyful heroism, away from passionate intensity and catastrophe, towards forbearance and endurance and self-control and acceptance. The white heat of *Macbeth* has been diluted to the *Tempest*, like the *Odyssey* a play of sea-faring—which, rather than war, Sophocles was to rank as the first of man's achievements.[8]

Mind and character now prevail over circumstances: the wisdom, or caution, of Penelope and Telemachus as well as of Odysseus is stressed. Love of wife and home has started to take precedence over love of comrades and honour, and courtliness over chivalry. There is a keen new interest in the social circumstances of the aristocratic rulers and their dependants and household. And so, while there is less deep and tragic feeling than in the *Iliad*, there is emphasis on hospitality, friendship, acquired courtesy, and the forms and formalities of decorum; the story of Telemachus is the story of the education of a hero within this framework. Between the marvels and excitements, we are shown the cultural pattern of a social class settled on its estates and managing them—with some regard, even, for the evils of poverty and ill-treatment, but with more for fixed residence, ownership of land, and respect for tradition and for good breeding. This is an ideal picture, and like that different, more colossal picture in the *Iliad* it seems to portray a world which had never existed in such dimensions. Probably it is the tenth century BC or thereabouts—after the fall of the Mycenaean palaces (page 33)— rather than his own eighth century, which inspires the poet's visionary view. Yet if so the inspiration comes from a distance, for in all the book the archaeologist discovers few objects which can certainly be attributed to an epoch earlier than that of the finished poem.[9]

The imaginative nostalgia of the *Odyssey* expresses itself in cunning arrangement, in acute and truthful observation of people, and in exquisite embellishment. There is a keen, sensuous satisfaction in beautiful, rich things and places, such as Calypso's home (page 71) and Alcinous' dream-like palace: 'A kind of radiance, like that of the sun or moon, lit up the high-roofed halls of the great king. Walls of bronze, topped with blue enamel tiles, ran round to left and right from the threshold to the back of the court. The interior of the wellbuilt mansion was guarded by golden doors hung on posts of silver which sprang from the bronze threshold. The lintel they supported was of silver too, and the door-handle of gold. On either side stood gold and silver dogs, which Hephaestus had made with consummate skill, to keep watch over the palace of the great-hearted Alcinous and serve him as immortal sentries never doomed to age.'[10]

The heroes of the *Odyssey* have an eye on possible increases of property, and gifts have become very important. 'However eager we may be to start,' Pisistratus advises Telemachus, 'we cannot possibly drive in complete darkness. It'll soon be dawn. Why not wait and give the brave Menelaus, our royal host, the chance of putting some presents for us in the chariot and bidding us a civil farewell? A guest never forgets the host who has treated him kindly.'[11] And later: 'Nobody will send us away empty-handed: we can count on each of our hosts for at least one gift, a copper tripod or a cauldron, a pair of mules or a golden cup.'[12] The suitors, on the other hand, are disgraceful because they are a financial drain.[13]

Yet there is also a new sentiment in the description of Odysseus' old dog, lying on his dung-heap, 'obscene with reptiles' as Alexander Pope described him. While the hero was speaking,

> An old hound, lying near, pricked up his ears
> And lifted up his muzzle. This was Argus,
> Trained as a puppy by Odysseus,
> But never taken on a hunt before
> His master sailed for Troy. The young men, afterward,
> Hunted wild goats with him, and hare and deer,
> But he had grown old in his master's absence.
> Treated as rubbish now, he lay at last
> Upon a mess of dung before the gates—
> Manure of mules and cows, piled there until
> Field hands could spread it on the king's estate.
> Abandoned there, and half destroyed with flies,
> Old Argus lay.
>   But when he knew he heard
> Odysseus' voice near by, he did his best
> To wag his tail, nose down, with flattened ears,
> Having no strength to move nearer his master.
> And the man looked away,
> Wiping a salt tear from his cheek . . .
> But death and darkness in that instant closed
> The eyes of Argus, who had seen his master,
> Odysseus, after twenty years.[14]

Nevertheless, in this different and to some extent more humane world there is still the savage delight in bloodshed which had characterized the *Iliad*. The beating up of Irus makes the suitors laugh merrily;[15] whereas their subsequent slaughter (which Sir

James Frazer far-fetchedly linked with the sacred king's refusal to die at the end of his reign, page 342), and the mutilation of their henchman Melanthius—the only thrall in these poems to betray his lord—are more brutal than anything in the *Iliad*. So is the mass-execution of the girls who had been their concubines. ' "I swear I will not give a decent death," he said, "to women who have heaped dishonour on my head and on my mother's, and slept with members of this gang." With that he took a hawser which had seen service on a blue-bowed ship, made one end fast to a high column in the portico, threw the other over the round-house, and pulled it taut at such a level as would keep their feet from touching the earth. And then, like doves or long-winged thrushes caught in a net across the thicket where they come to roost, and meeting death where they had only looked for sleep, the women held their heads out in a row, and a noose was cast round each one's neck to dispatch them in the most miserable way. For a little while their feet kicked out, but not for very long'.[16]

4 Beyond the World's End

In spite of such acts of cruelty which equal or exceed those of the *Iliad*, the poet of the *Odyssey* endows his gods from time to time with a somewhat higher philosophical content. They 'know everything'[17], but they cannot be blamed for misfortunes incurred by men against their better judgement. They still punish people for forgetting the ritual rules—that is why Menelaus was kept dawdling in Egypt—but there has been a shift, in determining divine responsibility, from individual deities to a more pantheistic view of god or the gods as indeterminate beings, daemons or half-abstractions (page 105).

Yet Athene, in particular, intervenes continuously on behalf of Odysseus, treating him with a humorous, admiring familiarity. This goddess, later the bold champion of Athens (page 193), stood in the Olympian pantheon for protection, intelligence and virginal independence. She was also reputedly the inventor of many fine and clever things such as the flute, trumpet, earthenware pot, plough, rake, ox-yoke, chariot and ship—together with all woman's arts.

In Homer she still occupies her basic role of the protectress of cities, the beloved daughter of Zeus.[18] Her name has been found on a 'Linear B' inscription from Cnossus (page 33), and she seems to be the heir of a Cretan snake-divinity whose snake she inherited as companion. Probably the shield-bearing goddess on a painted limestone tablet from Mycenae is her forerunner; and her sacred olive-tree on the Acropolis suggests that she likewise inherited the functions of another deity who protected these trees, without which no Greek community can survive. Ruskin in his *Queen of the Air* expanded the myths of Athene with exuberant, far-fetched fancy. There are also more recent echoes of her warlike role in the visions of the embattled Virgin seen by Greek soldiers marching ahead of them, during battles of the Second World War.

But ridicule of the Olympians, as in the *Iliad*, was still by no means impossible. The *Odyssey* contains that famous tale of Aphrodite caught in bed with her lover, Ares, by her husband Hephaestus, the divine lame craftsman. Hephaestus entangled them in a net so that all the gods might see and laugh—though some of them would have thought it worth while, even in such conditions, to be in Ares' place. 'His shouts brought the gods trooping to the house with the bronze floor. Up came Posidon the Earthshaker; Hermes, the bringer of luck; and the archer king, Apollo; but the goddesses, constrained by feminine modesty, all stayed at home. There they stood then, in front of the doors, the immortals who are the source of all our blessings, and when they caught sight of Hephaestus' clever device a fit of uncontrollable laughter seized these happy gods.'[19] This incident has kindled many a great painting, not only in ancient times (as is somewhat dimly apparent from copies at Pompeii) but especially from the brush of Titian, who presented the myths with such apparently heartfelt fire and feeling—although his erotic themes, including also many studies of Aphrodite (Venus) with Eros (Cupid) or Adonis, were prompted by the taste of royal and other patrons (page 399). Tintoretto, too, in his no less colourful but more factual and detached presentation of mythology, perpetuated the old story in various forms, and it is echoed in our own day by the title of Iris Murdoch's novel *Under the Net*.

Even if a goddess could still be laughed at, there is no lack of honour for women in the *Odyssey*. Penelope's place at the centre of the great mansion is appreciated, and her loyalty throughout twenty years is extolled. Circe is predatory, but Calypso is affectionate; and Nausicaa is brave, sensitive and resourceful. She is a characteristically Greek improvement upon the snake, with skin of gold and lapis lazuli, which in an Egyptian version saved the castaway. In one of the most entertaining quirks of Homeric criticism, Samuel Butler (followed by Robert Graves) believed Nausicaa to be a self-portrait of the 'authoress' of the *Odyssey*, whom he identified as a young and talented Sicilian noblewoman.

Yet Samuel Butler's reference to the central Mediterranean is not altogether beside the point. The wanderings of Odysseus cannot be placed with any exactitude upon the map; and, as the geographer Eratosthenes of Cyrene pointed out, it was not Homer's intention that we should do so (though Scheria, for example, was later identified with Corcyra, page 296). Ithaca, if rightly identified with the modern Thiaki (in preference to Leucas), has not yielded much to the archaeologist—it was little more than a symbol of the rugged life against the easy wiles of Ogygia—but across the sea there were persistent traditions associating features of the story with Italy. At a date scarcely, if at all, later than the *Odyssey*, Hesiod (page 103) brings Odysseus to that peninsula.[20] Cumae, at the northern end of the Bay of Naples, was colonized from Greece in the eighth century BC, and pottery of that century is found there; and Hesiod may also have known of merchant adventurers who explored the Italian and Sicilian coasts even before the colonization. At all events, among the 'returns' of the heroes from Troy, the west coast of Italy tends to be the preserve of Odysseus, although that does not exclude the importation into the poem of many stories from various other regions.

One of the Italian links with the story was perhaps the visit of Odysseus to the underworld; for one longstanding tradition associated the beginning of such journeys with Lake Avernus (near Cumae), where Virgil was to locate the descent of Aeneas and the

Sibyl (page 328). Yet Odysseus, unlike Aeneas and others such as Orpheus (pages 272, 305), does not go to Hades but to the End of the World and the Bounds of the Ocean, the land where the fog-bound Cimmerians (who, in history, entered Asia Minor across the Caucasus in the late eighth century BC) live in mist and darkness.[21] 'Set up your mast, spread the white sail and sit down in the ship. The North Wind will blow her on her way; and when she has brought you across the river of Ocean, you will come to a wild coast and to Persephone's Grove, where the tall poplars grow and the willows that so quickly shed their seeds. Beach your boat there by Ocean's swirling stream and march on into Hades' Kingdom of Decay. There the River of Flaming Fire and the River of Lamentation, which is a branch of the Waters of Styx, unite round a pinnacle of rock to pour their thundering streams into Acheron. This is the spot, my lord, that I bid you to seek out.'[22]

Yet then, by a conflation of contradictory myths, Odysseus is transported into the Hades of King Minos (page 342)—an underworld that had been mentioned in the *Iliad*.[23] By another contradiction—which greatly worried the ancients—we move from the normal Homeric and primitive afterlife of shadowy ghosts into a new place of rewards and punishments: the latter reserved here for conspicuous sinners only, though there is a reference in the *Iliad* to posthumous penalties for perjury.[24] Such an afterlife of pleasures or torments belonged to the age that lay ahead (page 148). Before the *Odyssey* touches on this novel set of ideas, the visit of its hero to the end of the world has been one of necromancy. Tiresias is raised by being given blood to drink—subterranean prophets, in his native Boeotia as elsewhere, could be summoned by this means—and the other ghosts become vocal only by having some too.

Necromancy was a widespread phenomenon, yet the Other World in the *Odyssey* is unusual, contrasting both with earlier Mycenae and with later Greece, since its dead are denied all intervention among the living. This might be thought incompatible with other references in these poems to sacrifices for the dead—a prominent part of Greek hero-cult (page 235) which implies that they can be potent to help or hurt. The burial customs of Palaeolithic days, and even of the

Australopithecines of South Africa, seem to show that the dead were treated with reverence even by the most remotely early human beings: and this reverence—probably implying belief in their capacity to intervene, though, even so, various forms of magic were practised to *ensure* survival—continued to be felt as a strong human need. Offerings to the dead have been found in Mycenaean graves, where inhumation had been the normal practice; and yet, with seeming inconsistency, they continue to be recorded in the Homeric poems when heroes such as Patroclus are cremated. But the distinction between the two methods of disposing of the dead is not necessarily reflected in differing beliefs about the afterlife, though deductions about these beliefs have often been drawn from them. More about the whole of this subject will be known when we can better compare Homeric practices with those that prevailed across the Aegean. For instance, Patroclus' funeral (like Hector's) provides resemblances with the procedures of the Hittites who were Mycenae's contemporaries in inland Asia Minor (page 34)—and who (like the Trojans) practised inhumation and cremation alike. For the rites in the *Iliad* display a number of similarities to descriptions, found at Boğazköy, of Hittite funerary ceremonies, which sometimes lasted thirteen days or more, longer even than Homer's. Mycenaeans and Hittites may have gone back to a common tradition of such ritual practices.

Homer's place of ghosts is a place of unrelieved gloom and horror. 'When I had finished my prayers and invocations to the communities of the dead, I took the sheep and cut their throats over the trench so that the dark blood poured in. And now the souls of the dead who had gone below came swarming up from Erebus—fresh brides, unmarried youths, old men with life's long suffering behind them, tender young girls still nursing this first anguish in their hearts, and a great throng of warriors killed in battle, their spear-wounds gaping yet, and all their armour stained with blood. From this multitude of souls, as they fluttered to and fro by the trench, there came a moaning that was horrible to hear. Panic drained the blood from my cheeks.'[25]

Achilles, whom Odysseus meets there, has no illusions about the relative merits of life and death. ' "For you, Achilles, death should have lost his sting." "My lord Odysseus," he replied, "spare me your praise of death. Put me on earth again, and I would rather be a serf in the house of some landless man, with little enough for himself to live on, than king of all these dead men that have done with life." '26 For the life of a ghost is wholly insubstantial.

> This is the law of mortals: whenever anyone dieth,
> Then no longer are bones and flesh held together by
>   sinews,
> But by the might of the blazing fire they are conquered
>   and wasted.
> From that moment when first the breath departs from
>   the white bones,
> Flutters the spirit away, and like to a dream it goes
>   drifting.[27]

Yet to visit these dead is a natural human desire, for all men wish to see their former comrades and kindred again. Love and friendship are enhanced by separation, and the reunion gives a feeling that death, the worst of Homer's enemies, has in some measure been overcome. Very many myths of numerous peoples describe the difficulties of gods and heroes in this supreme task of reaching the forbidden domain, penetrating the narrow door, the eye of the needle, and entering the transcendent place to win transcendent knowledge. In archaic societies boys and girls act out this supreme trial by leaving their homes and living for months or years in the bush, suffering tortures and trials culminating in symbolic death (sometimes represented by burial alive), which they surmount to be born again as new men and women.

The visit of Odysseus to the dead has unmistakable resemblances to the epic of Gilgamesh, legendary king of Uruk, a city of the Sumerian civilization which had flourished on the lower Tigris and Euphrates since the fourth millennium BC. The epic poems of this people, who themselves spoke an agglutinative language of uncertain affinities, were perhaps first written down not far short of two thousand years later. Then, fragments of a Semitic Babylonian (Akkadian) version (perhaps combining Sumerian episodes into longer epics) circulated widely in the Hittite empire of Asia Minor (page 34) and were translated into Hittite as well as Hurrian (page 114) versions, of which portions survive. These Mesopotamian epics have much less character, psychology and movement than those of Greece; for one thing the authors were endowed temple priests, who did not need to think of entertainment. Nevertheless, there emerges from them the personality of Gilgamesh, a human being of heroic stature, and the first literary hero of whom anything is known. The Gilgamesh epic, a mixture of pure adventure, morality and tragedy, is a classic quest which has much in common with the later Homeric myths. He and his friend Enkidu seem to foreshadow Achilles and Patroclus. But in particular, when on Enkidu's death Gilgamesh goes on a long journey, meeting Siduri who is like Circe and searching at the 'mouth of the rivers'—next to the abyss—for what lies beyond the grave and for immortality, it is necessary to conclude either that the author of the *Odyssey* knew the Gilgamesh epic, or at least, and perhaps more probably, that the two poems had a common cultural denominator. At all events, there was clearly a strong Asian element in this Homeric tradition.

Among the Greeks, the Hero's departure for the other world, or descent to Hades, became an abstract of this world's problems—the collective answer to all riddles (page 221). Occasionally, the echo of Homeric nihilism still sounded, as in the words of the poetess Erinna of Telos at the end of the fourth century BC.

> Naught to the far-off Hades but an empty echo cries.
> There, mid the dead, is silence. My voice in the
> darkness dies.[28]

Yet even in the *Odyssey*, quite separately from Odysseus' visit to the dead, there had been a reference to much less negative and nihilistic beliefs concerning the afterlife. For the poet refers to a paradise—also at the end of the world; it was the destined haven for Menelaus. ' "And now, King Menelaus, hear your own destiny. You will not meet your fate and die in Argos where the horses graze. Instead, the immortals will send you to the Elysian plain at the world's end, to join red-haired Rhadamanthus in the land where living is made easiest for mankind, where no snow falls, no strong winds blow and there is never any rain, but day after day the west wind's tuneful breeze comes in from the Ocean to refresh its folk. That is how the gods will deal with Helen's husband and recognize in you the son-in-law of Zeus." '[29] So Proteus foretells.

After Homer this note of rewards—with its corollary of punishments—came to dominate the faith of archaic Greece (page 148).

PART II

ZEUS, APOLLO, DEMETER

CHAPTER 3

THE RISE OF ZEUS

1   The Story Told in the THEOGONY

LET US first invoke the Muses of the great and holy mountain of Helicon, who sing praises of Zeus and Hera and the other gods. 'One day they taught Hesiod glorious song while he was shepherding his lambs under holy Helicon, and this word first the goddesses said to me—the Muses of Olympus, daughter of Zeus who holds the aegis:— "Shepherds of the wilderness, wretched things of shame, mere bellies! We know how to speak many false things as though they were true; but we know, when we wish, to utter true things." And so the ready-voiced daughters of great Zeus . . . bade me sing of the race of the blessed gods that exist eternally, but always to sing of themselves both first and last.'[1]

Let us begin, then, with the Muses, the daughters of Zeus and Memory, who sing of all things in heaven and earth. When they honour and behold someone at his birth, they pour sweet dew upon his tongue. All the people look to that man while he settles causes with true judgements, and when he passes through a gathering, they greet him as a god with gentle reverence.

Hail, children of Zeus! Tell of the everlasting gods. Tell how, in the beginning, gods and earth came to be, and rivers, and the boundless sea with its raging swell, and the gleaming stars, and the wide heaven above, and the gods who were born of them, givers of good things; and how those gods divided their dignities, and also how at the first they took Olympus.

First Chaos came into being, next wide-bosomed Gaea (Earth), Tartarus and Eros (Love). From Chaos came forth Erebus and black Night. Of Night were born Aether and Day (whom she brought forth after intercourse with Erebus), and Doom, Fate, Death, Sleep, Dreams; also, though she lay with none, the Hesperides and Blame and Woe and the Fates, and Nemesis to afflict mortal men, and Deceit, Friendship, Age and Strife, which also had gloomy off-spring.

And Earth first bore starry Heaven (Uranus), equal to herself, to cover her on every side, and to be an ever-sure abiding place for the blessed gods. And Earth brought forth, without intercourse of love, the Hills, haunts of the Nymphs, and the fruitless Sea with his raging swell. And Earth lay with Heaven and bore their children the Titans: Oceanus (who had three thousand neat-ankled daughters, one of them the mother of Thetis), Hyperion, Iapetus, Themis, Memory (Mnemosyne), Phoebe (whose daughter by Coeus was Hecate, whom Zeus loved most of all), also Tethys, and the one-eyed Cyclopes, and Cronus the wily—youngest and most terrible of her children.

Cronus hated his lusty sire Heaven (Uranus). And Heaven hated others whom Earth had borne him, the hundred-armed and fifty-headed Cottus and Briareus and Gyes; and Heaven would not let them come up into the light. But Cronus answered his mother's plea and, as his father Heaven lay upon Earth, he castrated his father with a jagged sickle. Cronus cast the severed members behind him, and from the bloody drops Earth conceived the Furies, Giants and Nymphs of the Ash-Trees. And as the members were swept away in the sea, the foam that spurted around them gave birth to Aphrodite.

To Cronus, Rhea bore Hestia, Demeter, Hera, Hades, Posidon. But Cronus devoured them all as soon as each had left its mother's womb, for he had learnt from Earth and Heaven that he was destined to be overcome by his own son. But when Rhea was about to bear

Zeus to him, Earth and Heaven sent her to Lyctus in Crete; and there Zeus was born, and hidden in a mountain cave. To Cronus she gave instead of him a stone wrapped in swaddling clothes, and he swallowed it instead of his son. When Zeus grew to manhood, Cronus was conquered by him, and Cronus spewed up not only this stone, but the children he had devoured. Zeus also released the brothers of Cronus from beneath the earth; and they gave him the thunderbolt and lightning by which he rules.

To one of Cronus' brothers, Iapetus, a daughter of Ocean named Clymene bore Atlas who upholds the sky, and wily Prometheus. At Mecone the Field of Poppies, while gods and men were met together there, Prometheus sought to deceive Zeus. When Prometheus was cutting up a great ox to be divided among them, he separated the flesh and entrails from the bones. He enclosed the meat and entrails in the stomach, and the bones he concealed in a wrapping of fat. Then he gave Zeus his choice of the two portions, and Zeus, though in his wisdom he saw through the trick, chose the bones. Out of anger for what Prometheus had done, he deprived mankind of fire; but Prometheus stole it in a hollow fennel-stalk and gave it to men. So Promethus was bound by Zeus to a rock, and each day an eagle flew over and ate his liver, which grew again during the night—until later Heracles, by the will of his father Zeus, released him from his bonds.

Zeus punished man in another way also, by creating an evil thing, woman, as the price of fire. Hephaestus made her out of clay; Athene adorned her, setting upon her head a golden crown which Hephaestus himself had devised; and Zeus brought her out to be shown to gods and men, and gave her to Prometheus' scatterbrained brother Epimetheus. 'And wonder took hold of the deathless gods and mortal men when they saw that which was sheer guile, not to be withstood by men. For from her is the deadly race and tribe of women who live amongst mortal men to their great trouble.'

But strife broke out between the young gods on one side—Zeus and his brothers and sisters, the children of Cronus dwelling on Mount Olympus—and on the other side the older gods, the Titans, children of Heaven and Earth, dwelling on Mount Othrys. With the help of the hundred-armed three, Cottus and Briareus and Gyes whom he had brought up from beneath the earth, Zeus assailed his Titan enemies. 'The thunderbolts flew thick and fast from his strong hand, with thunder and lightning, and flame unspeakable rose to the bright upper air; and his hundred-armed allies hurled three hundred rocks and felled the Titans to as far beneath the earth as heaven is above it.' For so far is the distance from earth to Tartarus with its gates and walls of bronze, the murky home of Night, Sleep, Death, Hades, Persephone and their guardian hound, and of the eternal, primeval water of Styx. At the entrance to Tartarus stands Atlas upholding the sky, where Night and Day draw near and greet one another as they pass the brazen threshold.

After the Titans had been driven from heaven, Earth bore to Tartarus her youngest child Typhoeus. A hundred snakes' heads sprouted from his shoulders, and flames flashed from his eyes. At times his voices were understood by the gods, but sometimes they were like the roar of a lion or bull, or the baying of a hound; and sometimes there came from him a hissing or whistling that echoed from peak to peak. Typhoeus threatened the earth and the sea and Olympus itself, but Zeus struck at him with thunder and lightning until the whole universe seethed, and the earth was scorched and melted. His hundred heads perished in flames, and he was hurled down, a maimed wreck, to Tartarus.

Now that Zeus had overcome all his enemies, the gods chose him to be their king, and he divided their powers and privileges among them. He made Wisdom (Metis) his first wife, but swallowed her before she could give birth to Athene so that none but he could be Athene's parent. Then he lay with Themis, who bore him the Hours, Order, Justice, Peace and the Fates; with Eurynome, who bore him the three Graces and other daughters; with Demeter who bore him Persephone; with Mnemosyne, of whom the Muses were born; with Leto, mother of Apollo and Artemis. Then lastly he made Hera his wife, and she bore him Hebe and Ares and Ilithyia, goddess of child-birth. Hebe became the wife of Heracles, son of Alcmene—

'happy man! For he has finished his great work and lives among the undying gods, untroubled and unageing all his days.'

But being angry with Zeus, Hera, conceiving without him, bore Hephaestus, 'who is skilled in crafts more than all the sons of heaven'*. And there were also immortal goddesses who lay with mortal men and bore them children who were like gods: Demeter whose son by Iasion, conceived in a thrice-ploughed fallow in the rich land of Crete, was Plutus who makes man rich; Harmonia wife of Cadmus and mother of Semele, who was to bear Dionysus to Zeus; Eos, who bore Memnon and Emathion to Tithonus, and Phaethon to Cephalus; Medea the daughter of heaven-nurtured Aeetes, from whom Jason took her; Thetis who bore Achilles to Peleus; Aphrodite (Cytherea) who loved the hero Anchises and gave birth to their son Aeneas on the peaks of Ida; and those who bore children to Odysseus—Circe gave birth to Agrius and Latinus, rulers of the Etruscans, and Calypso to Nausithous and Nausinous.

2 Myths of Creation

Creation myths are for society what early memories, true or fictitious, are to the individual. At Zuni in New Mexico, and in Fiji and elsewhere, such myths are recited during ritual performances, and that appears also to have been true of the earliest of such myths known to us. This is the Babylonian epic of Enuma Elish ('When on high—'). Though comparable to the Gilgamesh epic (page 94) as one of the most significant expressions of Mesopotamian religious literature, the Enuma Elish has not come down to us in any text earlier than the first millennium BC. Yet its origin is assigned to the Old Babylonian period of the second millennium; and indeed its inclusion of non-Semitic names suggests that the story may go back from this Semitic (Akkadian) literature to non-Semitic, Sumerian originals two thousand years earlier.

The Enuma Elish, like the later *Theogony*, achieves an imaginative feat by amalgamating a myth of origins with a myth of victory over

* But Hephaestus has already appeared (page 101): here is an imperfect fusion of two stories.

disorder. It displays the first known conception of a hero chosen as champion of the elder deities against the powers of darkness: Marduk fights and overcomes the sea-monster Tiamat, and man is made out of clay mixed with the flesh and blood of the defeated one. The separation of the firmament, described in the *Theogony*, is already found here in the Enuma Elish, for the divided portions of the monster's body become heaven and earth. Just as in Egypt the sun god Re still *every night* faced destruction from the demon-dragon lurking in the underworld, so the Babylonian myth also is brought into the present: 'may he continue to conquer Tiamat and cut short his days'. And the scene was in all likelihood annually re-enacted, and the epic recited, during the twelve-day New Year Festival at Babylon. It is not probable that the *Theogony*, at any rate in its present literary form, was likewise recited as a part of ritual; but that this poem too contains elements which had long featured in such ceremonials is beyond doubt (page 158).

These myths are the response to a natural curiosity about the causes of the world and the manner of its creation, a curiosity which is the mark both of primitive or instinctive man, and of sophisticated societies. But to instinctive man the myths are a good deal more than that. To him they are a necessity supporting his life, a guarantee for the continuance of our own order of things and all that is around us: and this is reflected in the Babylonian Festival, which guaranteed the annual renewal of the kingship, as the Abrahamic covenant guaranteed the future of Judaism. Creation myths are the Magna Carta of our universe and are deeply felt to ensure its perpetuity. Their variations and remodellings from place to place are governed not only by differences in social customs but by such factors as climate or even political revolutions or invasions. It has been supposed, quite plausibly, that Hesiod's story reflects such factors, and that the supremacy of Zeus echoes the success of invaders over earlier inhabitants of Greece (page 126).

Like Homer, Hesiod begins with an invocation to the Muses. But Hesiod's is the most elaborate and also one of the most heartfelt in poetry, comparable in grandeur to the portrayal of these goddesses with Apollo over two millennia later by Raphael, who in the Stanza della Segnatura at the Vatican lavishes upon them his talent for flowing and harmonious figure compositions. At the other extreme is the final flatness and conventional decay of such invocations, jokingly recorded by Byron who begins one canto of Don Juan: 'Hail, Muse, et cetera!'

That is infinitely far from the earnestness of the *Theogony*. This poem, as it has come down, combines no less than three invocations, variously enlarged, altered and arranged: and so imposing a length is fitting, for the poet regards the Muses as among the most potent of the personifications to whom he gives life. Others include the Fates, still today believed to visit houses in Aegina and elsewhere where there has been a birth; and Rumour,[2] for in a shame-culture the voice of one's peers has indeed the power of a god (page 51); and Justice. The masculine and feminine genders of Greek tend to such ideas, and these personifications played a real part, difficult for us to grasp, in Hellenic thought. Rather as the Choctaw Indians treat all objects worthy of thought as alive, the Greeks envisaged their personifications as daemons or demi-gods. Such beings gave those who defined them a livelier concept of the conditions ruling the universe and the human race and, by presenting abstractions concretely, satisfied a rising urge towards the abstract thinking which was soon to lead to philosophy.[3] These were the conceptions which Goethe described as 'free children of God', and Valéry sought to embody in his *Chant de l'Idée Maitresse*.

The gods, said the Greeks, had bidden Zeus create beings who would beautify with words and music all the great deeds and institutions for which he was responsible. The Muses brought to humanity the purifying power of music, the inspiration of poetry and the wisdom needed also by others who were not poets—needed, for example, by judges remembering precedent, for their mother was Memory. But Hesiod felt them particularly close to himself because their abode was on Helicon, near his home Ascra (page 108)—where, indeed, one of their oldest cults was to be found.

He identifies these deities of his Boeotian homeland with that faculty of inspiration which poets after him have from time to time endeavoured to define; refusing to admit with William Morris that 'it is a mere matter of craftsmanship', and instead feeling that some superior force from outside himself—in our day it is rather called an involuntary element *within* one's self—is acting upon his own imagination and spirit. Plato agreed (thinking this perilous at times) that poets 'do not utter the words they do through art but by heavenly power'—creating the almost fearful awe felt by Wordsworth, the rich melancholy of Tasso, or the anguish of Rilke. By turns, as William Collins describes the ardours of poets,

> they felt the glowing mind
> Disturbed, delighted, raised, refined—
> Filled with Fury, rapt, inspired.

And so Pindar called upon the Muses to swell the gale of his song, and two or three centuries before him Hesiod tells they they singled him out too.

> . . . and they handed me a staff
> Of strong-growing
> Olive shoot, a wonderful thing;
>   They breathed a voice into me,
> And power to sing the story of things
>   Of the future, and things past.
> They told me to sing the race
>   Of the blessed gods everlasting,
> But always to put themselves
>   At the beginning and end of my singing.[4]

Hesiod makes it as clear as any of his poetic successors that this inspiration, conferred by Apollo (page 137) as well as the Muses, raises a man above his fellow-men: even the mourner casts off his load by the Muses' gift.

But the manner of their visitation upon Hesiod was unusual.

> These were the first words of all
>   the goddesses spoke to me—
> 'You shepherds of the wilderness, poor fools,
>   nothing but bellies,

we know how to say many false things
that seem like true sayings,
but we know also how to speak the truth
when we wish to.'[5]

This utterance, beginning with an echo or forecast of the *Odyssey*, has been described as the first literary manifesto of Europe. Though obscure, it seems to imply a recognition, first, that there is factual content as well as artistic form in poetry; secondly, that although Hesiod is concerned with poetic creation, he cannot dissociate himself from the question of truth and falsehood, from the facts of religion, morals and daily life: facts which it is his duty to transmit. This is a new sort of poetry, very different from the Homeric school, which (if we knew more about their relative dates, page 109) the strange words of the *Theogony* could be regarded as criticizing.

Hesiod is *engagé* and didactic; he uses his myths to edify, as a priest or as a prophet like Amos, who must have been nearly his contemporary. The Greek is something of an inspired *shaman*, with quasi-biblical authority—the 'oracle of the neighbourhood' as Addison called him—and so it was with solemnity that he and his hearers approached the tale that was to come.

The message which the poet feels inspired to convey is a mixture of several themes relating to origins. After his lengthy preludes, and the creation myth and stories of failed rebellion which are the central subjects of the poem, there follows an account of the gods according to their relationships and a similar brief account of the heroes born to goddesses and men, leading on to a list of heroines and women which formed the subject of a lost poem. This is a practical, moral, matter-of-fact treatise, a theological and mythological pageant, revealing lasting values rather than a system. A sort of introduction to universal history, the *Theogony* is also the work of Europe's first religious thinker, displaying an interest in priestly piety, a concern for order, a preoccupation with divine genealogy, a desire to instruct in the sacred remnants of the past, and an enthusiasm to praise the governance of Zeus.

The poem blends tradition and respectability, and differs therein from Hesiod's poem *The Works and Days*. That was the work of a man whose father had left Cyme across the Aegean—to flee from evil poverty—and settled in 'a hole of a village' at harsh Ascra in Boeotia: near Helicon, but far from it in spirit. The *Works and Days* summon us not to Homeric glory, but to hard work, honesty, sobriety and thrift, in a world where life was grim, the spirit had degenerated, and there were extortions to be protested against. 'New is the race of iron'—the successor of happier ages (page 126)—and Hesiod's brother was an idle litigator who plagued him.

> There are other troubles by thousands
> > that hover about men,
> for the earth is full of evil things,
> > and the sea is full of them;
> there are sicknesses that come to men by day,
> > while in the night
> moving themselves they haunt us,
> > bringing sorrow to mortals—
> and silently, for Zeus of the counsels
> > took the voice out of them.[6]

That is the poet who has been hailed as so many different things—as Europe's first realist; the George Crabbe of the Greeks; the forerunner of Chaucer's *Parson*; a 'prudent clown'; the first preacher of labour and the rights of the poor; the first poet of individuality; the prophet of that righteousness which makes it possible for men to live together.

But to ascribe the *Theogony* to the poet of the very different *Works and Days* begs a substantial question. Not only is the hierarchical *Theogony* far more correct and conventional than the other, somewhat truculent poem. But it also, as Sir John Forsdyke has remarked, 'has the appearance of being like the Athanasian Creed, the work of a long series of committees'. Thirdly, the poem is itself not wholly unequivocal on this subject of authorship. It speaks of the Muses 'teaching Hesiod glorious song' (*The Works and Days*) and then making a statement 'to me',[7] the author of the poem, who is not in so many words identified with Hesiod. Both Herodotus[8] and Plato[9] attribute a *Theogony* to Hesiod, though this was no longer believed locally in the time of the Roman empire.[10] Yet the myth of Prometheus is conveniently divided between the two poems, and we may speak of Hesiod, rather as we can speak of Homer (page 36), as the culminator of a long line of oral transmission leading to *Theogony* and *Works and Days* alike. In parts the *Theogony* presupposes Homer—whom it appears, as has been said, to criticize (page 107)—and yet the Homeric poems also in places seem to echo the *Theogony*. Perhaps, like them, the Hesiodic poem can be attributed in something like its present form to the later eighth century BC; and the reciters can be thought of as transferring passages from the Ionian to the mainland corpus, and vice versa.

The central part of the *Theogony* is introduced by an attempt to tell how the first gods and earth came to be. The answer is that in the beginning there was Chaos: the gaping void, the primordial abyss. This corresponds, to some extent, with most near-eastern ways of envisaging the ultimate source of the universe. But the Babylonians, like the Old Testament writers whose God created heaven and earth, believed in some sort of a creation by gods. This the Greeks did not believe, with far-reaching consequences upon their view of divinity.

There were no cults of Chaos; but it is rare in polytheistic religions (except in the cases of the Indo-Iranian Varuna and Ahura Mazda) for the earliest powers to be worshipped. They belong to cosmology rather than religion. Nor have they a place in any highly developed or anthropomorphic mythology, since it is so difficult to imagine such lofty concepts. For example the Australian Maker (Baiame) is again not a highly developed monotheistic god with a cult, because of the indolence of primitive imagination.

Yet even Chaos is not a real starting-point, except that Hesiod starts his story with its name. On the beginning of all things he reserves his judgement, for Chaos itself 'came into being'[11]— henceforward there was space but not disorder.[12] In Hesiod, Oceanus (like Heaven) is the progeny of Earth—yet he surrounds her so that she floats upon a watery waste. But there was another very early tradition, recorded in the *Iliad*, that the primeval gulf or gap itself was not an undifferentiated mass but was water, Oceanus,[13] and that this was the 'genesis' of the gods as the sea-deity Tethys was their 'suckler' or mother. Like Oceanus was the Egyptian Nun—believed to survive in the waters which are still everywhere above, beneath and around the earth—and the Babylonian Apsu. For in Egypt as in Mesopotamia it seemed literally true that water was the primary element.

This brings us close to the beginnings of natural science. For in the early sixth century BC Thales of Miletus, classically described as the first of the Ionian philosophers, asked himself what is the one thing at the basis of all nature, and answered that this was water. Despite his search for natural causes verifiable by observation, Thales was still bound up with mythological ways of thinking; his native Miletus was in close touch with Egypt and Babylonia. Yet he, like Hesiod before him, helped to make the bridge between the myths and Ionian, rationalistic, natural philosophy. 'The races,' remarked Cesare Pavese, 'who possess a rich mythological background are those who thereafter become the most dogged philosophers: the Indians, the Greeks and the Germans.'

Hesiod represents a variant tradition from Ionia. Living inland in Greece itself, this school of writers had less concern with water; indeed, the *Works and Days* deplores sea-faring. But the poet of the *Theogony* evidently believed, like the Ionians, that the Greek gods were not mighty enough, were too strongly anthropomorphic, to have created the world. Yet his Chaos is not in human form and indeed is not much more than an explanatory principle. 'Next to it', but not specifically mentioned as its offspring, originated Earth of the broad breast (identified with the Mediterranean Great Mother, as well as with Demeter, page 145), and Tartarus the foggy in the pit of the earth—already in the underworld (page 92).

And then came Love (Eros). Love is the procreative force not apparent in Chaos; Hesiod begins to perceive the distinction between matter and force when he gives the driving urge of generation, the principle of attraction, its place as a cosmic power. This was an idea profoundly stimulating to later thinkers. Pherecydes of Syros, one of the first Greek prose writers (*c.* 550 BC), made a theological advance when he held that Zeus, about to accomplish the creation, transformed himself into Eros[14]—placing, as Aristotle commented, the best at the first,[15] and by implication adding a benevolent purpose to the primordial rule of nature. Then in the next century the Sicilian philosopher-scientist and wonder-worker Empedocles of Acragas named Love and Strife as the natural basic forces of binding and separation.

There was a very ancient 'unwrought stone' of Eros at Thespiae, in Hesiod's home country.[16] We are still a long way from the numerous personifications of Eros (Cupid) and pretty tales about him (page 408). Yet Hesiod himself—unless this is an interpolation—switches for a moment from cosmogony to psychology (as he did in writing about Aphrodite, page 116), when he describes Eros not as a procreative power but as a dread force within man's souls and bodies.

> Eros, who is Love, handsomest
>   among all the immortals,
> who breaks the limbs' strength,
>   who in all gods, in all human beings
> overpowers the intelligence in the breast,
>   and all their shrewd planning.[17]

Herein he anticipates the fifth century when men more conscious of the forces at work in men's minds echoed his conclusions.[18]

After this parenthesis or interpolation, the poet tells how from Chaos came forth Erebus and black Night, the mother by Erebus of Aether (the bright, untainted upper atmosphere) and of Day. Night is the mother of Day or Sun,[19] because the Greeks reckoned from sunset to sunset, and there was need to personify what happened during the dark half of time.[20]

We are now in a realm of more developed personification in which the powers marry and beget and conceive. Hesiod is strenuously selecting out of a mass of inconsistent myth and folk-lore, and not all the incompatibilities are removed. Yet this is one man's picture, at least as consistent as the cosmologies in many people's minds today.

The poet has not got a systematic method, but is already feeling his way towards ordered concepts. Hesiod's theology was far more self-conscious than Homer's. Between them the authors of the two very different sets of poems, as Herodotus observed, 'have composed for the Greeks the generations of the gods, and have given to their gods their titles, and distinguished their several provinces and special powers, and marked their forms'. [21]

'And Earth (Gaea) first bare starry Heaven (Uranus), equal to herself, to cover her on every side'; and she cohabited with him and bore numerous offspring. With this sacred marriage we are right back from incipient rationalism to much earlier picturings of the primeval powers. They are described in something like human shape, and listed in a series of genealogically presented procreations. The 'birth' of the sky reflects beliefs in an original physical separation between the two elements; and the Union of Father Sky and Mother Earth, so different from *Genesis* with its creation of heaven and earth by one god, is one of the most widespread mythical themes. It is found, for example, throughout Oceania, notably in New Zealand with its comparable Maori story of Rangi and Papa. The Kumana of South Africa, too, call their earth their mother and the sky their father, and the Navajo Indians reverence a sky-man (Yadilqil Hastqin) and his wife the earth-woman (Nihosdzan Esdza). The Ewe of Togoland believe that the union takes place again each year, in the season of the rains. There was a Hittite goddess Arinna, 'queen of the lands', and her husband U or Im, the god of storm. So also the ancient Egyptians believed in a marriage between Keb (earth) and Nut (heaven)—though there the roles are reversed, since the word for heaven is feminine.

The myth of the sacred marriage originates from the desire to show dramatically why these two regions of earth and sky, though separate, so obviously interact. Such stories have been attributed to a primeval division of the original tribal hordes into two inter-marrying groups, although there is no direct evidence to support such conclusions. At any rate Greek mythology included this widely familiar tale. Several strands of thinking developed from it. On the mythical side, the belief is recorded by Plato, who repeated (and sometimes invented) such stories for their symbolic value, that Eros, the procreative principle, appeared from an egg, fashioned in Aether; the two halves of the egg were earth and heaven. Yet, two centuries before Plato, the separation of heaven and earth had also contributed to the revolutionary astronomy put forward by the second of the so-called Ionian philosophers, Anaximander of Miletus, who in the quasi-scientific theory of beginnings that he was the first to formulate regarded the universe as a sphere in which water and air had become differentiated from the land.

3 Zeus Was Not Always There

The last of the offspring of Earth (Gaea) and Heaven (Uranus) was Cronus—perhaps originally a harvest deity, transformed by mythographers into the lord of the universe. There follows the savage story of how, at his mother Earth's prompting, he castrated his father Uranus.

> And from his hiding place his son
> reached with his left hand
> and seized him, and holding in his right
> the enormous sickle
> with its long blade edged like teeth,
> he swung it sharply,
> and lopped the members of his own father,
> and threw them behind him
> to fall where they would.
> But they were not lost away when they were flung
> from his hand, but all the bloody drops
> that went splashing from them
> were taken in by Gaea, the earth,
> and with the turning of the seasons
> she brought forth the powerful Furies
> and the tall Giants
> shining in their armour
> and holding long spears in their hands.[22]

Here is an unmistakable resemblance to a cycle of myths preserved for us in the Hittite language, going back to the culture of the Hurrians. This Hurrian people, with a language of prolific suffixes of which the affinities are uncertain, had originated (as far as we know) from near Lake Van, and conquered north Syria. There they established the state of Mitanni, based on a capital not far from the source of the river Khabar and on a culture revealed at Tell Halaf and Mari as intermediate between the Assyrians and the Hittites. For a time in the fifteenth and fourteenth centuries BC this Hurrian kingdom was the dominant power in western Asia. Before its power was broken, the Hittite theologians of Yazilikaya and Bogazköy in Asia Minor, whose records survived thirteenth century destruction (page 33), had adopted the Hurrian pantheon—and Hittite inscriptions begin with the formula 'this is what the singer of the land of Hurri sings'.

One of these stories, evidently translated into Hittite from Hurrian, is the Epic of Kumarbi; and it is distinctly similar to the Uranus-Cronus myth. Here, too, is the impregnation of the earth-goddess, the emasculation of the sky-god (Anu) by Kumarbi, the birth of a goddess as (in Hesiod's story) Aphrodite is born, and the swallowing of a stone; as well as the struggle with a monster (Ullikummi). Moreover, an alternative Greek version of the Uranus-Cronus conflict (recorded by Apollodorus) actually localizes this at Mt Casius (Hazzi) in north-western Syria (on the Turkish border) just as the Hurrian-Hittite story does. There are many differences, it is true; yet the resemblances are still so striking that a direct borrowing is perhaps more probable than a common source.

If, then, there was this borrowing, when did it take place? Perhaps the Mycenaean forerunners of the Greek poet had direct cognizance of the Hurrians or Hittites in the fourteenth or thirteenth centuries. Yet it is also possible that the link was established five or six hundred years later—that Hesiod and his contemporaries learnt these stories in the Levant in about the eighth century BC, for example from the Phœnicians whose kingdoms of Tyre and Sidon then dominated these seas, and whose alphabet was borrowed by Greece (page 37). As in the case of oriental elements in the *Iliad*, we cannot yet determine at which of these two epochs (if, indeed, it was not at some period between them) the common ground was established (p. 50).

Heaven (Uranus) had begotten monsters, and this was his reckoning —there is already a nexus of evils and punishments. Though Uranus remained purely mythological and was not thought of in such definite terms as his Indo-Iranian homonym Varuna, Hesiod may be indirectly influenced—though this cannot be proved—by early Indian rites of divine kingship, in which the ritual for the sovereign's investiture reflects a primitive slaying of the reigning monarch when he has lost his virility (page 342).

But above all, here is the original sin—which, say the psychoanalysts, since it occurred, has not allowed mankind a moment's rest: here is Hesiod grimly tolling the knell of our primeval crime. The castration of Uranus is a reflex of unconscious desires. Freud, whose views are discussed elsewhere (page 229), specified that the castration complex, which to him (by 1926) seemed present in every neurosis, becomes profoundly important at the climax of infantile sexual development (age 4–5) (page 230). This complex, caused by social depreciation of the genitals and by the now perceived differentiation between the sexes, develops—unless the advent of the super-ego fully transforms it into a more undefined social or moral anxiety—into such evils as anti-semitism (in which circumcision is equated with castration) and the narcissistic rejection of women. But in the story of the *Theogony* this universal fear of being castrated is transformed into the castration of the father, symbolizing the son's attainment of sexual freedom through the removal of his father-rival.

The member was cast into the sea, where from the surrounding foam it begot Aphrodite, whose name was believed to be derived from *aphros*, foam. She came to Cythera and then Cyprus, but both claimed her as their own, and the *Theogony* is contradictory about the place of her birth. Botticelli's painting of this event (also represented by Matisse in bronze) shows her rising from the waves as young and ethereal, very unlike the more mature and determined

Venuses of Apuleius, Titian, Velasquez and Racine. Botticelli's version, compared with Hesiod's savage tale, is a startling example of the different points of view from which the same myth can be depicted. Nor is the painting of Botticelli nearly so close to the *classical* spirit as Walter Pater believed—it shows a more introspective, almost morbid, hunger for physical beauty, and a non-Greek spiritual tension.

Aphrodite is in origin an un-Hellenic, western Asiatic deity, akin to Ishtar and Astarte in her incarnation of the maternal principle; perhaps she was once a Cypriot mother-goddess. Her birth proclaims an end to the era of unproductive monstrosities, and introduces a new order and fixedness of species. Accompanied by Eros[23] and with his aid, she is the irresistible force impelling procreation and production, who 'strikes fond love into the hearts of all, and makes them in hot desire to renew the stock of their races'.[24] As Euripides was to tell in his *Hippolytus*, she also strikes down those who exercise their pride to resist her.

And yet Hesiod strangely, in his poem of grim, portentous happenings of the distant past, pauses to speak not of such things, but of the pleasant frivolities that accompany the power of Aphrodite.

> Here is the privilege she was given
>   and holds from the beginning,
> and which is the part she plays among men
>   and the gods immortal:
> the whispering together of girls,
>   the smiles and deceptions,
> the delight, and the sweetness of love,
>   and the flattery.[25]

As Cronus overcame his father Uranus, so Cronus in his turn was overcome by his son Zeus. The two stories almost seem, in their main facts, to duplicate each other; and they indicate changes in the supreme governance of the universe which are unthinkable to ourselves. The attempt of Cronus to swallow his son Zeus, as he had swallowed his other children (the subject of a nightmare picture by

Goya) is described by Freud as 'typical age-old childhood material', since very often little boys are afraid of being eaten by their father. And the swallowing of a stone instead of the child is paralleled in the Maori tale of Tane Mahuta.

The myth of Zeus' birth, in Crete, goes back to the religion of its Minoan peoples in the second and earlier millennia BC (page 32). The divine child was prominent in this religion; it is uncertain if he ever grew up. A fertility spirit of vegetation, born and dying annually —like Adonis and Attis who became attached to the cults of Aphrodite and Cybele respectively—he personified the cycle of the seasons, and so he was thought of as the child of the Earth Mother (page 146). Hesiod says Earth hid him in a remote cave, and the mountain caves of Crete, especially Dicte and Ida, reveal the remains of shrines of the second millennium BC. Those cavernous holy places, the sites of annual ceremonies—and, before that, of human habitation—provide one of the most significant links between the Bronze and later ages in Crete.

This Cretan Zeus was a Mediterranean deity more primitive than the Indo-European sky-god, embodying the processes of fecundity within the earth rather than renewing them by the dispatch of vitalizing rain. Yet the two traditions are found alongside here in the *Theogony*. For it is above all the sky-god who triumphs over Cronus; and Cronus from that time onwards, according to one tale, sleeps for ever with his followers upon a remote holy island near Britain).[26] The strange, disturbing series of triumphant universal revolutions was over—and the poets dwelt upon its effects:

> Old song I will not sing,
> Now better songs are sung.
> Zeus reigns now, and is young,
> Where Cronus once was king.
> Old Muse, your knell is wrung.[27]

In origin, this Zeus was the Indo-European weather-god—the Germanic Tiu—a nature deity like Varuna or Ahura Mazda who lived in the sky. But Zeus was also head of the pantheon upon Olympus, its summit lost in the clouds of the divine cloud-gatherer.

His name means 'bright'. This conclusion was a success for the philological school of mythologists such as the Sanskritist Max Müller (1856–1865), who (calling myth a 'disease of language') deduced religion from word derivations. Muller believed that religion and myth (and so the attribution, for example, of evil to divinity) arose from the unavoidably metaphorical nature of speech and language, giving rise sometimes to erroneous conceptions. Thus there was once a time, he argued, when the words that have survived as the names of Vedic Gods had other meanings (mostly related to the sun); but that these meanings were forgotten and what had originally been metaphors about the sun, etc., were subsequently interpreted as the names of gods. That seems to us fanciful—and it places the origin of the myths too late, for whether language or thought are to be regarded as coming first (a disputed matter) both language and myth represent a very general and early experience of mankind. Nevertheless *sometimes* an etymological explanation is correctly discernible, and that is the case with the name of Zeus, the superseder not only of Cronus, but also of Heaven (Uranus) as the age-long concept of the animate sky.

Yet, although 'the bright one', Zeus is also the giver of life-giving rain and the weather-god of all the atmospheric phenomena, bright or dark, revealed by signs from the mountain-tops, and so of all natural phenomena whatever. In the words of an unknown poet:

> Distinguish god in your imaginings
> From men that die, think not of him as flesh.
> You know him not. Sometimes he leaps in fire,
> Swift, unapproachable; sometimes in water
> Comes, or in the darkness clothed about,
> And still is god in likeness of a beast,
> In wind, cloud, lightening, thunder and rain.
> The sea and all the rocks therein obey him;
> Springs, rivers, tributaries all are his.
> The mountains tremble, earth and the nethermost depths
> Of monstrous ocean, earth and the mountain-tops
> Tremble before the terrible eye of god.[28]

As Aeschylus sums up his powers:

> Zeus is the air, Zeus earth, and Zeus the sky,
> Zeus everything, and all that's more than these.[29]

He was also protector of the household; of this we hear nothing in the *Theogony* except, perhaps, by the implication that his conquest of many rebels protected the safety of everything in the universe. Thus good prevails over evil, and the moral—that Zeus can strike men down or raise them up—is much more explicitly drawn in the *Works and Days*.

> Men are renowned or remain unsung
> as great Zeus wills it.
> For lightly he makes strong,
> and lightly brings strength to confusion . . .
> He, Zeus, of the towering thunders,
> whose house is highest.[30]

For all his sometimes inscrutable and arbitrary workings, he somehow became the guardian of justice, with an almost Hebraic concern for the humble.

> The eye of Zeus sees everything. His mind understands all . . .
>   Nor does he fail
> To see what kind of justice this community keeps
> inside it.[31]

From this moralizing vein, so much stronger than Homer's, stemmed a whole tradition of Hymns to Zeus, such as that of Archilochus of Paros.

> Zeus, father Zeus, the sky owns thy command;
> Thou overseest what men do
> Both right and lawless, and in wild beasts too
> Pride and right doing feel thy hand.[32]

There is an almost universal belief in a celestial divine being, whose transcendence is directly perceived in the inaccessibility, infinity, eternity and power of the sky. Among the Iroquois the words 'high up' and 'powerful' are synonymous, and to the Ewe 'there where the sky is, God is too'. This belief, not logical or rational, derives from the sky's unfathomable height. 'Deep sky', observed Coleridge, 'is of all visual impressions the nearest akin to a feeling. It is more of a feeling than a sight, or rather, it is the melting away and entire union of feeling and sight.' By the middle of the first millennium BC, in Greece as elsewhere, the sky-god had become the Creator and prototype of mankind, the eternal and primary being in whom all things lived and moved. But that was not yet, although he was already supreme over the Olympians, and father of gods and men.

In the mid-nineteenth century, as has been suggested (page 120), the evident character of Zeus as a nature deity led to a theory generalizing all myths into symbols and reflections of natural processes, and particularly of the sun. This sort of interpretation works not too badly with Vedic material, but—like most other generalizations—has only limited application to the myths of Greece. Yet in the literary field, the translation of natural phenomena into mythological language—describing the sun as Phoebus Apollo, and so forth—had persisted right up to that epoch. For example, Milton, though he might view the gods as devils disguised, generally described nature in mythological terms. Indeed, in 1739 Lord Chesterfield advised his son: 'In prose, you would say very properly, "It is twelve of the clock at noon", to mark the middle of the day; but this would be too plain and flat in poetry; and you would rather say, "the Chariot of the Sun had already finished half its course"—this is what is called poetic diction.' Fortunately this view of how a poet ought to proceed is now outdated, but in its eighteenth-century manifestations it did much to make mythology seem banal and threadbare; and Coleridge and Wordsworth expressed their disgust with such hackneyed, decayed remnants of the classical tradition.

4 *The Destruction of the Rebels*

The aspect of Zeus' moral command on which the *Theogony* concentrates throughout a large part of the poem is the destructiveness

of the weapons which his power over physical forces affords him—
the thunder and the glowing thunderbolt and the lightning,[33] like
the storms in which Jehovah, too, displays his power.[34] For there are
successive threats to the sovereignty of Zeus, and one rebel after
another is shattered. First fall the grandsons of Oceanus—Menoetius,
Atlas and Prometheus. The clash between Zeus and Prometheus,
which is the only one of these stories told at length, is the
central feature of the *Theogony;* for it is preceded by the two
struggles for leadership among the high gods, in which Cronus
defeats Uranus and Zeus defeats Cronus, and it is followed by two
battles in which Zeus defeats others who, like Prometheus, rebel
against him.

Prometheus seeks to outwit Zeus by allowing him to choose an
inferior offering. Though, in deference to the god's omniscience,
Zeus is said to have known the trick beforehand, he chose the
offering wrapped in fat, which only contained white bone, instead
of the superior portion of flesh and fat which had been deceptively
covered with an ox paunch.

This strange tale represents an important type of myth: the story
that is aetiological, that explains how something, whether a natural
or a human phenomenon, came about. By ancient custom, when the
Greeks sacrificed to the gods, they kept the best part for themselves.
That was sensible enough—especially in a country where food was
scarce—and if there was any other reason, it had long been forgotten.
Yet people felt that an explanation was needed, and so this myth
was invented to provide one. Primitive man, as Sir Maurice Bowra
said, feels the need to have 'a story which attempts to illuminate
obscure subjects by providing a kind of historical antecedent or
parallel to them. Something happens in the present because something not very unlike it has happened in the past, or happens outside
the familiar scheme of time.' Men saw gods and spirits at work
everywhere, and attempted to explain what they saw—their
explanations taking the form of aetiological myths. A very large
number of myths in all countries, but particularly among the
inquiring Greeks, come into this category, and indeed the view that
most myths are aetiological has been held by many. This theory

cannot, it is true, be applied to the whole of classical mythology since no one theory will suffice to explain such varied material; yet aetiological elements are often strong.

Lately, other theories have tended to elbow out such interpretations, on the grounds that, although primitive people are speculative, the lore they transmit does not 'answer questions' but is another order of knowledge altogether (page 160). Supporters of this view, however, are obliged to concede that many a myth (such as this one) has unmistakably, at some stage, become invested with an aetiological purpose. But they would maintain that in such cases a community, faced with the desire to explain a phenomenon, did not invent a myth to provide this explanation, but ransacked its *already existing* mythology until an explanation was found in it. The example is quoted of the Fijian myth of the culture-hero Mberewalaki. This story was used aetiologically by the Fijians to explain the mountainous nature of an island, but it did not originate in that attempt. The myth was much older (and of unknown meaning), but people studied it until they *found* in it a possible explanation of the island's nature—or, alternatively, as they heard the tale over and over again it struck them that this was the explanation that they needed.

Does the story of the Promethean sacrifice come under this heading (its real cause and origin remaining unknown), or is it instead a genuine aetiological myth, actually invented to 'explain' the phenomenon? We cannot tell. However, it would be premature, as in many of these cases, to reject the latter possibility out of hand. Whether the poet himself still consciously offers it as aetiology is another matter; this was frequently done by archaeologically minded poets of later times (page 300), but we are still in a less sophisticated age. The poet of the *Odyssey*, for example, reproduces an aetiological myth about the three hundred and fifty cattle of the Sun[35]—a number which represents the days of the year in the ancient calendar—without apparently noting or caring for this correspondence and the explanatory element. There we have an 'explanation' of the causality of a *natural* (or supernatural) phenomenon. Here Hesiod is 'explaining' a feature of *human* life, a ritual custom of forgotten origin; just as there are many other stories which indicate, more or less conjecturally, how cult foundations and festival procedures come about.

Aetiological myths try to answer, by imaginative means, the questions which science or historical research were later to approach by inductive reasoning. Such myths are a response to the sense of wonder which lies at the root of knowledge,[35] an answer to the questions how and why. Events or customs have aroused curiosity and appealed to the intelligence, and these are attempts, in the special, universal language of mythology, to say what these events or customs mean and thus to alleviate perplexity. The stories do not, of course, scientifically explain cause and effect, but they fumble towards scientific method by suggestively linking one kind of experience to another. Nor is it, again, their intention to give an artistic picture; but myth is the half-sister of art, and seeks to translate and visualize in concrete terms the process which it is depicting. The provision of such apparently cogent answers conferred power upon the providers, and so their myth-making and myth-repeating ability made for a conservative strengthening of social systems and traditional customs, of which these men were the spokesmen.

For the trick of Prometheus, Zeus punished mankind by withholding the gift of fire; but Prometheus stole fire in a hollow fennel stalk and gave it to them. Prometheus was probably in origin a fire-god. The oriental Hephaestus, quickly naturalized, later eclipsed him in this capacity. Yet although not worshipped by the Greeks, and without temples, Prometheus remained popular, the patron saint of the proletariat, handed down in folk-memory. He is the supreme non-moral trickster, like Coyote and many others among the American Indians. Indeed Prometheus (though this is not fully accepted in the *Theogony*) even outwitted Zeus.

Although the myth was constantly reinterpreted (so that more will need to be said of it in a later chapter, page 200), the fire symbol remained constant. In the *Rig Veda* too, fire (*agni=ignis*) is linked with wisdom as 'the friend of man, the immortal among mortals, who is brought down from heaven to human kind'. Similarly, in an Amerindian tribe, a fish stole fire from the Creator. For fire is the material basis of civilization. According to varying ancient versions, Prometheus stole it by applying a torch to the Sun's wheel, or by robbing the forge of Hephaestus. The giant fennel in which he carried the flame is a stalk about five feet high filled with a dry white pith like a wick, which is still used in parts of Greece to transport fire.

The story is an optimistic one, and conflicts with the other Hesiodic view, in the *Works and Days*, of degeneration from every age to its inferior successor (page 126). Plato was to develop the tale of Prometheus into a theory of the origins of human civilization (page 208). But the implications of Prometheus' great gift are already present in the *Theogony*. Because of this gift, according to Aeschylus (page 200), or because of his trickery over the sacrificial meat in Hesiod's version, Zeus chained him to a rock, where his liver was perpetually eaten by an eagle—and the sufferings of this archetypal culture-hero, examplifying the frequent mythological theme of man's punishment for undue audacity, have reverberated through the centuries (page 209).

According to the *Theogony*, it was mankind whom Zeus punished for Prometheus' gift, by creating women; the first of them was allotted to Prometheus' scatter-brained brother Epimetheus.[38] For woman was the greatest of evils, just as Eve too was the root of all evil. In the *Works and Days* (in which Prometheus is little better than a common malefactor) that sour pessimistic belief, less generous than Homer's estimate of Helen, is elaborated by a further tale of this first woman. She is called Pandora, the all-giver—perhaps because she was originally an earth-goddess (page 145).

Hephaestus created Pandora,

> But into her heart Hermes, the guide,
> the slayer of Argus,
> put lies, and wheedling words
> of falsehood, and a treacherous nature . . .
> to be a sorrow to men who eat bread.[39]

Evil things were collected in a casket or box—familiar to the psychologists as a symbol for the mother's womb—which Pandora opened.

After that only Hope or Foreboding (Elpis) remained in the box, since this, for good or harm, remains within our own control. But everything else escaped from the box: all the ills of which the world is full, the maladies that stalk at noonday bringing men misery, and the maladies that steal through the darkness unlooked for and unheard. So beware of women—and the poet of the *Works and Days* echoes those many myths in which the primal Fall is blamed on sexual desire.

> Do not let any sweet-talking woman beguile your
>   good sense
> with the fascination of her shape. It's your barn
>   she's after.
> Anyone who will trust a woman is trusting flatterers.[40]

For women, as Semonides of Samos echoed in the seventh century BC,[42] are the biggest single bad thing Zeus has made for us. So say the tragedians too, and especially Euripides,[42] though his Medea declares that their name shall regain its honour.[43] To the early Christian church all women were again *instrumenta diaboli*, and the thought continued to find expression:

> When Eve upon the first of men
>   The apple pressed with specious cant,
> Oh! What a thousand pities then
>   That Adam was not adamant!

The parallel between Eve and Pandora was drawn by the sixteenth-century painter Jean Cousin the elder of Sens, in a picture entitled 'Eva Prima Pandora'.

After the punishment of Prometheus has been stressed again, the *Theogony* passes to the rebellion of the Titans, the monstrous progeny of Uranus, which is also the subject of a separate lost poem the *Titanomachy*. Hölderlin saw them as a weird sport of nature:

> There is created still another race,
>   So there flowers many a luxuriant weed,
> Which seems more than it is, rises quicker

Out of the earth, awkwardly: for the Creator
Jests, and men do not understand it.

But the theme of such monsters coming into existence, and rising
against the divine power, is ancient and almost universal. So too the
Sumerian demon-dragons Asag and Humbaba, the Hittite Illuy-
ankas, the creatures organized by the Babylonian Tiamat, and
numerous figures in North American myth attack the powers of
heaven.

The Titans on Othrys pit themselves against the gods of Olympus;
and Hesiod's tale of terror continues. Our primary source of information about Greek Dark Age beliefs (page 36), it is written with
a compulsive, nightmarish conviction. This was a time when demons
were almost palpable: the universe was violent and mysterious, and
so were the impulses and passions of men. The horrors of these
almost continual rebellions are menacingly close, dumbfounding
us by the vastness of the mighty forces at war. The Titans, an older
generation of nature powers of obscure pre-Greek origin and
derivation, may—according to an 'historical supersession' view,
fashionable some decades ago—stand for the gods of peoples whom
the invading worshippers of Zeus conquered, superseding yet
incorporating their pantheon (page 104), rather as Pan's legs and
cloven hoof survived in the Devil of Christendom. But what we have
here, above all, is a further grim phase of the victory of good over
evil: of the gradual, yet often also sudden, triumphs of ordered
justice, rationality and enlightenment over the monstrous wildness
of age-old elemental disorder. This is a different spirit from the
gloomy dream in the *Works and Days*[44] of decline from Golden Age,
through the Ages of Silver and Bronze and Heroes, to the Age of
Iron—paralleled in Indian and Babylonian myths, and characteristic
of a widespread belief in prelapsarian Paradise.

But Zeus, despite his supreme intelligence, cannot prevail alone;
the Greeks knew well that reason can easily succumb to anarchy.
So he must mobilize to his support the hundred-armed, fifteen-
headed giant sons of Uranus and Earth (Cottus, Briareus and Gyes),
more fantastic than the savage race of giants who in the *Odyssey*

died with King Eurymedon.[45] With their aid the life instinct, as Freud expressed it, could battle against the death instinct, in the struggle between creation and destruction that has been present in living organisms since the beginning.

> The infinite great sea
>   moaned terribly
> and the earth crashed aloud,
>   and the wide sky resounded
> as it was shaken, and tall Olympus rocked
>   on its bases
> in the fan of the wind of the immortals,
>   and a strong shudder drove deep
> into gloomy Tartarus under the suddenness of
>   the footrush,
> and the quenchless crashing of their feet and
>   their powerful missiles.[46]

Titans and Giants were sometimes mixed in tradition; there were also hostile giants led by Porphyrion and Alcyoneus, and Aloads— Otus and Ephialtes who piled Pelion on Ossa. The bones of prehistoric animals were attributed to a variety of these monsters. They were a favourite theme of archaic art; a vase of *c.* 680 BC, from Corinth, shows Zeus attacking a man-horse giant, and the Siphnian Treasury at Delphi, early in the sixth century, displays a struggle between gods and giants. Such designs, like the conflicts with Centaurs on the metopes of the Parthenon and the tortuous battles with giants on the baroque Hellenistic altar of Pergamum, stress that man must struggle heroically against the bestial element. But Zeus deals as fiercely with pride from below as he has dealt with pride from above, and amid shattering convulsions his foes are plunged into the pit.

Ovid retold this story, and Spenser expressed in the *War of Gods and Titans* his deepest thoughts and feelings about the riddle of the one and many. The seventeenth century provided magnificent new versions: the downfall of Satan in Milton's *Paradise Lost* incorporates many details from the *Theogony*, and so does the picture of

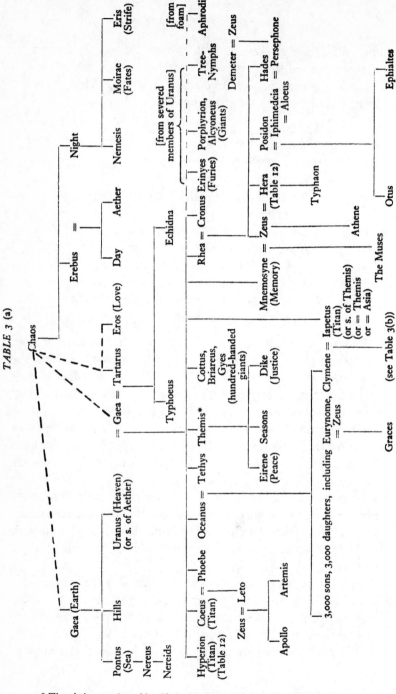

TABLE 3 (a)

* Themis is sometimes identified with Gaea as the mother of Prometheus.

TABLE 3 (b)

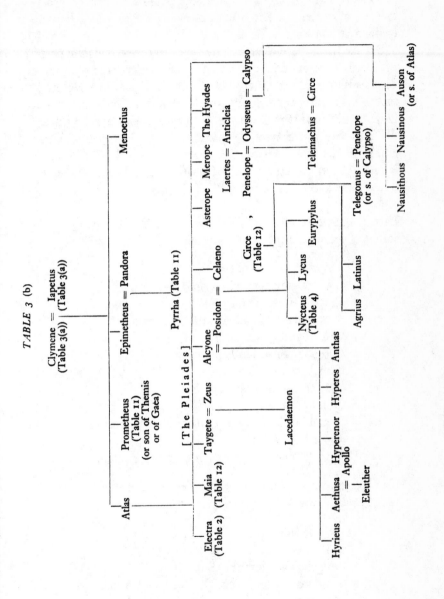

the Titans' Fall which Rubens, with his genius for catching instantaneous movement on the wing, designed for Philip IV's hunting
pavilion at Torre de la Parada (1636).

But the heroic revolt particularly appealed to the romantic poets,
with their hopeless desire to return to Eden. For more than three
decades William Blake was engrossed with the Titans' fate. Hölderlin
too, as his mind was collapsing, dwelt upon this theme, and so did
Goya (pages 125, 117). Leopardi, at the age of eighteen, translated
the *Theogony's* version of the battle, and the *Hyperion* of Keats
(1818–19) adapts and revises the account, making the Titans a link
in the upward succession. In our own century, Braque has illustrated these and other scenes of the *Theogony*.

Last in the poem comes the suppression of Earth's youngest offspring, Typhoeus, a monster described in obsessive detail.

> Up from his shoulders
>   there grew a hundred snake heads,
> those of a dreaded dragon,
>   and the heads licked with dark tongues
> and from the eyes on
>   the inhuman heads fire glittered
> from under the eyelids.
>   From all his heads fire flared
> from his eyes' glancing;
>   and inside each one of these horrible heads
> there were voices
>   that threw out every sort of horrible sound.[47]

The imagery of the battle, in which Zeus pounced on him, recalls
dread earthquakes and eruptions:

> Seizing
> his weapons, thunder, lightning,
>   and the glowering thunderbolt,
> he made a leap from Olympus, and struck,
>   setting fire

> to all those wonderful heads set about
>   on the dreaded monster.
> Then, when Zeus had put him down
>   with his strokes, Typhoeus
> crashed—crippled—and the gigantic earth
>   groaned beneath him,
> and the flame from the great lord
>   so thunder-smitten ran out
> along the darkening and steep forests
>   of the mountains
> as he was struck, and a great part
>   of the earth burned
> in the wonderful wind of his heat,
>   and melted . . . . in the flash
> of the blazing fire.[48]

According to Pindar and Aeschylus, Typhoeus was buried beneath Etna. The *Iliad*, however, had linked him with south-eastern Asia Minor,[49] and his fate may, perhaps, be interpreted as a Greek supersession of the weird gods worshipped by Hittites and Semites (page 126). Zeus is the forerunner of many dragon-slayers, such as Saint George of Cappadocia in the same peninsula. But Zeus is also the successor of Babylonian Marduk who overcame Tiamat (page 104); and each year when the king of Babylon ritually discomfited the demon to ensure the crops, his action was presented as a new defeat of the monster. In Greek tradition, the slaying of Typhoeus or Typhon is often blended and confused with the killing of Typhaon or Pytho at Delphi by Apollo (page 135).

And so when these convulsions were over, the gods, at Earth's prompting, called upon Zeus to rule over them, and he divided their powers and dignities among them. There follows a list of the goddesses who shared his bed, and of the goddesses and women who bore children to other gods. These polygamies, alien to Greek custom—though kings, like gods, could take women from the lower orders—are efforts to unite local cults and tales to the central religion, and to find distinguished ancestries for the families observing these cults. They are also echoes of the marriage of Heaven and Earth (page 112), for many of the female deities (Dione, Demeter, Semele, Persephone-Kore) are goddesses of earth and corn.

Zeus himself, in a laughable passage of the *Iliad*, lists some of his amours for Hera before making love to her. 'Today let us enjoy the delights of love. Never has such desire, for goddess or woman, flooded and overwhelmed my heart; not even when I loved Ixion's wife, who bore Pirithous to rival the gods in wisdom; or Danaë of the slim ankles, the daughter of Acrisius, who gave birth to Perseus, the greatest hero of his time; or the far-famed daughter of Phoenix (Europa), who bore me Minos and the godlike Rhadamanthus; or Semele, or Alcmene in Thebes whose son was the lion-hearted Heracles, while Semele bore Dionysus to give pleasure to mankind; or Demeter Queen of the Lovely Locks, or the incomparable Leto; or when I fell in love with you yourself—never have I felt such love, such sweet desire, as fills me now for you.'[50]

The polygamy of Zeus was what offended, as much as anything else in paganism, the early Christians. 'Was Juno (Hera) not enough for him?' protested Arnobius of Sicca (*c.* AD 296–311), deploring the lusts attributed to the god—and his conversion, for such purposes, into a swan or a bull, and his begetting (by Leda) of the white egg from which Helen was hatched.[51] But throughout the centuries what has especially produced dramatic exploitation is the *affaire* of Zeus with Alcmene, the mother of Heracles.[52] Giraudoux, in his *Amphitryon 38* about the cuckolded husband, indicates that this play is the thirty-eighth attempt throughout the centuries. The latest comment on Zeus, in his capacity as lover, comes from Graham Hough:—

> Ageless, lusty, he twists into bull, ram, serpent,
> Swan, gold rain; a hundred wily disguises
> To catch girl, nymph or goddess; begets tall heroes,
> Monsters, deities. . . . . All that scribe or sculptor
> Chronicles is no more than fruit of his hot embraces
> With how many surprised recumbent breasts and
> haunches.

CHAPTER 4

APOLLO AND DEMETER

1 The Story Told in the HYMN TO APOLLO

I WILL remember Apollo who shoots far. 'He goes through the house of Zeus; and the gods tremble before him, and all spring up from their seats when he draws near, as he bends his bright bow.'[1] Leto alone stays by the side of Zeus; she unstrings Apollo's bow, and closes his quiver and takes his arrows. Rejoice, Leto, for the children that you bore!—Artemis in the Island of Quails, Ortygia, and Apollo on rocky Delos as you rested against the Cynthian hill.

In her wanderings the pregnant goddess Leto had visited many mountains and islands of Greece, in order to find some place to give birth to her child. But no land dared to make a dwelling for Phoebus Apollo. At first Delos too feared to allow her refuge, afraid that her son would despise the desolate, rocky island and thrust it with his foot down into the depths of the sea. 'For then', said Delos, 'will the great ocean wash deep above my head for ever, and he will go to another land such as will please him, there to make his temple and wooded groves. So, many footed creatures of the sea will make their lairs in me, and black seals their dwellings, undisturbed; for people there will be none.' But when Leto swore, in response to the island's demand, that it should have the god's great temple, she was allowed to give birth to him there.

For nine days and nights she suffered grievous birth-pangs.

133

Many great goddesses assembled with her—but not Hera, who stayed in her own home and kept Ilithyia, goddess of child-bearing, away from Leto. However, the other goddesses sent Iris the messenger to fetch Ilithyia, and, casting her arms about a palm-tree, while the earth laughed for joy beneath her knees, Leto gave birth to Apollo. The goddesses bathed the child in water and swaddled it in white cloth with a golden braid. Fed by Themis on nectar and ambrosia, the infant god burst his swaddling-clothes and declared: 'the lyre and the curved bow shall ever be dear to me, and I will declare to men the unfailing will of Zeus'. The goddesses were amazed; Delos shone golden and its earth blossomed.

And so Apollo, lord of the silver bow, walked upon Cynthus. 'Many of your temples and wooded groves, Phoebus Apollo, and all peaks and towering bluffs of lofty mountains and rivers flowing to the sea are dear to you. Yet it is Delos that most delights your heart.' For there the long-robed Ionians, with their swift ships and abundant wealth, gather in Apollo's honour with their children and shy wives and delight him with boxing and dancing and song, as often as they gather on the island. After they have praised Apollo, Leto and Artemis, they sing a song of men and women of past days; and they know how to imitate the tongues and clattering speech of all men.

And you, maidens, if you are asked who is the singer here in whom you most delight, answer with one voice: 'he is a blind man, and dwells in rocky Chios: his songs will be supreme for ever'.

The glorious son of Leto went to rocky Pytho (Delphi) and to Olympus, where he joined the other gods and played to them upon his lyre, as his tall sister Artemis sang, and the Graces and Seasons and Harmonia and Hebe and Aphrodite danced. Then he descended from Olympus and visited many regions, seeking a place for his temple and wooded grove. Finally Telphusa found favour in his eyes. But in order that she alone, and not he, should have renown there, she persuaded him that the trampling of horses and noise of mules watering in her stream would disturb him, and that the horses and chariots would distract men from his temple. So at her suggestion he went on to Crisa beneath snowy Parnassus: a cliff hangs over the place from above, and a hollow, rugged glade lies at the foot. There Apollo laid the foundations of his temple, to be celebrated in song for ever. And at a spring near by he slew the bloated she-monster Typhaon, a plague to mankind, whom Hera without intercourse had borne, out of anger for Zeus, seeing that he himself had given birth to Athene. As the body of Typhaon rotted away, the place was called Pytho, signifying corruption in Greek.

As Apollo wondered whom he should make his priests, he saw in the distance a ship bringing many men from Crete on their way to do trade with Pylos. In the shape of a dolphin (after which he was called Delphian), the god leapt into the ship and steered it into Crisa. There he sprang like a star straight from the ship into his shrine, from which he appeared, in the shape of a young man, to the Cretans and enrolled them as his priests. When they saw the rocky wilderness, they were afraid they could not live there, but Apollo comforted them with the assurance that they would always have the rich gifts which men would be bringing for himself. He told them to show others his will, and to refrain from wrongful deeds or words; for if any did not heed his warning, they would be conquered by others, who would make them subject for ever.

2 The Brilliant God of Hellenism

The Greek hymns of the eighth and later centuries BC, which we know as the 'Homeric Hymns', have come down to us in a form which is literary rather than devotional. They are closer to ritual than the epic poems were, yet they are not in themselves a part of ritual (page 159): the elements of praise, thanksgiving and prayer are perfunctory, and the main content is the narration of myth. The ancient attribution of these hymns to Homer, and their careful imitation of his style, suggest that they belong to the aristocratic epic tradition. The *Iliad* includes a reference to a hymn.[2]

The Homeric Hymns were probably recited and sung by pro-fessional bards (rhapsodes), in competitions held publicly at festivals or thanksgiving ceremonies or privately at funeral games. Although a recitation is referred to in the *Works and Days*,[3] and the Delphic (latter) part of the present hymn comes from the mainland, most of these poems belong to the Ionian rather than the mainland tradition. Their authors have a better gift for narrative than the Hesiodic school, and a more fanciful imagination—to which their biographical themes gave full rein. It was formerly argued that the Hymns, as we know them, are all invocations which served as preludes to the recitation of epics (such as the Homeric poems) or of other long works. This may well apply to some, which are very short, but probably not to the longer works such as this Hymn to Apollo. Besides these compositions in the Homeric metre and style, there were choral hymns in lyric metres; and in the sixth century BC Sappho's invocation to Aphrodite, though not choral but a solo, is cast in the form of a hymn.

The Homeric Hymns are not, as far as we are aware, mentioned as a collection until the first century BC. Of their authorship, apart from the Hymn to Apollo, little can be said, though there was a tradition that the founder of the genre was called Olen, and that it was he who brought the worship of Apollo and Artemis from southern Asia Minor (Lycia, page 137) to Delos. The bards who composed and perpetuated the hymns did much to keep mythology alive, for after writing returned to Greece in the eighth century these poems were rapidly recorded and, before long, their themes appear as the designs of vases. In general, they are somewhat neglected today; and they were neglected in antiquity.

The hymn to Apollo was more appreciated than the rest. It is divided into parts relating to Delos (line 1–178) and Delphi (179–546) respectively. The two parts bear no relation to one another and are, no doubt, the work of different poets. The Delian part is self-ascribed to a blind poet of Chios.[4] It was attributed to Cynaethus of that island,[5] who worked at the end of the sixth century BC; but although Chios may well have been its place of origin, linguistic factors suggest an earlier date, before 700 BC—perhaps a little later than the *Odyssey*, since the poet seems to have forgotten the stiffness of the Homeric bow.[6] The Delphian portion of the poem, again, does not seem later than 582 BC, since there is no mention (as might have been expected) of the chariot races introduced in the reorganized Pythian Games at that date.

Apollo's origin is uncertain. He may have come to the Delian Greeks from Asia by way of Asia Minor (especially if his title 'Lykeios' means Lycian, as many believe, rather than 'wolf-god', as is also argued). Perhaps at first he was a god of herdsmen. Yet he became the essential symbol of the Hellenic spirit as it wished to be, embodying in his purity and stateliness distinctive features of its ideal. He is the god of light (later identified with Helios the Sun) and so of inspiration (page 106), which does for the soul what light does for the world: swift and powerful as the sun's rays, he was also the dazzlingly splendid young Lord of music and song. Accordingly, he was the giver of prophecy as well. He was also the healer of bodies with medicine; his name Paean—like Paieon the physician of the gods in Homer—appears as Paiavon on a tablet found at Cnossus (page 33). 'I am the eye,' Shelley makes him declare,

> With which the Universe
> Beholds itself and knows itself divine.
> All harmony of instrument or verse,
> All prophecy, all medicine are mine,
> All light of art or nature—to my song
> Victory and praise in their own right belong.

Within Apollo's province, too, was the approval of codes of law inculcating high moral and religious principles.[7] In particular, his was the jurisdiction over cases of homicide (page 193); he was the purifier and patron of the juridical aspect of religion. Know thyself, his priests taught—understand your station as man and do not overstep it; bow before the divine. His fifth-century statue at Olympia, one of the most triumphant evocations of Greek divinity, trails an idle bow, but it was there: he is dread and strange, as well as beneficent. 'In Apollo,' says Karl Kerenyi, 'sublimest clarity and the darkness of death face one another, perfectly poised and equal, on a border-line.'[7]

His centres of worship at Delos and Delphi were originally

distinct. The scene of his nativity—so utterly different from the Christian story—is Delos; his birth upon the island is familiar to the psychoanalyst as the 'night journey on the sea'. Upon the one and a third of a square mile of granite and yellow sand that is Delos, regarded as the centre of the Cyclades archipelago, there are remains of pre-Greek stone huts of the third millennium BC. Greeks from the mainland, coming to this island, inherited the sacred grotto on Mount Cynthus, and added their own religious contribution. Homer knew Delos, and at the date of the Hymn the great Delian festival was already established: for the bard tells of its songs and dances and sports, and of the long-robed Ionians who gathered in Apollo's honour.[8] By about 750 BC we know that a chorus from Messene in the Peloponnese had visited Delos, and less than a century later the sculptors Tectaeus and Angelion made a nine-foot image for the god's great new temple.

The Delphic part of the Hymn is as separate as were, in origin, the two centres of worship. This section is less skilful poetry but reveals much about Apollo. Its author could have been a Boeotian of Hesiod's school; he knows the country well. Pytho, as the place is called in this poem (though Apollo is called 'Delphic', with a conjectural etymology, and 'Delphi' appears in another hymn),[9] had been mentioned once in the *Iliad* as Apollo's shrine, and once in the *Odyssey* as the seat of an oracle. The story seems to be carried farther back still by the Hymn, which tells of paean-singers coming to Delphi[10] from Crete where, as was mentioned, the name 'Paiavon' has now been found on a tablet (page 137). There was said to have been at Delphi, before Apollo, an oracle not only of Themis but of Earth (akin to or identical with Themis, page 128, or her mother, page 205) which had once been the typical deity of all such places of prophecy: for example, of the oracle at Dodona (Epirus) taken over by Zeus. According to another theory such early Mycenaean cults were supplanted by a cult of Neoptolemus (Pyrrhus), known in Homeric myth as the son of Achilles. Then came Apollo, and by slaying the monster Typhaon or more usually Python—as Zeus slew Typhoeus or Typhon (page 131)—vanquished the forces of disorder so that enlightenment should prevail. This specimen of the Combat Myth is found in ten variant versions, embodying forty-two motifs.

Here, beside the stream of Castalia, 1,880 feet above the Gulf of Corinth on a ledge beneath two sheer spectacular crags of Parnassus, was this shrine lying at the very heart of Greek religion, politics and morality, where Apollo's representatives expounded the will of his father Zeus. Almost everyone in antiquity believed that the future could be foretold; and throughout the history of the Greek states, both before and after the establishment of the Pythian Games, the oracle exercised a decisive effect upon all branches of activity.

Its prestige, maintained by envoys in each city, was based upon good Intelligence and psychology, upon a local talent for interpreting ancient rituals and customs and recommending efficient laws and constitutions, and upon an impressive blend of dignity and excitement as well as a priestly gift for riddling formulas. These formulas suggested risks and offered warnings rather than initiating action, and were ambiguous enough to guard against failure. Yet the oracle's advice usually favoured advanced morality, and sometimes humbled the proud and justified the lowly; though it was not unknown for human sacrifice to be enjoined, and there was also a good deal of time-serving opportunism—notably in the Persian Wars. This was due to the military weakness of Delphi, which although dominant in a powerful religious League was always looked at by others with covetous eyes—as Apollo hints at the end of the Hymn.

There was, no doubt, room for ambiguity in what the priestess, the Pythia, uttered, as well as in the subsequent priestly interpretations of these sounds. To us, the trances of these women are incomprehensible and alien. Yet prophets and *shamans* and necromants, launching themselves into controlled ecstasies which (accompanied by symptoms like those of nervous breakdowns) precipitate a rupture from the world, are still found among many peoples of Asia, and notably among the Tartar tribes of Siberia. Around these Asian seers are woven underworld myths startlingly similar to those of Homer and Virgil (page 340); the intermediate link was perhaps the north-west Indian kingdom of Kanishka in the second century AD. The Turkish Howling Dervishes, forbidden but still existing, dance and yell in a tranced condition, and there are 'churches' in north America, like the Holy Rollers, in which similar ecstatic trances are induced (page 283).

English religion, too, in the last four centuries has known some 'speaking with tongues'. The phrase is a New Testament one, and the subject was very real to its authors.[11] Later, in the Middle Ages, its abundant appearances ranged all the way from the contemplative dis-association of St Teresa of Avila to the mass hallucinations of whole communities. Today, the trances of dervishes and *shamans* vary from the hysterical and pathological to the performances of gifted individuals possessing excellent concentration, strength and health. With such parallels in mind it is not necessary to ascribe to the Pythia the chewing of laurel leaves, or the inhalation of natural gases (excavations suggest that these were none), or even the magic of wine which, following another Greek tradition (page 174), Keats in his *Hyperion* saw as analogous or contributory to these strange gifts:

> Knowledge enormous makes a God of me.
>   Names, deeds, grey legends, dire events, rebellions,
> Majesties, sovran voices, agonies,
>   Creations and destroyings all at once,
> Pour into the wide hollows of my brain,
>   And deify me, as if some blithe wine
> Or bright elixir peerless I had drunk,
>   And so became immortal.

The Hymn also refers to the birth of Apollo's sister Artemis, in Ortygia (the island of quails), which is here implied to be distinct from Delos but was later regarded as the same place. Originally Artemis had nothing to do with Apollo, though later his Hymn was inscribed upon the walls of her Delian temple. Already in the *Iliad* she is the daughter of Zeus, 'lady of wild things'.[12] She appears in this capacity on an Athenian vase of *c.* 800 BC, and her worship seems to go back to the Mistress of Animals in Cretan, non-Greek religion.

On a Cnossus seal a goddess of this kind is accompanied by lions, just as lions at Mycenae (where the name of Artemis occurs on an inscription) flank a pillar which symbolizes her cult. She plays a rather inglorious role in the *Iliad*, and it has been suggested that this may be because she was, to the Greeks, the goddess of a conquered race (page 126).

To the historical Greeks, however, with their fascination for man-ruling, battle-fit Amazons (whose like they had perhaps seen in the women soldiers of the Phrygians and Carians), Artemis was the beautiful virgin huntress of the mountains. This was a very different conception from the underworld Hecate with whom she was some-times identified (page 256)—and the great goddess of Ephesus, the many breasted one (unless what seem to be breasts are clusters of eggs or dates!), called Artemis too, whose worship as mother-deity and birth-goddess affronted St Paul and was affronted by him.

In Artemis, as Kerenyi sees her, the wildness of young animals and the terrors of birth are in equilibrium, *joie de vivre* is balanced against murder-lust. A separate Homeric Hymn addressed to her tells of the terror of her arrows.[13] It is also a destructive deed of Artemis that has captured the world's artistic fancy. When Actaeon, son of Aristaeus, came upon her bathing naked (according to another version his crime was to claim he was a better hunter than the goddess),[14] she turned him into a stag, and he was run down and killed by hounds.[15] The scene of her surprise engaged the vivid attentions of Tintoretto, Veronese and Titian, whose versions are among his most sombre and terrifying pictures. Shelley in his *Adonais* rather elaborately saw Artemis as Nature, Actaeon as his own mind, and the hounds as his thoughts: he himself, in his mind,

> Had gazed on Nature's naked loveliness,
>   Actaeon-like, and now he fled astray
> With feeble steps o'er the world's wilderness;
>   And his own thoughts, along that rugged way,
> Pursued, like raging hounds, their father and their
>   prey.

3 The Story Told in the Hymn to Demeter

I sing of the revered goddess Demeter and of her daughter Persephone, seized from her by the Host of Many, Him who has Many Names, by leave of his brother Zeus.

Away from Demeter lady of the golden sword and glorious fruits, Persephone, with her companions the daughters of Oceanus, was picking flowers in a soft meadow. She reached out her hands for an especially beautiful flower: for 'from its root grew a hundred blooms and it smelled most sweetly, so that all wide heaven above and the whole earth and the sea's salt swell laughed for joy!'[16] But the earth suddenly opened, and Hades who has many names, the son of Cronus, sprang out at her and carried her off in his golden chariot. As Persephone cried to her father Zeus, no one heard her except Hecate in her cave, and the Sun. Zeus was seated in another place, receiving sacrifice from men, and did not object to the rape of his child by his brother.

Yet as long as she could see heaven, earth, the sea and the rays of the sun, she went on crying out; and her mother Demeter heard her. For nine days Demeter wandered over the earth in mourning, and on the tenth day she met Hecate, who told her that she had heard the girl's cry, but did not know who the seducer was. Then Demeter came to the Sun, who disclosed to her that it was Hades—a worthy husband for her daughter. Full of hatred against Zeus, Demeter grieved, wandering among men in disguise until she reached the house of King Celeus of Eleusis. She found the King's daughters fetching water, and told them that she was a Cretan, and that Doso was her name. They took her into the home of Celeus and his wife Metanira, where she sat upon a lowly seat, never smiling nor eating nor drinking—except for a mixture of barley-meal, water and mint, which she drank as a sacrament.

Metanira then gave her the care of her own son Demophoon. He grew like a god: because Demeter anointed him each day with ambrosia, and held him each night in the fire. She would have given Demophoon immortality and eternal youth, if Metanira had not kept watch one night and seen him in the flames. She screamed, and

Demeter snatched the boy from the fire and cast him to the ground. 'You have done an act of folly,' she said, 'that is beyond repair! Now he can no longer escape death and the fates, though he will always be revered since he has rested in my lap; and the sons of the people of Eleusis will stage contests in his honour. I am Demeter, the greatest of joys and blessings to gods and to men. Build me a temple and altar upon a hill beneath the city, and I myself will teach you the rites you must perform to win my favour.' Thereupon Demeter was transformed into the dazzling beauty of a goddess; and she went out from the place. Metanira stood speechless. Her daughters finally lifted the wailing child, and embraced him lovingly. But they could not comfort him, because he was used to a more skilful nurse.

A temple and altar were built as Demeter had ordered. She came back, and stayed inside the shrine, away from the gods; and she sent a year of barrenness upon the earth. Indeed, Demeter would have destroyed the whole human race. But Zeus intervened. At his order, Iris came to Eleusis and, finding the dark-cloaked goddess in the temple, summoned her to Olympus. She refused, and when all the gods came to her one by one with gifts, that did not make her change her mind. Demeter would never set foot on fragrant Olympus, nor let fruit spring out of the ground, until she had seen her daughter again.

Then Zeus dispatched Hermes to Tartarus to persuade Hades to release Persephone. Smiling grimly, the god agreed to let her go, but secretly gave the girl a pomegranate seed to eat so that she would have to come back to him, since the pomegranate was sacred to the underworld. Hermes brought Persephone to her mother at Eleusis, and Demeter learnt from her all that had happened. But she suspected the snare. Happy though she was to see her daughter again, the goddess knew that because Persephone had eaten the seed she must spend one-third of each year in the underworld. 'But when the earth shall bloom with the fragrant flowers of spring in every kind, then from the realm of darkness and gloom you shall come up once more to be a wonder for gods and mortal men.'[17]

Now Zeus sent Rhea to bring Demeter back to the assemblage of the gods. As Rhea came down to the plain of Eleusis, the soil was barren and leafless; but soon it would be waving with long ears of corn. For Demeter accepted Rhea's appeal, and made the land fruitful again. To the Kings of Eleusis, of whom Triptolemus was one, she showed her rites and 'awful mysteries which no one may in any way transgress or pry into or utter, for deep awe of the gods checks the voice. Happy is he among men on earth who has seen these mysteries; but to him who is uninitiated, and who has no part in them, such good things do not befall once he is dead, down in the darkness and gloom.'

And so Demeter and Persephone went to dwell beside Zeus. Blessed are the men whom they love! Be gracious, lady of sweet Eleusis and sea girt Paros and rocky Antron, giver of good gifts, bringer of seasons, you and your daughter, the most beautiful Persephone!

And, for my song, reward me with cheering prosperity.

4 Mother Earth

The greatest and perhaps the earliest of Greek mother goddesses was Demeter. This Second Homeric Hymn, of which she is the subject, only survives in a manuscript found at Moscow in 1777. It cannot have been written later than the seventh century BC; that is indicated by its language as well as by the absence of Dionysus and the relative insignificance of Triptolemus, both of whom thereafter were prominent in the cult (pages 282, 148). Moreover, there is no word about Athens, which in that century absorbed Eleusis and would have been mentioned in a later poem of this character. The Hymn is a poetical and reverent combination of human warmth and divine gravity, more heartfelt and less gay than other works in the collection. Its threefold structure comprises an opening invocation, a mythological central movement, and an epilogue or final benediction like the *quête* of European mummers' plays.

Demeter's name may mean 'grain-mother' rather than earth-mother; in thirteenth-century Pylos a word rather like it *may* have meant both a deity and a measure of arable land. Yet, as goddess of the crops, she was almost the personification of the Earth whom Hesiod also had placed in his cosmogony (page 110). 'She is the Earth,' says Euripides of Demeter, 'call her what you will';[18] and at Athens, Demeter and Earth shared the same shrine. Moreover, earth-goddess means mother-goddess. Woman, according to Plato, imitates the earth[19] and not vice versa, but at all events the identification of motherhood with the ploughed soil is very ancient and widespread. 'Creep back to the earth thy mother,' says the *Rig Veda*,[20] and the identification is repeated in many Greek writings.[21] 'It is a sin', said the American-Indian prophet Smohalla of the tribe of Umatilla, 'to wound or cut, or tear or scratch our common mother by working at agriculture'; but this was an extreme view.

Palaeolithic, Aurignacian deposits over a vast area, from southern France and mid-Rhine to Siberia—with the Ukraine perhaps as the central point—have disclosed bone or ivory female figurines. These were emblems of fecundity (often sexually exaggerated), and *possibly* they are evidence of worship. Among primitive societies, in which the role of the father was vague or non-existent, feelings of awe may well have been inspired by the relationship of mother to child. True, recognizing reluctantly that we have, before 3,000 BC, no direct evidence for the thoughts and beliefs of mankind—although vigorous attempts are being made to deduce them for earlier epochs (page 93) —we can no longer feel convinced, like Bachofen von Echt, that a certain stage in human history was characterized by the absolute ascendancy of woman and by an exclusively feminine religion. Malinowski's studies of the Trobriand islanders suggest that any assumption of the absolute priority of mother-right can be called a delusion. Yet the first fully formed religious image to take shape in a mind of man, some thirty thousand years ago, *may* well have been the Great Mother. Woman, with her unaccountable phenomena personifying life, was mysterious and awe-inspiring—especially at times when, human kind being rare and weak, fertility was the community's most highly prized value.

Reverence became stronger and more universal after the discovery of agriculture—which is often ascribed to women—and its identification with the feminine principle; for the earth was the mother of every man's village and community. An extraordinary variety of naturalistic female statuettes of clay, datable to the sixth millennium BC, have recently been found at Hacilar in Anatolia, and other possible prototypes of the mother-goddess, not more than a few centuries later, have come to light at Jarmo in Iraq. These are more shapeless than the slim (but snake-faced) female deities of Ur, before 3,000 BC. In the following millennium, if not a good deal earlier, the procreative principle as a female deity—with phallic symbols, and a secondary male idol the future 'boy-god' Adonis with Aphrodite, Attis with Cybele—was elaborately worshipped, with mass-production of statuettes, in the temple of Ishtar goddess of fertility at Ashur.

The principal object of Minoan worship in Crete, emerging as an individualized figure just before 2000 BC, was a mother-goddess akin to Cybele the Great Mother of Asia Minor; and from Mycenae there is a representation of a goddess approached by worshippers bringing flowers and ears of corn. It is not, however, certain whether we should regard these Cretan and Mycenaean female divinities, with their varied attributes, as one or many. At all events, the Earth was apparently believed to guard the dead, as the funerary design of a sarcophagus (from Haghia Triada in Crete) seems to show, and as other fertility goddesses, such as the Roman Feronia, were to guard them in time to come. The Mediterranean Earth-Mother fulfilled many potent roles.

Subsequently, the mother-worshipping structure of this settled, agricultural society was merged with the pastoral, patriarchal sky-worshipping invaders (page 32)—a mixture found also in Egypt, Mesopotamia, India and pre-Columbian America. The poets are aware of the juxtaposition, and sometimes the incompatibility, of old and new gods (page 192). Yet great power always remained in the old worships, and particularly in their intoxicating belief in the fecundity of the earth. To Freud, this worship was still so persistent because the cultivation of mother-earth satisfied the incestuous libido (page 230); as the son's importance—in the patriarchal, Indo-European family—increased, his efforts to take the place of his father, and so his attachment to his mother, became ever stronger.

This widespread conception of a female power with inexhaustible fertility as its chief characteristic, a conception based on nature's observed order and regularity, could give rise to mysticism; or to excitement and sexual licence; or to the lofty ideas of super-human motherhood that are contained in another Homeric Hymn, dedicated to Earth.

> O universal Mother, who dost keep
> From everlasting thy foundations deep,
> Eldest of things, great Earth, I sing of thee!
> All shapes that have their dwelling in the sea,
> All things that fly, or on the ground divine
> Live, move, and there are nourished—these are thine;
> These from thy wealth thou dost sustain; from thee
> Fair babes are born, and fruits on every tree
> Hang ripe and large—revered divinity![22]

And so the sculptor of Demeter's statue from Cnidus, in southwestern Asia Minor, represents her as a mother who is grave, tender and sympathetic.

Her sorrowing search for Persephone is like the search of the bereaved Egyptian goddess Isis for her husband Osiris; Isis, just like Demeter, looked after the son of a queen (Astarte at Byblus in Phoenicia) and placed him in the flames, only to snatch him out when his mother interrupted. The influence of the mother-goddess played upon the earliest Christian veneration of Mary, not so much in lands where the patriarchal Hebrew tradition was followed, but strongly in Asia Minor where the chief divinity had, since immemorial antiquity, been the Mother. Today, perhaps for the first time, seasonal festivals in honour of the earth-mother (in one of her many guises) are alien to many people, since our life has at last weakened its contact with seasonal rhythms. But throughout the ages this worship has touched every pinnacle and depth, all the grandeur and degradation, of the human spirit. Its rites have a general resemblance; in most parts of the world, as Frankfort says, they show 'a broad sequence of mortification, purgation, invigoration and jubilation'.

147

At Eleusis the myth of Demeter was acted out in the Telesterion, the antique place of Initiation. Here, at the time of the autumn sowing, the Mysteries took place annually*; in an earlier age too, at this season, an agrarian rite had celebrated the bringing up of corn from the silos in which, after the June threshing, it had been stored. But the fact that the reviver of the crops was the earth, which also has the dead in its charge, came to associate the occasion with thoughts of the afterlife; for the link of seasonal cycles with death and resurrection was very prominent in the Greek mind. 'Happy is he among men upon earth, who has seen these Mysteries,' says the Hymn[23]—happy because in the next world he will enjoy bliss, a conception in general unfamiliar to the *Iliad* and *Odyssey* though it is briefly mentioned (in connection with Menelaus alone) in the latter poem (page 95). 'But to him who is uninitiated and has no part in the mysteries, such good things do not befall once he is dead, down in the darkness and gloom.' This promise of rewards for the initiated in the afterlife, a response to men's longings which made a wonderful change from the traditional gloom of Hades, was the keynote of post-Homeric, archaic Greek religion in the sixth century BC: and particularly of the Mysteries of Demeter, and the movement called Orphic (page 312).

Starting with ritual purity, the Mysteries acquired the wider morality of human brotherhood; for women and even slaves, excluded from so much else, were admitted to these performances. In the fifth century, Pindar more clearly linked rewards with moral deserts,[24] and Aristophanes makes his initiates speak of themselves as 'us who have been initiated and have led a righteous life'[25] —though Diogenes, the Cynic, could still comment that an initiated thief was unfairly better off than an uninitiated great man. At Eleusis, an added element was the glorification of agriculture as the basis of civilized and peaceful life, with Triptolemus (like Longfellow's Hiawatha) as its hero.[26]

The secret of the Mysteries has been well kept; Eleusis set a jealous value on the cause of all its fame and fees. But the central part of

* Persephone may have had both an autumn and a spring Ascent (page 143).

the ceremonies was probably a sacred drama re-enacting the story of Demeter and Persephone (Kore) that is told in the Hymn—with music and dancing added,[27] and sacred objects displayed. There is always renewal, but always it must be ensured by such collective dramatization of the sacred stories. These mimetic and symbolical representations seemed to give the participants contact with the divine power, releasing them from fear and providing comfort—and an assurance of escape from the terror or gloom that awaits the soul after death. 'The soul at the point of death,' said Themistius (in about AD 310), 'suffers the same feelings as those who are being initiated into great Mysteries. First there are wanderings and weary devious hurryings to and fro; journeyings full of fears and uncompleted (*atelestoi*, which also meant "uninitiated"); then, before the end, every sort of terror—shuddering and trembling and sweat and horror. And after that a marvellous sight meets you, and pure regions and meadows receive you, and there are voices and dancing, and wonderful and holy sounds and sacred lights. And he that is completed and initiated wanders free and unrestrained, and is crowned and joins in the worship, and is among pure and holy men; seeing those who live here uninitiated, a foul horde, trodden under his feet and rolled in filth and fog, abiding in their miseries through fear of death and lack of faith.'[28]

The central theme of the drama that inspired and enacted these experiences, and the central theme of the Hymn, is the carrying away of Persephone by Hades or Pluto or Dis (not mentioned by name in the poem since Greeks feared to name him), of which our earliest account is in the *Theogony*.[29] Pluto, the inexorable, severely just lord of the dead, the subterranean brother or darker aspect of Zeus, was confused and merged with Plutus, god of beneficence and giver of the riches of the soul. His bride is called Persephone (a pre-Greek name), and Kore as the Greek corn-maiden whose new crop means eternity of life. In the Greek summer she goes underground, since the fields are bare until the autumn rains and ploughing. But she loves the sun and rain, and longs to return; and perhaps there was an alternative version in which Demeter compelled Pluto to come to terms. At all events, the association of Persephone with

Pluto symbolizes the interplay of life and death, and the decision that she must divide her home responds, in the language of affection and separation, to our certainty that we must come to terms with life and death alike.

The story was an old one. There are cuneiform texts, dating from c. 1000 BC onwards, which record the detention of Mesopotamian goddesses of fertility—the Sumerian Inanna and the Semitic (Akkadian) Ishtar—in the realm of the dead, and their eventual return to the land of the living. Demeter and Persephone are 'the two goddesses'; sometimes they are two aspects of a single nature, and in a version from Arcadia it was Demeter, not her daughter, who was snatched away. The Hymn's story that, because Persephone ate the pomegranate seed, she must return to the lower world, echoes a widespread belief that the partaking of food in the world of the dead condemns one to that world. The Egyptian Hathor offered such food, and so do other deities in New Caledonia (eastern Melanesia) and New Zealand—and the subject recurs in the story of Cupid and Psyche (page 408).

The myth of Demeter and Persephone is of interest to psychoanalysts since in dreams there appear time after time the over-life-size demonic, superordinate mother, and her Gretchen counterpart the maiden, or the unknown young girl, or the mother who is unmarried. Although psychoanalysis cannot account for every myth or even for most of them, it would now be rash to reject, on principle, the validity of the psychoanalytical approach to myth. Psychology, as Thomas Mann remarked, contains within itself an interest in myth 'just as all creative writing contains within itself an interest in psychology'. In this field, as in others, we must discard some of the rationalism of the enlightenment and find room for instinctive images of the imagination as well.

Following upon writers who, in the nineteenth century, had deeply probed man's unconscious (page 229), a few years later psychologists and psychoanalysts were beginning to reinterpret the Greek and Roman mythology; and even after all their exaggerations and misconceptions have been removed, these retellings have drawn out meanings vital to ourselves, and have illuminated dark places of the soul. Nietzsche observed that 'in our sleep and in our dreams, we pass through the whole thought of earlier humanity', and provided that the differences are borne in mind between the fantastic artistry of the former and the more incoherent irrationality of the latter, a comparison of myth to dream is valid. When we study the myths with dreams in mind, we are like men remembering a childhood tale, and at last grasping aspects of its significance that had eluded us before.

The first decade and a half of this century was a time when not only dreams in general, but also the mental products of neurotics were brought under comparison, as well as the myths of primitive peoples which Andrew Lang had noted and social anthropologists were studying (page 82). As the horizon thus widened, the myths seemed to C. G. Jung to be 'still fresh and living . . . in the hidden recesses of our most personal life'. Yet, as he observed and as is even more true today, 'unfortunately, we acquire in school only a very paltry conception of the richness, and immense power of life, of Grecian mythology'. Seceding from Freud in 1912 so as to avoid over-stressing infantile sexuality and its traumas—by which Freud had sought to explain the myths (page 230)—Jung also wished to transfer attention from the personal to the collective unconscious. Here he was developing the ideas of Adolf Bastian (1826–1905), who recognized the universality of mankind's 'elementary ideas'. Present in every individual, in Jung's view, are not only personal memories but the inherited, shared products of the human imagination; the basic, primordial images or motifs or archetypes or dominants—some universal, others (less deep, yet still powerful) belonging to family, tribe, or race. For the personal psyche rests 'upon the broad basis of an inherited and universal psychic disposition, which is unconscious and from the darkness of our soul sends up its dark and unrecognizable urges—deposits of the constantly repeated typical experiences of humanity by which the psychic energy regresses into the legacy of ancestral life'. This objective or autonomous psyche, as he later called it—a development of Kant's 'deep abyss of human knowledge for ever beyond our reach' (1889)—is not a state but an activity, representing a dynamic view of the unconscious which is not just a cupboard full of mental skeletons but an integral, functional part of the human being.

When the collective psyche becomes conscious, it (like the psyche of the individual) needs repression for the development of personality, and this victory is symbolized by myths telling of successes in a quest, or of the winning of treasures, invincible weapons, magic talismans. Indeed Jung believed that no expressions of the collective unconscious are more important than those to be found in the familiar myths. To him, as to other early psycho-analysts such as Abraham and Rank and to literary critics who have followed them, these are involuntary statements about unconscious psychic happenings—group-fantasies reflecting impulse repressions; wish-fulfilments not only of individuals but sometimes of whole societies suppressing the individual (page 231); and symbols of the desires and passions which mankind feels but does not acknowledge. Jung gave myth this vital role in his collective unconscious for several reasons. First, because the same mythical themes are found everywhere. Secondly, because the fantasies of psychotic, especially schizophrenic, patients strikingly resemble the myths: psycho-analysis shows how each experience of its patients is traceable back to the primitive and universal forms which are the mythological material.

Others have disputed and minimized these analogies. Moreover, since Jung formulated the theory, a very great many correspondences between myths in widely separated lands have been convincingly ascribed, not to coincidence, but to actual transmission (page 82). This means that the minds of those concerned have had external influences at work on them and have not dredged up the myths wholly from their own unconscious; although it still remains remarkable that so many different communities should have chosen to borrow similar myths. Indeed, the same must be said of the theory as of the whole psychological approach which it exemplifies: so long as the theory is not held to explain *everything in every myth*, it is valid —and so long as it does not lead to such a complacent reliance on the 'collective' that individual myths are not studied for their own peculiarities. In many myths, however, the collective unconscious is a helpful concept. For example, the story of Demeter and Persephone reaches back, as has been said, to archetypal images which are easily recognizable in the material available to psychoanalysts. Again, there are resemblances between myths in widely distant lands which still cannot be made explicable by any easy theory of transmission.

We have, it is true, been taught by social anthropologists not to use the word 'primitive', or phrases like 'infantile soul-life of the people' (Abraham), as freely as they were employed half a century ago, since there is an infinity of opinions about the yardstick which can be used to measure such primitiveness. Yet the vitality of many societies, *primitive and advanced alike*, has indeed depended upon the continued affirmation of the mythical symbolisms rearing up from the collective unconscious. They are not just stories: they establish a sociological charter, a moral pattern, a miracle perpetually renewed. In the words of Mircea Eliade, 'every primordial image is the bearer of a message of direct relevance to the condition of humanity; for the image unveils aspects of ultimate reality that are otherwise inaccessible'—kinds of knowledge that are unknowable in any but mythical form. For these mythical symbols, felt *true* (though not necessarily historically true) by those cognisant of them, give a concrete, particular shape to unformulated, unconscious or half-conscious memories, desires and emotions that would otherwise escape our grasp. Myth, says Eric Dardel (1954), is 'that pang which comes upon man in the midst of things'.

The tale of Demeter and Persephone, perhaps more than any other classical myth, has embodied and directed man's accumulated thoughts about being born and dying. It anticipates both Easter (in which life and death co-exist) and Christmas (the time of annual rebirth and hope). The story has received resplendent artistic expression. Repeating an ancient location of the Rape at Enna in Sicily, Milton weaves the theme into his symphonic pattern of association-laden musical parallels.

                    Not that fair field
Of Enna, where Proserpine gathering flowers,
Herself a fairer flower, by gloomy Dis
Was gathered, which cost Ceres all that pain
To seek her through the world; nor that sweet grove
Of Daphne by Orontes, and the inspired
Castalian spring, might with this Paradise
Of Eden strive.

Bernini was one of those who told the story in sculpture, and his
version was challenged by the sculptural group of François Girardon
at Versailles (1677–9). There is Goethe's drama *Proserpina* (Persephone) of the mid-1770's, and Schiller's *Complaint of Ceres*
(Demeter), and then Shelley's *Song of Proserpine*:

        Sacred Goddess, Mother Earth,
        Thou from whose immortal bosom
        Gods, and men, and beasts have birth,
        Leaf and blade, and bud and blossom,
        Breathe thine influence most divine
        On thine own child Proserpine.

The mellow masterpiece of Tennyson's old age, written in 1889 when
he was eighty (six years after a version by Meredith), is his *Demeter
and Persephone*. With warm human sympathy, he embroiders upon
the Homeric Hymn to convey his thoughts upon the mysteries of
love and life and death, and the primitive greatness of maternal
passion. Swinburne, too, was attentive to the story, in his *Hymn to
Persephone* and *Garden of Persephone*. In our own century, Stravinsky's opera *Persephone* (1934) is set to words by André Gide;
though he and his composer by no means felt alike about the production. In this version Persephone *chooses* to enter the underworld—
through self-sacrificial pity—and is not forced by Pluto.

    The seasonal myth is the basis of T. S. Eliot's *Waste Land*, and
François Mauriac draws strength from the relationship between the
Church Year and the cycle of summer and winter, sowing and
reaping, birth and death. Robert Graves detects the cults, rituals and

art forms of the earth-mother in so many places and guises that he has accepted them as the prime source of poetry, maintaining (with emphasis upon a primeval, universal matriarchy, page 145) that the language and mythology of a poet are bound up with the female principle of divinity rather than with the rational Apolline patriarchal principle by which, in his view, the myths were later contaminated.

5   Myth and Ritual

Although the Homeric Hymns themselves are literary rather than ritual (page 135), much of the material which they contain was related to cult-acts. This is pre-eminently true of the Hymn to Demeter, of which the story was so integrally connected with the subject-matter of the Eleusinian Mysteries. Parallels are not hard to discover; the Spartan lyric poet Alcman's *Maiden Song* (*c.* 630 BC)[30] again clearly has some relation to the festival for which he is writing (whether this ceremony was in honour of Artemis, Helen, Castor and Polydeuces, Dionysus, or more probably a local goddess Orthia).

For the link of many Greek myths with Greek religious practice is intimate. This was seen by the European romantics when myths were regarded as an essential element in the philosophy of religion, representing the alleged creed or dogma of paganism. But when it came to be understood that Greek religion, unlike our own, does not depend on dogma, another mistake was made: the myths were regarded as entirely literary or artistic tales, unconnected with religion. Nowadays it is better appreciated that, although they have come down to us in literary or artistic form, they are profoundly illustrative of Greek religion. Ambiguity has arisen here owing to a problem of definition: some social anthropologists, such as Durkheim and Kluckhohn, want to restrict the term 'myth' to sacred stories, using 'folk-lore' not in the wider sense of popular folk-tales in general (page 81) but for profane, non-religious tales in particular. But it is going too far to regard *all* myths as of religious origin; although it remains true that many of them are.

This link between myth and religion is scarcely surprising, seeing

that religious sentiment naturally employs a mythologizing imagination, based on the habit of conceiving the deity in an individual
shape. H. Thielicke observes of mythology that it is 'the form of
human apprehension peculiarly fitted to deal with religious truth'.
In our own day, one of the most vital issues in Christianity relates
to the mythological elements contained in the New Testament.
Like the Old Testament, this is full of poetry and poetic allegory
(page 419). According to Rudolf Bultmann, we are ill-fitted to
assimilate these elements, since (apart from certain quasi-myths,
Marxist, Nazi and so on, of a political nature) our twentieth century
is a non-mythical and post-mythical age. If, therefore, we are to
grasp the New Testament and understand its central message, we
must first, he says, subject this to a 'demythologizing' process
(*Entmythologisierung*); when that has been done, but not before,
Christianity will conserve only those elements 'relevant to the
intelligence of man and his existence before God', notably the
proclamation of God's decisive act in Christ. This whole controversy
has brought the sharpest light to bear upon the intimate relationship
of myth and religion.

In dealing with ancient Greek paganism, ritual is of prime significance. The framework of these rites was satisfying and soothing:
to perform the proper act was the safest and most comfortable
course, because this had always been done. So it is with ritual,
rather than any other aspect of religion, that Greek myth may be
expected to have the most potent connection. Human needs are met
by the life-giving potency of the sacral act; the myth translates
that situation into permanent literary form.

At the stage before sophisticated religion transformed myth and
ritual alike into symbolism of various kinds, it ought to be possible
to trace a relationship between them—such as existed in regard to
the stories and rites of the central Eskimos, and between the creation
myths and rites of the Babylonians (page 103); a relationship such
as is apparent also in the Jewish scriptures where we read first of
Aaron splashing the blood on the altar (story)[31], and then of an
instruction that the priest should splash the blood on the altar

(rite)[32]. In Greece, however, this process of tracing myth-rite relationships presents difficulties. For as among the Bushmen, in contrast to the ancient Romans (page 368) and many north American Indians, our knowledge of the ritual system of the Greeks is much scantier than our knowledge of their myths, of which, as the Plates in this book show, we have evidence from sculptures, vase-paintings, and other visual arts as well as from literature.

A question that has been often asked recently is this: which came first, Greek ritual or Greek myth? F. C. Prescott wrote in 1927: 'myth must always come first to generate the rite.' But this now appears an excessive generalization. Exponents of myth as products of Jung's collective unconscious (page 151) do not support Prescott's view as fully as they might, since they are inclined to attribute the origins of ritual to the same collective unconscious, in which case it need not be later than myth. The priority of myth is, however, true in certain cases—notably the rape of Persephone by Pluto, which no doubt remodelled the ceremonies at Eleusis (page 148). Malinowski and other social anthropologists have blamed classical scholars for not extending much further the identification of myths as the sources of ritual texts. About this opinion there is disagreement. Professor H. J. Rose, on the other side, pointed out that in the scanty remains of Greek ritual texts myths are hardly referred to, and that even the chants at festivals (pages 104, 135) were poetic, not liturgical, compositions. Against his sceptical view it has been protested that, even if this is so, such literary compositions do not justify Rose's objection, since if there is evidence of a *resemblance* between myth and ritual even without proof of actual recitation, that in itself is enough to suggest that myth-based liturgies existed. But they are nearly all lost, so we cannot tell.

Much more fashionable, in the past four decades, has been the opposite opinion that ritual comes first, and that mythology comes later and explains it; that myth is the stage direction of the ritual drama, or a kind of libretto composed to make sacro-magical acts intelligible. Some have gone farther still, and claimed that ritual is the origin of all forms of social organization, of philosophical and religious thinking, of processes of law, and of the arts. With regard to mythology, Jane Harrison (1903) and Robertson Smith believed that this was invented, or adapted from folk-lore, in order to explain obscure, forgotten rites, and that such interpretation of rites, imposed on them *after* their creation, was an important and central manifestation of the aetiological, explanatory sort of myth (page 121). During the last few years the basis for this view has been extended; texts from Ugarit (page 49) and Israel[33] have suggested to scholars, especially in Scandinavia, that many myths received their whole frame and content from already existent rites.

Although the Ugarit deductions are contested, and much still has to be explained about the processes which create ritual (as well as those which turn it into a story), this conclusion supplies a valuable clue to the sources of mythologies. That is to say—and this applies to so many other theories also—the theory is tenable provided it is not generalized to account for *all* myths. With the same all-too-rarely observed proviso, it is applicable to Greece, where myths, as Sir Maurice Bowra expressed the position, 'did for a choral song what sculpture did for a temple, illustrating the importance of a rite'. The Greek popular philosopher Lucian of Samosata, in his essay *On the Dance*, lists many ritual mimes—in which the ritual is translated into narrative, mythographic form—still performed in his own second century AD.

Whether a myth *correctly* explained the origins of the rite which it interpreted is, of course, quite a different matter; for example a number of rituals of apparently distinct origins were eventually explained by a single myth of Combat (page 131). But when a myth possessed, or even seemed to possess, this rite-explaining character, it was endowed with religious force, since its narration vouched for the efficiency of the ritual from which the story was ostensibly derived.

That is an attempt to deal briefly with the questions whether, and to what extent, ritual comes out of myth, and myth comes out of ritual. But one must add that this is probably a not very helpful way to formulate the problems. In the early stages of communities—the Greek community among them—it is doubtful how far worshippers distinguished between the two things. At any rate, what was performed (*dromenon*) and what was said (*legomenon*) were not only parallel but interdependent, interpenetrating (says Roger Hinks) like time and space, distinct in kind yet forming a single reality, providing a variety of clues to the same permanent and universal features in human nature. And indeed, the interpenetration between the two things, the reciprocal action, remains, continues and develops, though it takes different forms in different cultures, and probably at different times in the same culture. To the psychoanalysts, ritual is a sublimated compulsion, myth a sublimated obsession. Or ritual is an obsessive repetitive activity, often dramatizing symbolically the 'needs' of the society, whether economic, biological, social or sexual; mythology is the rationalization of these needs. Both myth and ritual are stabilizing elements in the *group*. Yet at the same time they may well be cherished by the *individual* as an individual (at the expense of reason), because, as Kluckhohn suggested, as mechanisms of defence they reduce his 'anticipation of disaster'.

Ritual gives myths their names, a lot of detail and much of their explanatory character. Myth acts more slowly upon the conservatism of rites—interpreting (rightly or wrongly) their elements, and gradually imposing features of its own. Yet myth is also potentially inherent in ritual from the beginning, not only as the spoken correlative of what was performed, but as a translation of the real, static, temporal, immediate ritual into terms of the eternal and transcendental. Myth is the projection of rites on to the plane of ideal situations. Gaster (1950) has worked out how myths go through successive stages, each leading them one step farther away from ritual, and how certain myths belong to one or more of these stages, but not to others. When there is a dramatic or pantomimic presentation of ritual (such as the Egyptian coronation drama of the First Dynasty—enacted by the protagonists themselves), the two are quite close; when a liturgical recitation is included in a religious ceremony as an explanatory background (like Christian hymns sung at saints' day services), they are farther away; and then there are literary performances in which the story has been removed so far from ritual that it has become an artistic creation. In this last category are the Hymns to Demeter and Apollo and most other Homeric Hymns—or all of them.

At each of these stages of proximity and remoteness, myth shares something of the potency of ritual and religion. Although the mythical stories, as we know them, have become artistic, literary creations, and have reached their supreme expression in this form, the myths behind them remain far more than mere narrations. What took place once upon a time, as told in the myth—that is to say what took place in the primordial or timeless fluid past, the original time which is the model for all times—is located by ritual in the present. From this parallelism of the eternal (myth) and the topical (ritual) comes the Jewish tradition that all the generations of Israel, not only the actual fugitives from Egypt, were present in spirit on Mount Sinai when the Covenant took place.

But in any case myths, with or without the partnership of ritual, are lived and re-lived, as well as told. Thomas Mann spoke of the 'quotation-like' life of mythopoeic man, who steps back a pace before doing anything, seeks an example from the past and slips into it as into a diving-bell in order to plunge, at once protected and distorted, into the problems of the present; and thus his life achieves its own expression and harmony. Myths also, as has been said, safe-guard and enforce morality (page 123): they contain practical rules for the guidance of man, and supply a pattern of social values. But to ascribe their power, as Malinowski did, *solely* to the validation of traditional usage is not enough, for the recital of the myth, like the performance of the rite, has also—in times before the myth becomes too remotely literary—the active power to strengthen in people's minds the precarious existence of the community, to preserve it from chaos and give increase of life.

Now the epoch in which Greek literature enshrined its myths was one in which, as among the contemporary Israelites, these values and this salvation were linked with divine control; so that most of the stories are about the relations of man to his gods.

PART III

AGAMEMNON AND PROMETHEUS

CHAPTER 5

THE HOUSE OF AGAMEMNON

1   The Story of the ORESTEIA *Told by Aeschylus*

THE *Oresteia* is a sequence of three plays, the *Agamemnon, Choephori* (*Libation-Bearers*) and *Eumenides* (*Kindly Ones*).

As the *Agamemnon* begins, a watchman is seen on the palace roof at Argos, a little before dawn. For a whole year now, he says, he has watched for the beacon which will announce the fall of Troy. All other stars he has seen in his vigil, except this. Its declaration would bring great news for Queen Clytemnestra, the wife of Agamemnon, who is for so long absent at Troy. Yet the watchman goes on to tell how his songs to keep awake have turned to weeping—since all is not well within the house. At this moment the beacon suddenly shines out. But his cries of joy, and his prayers that the gods may now bring Agamemnon safe to his home, are stifled by a moment of fear.

Clytemnestra comes out of the palace to sacrifice and pray in silence before the statue of Zeus. Out come the chorus of Argive elders also. They do not see her, and do not know the good news yet. They tell the story of how Agamemnon and his brother Menelaus, because of the guilt of Paris and Helen, once mustered the fleet for Troy; and, now, Greece and Troy have equally paid their share of sweat and wounds and death. The elders explain how they themselves had been left behind by the expedition because of their advanced age. But then they break off, because they see the

163

queen. Begging her to explain why the altars are ablaze with offerings, they appeal to her to relieve their haunting fears. She does not speak, but the chorus go on to tell of the past which weighs upon their minds. They recall how at Aulis, as the army was setting out, men had beheld the omen of two eagles devouring a pregnant hare. Calchas, the wise prophet, had understood the sign, and foretold that one day the army would capture Troy. But he had also said that Artemis was angry with the eagles and pitied the hare; and that if she were not to delay the host with adverse gales, those two eagles, the princely commanders Agamemnon and Menelaus, must sacrifice a child, whatever the evil consequences for their house.

'Sorrow, sorrow! Yet let good prevail!' That is their refrain, but they stop to ask—what is good? And who is God, whom men call Zeus? They recall how in turn old Uranus (Heaven) and Cronus passed away, and how Zeus is now lord; and he has appointed a law that man, in sorrow, shall learn by suffering.

As the men starved and ships rotted at Aulis—the Argive elders continue—Calchas had spoken again, disclosing that, in order to appease Artemis, Agamemnon must sacrifice his own daughter Iphigenia. Agamemnon had prayed, and bidden the attendants lift her, like a goat, above the altar; he had told them to gag the cry that would curse his house.

> Letting fall her saffron robe to earth
>   She turned and looked upon each of them that
>   slew her,
>   She smote each one with the piteous glance of
>   her eyes . . .
> For the rest, as I saw it not neither do I speak of it.
> But the arts of Calchas were not unfulfilled.[1]

Yet the killer will be killed. 'Time may show, but cannot alter, what shall be. Meanwhile, let good prevail—good news, to gladden Clytemnestra's heart!'

Day has now come, and the queen turns and faces the elders. She describes the scene at Troy as she imagines it, and gloats over the sufferings of the conquered. If the fleet sails free from taint of sin, she adds, and if there are no dead to take vengeance, the Greeks may have a safe passage home. She goes indoors, and the old men of Argos, instead of celebrating the victory, resume their meditations on Zeus, who is just—and punishes the proud and over-prosperous. Destiny lures the wicked to their ruin; that was the fate of Paris, who caused misery to Menelaus and the horrors of war to Troy. They feel a desperate foreboding of evil and retribution, and declare that to be neither conqueror nor captive is best. Meanwhile, are the glad tidings of the beacons true, or only a delusion?

But now a cheerful herald enters, and confirms the news of victory, telling also of the hardships and discomforts that the army has suffered during its ten years before Troy. Clytemnestra declares that she has already rejoiced for the victory; next she will prepare to receive Agamemnon. He will find her, she says, as faithful as when he left—and implacable to those of ill will. 'Of pleasure found with other men, or any breath of scandal, I know no more than how to dip hot steel.' As she turns back into the palace, the herald is first perplexed at something in her tone. But then he reports further news. The fleet has been scattered by a storm—where Menelaus is, no one knows. So Agamemnon has come home unaccompanied.

The chorus sing of Helen, and of her marriage-song with Paris, which was drowned in wailing. To Troy Helen, coming there in all her beauty, was like a lion's whelp, which is gentle and playful when you rear it, but soon the beast ravages the flocks, filling the house with blood. It is sin, the elders suggest, not prosperity, that begets grief and evil and recklessness: 'whose menace like a black cloud lies on the doomed house hour by hour, fatal with fear, remorse and pain'. But Justice, averting its eye from guilty golden palaces, will guide good and evil to their sure destinations.

Agamemnon now enters in his chariot, followed by another chariot bearing, among various spoils of war, King Priam's daughter Cassandra. The chorus greet him, and he coldly gives thanks. Expressing mistrust of false friends—among his companions at Troy he has praise only for Odysseus—the king promises that suspected disaffection at home will be rooted out with well-inten-

tioned fire or knife. Clytemnestra now arrives. But first she describes to the elders her fidelity and wretchedness while her lord
was away, and while travellers told their tales.

> It is evil and a thing of terror when a wife
> sits in the house forlorn with no man by, and hears
> rumours that like a fever die to break again,
> and men come in with news of fear, and on their heels
> another messenger, with worse news to cry aloud
> here in this house. Had Agamemnon taken all
> the wounds the tale whereof was carried home to me,
> he had been cut full of gashes like a fishing net.[2]

Explaining to her husband that she has sent their son Orestes elsewhere—in fear of a plot against his father at Troy or in Argos—she
concludes by inviting him enter the palace on a crimson carpet,
which her maids now lay down. Agamemnon, with increasing
roughness, rejects these Persian adulations as fit for gods, not man.
Yet he gives way, and marches indoors upon the carpet: to a cry of
victory from his wife, who begs Zeus answer her prayers.

The elders sing of the persistent terror which haunts their hearts
and nerves, even though the departure for Troy is long past and the
fleet is back. In health, disease is close: in prosperity, beware of a
concealed reef. But wealth can be saved by timely sacrifice, coming
like the harvest after famine. Only the dark, unfading stain of blood
cannot be recalled—when Asclepius gave the dead flesh of Hippolytus
a second lease of life, Asclepius was struck down by Zeus. Were not
events and causes and results divinely ordered, the leader of the
chorus adds, I should have spoken out; but, as it is, I hide my distress within my dumb and smouldering spirit.

Cassandra is still waiting in the chariot before the entrance.
Clytemnestra orders her indoors, and herself passes into the palace.
Cassandra has not answered her, and remains where she is. But now
she is suddenly racked by an appalling vision of the house's doom.
Crying for mercy from Apollo, god of her prophetic art, she sees
from the past the children's gobbets of flesh served up by Atreus,
sire of Agamemnon, for their father Thyestes to eat:

> Look there, see what is hovering above the house,
> so small and young, imaged as in the shadow of dreams,
> like children almost, killed by those most dear to them,
> and their hands filled with their own flesh . . .[3]

Into her brain, then, comes the picture of Clytemnestra:

> King of the ships, who tore up Ilium by the roots,
> what does he know of this accursed bitch, who licks
> his hand, who fawns on him with lifted ears, who like
> a secret death shall strike the coward's stroke, nor fail?[4]

Cassandra sees how Clytemnestra will approach her victim, entangle him in a net, and strike; and he will crash to the ground. Her vision next ranges back to the sacrifice of Iphigenia, the tragic passion of Paris, the sack of Troy, and the seduction by Thyestes of Aerope, his brother Atreus' wife. And then her thoughts return to the slaughtered children, and again to the imminent fate of Agamemnon himself. Finally, she appeals desperately to Apollo to avert what she already knows must come—her own death at Clytemnestra's hands. Telling of 'the third' who shall avenge his father, and praying that her own death too shall be avenged, she goes into the palace.

A scream is heard, and then another. As the elders debate what to do, the palace doors open, revealing Clytemnestra standing over her victims. Agamemnon lies in a silver bath, wrapped in a heavy robe; upon his body lies Cassandra. The queen is satisfied by what she has done.

> Inextricable like a net of fishes
> I cast about him a vicious wealth of raiment,
> And struck him twice, and with two groans he loosed
> His limbs beneath him, and upon him fallen
> I deal him the third blow to the God beneath the earth,
> To the safe keeper of the dead a votive gift.
> And with that he spits his life out where he lies,
> And smartly spouting blood he sprays me with
> The sombre drizzle of bloody dew—and I

> Rejoice, no less than in God's gift of rain
> The crops are glad when the ear of corn gives birth.[5]

The chorus express their loathing of Clytemnestra, but she fears no threat of an avenger while her lover Aegisthus remains by her side. When they blame Helen, she rejects this; but when they see the workings of an ancestral curse, she agrees.

> You now speak more in wisdom,
> Naming the thrice-gorged Fury
> That hates and haunts our race.[6]

And the elders must despairingly admit that even these horrors could not be, if they were not the will of Zeus.

Now, at the very end, Aegisthus appears. He too recalls how the children of Thyestes were set before their father to eat, for they were his own brothers. And this is what prompted himself, the survivor, to plan the killing of Agamemnon. Justice, he asserts, is on his side, and the play concludes with a torrent of threats and insults directed against the Argive elders. They leave the scene, to Clytemnestra's final words:—

> Pay no heed to this currish howling. You and I,
> Joint rulers, will enforce due reverence for our throne.[7]

In the *Choephori* (*Libation-Bearers*), we are outside the walls of Argos. Orestes is standing beside the grave of his father Agamemnon, having returned from Phocis with his friend Pylades. Orestes lays a lock of hair on the murdered man's tomb. But then, seeing his sister Electra approach with a procession, he draws aside. Electra and the chorus of libation-bearers—probably captive women brought by Agamemnon from Troy—are appeasing the dead; for Clytemnestra has had a horrible dream.

> She woke screaming out of her sleep, shaky with fear,
> As torches kindled all about the house, out of
> The blind dark that had been on them, to comfort
> the queen.[8]

She has ordered these libations to avert disaster. But all the water in the world, say the chorus, cannot clean hands stained with unrequited blood.

As Electra pours the libations and prays bitterly for vengeance, suddenly she sees the lock, and the strangers' footprints, and understands that Orestes has come. He appears, and completes her recognition by producing a robe which Electra remembers having embroidered. They rejoice together and pray to Zeus, and Orestes reveals an oracle of Apollo: shed blood for blood. If this oracle be neglected, the price will be plagues, leprous ulcers, maddening Furies and banishment.

Orestes, Electra and the chorus pray for justice and divine aid, and the chorus discloses to Orestes what Clytemnestra had dreamt: she was suckling a snake which drew blood from her breast. Orestes interprets the snake as himself, and elaborates his plans to murder Clytemnestra and Aegisthus. The chorus sing about the power of reckless, blinding passion in women—in Althaea, who was told that her son Meleager would live till the brand on the hearth was burnt, but then, angered because he slew her brothers, threw the brand into the fire so that he died; Scylla, daughter of Nisus of Megara besieged by Minos of Crete—the girl who was bribed by a golden necklace to pull out of her father's head the immortal hair on which his life depended; and the women of Lemnos who slew their husbands through jealousy of Thracian slave-girls. Worst of all, they say, is Clytemnestra's deed. Yet:

> Right's anvil stands staunch upon the ground,
> And the smith, Destiny, hammers out the sword.
> Delayed in glory, pensive from
> The murk, Vengeance brings home at last
> A child to wipe out the stain of blood shed long ago.[9]

Orestes, disguised as a stranger from Phocis, is now welcomed by Clytemnestra and gives her a message that he himself is dead. She receives this with assumed grief and, as he is conducted into the palace to be entertained, goes to tell Aegisthus and their friends—'for we have many'. An old nurse, whom the queen has sent to fetch

Aegisthus, appears on the stage and laments, abusing Aegisthus and recalling the childhood of Orestes. Reassuring her with dark hints, the chorus urge her to see that Aegisthus comes alone; and they pray that Zeus, Apollo and Hermes will guide and assist the plotters.

> For things done in time past
> Wash out the blood in fair-spoken verdict.
> Let the old murder in
> The house breed no more . . .
> Be not fear-struck when your turn comes in the action,
> But with a great cry 'Father',
> When she cries 'Child' to you,
> Go on through with the innocent murder.[10]

Appearing for a moment in response to the summons, Aegisthus, after a contemptuous reference to female incredulity, returns to the palace so as to interrogate the supposed Phocian traveller.

Then, from inside, the dying cry of Aegisthus is heard. A servant calls for Clytemnestra, though

> Her neck is on the razor's edge
> And ripe for lopping as she did to others before.[11]

Confronted by Orestes with his blood-stained sword, she appeals to her son for mercy. But in vain: she is driven within to her death. The chorus rejoice that justice has saved the house, and as the doors open and reveal the two corpses, Orestes displays Agamemnon's bloody robe.

But now, at the very moment when he is justifying the retribution he has inflicted, Orestes is overcome by torments and visions of the Furies—Gorgon-like, grey-cloaked, their bodies swarming with snakes' coils. As he rushes away in agony, the chorus anxiously look ahead to discern the results of these latest violent deaths in Atreus' house. 'We hold our breath seeking the hopeful word—act of deliverance? Or another death?'

The *Eumenides* ('Kindly Ones', page 192) opens at Delphi, before the temple of Apollo. The Pythian priestess enters and invokes the powers of the shrine—Earth, Earth's daughter Themis who once ruled the oracle, and Apollo its present ruler; Athene, Dionysus, Posidon and Zeus the Supreme Fulfiller. Entering the shrine, Pythia rapidly reappears horror-stricken. For she has seen the fugitive Orestes taking sanctuary at its sacred stone, and the hideous, stinking Furies asleep and snoring round him.

The priestess returns within, and the curtains open, revealing the Temple of Apollo. The god himself, with Hermes, stands beside the Furies and Orestes. Promising that his wanderings hounded by 'these ancient, ageless hags, born for the sake of evil, abhorred by men and gods' will eventually end, Apollo directs Orestes to supplicate Athene at her own city of Athens. Hermes leads Orestes away. But the ghost of Clytemnestra appears, and rouses the Furies to their duty of revenge. They wake to see that their prey has departed, and for this they revile Apollo and the 'younger gods' who rule in the place of those who had ruled before. They foretell that Orestes shall be struck down by an Avenger; and while they renew Fate's curse upon his branded head, Apollo savagely orders them from the temple.

The encounter at Delphi ends without reconciliation, as the Furies threaten Orestes and Apollo promises to help him. Then the scene changes to Athens. A long interval has passed, and Orestes, hunted far and wide, has come to the sanctuary and statue of Athene. But the Furies are soon there too, and they menace him savagely and with increasing anger, singing a magic song which will bring him within their power.

> Over the beast doomed to the fire
> This is the chant, scatter of wits,
> Frenzy and fear hurting the heart,
> Song of the Furies
> Binding brain and blighting blood
> In its stringless melody.
>
> He is strong, but we wear him down
> For the blood that is still wet on him . . .

For with a long leap from high
Above and dead drop of weight
I bring foot's force crashing down
To cut the legs from under even
The runner, and spill him to ruin . . .[12]

Athene appears from her temple. After both Orestes and the Furies have accepted her arbitration, she states that she will summon special judges, who shall judge Orestes and henceforth constitute a permanent court for homicide. But the Furies lament that, if justice and wholesome terror are set aside, sin will go unscathed and disasters follow: parents will soon await the death-stroke at their children's hands. Athene returns, with twelve Athenian citizens as judges, and Apollo brings in Orestes the accused, and speaks for him as witness and advocate. The god asserts, against the arguments of the Furies, that the father, not the mother, is a child's true parent; and that Orestes' deed is sanctioned by a Pythian oracle which carries the authority of Zeus.

Athene announces that it is here, on the Hill of Ares, that the new Athenian court will henceforward be established and will solemnly pronounce justice. When she demands the judges' verdict upon Orestes, the votes are equal, and she uses her casting vote for his acquittal. He offers thanks to Athene and Apollo, and promises eternal friendship between Athens and his own city of Argos. Giving vent to their anger and humiliation, the Furies utter abuse against Athens. But when Athene soothes them with promises of an honourable home in her city, finally they are appeased; they accept her offer, and at her request pray for blessings on the Athenian state. She, and all present, escort them in procession to their new dwelling-place.

2 Tragic Drama Chooses Myth

In the 'archaic' period of their culture, between the age of epic and the Persian Wars (490-79), the distinctive literary achievement of the Greeks had been, not yet tragic, but lyric poetry. This was written both for singing and for recitation; some odes were designed for solo performances, others—with verse patterns attaining a high degree of complexity—for chorus. Then, late in the sixth century at a fascinating and explosive time of evolution for the city states, this sort of poetry, in the hands of Simonides of Ceos and others, was beginning to change its emphasis from personal topics to social, religious and moralizing themes.

From these beginnings came the genre by which myth took on new life—Attic tragedy. How the development occurred has been endlessly and, in the lack of decisive evidence, inconclusively discussed. But there appears to be a basis of truth in Aristotle's statement that tragedy evolved in the hands of those who led songs of rejoicing, accompanied by dances in honour of the god Dionysus[13] of whom more will be said elsewhere (page 275). In due course someone was made to *respond* to the chorus, dramatizing an incident in the story,[14] and a play was on the way to being born. 'Tragoedia' means goat-song; these early chants began to incorporate a rudimentary dramatic action, in which initially a goat, the animal sacred to Dionysus and held to represent him, was torn to pieces in imitation of the rending of animals which formed part of the Dionysiac orgies (page 282). Aristotle ascribes tragedy to a 'satyr-like' beginning, and many vase-paintings of the sixth and fifth centuries BC show satyrs—creatures not goat-legged, but with bristly hair, broad noses, pointed ears and tails—dancing round Dionysus to the music of flute and lyre. There were also tragi-comic or semi-burlesque 'satyr plays', which seem to have been brought by Pratinas from Phlius in the Peloponnese in *c.* 500 BC. It became customary to perform these as an appendage to the main tragic performances at Athens. Euripides' *Cyclops* is the only complete example to survive, though we also have most of Sophocles' *Ichneutae* (*The Searching Satyrs*).

Some would go further and attribute the origins of tragedy not only to religious songs but to actual ritual (page 158)—perhaps seasonal rites of the fertility-god. These rites may have included a contest (in which the god was killed to rise again), acted out by countrymen wearing their ordinary goatskin cloaks—unless these were specially chosen because the goat was a symbol of virility.

However, in spite of Herodotus' comparison of Dionysiac ritual to that of the Egyptian Osiris,[15] we know too little about early Greek religious ceremonies to say whether ritual was the source of tragedy or not. What can be said is that traces of the old religious song-form remained in the importance of the chorus (page 177), the fewness of actors (page 178), the frequent passages of single-line exchanges of conversation (*stichomythia*).

Although, with a few remarkable exceptions, Dionysus did not provide the themes of the plays, some of the earliest of them may have dealt with his story (page 281). But in any case the subject-matter of tragic drama was at all times closely related to religion. Indeed, the ecstatic, maenad nature of the Dionysiac faith left its mark by the creation of an urgent, intense, religious spirit absent from our own drama. Archilochus of Paros had referred to his senses being 'thundered away by wine'[16] when he led the lyric, and now it was the wine-like intoxicant of spiritual surrender which—to varying extents that we cannot now estimate—assisted the actors to interpret these plays, and the audiences to participate in their performance. They were more understanding audiences than any other western dramatists have known; for this was an epoch in which a small and gifted society, with slave-labour to support its shared traditions and culture, truly entered into the achievements of its great writers and artists.

The subject-matter of the Athenian plays dealt with solemn fundamental matters concerning the relationship of mankind with the gods. That is to say, the subjects were mythological. The myths handed down from the Homeric and Hesiodic poems, as well as many more besides, had been retold by lyric poets writing in the intervening period (though some, such as Ibycus of Rhegium, had renounced such themes). And now remarkable further developments of this mythical material were on the way. The splendour of the dramatists' culture was far removed from saga, farther still from primitive memories (though these could still sometimes be detected in them): tragedy is unlike anything which developed from the myths of Polynesia or central Africa. Greek drama was a sophisticated symbol of profound, consciously appreciated issues, illuminating the universal problem through the individual case; just as the sculptors and vase-painters of this epoch, employing the same mythological themes, likewise attained new grandeur.

The Attic playwrights altered and transfigured the myths (as Shakespeare made use of Plutarch, the English chronicles, and the Italian romances), employing them as a traditional but elastic framework which gave the fullest scope for their originality. To Greek audiences these myths, although still capable of numerous variations (even at the hands of a single author), were familiar enough to enable much explanation to be saved. The tragedian could therefore concentrate on the essence of his task, which was the poetic, religious recreation of the past in the present. For the myths were the past to the Greeks, were real, and were therefore credible. Indeed distance aided contemplation, since although the first great tragedian Aeschylus was successful with his topical *Persae* about the battle of Salamis, his rival Phrynichus had earned condemnation for a tragedy about a painful contemporary happening, the capture of Miletus by the Persians. Universality was more easily attained by the treatment of myths instead, since they avoided any such concrete situation undetachable from topical events.

Yet, even in an age in which leading thinkers, with startling rapidity, were changing from mythopoeic to rational attitudes (page 110), mythology still gave expression to what engrossed or troubled people, and continued to provide the subject-matter for the great creative dramatists—rather as artists of the fourteenth century AD constantly repainted Biblical scenes and gained by doing so. Likewise, the Boeotian lyric poet Pindar of this same period (518–438 BC) interwove in almost all his odes—as an intimate part of his thought—some illuminating myth, in order to add surprise, universality and a moral (in tones either urgent or relaxed) to a topical occasion. Yet he was a contemporary of Aeschylus, and in spite of Pindar's lyric achievement it remains generally true that epic and tragedy, as creators and recreators of myth, are, as Jaeger says in a more general context, 'two huge mountain-chains, connected by an unbroken line of foothills'.

The stages of tragedy's development from choral song are lost.

We hear of a famous seventh-century lyre-player named Arion who was the first to compose songs, with a regular metre, in honour of Dionysus and to have them performed at Corinth;[17] and at neighbouring Sicyon, the sixth-century autocrat Clisthenes is said to have introduced choral singing in honour of the god. In the middle of that century an Attic box has a painting of a flutist playing to five skin-clad youths in tunics. Then, again in Attica, comes the name of the first known dramatist, Thespis. It may well have been he who converted 'the answer to the chorus' (page 173) into a regular actor impersonating a character; that is to say, responding to the chorus not in a choral metre but in the characteristic iambic verse-pattern of tragic narration, imitating the cadences of speech, which had evolved (notably in the hands of the statesman-sage Solon) in previous years. This extraneous element took the form of spoken dialogue or monologue interposed between the choral songs. And by thus representing and enacting a version of heroic myth, instead of merely singing about it, the new actor created drama and tragedy. Thespis came from Icaria (on Mount Pentelicon near Athens) where there was an old cult of Dionysus; and he introduced this novel variety of the choral art-form to Athens. There it was first given a public performance in *c.* 534 BC, presumably with the support of Pisistratus who ruled the state.

As citizenship and education were extended, drama rose to considerable heights in other cities too, such as Megara and later Syracuse. But it was at Athens that this art reached its zenith, and in the Attic dialect that the Athenian actors spoke—though not the chorus, which retained the Doric of the Peloponnese, home of great masters of choral lyric. Athens was at a geographically focal point, accessible to Ionia, Boeotia, the Isthmus and the Peloponnese alike. The city had been a cultural leader for at least five centuries. Its growing power and trade brought wealth; and this wealth was used to support elaborate festivals, comprising various sorts of vocal and instrumental performance—of which tragedy became the chief. For this art in honour of Dionysus was performed at the festival of the Great Dionysia in about March of each year, the main expense—the production of a chorus—being met by citizens of means (*choregoi*). After programmes of choral songs by men and boys, about three days were devoted to the competitive performance of tragedies. On each day, probably, were staged four plays by a single author: three tragedies and one satyr-play (page 173) or tragi-comedy, or maybe four tragedies.* Sometimes the tragedian's four plays do not possess any readily identifiable links one with another, whereas in other cases there are close connections, although the evidence for calling them a 'tetralogy' or 'trilogy' is of later date.

The historical development of tragedy explains what to us is one of the most unfamiliar features of this mythological drama, the prominent place it allows to the chorus and to choral odes. Alien to our own conventional realism, these odes were utilized (in different ways) by all the Attic tragedians; the choruses who pronounce them vary all the way from central figures in the play to peripheral observers. The chorus complements, illustrates, universalizes, or dramatically justifies the course of events; it comments or moralizes or mythologizes upon what happens, and opens up the spiritual dimension of the theme or displays the reaction of public opinion. 'It mediates,' says T. S. Eliot, 'between the action and the audience. It intensifies the action by projecting its emotional consequences, so that we as the audience see it doubly, by seeing its effect on other people. . . . The artistic emotion approximates to the emotion of the actual spectator.' So the twelve, or later fifteen, singers and dancers of the chorus played a vital part in the perpetuation and transfiguration of the myths which was tragedy's achievement.

Yet we cannot assess this role of the chorus fully, since we cannot reconstruct the musical accompaniment which was its integral constituent and which the Greeks regarded as their greatest art, inseparable from poetry and essential to the harmony of speech, song and dance which made tragedy what it was. Less than twenty more or less fragmentary scores have survived, and of these the only

---

* Comedies, the genre of Aristophanes (and later Menander)—likewise of religious origin—were also performed, first from *c.* 450 BC at the Dionysiac festival of the Lenaea (at which tragedies were also later exhibited), and then at the Great Dionysia. Their subjects blended mythological figures and new inventions.

unmistakable setting of a tragedy is the tattered score of a few lines of Euripides.[18] If more of this music had survived, the tragic treatment of mythology would assume a vital new dimension for us; though I doubt if this would make the plays more readily accessible to our minds, since alien music comes hard to western ears, as travellers to Asia know. Since the Renaissance, however, composers of operas on mythological themes have been free to display, according to their own talents, their recognition of the all-important role which music must have played in the original productions.

The titles of 525 Greek tragedies are known (at least a quarter of the titles, relating to familiar mythical themes, are used again and again), and of these only 34 plays are preserved complete or almost complete. Although we know the names of many playwrights, the surviving tragedies are by Aeschylus, Sophocles and Euripides. Their plays are short by our standards—shorter than two acts of *Hamlet*—but in the semi-circular theatres audiences of 10,000 and more sat watching and listening for seven or eight hours a day. The scene, usually simple, was rarely changed (twice, exceptionally, in Aeschylus' *Eumenides*), and the chorus seldom left the stage. The actors, men or boys (apart from mutes), gradually rose to three in number, with a fourth very rarely—only for a brief scene or two at the end of the fifth century: the doubling of nine to eleven parts in Euripides must have been a strain. Costumes and masks were conventional, stressing the religious awe felt for the strange world that was being enacted; and when Euripides attempted greater realism, he was criticized.

Poetry depicts the larger passions, and the permanent and universal themes enshrined in the myths, more effectively than prose. Indeed all the world's greatest plays, mythological or otherwise, have been in poetic language. Poetry rises beyond the limitations of the theatrical framework, and gives drama the opportunity to understand and present the great issues of life in a dimension which neither science nor theology can attain. The methods of the theatre are at once subtle and direct, and in the Greek open-air stage and the long daily sessions they had to be raised to the highest degree of dramatic vividness. Thus in Attic tragedy, although certain unfamiliar conventions such as the chorus seem to us to hold up the action, and although incident and movement are sometimes scarce in comparison with the physical activity of an Elizabethan or modern play, there was an immense economy and a concentrated, irremediably speeding ferocity of thought and meaning. The myths made this possible. Much of the action, as the audience knew (page 175), had already happened before the play began. This, as Dryden observed, 'set the audience at the post where the race is to be concluded'; and directed their eyes upon the sharply explicit foreground in which fundamental problems were presented in the most vigorous and concrete form.

Out of the ninety plays attributed to Aeschylus, and performed from c. 499–6 BC until his death in 456, seven have come down to us. We have not enough secure dates to draw any useful conclusions about the chronological development of his art; but his most important technical innovation was the introduction of a second actor, which created the possibility of a dramatic situation or conflict. Aeschylus is also responsible for a new seriousness, a lofty intellectual tone conveyed through a densely charged style of massive grandeur and stiffly gorgeous, exuberant complexity. For Robert Browning, as for others,

> Aeschylus' bronze-throat eagle-bark at blood
> Has somehow spoilt my taste for twitterings.

In veiled, oracular speech, loaded with a multiplicity of daring, inventive words and symbols, he mobilized his imaginative power to write into the myths almost incommunicable cosmic and human truths.

One of the most famous of the mythological cycles elaborated by the tragedies relates to the gory tale of the House of Pelops and Atreus. These stories were located at Argos by Aeschylus, as earlier (in the *Odyssey*) at its neighbour and forerunner Mycenae.[19] Perhaps the Pelopid tradition echoes a real Mycenaean ruling house, whose alleged foreign origin may reflect early immigration from Asia Minor. After grim preliminaries in previous generations,[20] the story comprises six crimes: the seduction by Thyestes of Aerope, the wife of his brother Atreus; the murder by Atreus of Thyestes' children (whose remains were set before their own father to eat); the abduction to Troy, by Paris, of Helen the wife of Atreus' younger son Menelaus; the sacrifice by Agamemnon (Menelaus' brother) of his own daughter Iphigenia; the murder of Agamemnon, on his return from Troy, by his wife Clytemnestra and her lover Aegisthus (in the quasi-Homeric *Returns*, Aegisthus alone was the slayer); and the murders of Clytemnestra and Aegisthus by her offspring Orestes and Electra.

The plays in Agamemnon's trilogy known as the *Oresteia* deal successively, as has been seen, with the death of Agamemnon, the deaths of Clytemnestra and Aegisthus, and the termination of the blood-feud by divine intervention. This is the only surviving trilogy of any tragedian; it may have been accompanied by a satyr-play (page 173) about the wanderings of Menelaus.

Parts of the story must be very ancient—the sacrifice of Iphigenia, for example, no doubt goes back to times of human sacrifice. The *Odyssey* had held up the fate of Agamemnon as a warning and contrast to the destiny of Odysseus, and hinted at the murder of Clytemnestra by Orestes.[21] But the paucity of references to this story in the two principal Homeric poems shows that Aeschylus was too modest if he described his subjects as 'slices from the great banquet of Homer'.[22] The tragic implications of Agamemnon's story are far from Homeric, reflecting rather the religion and morality of the guilt-culture (page 188) which followed and largely superseded the shame-culture of *Iliad* and *Odyssey* (page 67).

From the later seventh century BC onwards, the theme inspired artists; sculptural reliefs from the sixth-century Treasury of the Heraeum on the river Silerus (Foce da Sele) in south-west Italy show Orestes killing Aegisthus, and Clytemnestra forcibly restrained —perhaps by Orestes' nurse—from attacking her son. The lyric poet Stesichorus (though transferring the scene to Sparta) introduced much of the material subsequently used by Aeschylus, and Pindar dwells on the dreadful Clytemnestra:

TABLE 4

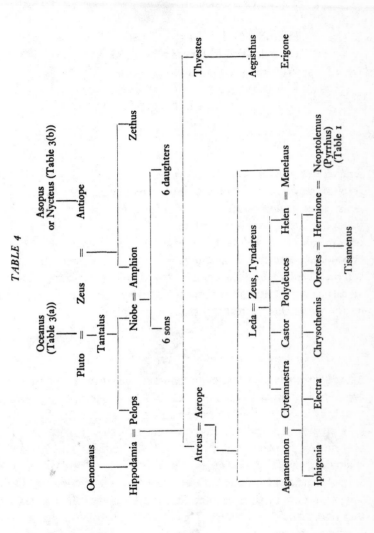

> That grievous traitress, whose grey bronze
> Made Cassandra, Dardanid Priam's child,
> Bear company with Agamemnon's spirit
> To Acheron's shadowy shore.
>
> Pitiless woman. Was it Iphigenia,
> Slain at Euripus far from her land,
> Who stung her to uplift
> The wrath of her heavy hand?
> Or was she broken in to a paramour's bed—
> And the nightly loves
> Turned her mind?[23]

The subject-matter of such myths seemed to H. G. Wells, in *The New Machiavelli*, 'the telling of incomprehensible parricides . . . of gods faded beyond symbolism, of that Relentless Law we did not believe in for a moment, that no modern western European can believe in'. Nevertheless, the *Oresteia* displays one of the world's outstanding arts in all its glory, presented to a vital, responsive community by an idiosyncratic genius of inexhaustible poetic versatility and strength. Swinburne described the plays as 'probably on the whole the greatest spiritual work of man'.

3   The God Who Exacts the Price

The *Agamemnon* contains, more than anything else in literature, the rumble of approaching doom, the palpably growing darkness of prophecy and fear. While through a short, simple series of events—separated by long and superb lyrics—the expected crime approaches ever nearer, suspense is accentuated by the frequent employment of dramatic irony. The speakers say things of which the full significance is not understood by their hearers, or is not understood by themselves but only by their hearers. Sometimes another character in the play understands; more often it is only the audience who grasp these meanings, and who are by this dramatic irony (page 222) indissolubly linked with the myth that is working itself out.

But the subject of the *Oresteia* is not only the myth, it is the pressing theme, drawn out of the myth, that crime must be punished by crime. As later in French tragedy, women play formidable parts —it is hard, after this, to believe that their role in Athenian life was insignificant. But even Clytemnestra, the only character who appears in all three plays, is depicted with a massive simplicity and awful grandiloquence which rejects detailed characterization. With none of Lady Macbeth's repentant horror, she is dominated by a lust for vengeance. But she is also caught up in larger forces, and so, at a harrowing moment of the play, is Cassandra, entering with terrified, hallucinatory foreknowledge the house of her destruction. The *Agamemnon*, despite lyrical praises of Zeus, ends in utter disaster: there is no predictable halt to the chain of bloodshed.

In the *Choephori* the taint deepens, as the myth spells out the intolerable burden of the killing of a mother. Yet Orestes, like his sister Electra, is more than a killer, since he is the instrument of destiny. In his unfalteringly revengeful mind there are no conflicts, though his hardness softens after the repulsive duty. This has been called a statuesque, marble play, but the emotional and moral tension is sustained, the choral imagery resplendent, and the climax exciting and moving. Then, in the *Eumenides*, a new swerve of the dramatist's imagination resolves the grim series of myths in the stirring, exalted spectacle, not so much of the rule of law or of a new era, but of divine light and strength.

The Aeschylean conception of the supreme power is more definite than the gropings of the Hesiodic poems. The forerunners of Zeus are again recorded; but that there will be no end to Zeus is more explicitly stated.

> Zeus, whoever He is, if this
> Be a name acceptable,
> By this name I will call him.
> There is no one comparable
> When I reckon all of the case
> Excepting Zeus, if ever I am to jettison
> The barren care which clogs my heart.[24]

All that is done on earth is determined by the will or agents of him whom a more advanced theologian, Xenophanes of Colophon, had now called 'one god, the greatest among gods of men, like unto mortals neither in form nor in thought' (cf. page 264).[25]

The drama and religion of Aeschylus centre upon Zeus, who is overwhelmingly powerful. 'How,' asks Danaë, 'can I look into the mind of Zeus, that abyss where sight is lost?'[26] Yet his worship did not exclude the traditional polytheism, for he was the blessed king of kings:[27] other gods and goddesses reflected aspects of the order which stemmed from him. In the *Agamemnon*, a Hymn to Zeus stands between the omen of the eagle and the hare forecasting a just fate for Troy, and the appalling horror of Iphigenia's sacrifice for which payment was now being exacted. ✓

Aeschylus distils in his renderings of the myths the intense thought and feeling, and the unswerving regard for truth, which he has devoted to the relationship between gods and men and to the operation of divine laws upon the mortal condition. His gods are like the gods of archaic and early classical art, formidably worthy of reverence, humanity with a shattering difference: like the Apollo of the Olympian pediments who stands majestically guiding the struggles of men. God's power over man's life may seem crushing, although, as Pindar says, it can at times transfigure the human lot.

> Man's life is a day. What is he?
> What is he not? A shadow in a dream
> Is man: but when God sheds a brightness,
> Shining light is on earth
> And life is sweet as honey.[28]

Yet 'God bringeth every end to pass according to his desires',[29] for 'neither by libations nor by sacrifice will you bend the inflexible will of the gods'.[30]

Nevertheless, there is room for *some* free will in human affairs; and the tragedians devoted their talents to assessing and interpreting the traditional stories so as to see just how far this free will goes. There is still a measure of the Homeric confusion between fate and the gods (page 68): even Zeus cannot alter what is ordained[31]

(page 202), though the last lines of the *Oresteia* celebrate the union of
Zeus and Fate.[32] Fate was desperately strong; the sixth century
poet Theognis of Megara had stressed its mighty, almost malevolent
inscrutability.[33] So does Pindar—who sometimes contrasts but
usually interchanges god and fate—and yet he sees in the potential-
ities of human kind some freedom from complete servitude.

> There is one
> race of men, one race of gods. Both have breath
> of life from a single mother; but sundered power
> holds us divided, so that the one is nothing, while for the
>   other
> the brazen sky is established their sure citadel forever.
> Yet we have some likeness
> in great intelligence, or strength, to the immortals,
> though we know not what the day will bring, what course
>   after nightfall
> destiny has written that we must run to the end.[34]*

The tragic poets, too, were not so wholly fatalistic as Plato hinted,[35]
and were still some way from Stoic predestination. There may be a
total pattern, but since we have no means of knowing what it is we
must act according to our own best judgement.

For Fate plans only in general terms, allowing temporary, individual aberrations and dilemmas. The individual, it is true, might not
perceive either the causes or the consequences of his action; tragedy
is full of outcomes which proved the opposite to what was intended
(page 224). Yet in most situations man is regarded as free to choose
what course that action would take—even if it turns out that all he
can do is to make the best of what befalls him (page 69).

> For every one good thing, the immortals bestow on men
> Two evils. Men who are as children cannot take this
>   becomingly;
> But good men do, turning the brightness outward.[36]

Homeric endurance is still a noble aim, as it continued to be for the

---

* For another translation of this passage, see above, page 51.

Stoics and Shakespeare too. But Pindar, who wrote those lines, also represented Chance as one of the Fates[37]—rather before his time in this, since Chance was the religion of post-classical Greece (page 227). Accident, indeed, was an ever-present risk, adding to 'the perpetual jar of things', the gap between real and ideal. Within this gap occur the crises of mythology, moulded by the tragedians to illustrate their belief in humanity and fate alike. 'The absolute beginning of tragedy,' as Schlegel said, 'is the condition of freedom, the absolute end the recognition of necessity.'

Sometimes, indeed, it seemed that before the divine power humans were as flies to wanton boys, that theirs was a tale told by an idiot. The archaic sculptors convey these Shakespearean hints in their lofty, remote, interpretations of the gods; and Theognis, in pessimistic mood, had asked why Zeus visited the same fate on good and bad alike—the great riddle of moral theology.

> How then can thy wisdom look in so indifferent fashion
> On those whose deeds are evil, and who deal
>   righteously?
> Whether a man refrain his heart, or sate his passion
> In works of overweening and iniquity?[38]

Yet a century earlier, following the ideas of divine rewards and punishments that were current (page 148), the Spartan poet Alcman had foreshadowed Aeschylus by stressing that the thunderbolts of Zeus strike not arbitrarily, but in retribution.

> Vengeance is God's: he will repay.
> Lucky who, without a tear,
> Fills the pattern of one day
> With gaiety.[39]

At Athens Solon (*c.* 640–560), the national leader, reformer and poet to whom Aeschylus owed much, had conveyed the same urgent message.

> Zeus forever is watching the end, and
> strikes of a sudden . . .

He does not, like a mortal, fall in a rage
    over each particular thing, and yet
it never escapes him all the way when a man has a
    sinful spirit; and always, in the end,
his judgement is plain.[40]

In the words of the *Epistle to the Hebrews*, 'It is a fearful thing to
fall into the hands of the living God.'[41]

And what earned this punishment? Prosperity, success, pride.
The high peak, says the Aeschylean chorus, is blasted by the eyes of
Zeus; blessed is a life too low for envy. But Aeschylus refined upon
this old 'touch wood' idea, and, like Theognis[42] and Pindar but with
a new ferocious power, deduced that prosperity brings this fall
because the prosperous are so easily led to commit wickedness.

A man thought the gods deigned not to punish mortals
who trampled down the delicacy of things
inviolable. That man was wicked.
The curse on great daring
shines clear; it wrings atonement
from those high hearts that drive to evil,
from houses blossoming to pride
and peril.[43]

In a changed society, amid the fierce struggles that raged within the
growing city-states, the old Homeric self-assertion seemed all too
liable to Nemesis, the daughter of Night as Hesiod called her—the
Arbiter of Events, the Queen of all Causes, who binds men's pride
with the indissoluble bonds of fate. To Aeschylus the myths were
full of Nemesis—retribution upon unrighteous prosperity. His god
has this in common with the god of Isaiah who had said, 'I will
punish . . . the glory of his high looks. For he saith, "By the strength
of my hand I have done it, and by my wisdom.' "[44]

Men with high looks are occupied by *hubris*, overweening pride
(page 68). To Greeks, as to Jews and Dostoevsky's Alyosha
Karamazov, this brought the madness of *ate*, a hideous delusion
which even in the days of Homeric individualism had potently fused

curse, pollution and sin (page 69).[45] The archaic much more than the Homeric age was haunted by evil spirits, and this was the world of demons into which Aeschylus was born. Clytemnestra, tormented by a snake-dream that is a gift to psychoanalysts, sees *ate* itself as a personal fiend.[46] Agamemnon is acutely aware of the danger when the grandiose carpet is laid for him to tread on: he knows the risk of destruction, yet he is infected and succumbs. A sinful or hubristic act, whatever its motive (it took time for intention to appear relevant), taints and must be expiated.[47] Revenge may not come at once, but it will come.

> The gods are crafty:
> they lie in ambush
> a long step of time
> to hunt the unholy.[48]

The gods put before men the opportunity to sin,[49] and if they give way and commit the first sin[50] they are helped to their ruin.[51]

For gods are jealous of prosperous men. The idea had been voiced, in passing, by Calypso in the *Odyssey*,[52] and is described in the *Agamemnon* as venerable doctrine uttered long ago.[53] But it was amid the politico-religious anxieties of the post-Homeric age, with its deepening sense of human helplessness, that the jealousy of the gods (later denied by Plato[54]) had become an ever-present oppressive threat. Pindar's ethical system is founded upon it, and the gods of Herodotus are often jealous and disagreeable, for instance in their destruction of Croesus.[55] Among these profound mistrusts, creating so great a gulf between gods and men, the heroic self-assertive virtues sometimes seemed hazardous and readily tending to *hubris*. It is almost looked, in a frightening new world, as if divine envy would come upon all who followed their own inclinations. Many of the lyric poets took refuge in an escapist, hedonistic pessimism. But for those who did not withdraw from the struggle there grew up alongside the old self-assertion, not necessarily replacing but counter-balancing it, the reminders of caution inscribed on Apollo's Delphic temple, 'nothing too much' and 'know thyself'. Moderation is not an innate feature of the Greek character, but the dangers and tensions brought by the rapid upsurge of power and prosperity in those centuries made it a pressing plea. Many of the myths were employed to illustrate and interpret this moral: above all, it was reinforced by the story of Agamemnon and his house.

In their gloomiest moments, the tragedians still agreed with the lyric poets who, like Job, had thought it better never to be born.

> Never to have lived is best, ancient writers say;
> Never to have drawn the breath of life, never to have
>   looked into the eye of day;
> The second best's a gay goodnight, and quickly turn
>   away.[56]

But since we are here on earth, we had better observe moderation, whether we live in an insignificant situation and city (as Phocylides had recommended) or not. Whatever we do, however, suffering will be our lot. And the *Agamemnon* teaches the hard lesson, illustrated also by Solon[57] and Herodotus,[58] that it is by suffering that we have to learn wisdom. For Zeus,

> Setting us on the road,
> Made this a valid law—
>   That men must learn by suffering.
> Drop by drop in sleep upon the heart
> Falls the laborious memory of pain.[59]

The reconciliation of the *Eumenides* reveals the hidden harmony, the ultimate blessing, to which even desperate agony can lead in the presence of higher powers.

But this is not the limit of men's difficulties, for the pain and sorrow of the *Oresteia* come from a chain of wrongs each leading to another, an ancestral curse and pollution. The idea—to which we, who deny the efficacy of curses, can only with difficulty respond—was again inherited from Solon (as well as from Hesiod and the Hittites).

> One man has to pay at once, one later, while others
>   altogether escape overtaking by the gods' doom;

but then it always comes in aftertime, and the innocent
pay, the sons of the sinners or those born long
afterward.[60]

The ancestral evil takes effect at every stage of Aeschylus' story,
fatally corrupting even the beauty of Helen—

> That which first came to the city of Ilium,
> call it a dream of calm
> and the wind dying,
> the loveliness and luxury of much gold,
> the melting shafts of the eyes' glances,
> the blossom that breaks the heart with longing.
> But she turned in mid-step of her course to make
> bitter the consummation,
> whirling on Priam's people
> to blight with her touch and nearness.[61]

How far could each successive agent in this catastrophic series have
avoided his own contribution to its horrors? Could Agamemnon, for
example, have avoided sacrificing his daughter Iphigenia at Aulis?
Sir Denys Page said he could not, Professors Fraenkel and
Winnington-Ingram said he could. But perhaps the poet himself
did not intend us to find a clear-cut answer to this eternally
harrowing theological, and human, problem: for the principle of
Evil seems to be beyond the comprehension of logic. At any rate
Aeschylus finds that the guilt of fathers inclines children towards
guilt, transmitting a stain that is both morally and physically
infectious. Orestes is finally saved by superhuman agencies and
so the sequence is, on this exceptional occasion, ended. But the
rule is otherwise:

> The truth stands ever beside God's throne
> Eternal: he who has wrought shall pay; that is law . . .
> The seed is stiffened to ruin.[62]

Bloodshed, particularly, was irrevocable: for who can sing spells to
call it back again?[63] And the worst of all bloodshed was the slaying
of a close kinsman.

Through too much glut of blood drunk by our
  fostering ground
The vengeful gore is caked and hard, will not drain
  through . . .

Swarming infection boils within . . .
All the world's waters running in a single drift
May try to wash blood from the hand
Of the stained man; they only bring new blood guilt on.[64]

The family was a more ancient and stronger unit than the state, and
the blood-vengeance of Orestes reflects a 'heroic' time before the
regular courts for homicide had existed. In those days, the blood-
feud had to be carried on by the senior male of the family; as in laws
of Thuringia of the ninth century AD, and laws of Jaroslav two
hundred years later, and a Montenegrin code of not so long ago.
But why, a century and a half after Athens had solved the blood-feud
in its courts, did the matter still weigh so heavily upon Aeschylus'
mind? He lived at a time when the state was growing in strength at
the expense of the family; as today, family solidarity was diminishing.
So as the city took over many of the family's responsibilities he
asserts, in its fiercest form, the family's ultimate claim which could
not be ignored or forgotten.

In the manner of Hesiod's many personifications of demons and
powers (page 105), the agents of retribution were personified by
Aeschylus as the Furies (Erinyes). These are mentioned from the
Iliad onwards[65]—even the gods were subject to them[66]—and the
Odyssey had recorded their curses upon infringements of tribal law
such as offences against kindred, and particularly against parents
and eldest born.[67] If the Sun were to overstep his measures, said
Heraclitus of Ephesus (*c.* 500 BC),[68] the Erinyes, handmaidens of
Justice, would find him out. Though they are not seen to pursue
Clytemnestra (whose victims were not her blood-relations), their
intervention is foreshadowed in the *Agamemnon*.

There is something cowled in the night
That I anxiously wait to hear.

> For the gods are not blind to the
> Murders of many.[69]

In the *Eumenides* (meaning the 'gracious' or 'kindly' goddesses, a euphemism for the Erinyes), their appearance is accompanied by every circumstance of horror—

> children grey with years,
> With whom no god consorts, nor man nor beast,
> Abhorred alike in heaven and on earth,
> For evil born, even as the darkness where
> They dwell is evil, the abyss of Tartarus.[70]

Whether or not the Furies were, as some say, a survival of tribal beliefs in ancestral ghosts, they seemed a hideous, truculent reality justifying desperate terror. Interested not in motives—moral consciousness, accident, or *force majeure*—but only in the deed, they belonged to the primitive, infernal powers lurking within the earth. This was the place of the dead; but he who died by violence (as many die by violence in Greek tragedy) did not rest beneath the soil, and his spirit demanded vengeance, which the Erinyes, or *his* Erinyes, secured for him. Their appearance in the *Eumenides* points a dramatic contrast, the deepest contrast in Greek religion, between these black, bleary-eyed, snorting demons of the earth and the brilliant religion of Olympus.

Aeschylus brings the two forces into audacious collision. The Furies are open and savage in their abuse of Apollo the purifier (page 137), who has stolen away the godless matricide from the ancient powers.

> The executioner's cutting whip is mine to feel
> and the weight of pain is big, heavy to bear.

> Such are the actions of the younger gods. These hold
> by unconditional force, beyond all right, a throne
> that runs reeking blood,
> blood at the feet, blood at the head.

The very stone, centre of earth, here in our eyes horrible
with blood and curse stands plain to see.[71]

Apollo replies to them with a violence that may be latent, but is not
visible, in the sculptured serenity with which he calms Centaurs and
Lapiths on the pediment of Zeus' temple at Olympia. Get out, he
says:

> else you may feel the flash and bite of a flying snake
> launched from the twisted thong of gold that spans my bow,
> to make you in your pain spew out the black and foaming
> blood of men, vomit the clots sucked from their veins.
> This house is no right place for such as you to cling
> upon; but where, by judgement given, heads are lopped
> and eyes gouged out, throats cut, and by the spoil of sex
> the glory of young boys is defeated, where mutilation
> lives, and stoning, and the long moan of tortured men
> spiked underneath the spine and stuck on pales.[72]

There would seem no hope of reconciliation here. Yet by Apollo's
direction Athene intervenes, and the chain of vendetta comes to an
end. Her argument, in favour of Orestes, is a sophistic manifestation
of patriarchal societies, now as then.

> The mother is not the parent of the child,
> Only the nurse of what she has conceived.
> The parent is the father, who commits
> His seed to her, a stranger, to be held
> With God's help in safekeeping.[73]

However, Athene's decision is not just a blow for the rather un-
attractive Greek cause of male supremacy; it has a deeper national
significance as well. Orestes is vindicated by an appeal to patriotic
feeling. For the court which is given the glory of ending the vendetta
is the court of the Areopagus, the Athenian Hill of Ares, going back
to the days of the ancient monarchy.[74]

In 462–1 BC, some three or four years before the *Oresteia* was
first performed, the statesmen of Athens, curtailing the powers of

this historic court, had recognized as its proper task the application of the code of homicide to which in the past it had contributed much. But what Aeschylus is really saying is that the court's authority and wisdom mirror the authority and wisdom of Athens, embodied in the establishment of a system of justice dependent on equity; and that those institutions of Athens, in their turn, mirror the dispensations of heaven. This is, indeed, a patriotic twist such as every city tried to give to the traditional mythology. But none so effectively as Athens—whose citizen Pherecydes, for example, ransacked the myths, in this same century, to find divine origins for famous Athenian families.

And so, doubtless amid popular applause, the cumulative tensions are resolved, at the end of the *Eumenides,* in the peace and goodwill of the Panathenaic Festival. In this strange cross between a festivity and a trial, which seems to our different minds something of an anticlimax after the appalling magnificence of the preceding plays, the ancestral curse is miraculously repudiated, as Ezekiel repudiated it in Israel. But how, amid such an apparently irreconcilable conflict of moral obligations, could this come about? The Olympians win, yet it is conceded that the Furies are the agents of Zeus' justice; the light triumphs, but the principle that the doer must learn by suffering is not dead. Force is modified by persuasion, and the Furies at last agree to be reconciled. Unlocalized before, they are now, without losing their functions, to be transformed into the Reverent Goddesses (Semnai Theai): who were venerated in a cave beneath the Hill of Ares, just as the kindred (or synonymous) kindly Eumenides were worshipped, not only in parts of the Peloponnese, but also at Athenian Colonus near by (page 236).

A solution had seemed impossible; but nothing was impossible for the gods. And with their help, nothing seemed impossible for the rising democracy of Athens.

4 *To O'Neill, Eliot and Sartre*

The house of Agamemnon continued to fascinate Athenian dramatists. Sophocles wrote of Atreus and Thyestes, and also unlike

Aeschylus gave a grim prominence to Orestes' sister, Electra, who, in his play named after her, needs her brother's help but displays a fearful piety of vengeance.

> House of the Death God, house of Persephone,
> Hermes of the Underworld, holy Curse,
> Furies the Dread Ones, children of the gods,
> all ye who look upon those who die unjustly,
> all ye who look upon the theft of a wife's love,
> come all and help take vengeance for my father,
> for my father's murder!
> And send me my brother to my aid.
> For alone to bear the burden I am no longer strong
>   enough,
> the burden of the grief that weighs against me.[75]

Yet Sophocles enables Clytemnestra, also, to state her case. She appeals to Electra as the sister of Iphigenia, stressing, in contrast to Athene in the *Eumenides*, the cares and sorrows of motherhood.

> For this your father whom you always mourn,
> alone of all the Greeks, had the brutality
> to sacrifice your sister to the gods,
> although he had not toiled for her as I did,
> the mother that bore her, he the begetter only.[76]

But the appeal was in vain beside the claims of filial vengeance.

In Euripides' play *Iphigenia in Tauris*, and probably in his *Iphigenia in Aulis* too, the maiden was miraculously saved from the sacrifice—just as there was an alternative version of her aunt Helen's fortunes (page 49). But his *Orestes* and *Electra*, whatever their chronological relation to Sophocles' *Electra*, are painful studies of tragic waste and misery. The Furies appear in traditional guise, revelling in their vengeance.[77] Yet there comes also a suggestion, characteristic of a new and psychologically minded age (page 261), that the Erinyes are a subjective hallucination in the mind of Orestes,[78] who thus foreshadows Ibsen's enactment of the terrible effects of delusions. But the Euripidean Orestes is a deranged, inhuman prig. In the *Electra* he and his fanatically devoted sister are warped by brooding and agonized by remorse. Even the murder of Aegisthus is a bloody horror, with no resemblance to a glorious deed. While his head was bent over the sacrifice,

> Your brother stretched up, balanced on the balls of his feet,
> and smashed a blow to his spine. The vertebrae of his back
> broke. Head down, his whole body convulsed, he gasped
> to breathe, writhed with a high scream, and died in his blood.[79]

And Clytemnestra holds forth with a sinister, sordid logic.

> Oh, women are fools for sex, deny it I shall not.
> Since this is in our nature, when our husbands choose
> to despise the bed they have, a woman is quite willing
> to imitate her man and find another friend.
> But then the dirty gossip puts us in the spotlight;
> the guilty ones, the men, are never blamed at all.
> If Menelaus had been raped from home on the sly,
> should I have had to kill Orestes so my sister's
> husband could be rescued? You think your father would
> have borne it? He would have killed me . . .[80]
>   I am not so happy
> either, child, with what I have done or with myself.

> How poorly you look. Have you not washed? Your
>   clothes are bad.
> I suppose you just got up from bed and giving birth?

> O god, how miserably my plans have all turned out.
> Perhaps I drove my hate too hard against my husband.[81]

One of Euripides' motives is to show just why mother-murder is an even more intolerable deed than the other gory happenings.

In Roman times the most famous work of the Augustan dramatist Varius was his *Thyestes*, much praised[82] but now lost. Seneca (as well as composing a frigid *Agamemnon*) wrote a gruesome *Thyestes*, foreshadowing Renaissance and Elizabethan melodrama by the introduction of Thyestes' ghost. With greater restraint than the Elizabethans, Crébillon, in his *Atrée et Thyeste* (1707), avoids murder on the stage by showing an actor draining a goblet of blood; and Voltaire, in his *Oreste* (1750), tones down matricide, the fatal blow being intended for Aegisthus—Clytemnestra dies in his defence.

There was also continuous interest in the story of Iphigenia. Racine's *Iphigénie* (1647) shows how this 'ardent, passionate idealist', as Dostoevsky called the playwright, excelled at intimate portrayals of classical myth—the best known French renderings of these themes, and therefore a model for modern French dramatists using similar subjects. Then Gluck's *Iphigenia in Tauris*, based on an eighteenth-century version of Euripides' play, impressively illustrates his novel employment of the operatic medium to illustrate such themes (page 322). As regards the alternative version according to which Iphigenia was sacrificed, there is a fantastic contrast between the almost unendurable pathos of Aeschylus and the fashionable elegance of the same scene on Tiepolo's masterpiece (*c.* 1757) in the Homer Room of the Villa Vilmarana at Vicenza. The contrast underlines the obliqueness with which the inspiration of classical mythology operates; for Tiepolo's un-Aeschylean scene recalls the saying of George Moore that 'the eighteenth century is only woman . . . no servile archaeology chills the fancy; and this treatment of antiquity is the highest proof of its genius'. Besides, there was rationalism as well as woman in the eighteenth century; and the period was, on the whole, too lucid and orderly to understand tragedy. Yet Goethe reverenced Aeschylus' *Agamemnon* as if it were divine, and found in its pages the keystone of all ethical and aesthetic inquiry, particularly regarding the relation of moral to tragic guilt.

Early in our own century, the Athenians rioted in their streets when an effort was made to stage the *Oresteia* in a modern translation. Since then, several writers and dramatists have used the myth as a catalyst for their statements about life. The disastrous labyrinths of error in the writings of Faulkner are Aeschylean; and Eugene

O'Neill's *Mourning becomes Electra* (1931) takes over the family relationships, many incidents, and some of the moral dilemmas of Aeschylus, restating them in terms of nineteenth-century New England. There is more emphasis on sexual repression and less on the greater religious issues. As O'Neill himself remarked, we have no gods or heroes, but 'we have the sub-conscious, the mother of all gods and heroes'.

So the play is Freudian Vienna as well as ancient Greece. The mansion's temple portico—of Athenian but also federal American style—is like a 'incongruous white mask', fastened upon the house to hide its sombre grey ugliness. The daughter, Lavinia-Electra (who dominates the action) is fixated on her father, and loves her mother's lover. The mother, Christine-Clytemnestra, is told she can live, but kills herself. Her son, Orin-Orestes, is devoted to her and therefore all the readier to kill her lover. In the third play, there is no reprieve; Orin's remorse drives him to suicide, and his sister lets him die. O'Neill's adherence to the *Oresteia* as a model goes so far as adopting the same shape of a trilogy: the three plays are called, 'Homecoming', 'The Hunted', and 'The Haunted'. A rudimentary chorus of townspeople appears at the beginning of each play. Unlike Anouilh who uses classical myth as the framework for stories which he in any case felt impelled to tell, O'Neil seems to have started with the myth and then composed a story which would fit into its classical frame. *Mourning Becomes Electra*, with its closed situation and sternly simple dramatic structure, is the most deliberate attempt in the twentieth century to write tragedy of the traditional kind.

Of New England stock also is T. S. Eliot, who again, but this time in poetic prose, employs Aeschylean myth to present a profounder vision than naturalism can provide. After mythological foreshadowings in earlier poems, his plays, although they incorporate more action and a modern concept of climax, owe much of their form to Greek tragedies. Episodes, including such classical devices as the messenger, are linked by a full reinstated chorus. Ranging between bafflement and involvement, this is Aeschylean in its relation to events; although, in secular terms, it obliquely states Christian values. In partly romantic, partly realistic settings, Eliot retells the story of the *Oresteia*. *Murder in the Cathedral* (1935) is his *Agamemnon*; *Family Reunion* (1939) echoes the *Choephori*. This latter play also takes from the *Eumenides* the transformation of the Furies from Erinyes to Kindly Ones. But they are the promptings of conscience, instruments of divine grace, and the curse upon the House of Monchensey is no longer the ancestral blood-feud but the mark of Cain that murderously impels humanity.

In France, the Furies in the *Electra* of Giraudoux (page 60) are seen first as singularly disagreeable children and then as even more disagreeable young women. Claudel had modernized the *Oresteia*, and Sartre employed it, in *The Flies*, for a questioning of traditional morality. Blood-guilty Argos is infested with the Furies in the form of monstrous black blood-sucking blow-flies. They annoy and terrify, but with energy and decision one could survive their unpleasantness. The same is true of the rule of Aegisthus and Clytemnestra: in this war-time play (1943), Aegisthus stands for the Occupying Power, and Clytemnestra for collaborators. The Argive people are enslaved by superstition and habit, but the crisis turns Orestes into an authentic man who consciously assumes the responsibility and consequences of an act which convention denounces. The gods are not just, and redemption is not by Christian sanctity but by action— even action that seems criminal and brings with it isolation from the rest of one's kind. Man has to choose, each moment, how to see the world, and has to bear his own acts upon his shoulders.

Mythology no doubt helped to get the play past the censor. But in addition mythology alone, said Sartre, could supply a horrible enough action to provide an acceptable crisis; and the classical obsession with fate helped to bring out his idea of freedom. Men are free, observes an ironic, derisive Zeus, and they do not know it. They can save themselves by just refusing to let self-condemnation torment them—and so Orestes walks out at the end untouched.

CHAPTER 6

PROMETHEUS

—————⟫⟫⟫⟫⟫⟫⟫⟫⟫⟫⟫⟪⟪⟪————

1   The Story of the PROMETHEUS BOUND Told by Aeschylus

THE SCENE is a far-off rocky mountain-top. Power and Violence enter, dragging Prometheus. At the bidding of Power, Hephaestus, who follows them, reluctantly rivets Prometheus to the rock because of his kindness to the human race, and tells him that no man yet born shall set him free. Prometheus calls upon the sky, the winds and streams, upon Earth the mother of all life, and upon the all-seeing Sun, to behold the miseries that gods are inflicting on a god. Where will deliverance come? But then he corrects himself.

> Yet what is this I say? I know what is coming,
> all of it exactly, and not a single evil can
> reach me unforeseen, and I must bear the fate
> allotted to me as best I may, because I know
> one cannot fight with the power of Necessity . . .
>
> For I am he who sought the stolen fount of fire,
> stored in a stalk, which proved to be the teacher of
> all kind of craft to mortals and their great resource.
> This was the sin for which I pay the punishment
> nailed hard and fast in chains beneath the open sky.[1]

The chorus, daughters of Oceanus, approach in a winged ship or chariot, and join in his lamentations. Zeus, they assure him, will not relent until either his passion is sated, or he is overthrown by a plot. But Prometheus discloses to them that one day Zeus will need his help, for Prometheus knows a secret which could cause the king of heaven's downfall. And though the women are afraid since they find his words too free, he goes on to foretell that a pact of friendship between Zeus and himself will one day begin.

Next he describes how his present evils have come about. In the wars between Cronus and his son Zeus, Prometheus himself and his mother Themis or Earth, of one form but many names, had stood beside Zeus and advised him—because cunning and ingenuity, not violence, were bound to prevail. Their only reward had been suspicion, the disease inherent in a tyrant's soul. Then, says Prometheus, Zeus had distributed among the gods their various dignities. Yet he had given nothing to men, whom, on the contrary, he had planned to destroy utterly if Prometheus had not opposed him. Nor was this, he tells, his sole intervention in favour of mankind, for he gave them not only fire, the means of mastering many crafts, but hope as well.

As Prometheus promises to disclose what is still hidden in the future, Oceanus, riding in upon a winged beast, asks what help he can offer. But Prometheus bitterly charges him with coming only to gaze. Oceanus counsels submission, and offers to intercede.

> Meanwhile, keep quiet,
> Don't rage and storm. You are intelligent: full well
> You know that punishment falls on the unruly tongue.[2]

Prometheus, however, recalling the sufferings of others at the hand of Zeus—of his own brother Atlas, of hundred-headed Typhon crushed beneath Etna—bids Oceanus leave him and not risk his safety. As Oceanus goes, his daughters sing of the power of Zeus, imposed by self-invented laws, over the gods of the past; and they grieve for Prometheus and his brother Atlas.

Prometheus now describes the gifts he gave the human race.

> They were like
> the shapes we see in dreams, and all through their long life

they mingled all things aimlessly . . .
  till I revealed to them
the risings of the stars and settings hard to judge.
And then I found for them the art of using numbers,
that master science, and arrangement of letters,
and a discursive memory, a skill to be
mother of Muses. I was first to bring the beasts
to serve under the yoke and saddle, that they might
take on themselves the greatest burdens of mortals.
And it was I who brought and made them love the rein,
horses to chariot, the pride of lordly wealth.
And no one else but I discovered for sailors
the sea-wandering vessels with their canvas wings.[3]

He himself, he laments, lacks even one trick to win freedom from his own agony. Yet he had also given mankind healing herbs, and the power of prophecy, and the interpretation of dreams and of bird-flights and entrails, and the discovery of bronze, iron, silver and gold hidden deep in the earth. But all this is of little avail to him—

                          My lot
        Is to win freedom only after countless pains.
        Cunning is feebleness beside Necessity.
CHORUS: And whose hand on the helm controls Necessity?
PROMETHEUS: The three Fates; and the Furies, who forget nothing.
CHORUS: Has Zeus less power than they?
PROMETHEUS: He cannot fly from Fate.[4]

The chorus respond with a prayer that they may never be remiss in worshipping and sacrificing to the gods; and they point to the feeble infirmity of men, creatures of a day whom Prometheus, once a happy bridegroom for their sister Hesione, has so disastrously tried to help.

Now Io enters, wearing horns to symbolize her transformation into a heifer, and screaming in pain and terror. She is tormented by the stings of a gadfly and by the ghost of the many-eyed herdsman Argus, for she has incurred the anger of Hera by being the object of Zeus' lust. Prometheus, angered at this new story of Zeus' tyranny, foretells her endless wanderings. But he asserts also that Zeus will meet his doom—by marrying one who would bear him a son more powerful than his father—unless he is helped by Prometheus himself, whom a descendant of Io will free. As he tells her of her destined relief and settlement in Egypt, she interrupts with a savage cry of pain, and as madness comes upon her again, rushes away.

The daughters of Oceanus see in her plight a reason for not marrying above one's station, and when Prometheus again threatens Zeus with catastrophe, they urge him to speak humbly, in fear of Nemesis. But Hermes the messenger of the gods, who now enters, is assailed by Prometheus as 'the new tyrant's servant and lackey'. Hermes conveys a demand from Zeus that Prometheus should tell him with whom shall be this marriage, that will unseat the king of the gods. Amid mutual altercations, the demand is refused. Accordingly, Hermes declares the decision of Zeus: he will split the rock with lightning, entomb Prometheus in its midst, and send an eagle all day long to feast upon his liver, gnawing it black. Prometheus will have no release until a god be found who will take his pains upon himself, and of his own free will descend into dark Tartarus.

Rejecting the women's plea that he should submit, Prometheus remains defiant. Yet they decide to stay with him, come what may, and they too come under the lash of Hermes' tongue.

> Remember then my warning before the act.
> When you are trapped by ruin don't blame fortune:
> don't say that Zeus has brought you to calamity
> that you could not foresee.

>   . . . your own want of good sense
> has tangled you in the net of ruin, past
> all hope of rescue.[5]

And so the play ends in cataclysm. Amid thunder, lightning and earthquake, Prometheus cries out to his holy mother Earth, and to the Sky, to witness his wrongs; and with the daughters of Oceanus he sinks from view.

2 The Resistance Hero

The chorus, though its part is unusually short for Aeschylus (if this play is by him, as not everyone agrees), reflects in a novel way the pitiful contemplation of the audience itself: 'thus I have learnt from gazing on your ruinous fate'.[6] The maidens arrived in winged vehicles, and the fallen Prometheus around whom they grouped themselves was perhaps represented by some artificial figure, from behind which the actor spoke. Aspects of the play may have been suggested to Aeschylus during one of his visits to Sicily (perhaps the second, before he died there in 456), both by local tyrannies and by the sight of Mount Etna and the story of the giant imprisoned beneath it—'the rebel o'erthrown' of Matthew Arnold's *Empedocles on Etna:*

> Through whose heart Etna drives her roots of stone,
> To imbed them in the sea.

With such convulsions in mind, Aeschylus introduced weird and spectacular devices. The play opened with the clang of hammers upon chains, as Prometheus was riveted to the rock; at the end some means must have been found to portray his envelopment in a general convulsion of nature. Aeschylus and his collaborators were alive to such opportunities—the same dramatist's *Suppliants* contained movements of tens or even hundreds of noisy exotic figures.

The story of Prometheus was already an old one. Different parts of the myth had appeared in the two main Hesiodic poems, the *Works and Days* and *Theogony* (page 124). Aeschylus' play is the only extant tragedy based upon those works. His version is misleading unless it is realized that a sequel followed, the *Prometheus Unbound*, in which Prometheus was rescued by Heracles, who killed the eagle; but of this work only fragments have survived. Whether another lost play *Prometheus the Fire Bringer*, one of the satyr-dramas often written as an appendage to tragedies (page 173), belongs to the same cycle or not is disputed.

In view of these losses and uncertainties, it is difficult for us to grasp the whole picture as Aeschylus intended us to see it. But we

know how and why Zeus relented sufficiently to enable Prometheus
to be released.

> All tortured though I am,
> fast fettered here,
> he shall have need of me, the lord of heaven,
> to show to him the strange design
> by which he shall be stripped of throne and sceptre.
> But he will never win me over
> with honeyed spell of soft, persuading words,
> nor will I ever cower beneath his threats
> to tell him what he seeks.
> First he must free me from this savage prison
> and pay for all my pain.[7]

This is explained by a story told by Pindar,[8] that Zeus (as well as
his brother Posidon) had been a suitor for Nereus' daughter Thetis,
but abandoned his pursuit of her when Themis (Prometheus'
mother—the Earth—in Aeschylus, and giver of his prophetic powers)
foretold that she would bear a son stronger than his father. Evidently
in the lost sequel Prometheus purchased release by revealing this
secret: he was exchanged with the centaur Chiron, who longed for
death (to relieve his incurable wound at the hand of Heracles) and
offered himself to Zeus as substitute for Prometheus,[9] and thus took
his pains upon himself, and willingly descended to Tartarus. And
so Heracles, descendant of Io, freed Prometheus. This is a deal with
the gods, like the outcome of the *Eumenides*.

Did the *Prometheus Unbound* show a reformed, changed Zeus,
whose character had developed from raw young tyrant to mature
constitutional ruler—rather as the government of Athens could be
passing from aggressive young democracy to maturity? The fact
is rather that the gods have two faces. Both are inscrutable, but
whereas one is appalling, the other enables people to survive: like
the statue of Apollo at Delos, with a bow in one hand and statues of
the three Graces in the other. Matters turned out strangely, but at
least Zeus, without sacrificing any of his violent might, decided to
help Heracles[10] and let moderation prevail, though his reason for

doing so is disconcerting enough to wreck any sentimental conception of deity. Even Zeus cannot escape Fate (pages 184, 202),[11] yet he will exercise his own power to end the oppression,[12] and to that extent Prometheus' splendid sin has produced a change (as seemed possible to Greeks) in God himself.

The human mind could not tolerate the alternative to *eventual* release. Even the *Book of Job* (whether it is earlier or later than Aeschylus is unknown) has an abrupt happy ending—since the heavenly kingdom was the due of all who righteously observed the Law. So on Assyrian tablets Marduk intervenes to restore the utterly wretched *Righteous Sufferer*.[13] But Prometheus—like Jeremiah[14] but unlike the Righteous Sufferer, Job,[15] and Euripides' *Hippolytus*[16]—knows why he has caused the divine wrath; and it comes from a supreme deity as terrifying and startling as anything in either Greek or Jewish tradition. Io is allowed to paint a dreadful picture of the god, and well may Hermes say, in reply to Prometheus' groan, ' "Alas"? That is a word unknown to Zeus.'

Zeus had planned, but for Prometheus, to destroy the whole human race—as the Hesiodic Zeus had destroyed four successive races, one after another (page 126).

> As for long suffering men, he took no care at all;
> indeed his plan was to make the whole of their race
> extinct and then to form another race instead.
> Except for me no one opposed his purpose.[17]

It was the destiny of Prometheus to rescue man from ignorance—though he had to defraud heaven to do this. In the triumphant spirit of the Ionian philosophers, he proclaims the doctrine of human progress, terribly hard to attain, yet so different from the crustiness of Hesiod. We cannot be intended to think of Prometheus as wrong.

Yet to speak of 'sympathy' for him is perhaps beside the point seeing that his enemy is the supreme power. This is ruthless and vindictive—at best indifferent—basing its rule, not on moral right or superiority, but on personal sanction through conquest (page 131). Oceanus' talk of 'reconciliation' is too sentimental and shallow in dealing with the grimness of metaphysical power and what it means in human terms. Nevertheless, Prometheus is strong enough, as we are not, to compel or blackmail some concession. He is the culture-hero who in many communities is linked or fused—or sometimes contrasted—with godhead: not only the intelligence of the hero, but also the power of his opponent, has to concede something in the end. Moreover, Zeus, although indeed 'the paths of his mind extend thick and bushy',[18] is, after all, special champion of the rights of Justice.[19] She was his daughter according to Hesiod (page 102), and she had sided with him against his father.

However, despite the Hymn to Zeus in the *Agamemnon*, he does not look like an obvious champion of goodness. A glance at the world seemed enough to show this: 'it would be odd,' as a later writer remarked, 'if anyone were to say he *loved* Zeus.[20] Prometheus' defiance was unrealistic; like the Trickster of the Winnebago Indians (except that Prometheus, unlike such Tricksters, is dis-interested), his cunning overreaches itself. How should the supreme power be expected to show softness to such an enemy? Besides, perhaps Zeus when he proposed to destroy the human race had intended to create something better!—perhaps it was Prometheus' fault that he did not. But the mystery is too great for there to be any solution on a logical or intellectual plane. The Prometheus of Aeschylus was the noble conception of a mind and a community that had seen and honoured Harmodius and Aristogiton, killers for freedom's sake of Hipparchus, the son of Pisistratus. Yet Prome-theus is wrong to say that he himself will triumph 'in spite of' Zeus.[21] Zeus had not always been there, but he had broken the cycle of rise and fall, and he has come to stay; and Prometheus is again wrong to hint that this is not so.[22] His defiance seeks apparent justice, but at the expense of something higher—and bleaker and more incomprehensible.

Later, however, this defiance must somehow have been transmuted into a voluntary revelation of his secret.[23] It is by such means, possible not for ordinary humans but for him who is at and beyond humanity's culmination, that intelligence painfully coalesces with the divine might into a cosmic order where there is room, precarious room, for human striving. At least the violent, impervious Zeus of

Aeschylus left no place for the low-grade religion which makes relations with the divine power of God into a romantic moralizing tale, with a conventional, reassuring profit and loss account.

The agent of Zeus, Hermes, shows the two faces of divinity. He is a snarling, abusive lackey of the boss, remote from the affectionate smiling disrespect of the fourth Homeric Hymn dedicated to him, which Shelley translated—'a miracle-play written by Congreve', it has been called. Far, too, is the Aeschylean Hermes from that god's guidance of the living in the *Iliad*, and of the dead in the *Odyssey*; where he is the god's messenger, but in no such unpleasant guise as this. Hermes is generally the clever, non-moral, *dieu tzigane*—another aspect of the Trickster—who presiding over the mischief of the primitive animals he rules, turns this into the patronage of trickery in the common man. But he is not that here. Infinitely far, again, from the vituperator of Prometheus is A. E. Housman's divine Hermes 'with lips that brim with laughter'. There was no knowing which face a god would wear.

Writing a century later than Aeschylus, Plato, for all his hostility to degrading traditional tales,[24] told poetic myths to convey difficult truths beyond the range of the logical process[25] (as Arnold Toynbee has endeavoured to do in our century). Plato makes the sophist, or learned popular philosopher, Protagoras retell the Prometheus story yet again.[26] This time it reflects an evolutionary theory of human society. Partly based on Ionian philosophy and partly new—though whether the novelty comes from Plato or Protagoras we cannot tell—the Platonic version claims the teachability of virtue, and demonstrates the importance of law in human progress. The credit for this progress, however, is transferred from Prometheus, now in a subordinate role, to a fixed and stable Zeus. Plato, then, is in a minority among those fascinated by Prometheus, in that he gives the story a conservative instead of a revolutionary interpretation.

Men of most other times have seen in Prometheus a representative of human kind and its struggling spirit, and in Aeschylus' play (necessarily considered without its sequel) they have found one of the archetypal myths most applicable to man's destiny. The theme is linked not only with Job but with the crucified Christ, whom Tertullian saw as the 'true Prometheus': in Prometheus' agonies, the Fathers saw a mystical symbol of the Passion. The Renaissance was divided about him: Marsilio Ficino (d. 1499) treated him as the microcosm of man at his fullest development, Michelangelo drew him gnawed by an eagle and crucified on an enormous oak, and Ronsard (d. 1585) saw him, in medieval fashion, as a learned disguise for the sin of Adam. Prometheus then becomes the model for Milton's Samson—and above all of his Satan, who is as magnificent as the Greek hero, but less sympathetic.

The story, as Francis Bacon (page 423) said, 'demonstrateth and presseth many grave and true speculations'. Furthermore, in the age of Rousseau and of the revolutionaries who followed, men also dwelt on ancient stories—not told by Hesiod or Aeschylus—that Prometheus, like the Archangel Michael forming Adam from dust, was the creator of mankind: his material the clay and water of Panopeus in Phocis (into which Athene breathed life), or clay mixed with pieces of other animals.[27] Unlike Mephistopheles who denies, Prometheus is the creative spirit who affirms, with innocent, exhilarated effrontery. For Herder, he embodies 'the continued striving of the Divine Spirit in man for the awakening of all his powers'.

But above all, as the formal rococo spirit gave way to less restrained and stronger themes, Prometheus stood for the urge to revolt against static tyranny. For romantic poets, he was a glorious symbol of the human spirit struggling against priests and kings—one of the fallen yet noble Titans who engaged the imagination of Hölderlin and Blake (page 130). That is, in part, how he appealed to the young Goethe, whose play (1773) shows Prometheus exulting in the fullness of life. Nearly half a century later, however, Goethe was afraid that this youthful play might be a gospel for the revolutionary young (1820); and he now preferred to see the culture-hero in a less political light, as the personification of doing good—as opposed to dreaming it. But in the intervening years, almost every poet had claimed Prometheus as a symbol of rebellion. Vincenzo Monti, in his *Prometeo* (1797), compared Napoleon to him as a liberator from tyranny. To Byron, however, Napoleon was a desolator, but Prometheus an enhancer of life:

> Thy Godlike crime was to be kind,
> To render with thy precepts less
> The sum of human wretchedness,
> And strengthen Man with his own mind . . .
> Like Thee, Man is in part divine,
> A troubled stream from a pure source . . .

At about the same time, English poetry underwent a rich, if exotic, revival of classical myth. This was due to the advance of Greek scholarship, combined with new, explosive, primitivist ideas about nature and religion; and the movement drew strength from the sort of unclassical allegory and symbolism that had characterized the Middle Ages (page 423). Goethe had turned from heroic Greece (page 52), and centred his imagination upon Faust. But now it was Prometheus who occupied men's minds and feelings, and Shelley's drama *Prometheus Unbound*, written in Italy in 1818-19, was justly regarded by himself as one of the finest of his works. Like certain poems by Keats, the play demonstrates the use a creative artist can make of classical mythology. Remote, in his complex inventiveness, from the Greek tradition, and introducing echoes of Calderon, Goethe, Young's *Night Thoughts* and Robert Blair's *The Grave* (1813), Shelley retains the ideal of Prometheus as suffering champion of mankind. But now he is also the ideal type of mankind itself, the highest perfection of moral and intellectual evolution. He illustrates the millennial conflict of good and evil, and by his gift of fire he exemplifies the poet's own creative energy. Prometheus, thus recharged with feeling and freshness, becomes 'a more poetical character than Satan', because he is free from personal ambition and revenge. And no mere 'catastrophe as feeble as reconciliation' will be enough for Shelley: Jupiter, conventional deity, is overthrown by Demogorgon, Eternity, the Spirit of the Hour.

In America, the *Epimetheus* of Longfellow recorded poetic disillusion overcome by Hope, while his *Prometheus* (1858) showed the hero as 'poet, prophet, seer' made wise by suffering, carrying the torches of progress and fervid creation.

> Ah, Prometheus! heaven-scaling!
> In such hours of exultation
> Even the faintest heart, unquailing,
> Might behold the vulture sailing
> Round the cloudy crags Caucasian!

But the greatest of American Prometheans was Herman Melville. The maniacally brilliant Captain Ahab, in *Moby Dick*, is a latter-day Prometheus in the isolating Pacific wastes, with his egalitarian hatred for the White Whale, the leviathan standing for god. 'I now know that thy right worship is defiance.' However, Ahab would carry man down with him to destruction, unlike Prometheus; but at the end he is bound to the whale, by the ropes of his harpoon, as Prometheus was nailed to his rock and Christ to the cross. Yet Melville's individual fantasies and New-England-style allegories are alien to ancient archetypes, and he uses no classical names. Elizabeth Barrett Browning would have neither classical names nor subjects. Rejecting her future husband's suggestion of Prometheus as a poetic theme, she does so not merely because the myths seemed threadbare (page 120), but because she wanted them superseded by specifically Christian subject-matter. 'The old gods are dethroned,' she says. 'Let the dead bury their dead. . . . And then Christianity is a worthy myth, and poetically acceptable.' Yet, in the generations that followed, writers so different from one another as Hardy and Rimbaud continued to find the Aeschylean myth fundamental. Hardy is aware of it in the Dynasts, and at the end of *Tess*; Rimbaud laid claim himself, as poet, to Promethean powers—seeing that 'the poet is truly the thief of fire, charged with the government of humanity, the animals even, and he must make his discoveries felt, touched, heard' (1871). Nietzsche contrasted the 'feminine' values of the serpent-encompassed Fall in *Genesis* with the masculinity of the tale of Prometheus.

To André Gide, in his *Promethée mal enchaîné* (1899), the hero has left the crag, but still keeps the eagle (or vulture) as a pet—and continues to feed it on his own liver, for the bird is his conscience, to which he is faithful: he does not want to have a dead albatross round his neck. K. Abraham, in 1913, subjected the myth to the same treatment as Freud had given Oedipus (page 229), suggestively but without carrying conviction. More recently Camus wrote an adaptation of Aeschylus' tragedy, which was acted in Algeria but never published; the playwright's scorn for non-human solutions, and his love of life, were subsequently given voice in another myth of rebellion instead—the story (now very popular) of Sisyphus, one of those tormented in Hades, like Tantalus, Ixion and Tityus. The punishment of Sisyphus is eternally to roll a rock up a hill, from the top of which it always rolls down again.

But, unlike Sisyphus, Prometheus eventually finds release. The sculptor Jacques Lipchitz interpreted this release in his own fashion; for he made a statue of Prometheus strangling the bird which has been his attacker (1943).

PART IV

OEDIPUS AND ANTIGONE

CHAPTER 7

OEDIPUS

1 The Story of the KING OEDIPUS Told by Sophocles

KING OEDIPUS appears from inside the royal palace at Thebes. Upon its steps, and around the altars in its forecourt, many Theban citizens are seated in attitudes of supplication. The priest begs the king find some deliverance for the city from the plague which has attacked its people: he recalls how Oedipus broke the bondage of Thebes to the Sphinx, and urges him to act again. Oedipus swears he will do whatever is enjoined by Apollo's oracle, which Creon, brother of his wife Jocasta, has gone to Delphi to consult.

But Creon is back again. Apollo, he reports, demands the punishment of the unknown man who murdered the king's predecessor Laius, while he was away from the country on a pilgrimage. A single survivor had attributed the deed to a crowd of robbers. Oedipus again promises action, and after the chorus of Theban elders have called upon Apollo, Artemis, Athene and Dionysus to save them from the pestilence, he pronounces solemn sentence of imprecation and exile upon the killer. At Creon's suggestion he sends for the seer Tiresias, who refuses to speak but finally, goaded by taunts, accuses Oedipus himself. The elders denounce the slayer but refuse to accept that he is Oedipus. The king and his brother quarrel sharply: Creon denies that he has suborned Tiresias to denounce Oedipus. Queen Jocasta stops the dispute and reassures her husband by recalling that Laius, according to an oracle, was to have been murdered by his own son, but that his son, while still a baby, was exposed on a hill-side and died—whereas Laius, instead, met his death from robbers, at a place where three roads met.

This information arouses the first anxiety in Oedipus. After questioning his wife about the place and time of the murder, and the appearance and company of Laius, he begins to fear that it is he himself who has unknowingly done the deed. His father, he tells Jocasta, was king Polybus of Corinth; and Oedipus, angered one day by a slight on his paternity, had consulted the Delphic oracle and been told he would *kill his father and marry his mother*. That is why he left Corinth—and on his journey away from that city, travelling alone, he had killed an old man who had roughly ordered him from the road. Yet Oedipus takes some hope from the report, by the sole surviving witness, that many men, not one, had been involved in the incident. Jocasta, too, assures her husband that this proves the oracle wrong. Yet the king orders the survivor, a shepherd, to be sent for. The elders utter a prayer against two evils: arrogance, which provokes a fall, and the impiety of disbelieving Apollo's oracle.

A messenger from Corinth arrives to announce that his king Polybus is dead, and the Corinthian throne is offered to Oedipus. He and Jocasta exult in this refutation of the oracle which had declared that Oedipus' father would die at his own son's hand. But Oedipus still dreads the other prediction, that he would marry his mother: for fear of this, he will refuse to accept the invitation from Corinth. However, the messenger reveals that he need have no such fears—because Oedipus' father was not Polybus after all.

MESSENGER: All idle, sir; your fears are groundless, vain.

OEDIPUS: How can that be, seeing I am their son?

MESSENGER: No. Polybus is no kin of yours.

OEDIPUS: No kin? Polybus not my father?

MESSENGER: No more than I.

OEDIPUS: Come, sir; no more than you? Explain yourself.

MESSENGER: I am not your father, neither is Polybus.

OEDIPUS:	How comes it then that I was called his son?
MESSENGER:	I will tell you. You were given to him—by me.
OEDIPUS:	Given? And yet he loved me as his son?
MESSENGER:	He had no other.
OEDIPUS:	Was I . . . found? Or bought?
MESSENGER:	Found, in a wooded hollow of Cithaeron.
OEDIPUS:	What brought you there?
MESSENGER:	Sheep-tending on the mountain.
OEDIPUS:	Were you a hireling shepherd then?
MESSENGER:	I was;
	And by that happy chance, your rescuer.
OEDIPUS:	Why, was I in pain or danger when you took me?
MESSENGER:	The infirmity in your ankles tells the tale.
OEDIPUS:	Oh, that old trouble—need we mention it?
MESSENGER:	Your ankles were riveted, and I set you free.
OEDIPUS:	It is true. I have carried the stigma from my cradle.
MESSENGER:	To it you owe your present name.
OEDIPUS:	O Gods!
	Was this my father's or my mother's doing?
MESSENGER:	I cannot say. Ask him who gave you to me.
OEDIPUS:	Gave me? Did you not find me, then, yourself?
MESSENGER:	Another shepherd entrusted you to my care.
OEDIPUS:	And who was he? Can you tell us who he was?
MESSENGER:	I think he was said to be one of Laius' men.
OEDIPUS:	Laius? Our former king?
MESSENGER:	Why, yes; King Laius.
	The man was one of his servants.
OEDIPUS:	Is he alive?
	And could I see him?
MESSENGER:	Your people here should know.
OEDIPUS:	Good men, does any of you know the fellow—
	This shepherd of whom he speaks? Has anyone seen him
	In the pastures or in the city? Speak if you know.
	Now is the chance to get to the bottom of the mystery.

CHORUS: I think he will prove to be that same countryman
Whom you have already asked to see. The Queen
Is the one most able to tell you if this is so.

OEDIPUS: My wife, *you* know the man whom we have sent for.
Is that the man he means?

JOCASTA: What does it matter
What man he means? It makes no difference now . . .
Forget what he has told you . . . It makes no difference.

OEDIPUS: Nonsense: I must pursue this trail to the end,
Till I have unravelled the mystery of my birth.

JOCASTA: No! In God's name—if you want to live, this quest
Must not go on. Have I not suffered enough?

OEDIPUS: There is nothing to fear. Though I be proved
slave-born
To the third generation, *your* honour is not impugned.

JOCASTA: Yet do not do it. I implore you, do not do it.

OEDIPUS: I must. I cannot leave the truth unknown.[1]

Jocasta leaves him with a cry of despair. The elders, however, hope that this news may mean that Oedipus' real father was a god.

The shepherd, who had been sole survivor of the fight at the cross-roads, arrives, and is identified by the Corinthian messenger as the man who had given him the infant boy. Interrogated, the shepherd gradually discloses that the baby was the son of Laius, and that he himself had received the child from Laius' wife.

Oedipus now knows the truth. Crying that he is sinful in his begetting, sinful in marriage, sinful in shedding of blood, he rushes out. The Theban elders lament, and meditate upon his fall; and they wish they had never set eyes on him.

A messenger arrives from within to tell them that Jocasta has hanged herself, and that Oedipus has put out his eyes. The king is led forth, and, grimly lamenting, begs the elders to exile him or slay him. His brother Creon comes to lead him into the palace, and promises to care for his young daughters Antigone and Ismene.

Oedipus bids them what he intends to be a last farewell, for he urges his brother to banish him from the land. But Creon answers that Apollo must decide, and, finding Oedipus reluctant to cease his farewells, bids him not to seek to rule in everything; for those days are ended. And 'none', as the elders reflect, 'can be called happy until that day when he carries his happiness down to the grave in peace.'

TABLE 5

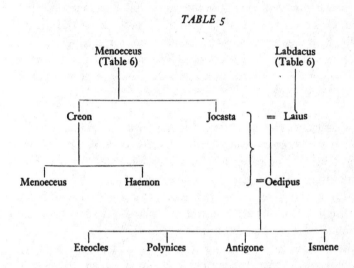

2   *Why is Oedipus Destroyed?*

Thebes, on the southern edge of the eastern plain of Boeotia, had been the chief Mycenaean city in central Greece, though the mention of only a subsidiary settlement in the Homeric catalogue[2] suggests that there was an interlude in its prosperity during which the town had been laid waste. The Thebans possessed good wheat and horses, and were agricultural and self-contained, having no part in overseas expansion. Though producers of fine poetry, they were reputed to be slow of wit.

Not only do we know little of Thebes itself, for it has not been excavated, but we have also lost the whole of the Theban epic cycle in which the myths of the House of Oedipus were handed down.

The cycle's two leading poems, the *Thebais* and *Oedipodia*, are con-jecturally attributed to the eighth century BC. The *Thebais* was early, though dubiously assigned to Homer,[3] and was greatly admired. The *Oedipodia* was ascribed to a certain Cinaethon of Sparta.

Oedipus may have been a real person: whose story absorbed, among other fabulous elements, the classic folk-tale situation of those who try to avert an unpleasant prophecy and believe themselves safe, whereas the prediction is, in the end, fulfilled in an unexpected fashion. Or he may be wholly mythical. In any case he is different from the Homeric heroes, because he is superior in intelligence and not in physical might (even Odysseus had both); and because he is not the son or direct protégé of a god but the individual member of a family, participating in its greatness and its faults of violence and anger.

Oedipus lacked physical strength because when he was a baby his father Laius, abandoning him, had thrust a spike through his feet, presumably to disable the ghost. Hence his name, 'swell-foot'. Not only were exposed children a phenomenon of Greek life with which many were familiar, but the recurrent myths of their survival symbolize defiance of fate. These stories may be derived from the initiation tests of early societies; in psychopathology, as Jung points out, they stand for the imaginative transformation of personal inadequacies into great pretensions and powers. The Maori hero Massi was thrown into the sea as an infant, and Vainamoinen, the hero of the *Kalevala*, 'floated above dark waves'. In the Mediter-ranean tradition there are Moses and Romulus and Remus (page 354) and many others, and as early as the third millennium BC King Sargon the Akkadian had told of his own exposure.[4] Not only has the foundling myth become familiar as a success story in comedy, but Shakespeare, in his last plays, illustrates the tragic helpless character of human life by showing many of his heroes and heroines as orphans, at the mercy of the storm. Like Oedipus, they are deliv-ered from the danger, but their lonely upbringing sets them apart from our common destiny.

Oedipus won his throne by defeating a female incubus from the underworld, the sphinx. Her name is usually explained as the 'throttler' or the 'choker', but more probably means the 'tight-binder', the demon of death. Sphinxes originated in Egypt, but became known throughout the near east. In Greece—where they appear frequently on orientalizing seventh-century friezes and vases—they have changed from male to female, the female fear-animal of nightmare that Freud attributed to the incest prohibition (page 230).

The Sphinx had been sent by Hera to Thebes, and had devoured its people, until Oedipus got the better of the monster by solving the riddle which others had failed to solve. Riddles, which may perhaps be of separate origin from folk-tales but circulate no less freely, are common in many lands from Mongolia to central Africa. In Greece, which loved them, these conundrums were the descendants of the parables and hard sayings in Hesiod's *Works and Days*. In particular, riddles often reflected the misleading darkness of divine utterances, and of the human choices which depended upon them. The riddle of the Theban Sphinx was this:

> A thing there is whose voice is one,
> Whose feet are two and four and three.
> So mutable a thing is none
> That moves in earth or sky or sea.
> When on most feet this thing doth go
> Its strength is weakest and its pace most slow.[5]

Oedipus recognized in this the three ages of man. Freud, however, conjectured that the question the riddle was really designed to answer related to the oldest and most burning question to the immature—the origin of babies. At all events, Oedipus solved the riddle and gained the throne of Thebes.[6] Tennyson, in his *Tiresias* (1885), tells how

> the fierce beast found
> A wiser than herself, and dashed herself
> Dead in her rage.

Although hardly anything 'happens' in Sophocles' *King Oedipus*—

other than the arrival of people with news—the play moves with intense, remorseless speed. Every word counts in this marvellously flexible dialogue and breath-taking choral poetry, and the issues are not intellectual abstractions but stamp themselves upon our hearts. To us it might seem an extraordinary improbability that Oedipus had never before heard, or inquired, how his predecessor had met his end. But in the dramatic tension of the performance, as it rapidly unfolded in the conditions of an open-air theatre, this aspect would be ignored. Besides, it is the self-appointed task of Sophocles to face the implausibilities of the myths—and display how such things nevertheless could have happened.

When first performed (at a date which we cannot determine), the play did not win first prize. But Aristotle handed it down to posterity as the model tragedy. Its continual imagery of blindness, light and darkness leads to a dramatic, harrowing conclusion. Yet the audience knew who the culprit was; it remained for Voltaire, in the preface of his *Mérope*, to advocate the virtues of suspense in regard to a plot. By the audience of Sophocles, on the other hand, the events that ineluctably take place are expected. Since, therefore, we are all in the secret but only the actors are not, the whole progression of events is a cumulation of the tragic irony (page 182) which is particularly associated with the name of Sophocles. In this process the chorus plays an essential part, for he is the dramatist who most closely integrates its utterances both with the action of his plays and with the emotions of the spectators. More than the poet's mouthpiece or a sympathetic onlooker, the chorus organizes and gives rhythm and background to Sophocles' version of the myth, and helps him to use the story as a concrete example of the harrowing hatreds and aspirations of life.

For it is in the myths, even the cruellest myths, that Sophocles sees the permanent human battleground, accepting their horrors with his dramatic (if not altogether with his moral) sense, and more than Aeschylus adhering to their traditional framework. Yet these stories would be nothing without the poetry, for there comes a point, and this is reached by Sophocles, where form is so nearly perfect as to achieve the autonomous originality of a new concept. This is also true of the contemporary Parthenon in which, likewise, the achievement depends not on lavish ornament but on a simplicity modified by subtle constructional and stylistic effects. These, like the effects of Sophocles, 'triumphantly escape, but just escape, the prosaic'.

The supreme moment of tension is the passage from ignorance to 'recognition' and knowledge, from success to despair. Oedipus is the most famous of all mythical searchers for truth behind illusion, and tragedy's function—in which Racine alone has approached Sophocles—is to display, and link with all that has gone before, the unendurable moment of truth in which the king knows who he is and what he has done. Sophocles is less interested in morality than in the human personalities which it exhibits. Yet in the rapid movement of the stage, comparable to the vivid breadth of a sculptural relief, the boldly contrasted dramatic lines in which character is presented are drawn not so much by psychological study as by concentration upon the qualities which prompted their decisions. As Aristotle saw, it is at one remove from ordinary men that the characters of Sophocles in their stark strength work out these crucial dilemmas,[7] determining—as, in an era of change and questioning, Sophocles and his contemporaries had to determine for themselves—what they owe to the gods, their state, their family, and their own minds and hearts.

Among these demonic and iron-willed, yet arrogant, obstinate, and fierce-tempered sufferers of Sophoclean drama, Oedipus stands out: the self-taught ruler who unaided, and through his noble qualities, has risen to mastery over adversaries believed insuperable before. Oedipus illustrates Aristotle's theory that, in tragedy, misfortune should fall on an eminent man not because he is vicious but because there is something wrong about him, an error (*hamartia*).[8] It has been endlessly discussed whether this meant, or should mean, a flaw, a moral fault or frailty; or the intellectual foolishness or error of judgement of one who like Deianira 'erred, intending well' (she killed Heracles with a supposed love-philtre in Sophocles' *Trachinian Women*); or a hereditary quasi-physical curse or blight—seeing that guilt, intentional or otherwise, was still regarded as such an infection.[10] If, on the other hand, a wholly virtuous man were brought from prosperity to adversity, there would be no material for a tragedy. Shakespeare's Richard III and Macbeth are wicked, but have the compensating *grandeur d'âme* which Corneille, too, required in a central tragic figure. The Aristotelian ideal hero, exemplified by Oedipus, presents a more subtle problem. He is not only a figure of this same general grandeur, but he also possesses many specific qualities far above the common level. True, in an age of fighting and killing he killed hot-heatedly at the cross-roads when provoked (though without knowing it was a kinsman that he killed), and he shows fits of *hubris* in his over-confident, rash handling of the present situation. Yet these things are not the main, or at least not the sole, cause of his disaster. He is also the fatal victim of an unfathomed blow, tainted by some alloy of which the painful refinement brings him to utter ruin—ruin incurred, moreover, in conducting an investigation which he believes a duty, and an unpleasant one at that.

What Aristotle is referring to as Oedipus' 'error' lies in his ignorance of material facts and circumstances: in his misconception that touches off the casually linked events which lead to catastrophe. This misconception may or may not be blameworthy; its relevance to the problem of undeserved suffering is cryptic. The catastrophe, besides being complete, is also, according to Aristotle, the sort most proper to tragedy, in that it proceeds from a 'reversal' of the situation (*peripeteia*: page 185)—an outcome contrary to the main actor's intention—combined with a dramatic 'recognition' (*anagnorisis*) when the nature of what has happened dawns on him.

Downfalls such as that of Oedipus are caused by the gods, to whom all things are easy. They come when the divine order has somehow been breached. But we cannot always detect the breaching, or see why the divine purpose works as it does, or how the ensuing destruction harmonizes with our own fragmentary view of human justice. As in Theognis (page 186), suffering often seems to exceed deserts. In his *Trachinian Women* telling of Heracles' end, Sophocles concludes with words that are more equivocal than any clear-cut victory of right over wrong.

You have seen a terrible death
And agonies, many and strange, and there is
Nothing here which is not Zeus.[12]

Men such as Oedipus are vulnerable and flawed since they are
victims of the unpredictability of events, which, by injudicious acts,
they often involuntarily help to deal them wounds.

Critics in the seventeenth and eighteenth centuries liked to stress
the poetic justice in Greek tragedy. But Joseph Addison rightly saw
that the ancient dramatists 'treated men as they are dealt with in the
world, by making virtue sometimes happy and sometimes miserable'
(1711). A tragedian's handling of the myths, therefore, may well
challenge or outrage our moral sense. Indeed, perhaps it must, in
order to be tragedy at all—the frustrations and futility of which were
dwelt upon by Schopenhauer. There is, in life, a stubborn residue
of evil which no moralizing can easily justify, and Sophocles accepted
this non-rational element, this lack of correlation between sin and
punishment, this tolerance or support of evil by the supreme power.
He did not feel obliged to resort to Manichaean dualism; Greece
lies outside the great region of the earth (from the Iranian plateau
eastwards to North America) which is the natural home of such
beliefs. Nor did he need the African doctrine that the kind Supreme
Spirit is followed about by an idiot brother who spoils what he has
done.

Christian doctrine also rejects dualism. But unlike Sophocles it
assumes that God is just. For this reason it is difficult to conceive a
truly Christian tragedy; in Racine's *Phèdre*, for example, Friedrich
von Schlegel (1807) saw a discrepancy between the tragic spirit and
Christian providence—although the fierce fatalism of the Jansenists
goes less badly with tragedy than, say, Rousseauist perfectibility.
There is a contrast, too, between the various failures of individual
human beings in classical drama and the Biblical doctrine of the
Fall, by which all men become leprous and unclean until Jesus
Christ redeems them. For Christians see evil as the harbinger of
blessing, as something which always permits of reconciliation and
atonement, a relief from what Dostoevsky saw as our complete and

terrifying freedom: 'O happy fault that has won for us so loving, so mighty a Redeemer.'[13]

Sophocles, like other Greek tragedians, found evil (expressed in suffering) beneficial for another reason—because of its educative power.[14] Before the gods, or the god as Sophocles also says,[15] man is nothing, and he must humble himself before their will; his mistakes and illustrations are on a far lower plane than theirs. *He* is entitled to understanding and compassion, yet *they*, however dreadful and inexplicable their manifestations, cannot ever be unjustified or wrong. For they embody the natural order of events.

The poet's piety is tranquil beneath the storms of action, and imperishable; his imagination wholly accepts the apparent evil in the divine dispensation. Yet man, in his gallant, losing struggle with necessity, is raised to a stature larger than life. For this is not only a pious but a humanistic creed, which incorporates the dilemmas of an optimistic and ambitious generation. Oedipus has extraordinary powers to match his extraordinary fate—and Sophocles also suggests that the forces which tolerate misery create, or augment, moral grandeur in the man who stands against them. There is, in defeat, a splendid heroism, peculiar to mankind and indissociable from their self-destruction. Thus, even at the appalling end, Oedipus is not wholly broken, and Creon says to him:

> Do not seek to be master in everything,
> For the things you mastered did not follow
> You throughout your life.[16]

Oedipus is reduced to utter destitution, stripped of everything—like Edgar, naked from the storm, of whom Lear asks: 'is man no more than this?' The doom, which he gradually and horribly recognizes, is fixed from the start, and it comes from the Delphic oracle—which *has* to be fulfilled. Aeschylus had stressed the ancestral curse and the Furies' pursuit; Sophocles transfers the working out of events to Apollo and his oracle, which he inexorably justifies—at a time when disbelief was in the air (page 265).

Accordingly, the *Oedipus* has been used more than any other play to support the view that Greek tragedy deals with puppets helpless in the grip of destiny. And indeed, since fate was believed to be as much part of a man's endowment at birth as his looks or his mental gifts, the odds are overwhelmingly against Oedipus, who is therefore a more helpless victim of destiny than his daughter Antigone (page 246). He committed parricide and incest in all innocence. Yet, as H. D. F. Kitto warned, if you mistake potassium cyanide for sugar, innocence and ignorance will not save you. Oedipus keeps his responsibility, for fate is the way life works out for a man, and he has a say in its working out. But fate also comprises the terrors of sheer ill-luck, of which Oedipus has much, and Sophocles seems to ask whether chance, or law, is at the root of the universe; later Greeks decided in favour of chance (page 186). And so Nietzsche calls tragedy the dancing ground of divine, unfathomable accident. Inexplicably cruel things do happen, but this only means that our knowledge of the universe's laws is fragmentary. Meanwhile, it is folly to neglect those which we do know. Such neglect is also disobedience to the gods. But Oedipus disobeys them without knowing it, and thus supplies an ever more terrifying manifestation of the divine will—irrefutable, sometimes incomprehensible, often unbearable.

The resulting events are painful, as their participants pass through anguish and are destroyed by forces they can neither understand nor master. Yet the plays which tell of these desperate, demon-ridden themes have appealed irresistibly to many generations. It has always been asked why this is; and the answers have been many. Aristotle,[17] thinking of Sophocles rather than Aeschylus (and not following Plato in his desire to stamp out tragic pity as poison for the soul),[18] said that tragedy, by actions arousing pity and fear, purifies or purges the corresponding passions in ourselves (*catharsis*). It arouses and then allays our pity and fear—pity prompted by unmerited misfortune, and fear caused by seeing the misfortune of man who is like, or not too unlike, ourselves. We share the mythical heroes' attempts to escape their dooms, comparing our desires and aims with theirs and hoping to avoid their catastrophes, and we depart in an emotional balance and equilibrium, all passion spent.

Yet St Augustine was still perplexed that 'this very sorrow is the spectator's pleasure', and some (like the Athenian comic dramatist Timocles) have thought of tragedy as a gloating over horrors, while others again have condemned it for justifying and commending sufferings. Or should we rather interpret Aristotle as postulating the *retention* in us of pity and fear, but the elimination from these feelings of what is impure and harmful, making of them *not* a selfish sort of gloating but sympathy for human sorrows? Yet probably that is to introduce too much morality into a question that is primarily aesthetic rather than moral. For it is only through the poetic words, into which the suffering is translated by the artist, that this is elevated and transfigured into what is pure and moving and stimulating and delightful.

Since immediacy is a necessary part of fear, and tragedy is less immediate than films and novels, it is harder today than it was to effect the transference of emotional conflicts through these plays. But some modern writers still see a function in tragedy. 'By its symbolic re-enactment,' said Giraudoux (page 59), 'it satisfies collectively the need of the public to commit a crime . . . To witness a tragedy in the theatre is to diminish in the heart of the spectator whatever murderous intention he may have had.' To Anouilh (page 248) on the other hand, tragedy is, paradoxically, restful: because you know that there is no more hope, dirty sneaking hope, and that you are caught, caught at last like a rat in a trap.

3   The Oedipus Complex

When tragedy, in Roman times, had become melodrama, Seneca used the story of Oedipus as a vehicle for gloomy sacrifices and necromancy.   In the Renaissance, the theatre at Vicenza was inaugurated by Sophocles' *King Oedipus* in Italian. The story was the favourite of sixteenth-century humanists, and then in the 1600s a subject for Corneille, Dryden and Lee. In the following century every would-be classicist turned to Oedipus, and Voltaire's *Oedipe* (1718), perhaps his best play, was especially popular because it enabled contemporaries to recognize allusions to current incest-scandals among French royalty. And now a version by Hölderlin has been adopted for Carl Orff's 1961 opera. For each age has continued to interpret the myth according to its own ideas—neo-classic, rationalistic, or romantic.

Very far from romantic is the increased attention which the tale of Oedipus received from psychoanalysts in the first decades of the present century. Oedipus murdered his father and committed incest with his mother[19]— entered, as W. B. Yeats paraphrased the lines, through the door that had sent him wailing forth. The same double crime appears in a Finnish tale, and with variations in the Ukraine and in Java; during the Middle Ages a version of the Oedipus story was told of Judas Iscariot. Incest, being a violation of one of the rules of exogamy, had been among the major crimes of a tribal society, and remained a major crime in a still predominantly patriarchal community which stressed, even amid state encroach-ments, the family and its laws (page 191). Jocasta was a difficult psychological problem for the dramatist, and she has had her character assailed by critics ('the arch-horror', 'a frivolous soul', 'coarse, reckless and impious'). But her guilt was back in early youth, and her 'blasphemies'—in respect of the oracle—are frantic attempts to reduce her husband's growing despair.

Oedipus, when all was known, blinded himself—expressing, according to Sigmund Freud, his deep-seated urge to make repara-tion for the death of his father, for whom his feeling was one both of love and of hate. For this was the myth which according to Freud expressed the most powerful of all instinctive drives, love of mother and jealousy of father. The sub-conscious areas of the mind had long been recognized by mystics and Neoplatonists. The Puritans, too, had been all too familiar with the undercurrent of unbidden suggestions through the voices of the devil and of witches. William Law (1686–1761) described—as poets in their own ways depicted— the hidden surges of desires, emotions and thoughts in the obscurer parts of the mind: parts which were far from unknown to Novalis, Schopenhauer, Kierkegaard and Nietzsche (page 151). The con-templations of such thinkers brought them 'glimpses of a great tide of life, ebbing and flowing, rippling and rolling, and beating about where we cannot see it'—in the depths of our memory, or in dreams;

and to William James (1897) it seemed that 'the recesses of feeling, the darker, blinder strata of character, are the only places in the world in which we catch real fact in the making'. But it was Freud who more than anyone else suggested that man's godlike intellect was 'no more designed for discovering the truth than a pig's snout' (H. G. Wells).

Freud worked on the repressed drives and wishes which appear in dreams, experiencing distortions—condensation, displacement, doubling—yet preserving a logic of their own.

In particular, he rightly pointed to many parallels between these dream-symbols and the stories of famous myths. Mythology, therefore, like dreams, seemed to him and his followers a royal road to our understanding of the unconscious processes, since myths contain thinly disguised representations of certain fundamental unconscious fantasies common to mankind. But Freud went further and concluded that the key to our comprehension of the unconscious was to be found in the story of Oedipus. First employing the term 'Oedipus complex' in 1910 (earlier he had written of a 'nuclear' complex), he was writing ten years later that 'every new arrival on this planet is faced with the task of mastering the Oedipus complex'. The two wishes in the complex—to commit the two crimes of Oedipus—represent, according to Freud, two main features of every son's efforts to replace his father; coinciding with 'the two principal prohibitions imposed by totemism', they are all-important among the neuroses caused by conflicts between instinct and society. So the fate of Oedipus moves us 'because it might have been our own, because the oracle laid upon us before our birth the very curse which rested upon him. . . . Our dreams convince us that we were all destined to direct our first sexual impulses towards our mothers, and our first impulses of hatred and violence towards our fathers. . . . Like Oedipus we live in ignorance of the desires that nature has forced upon us.' And it is true that out of fifty representative mythologies of the world no less than thirty-nine include incest among their subject-matter.

To be more specific, Freud believed the complex to be strongest when 'infantile sexuality' is at its height, between the end of a boy's third year of life and his fourth or fifth year; when his first choice of object is his mother. Then comes the process of overcoming this urge if normalcy, without infantile fixation, is to be achieved. The successor and conqueror of the Oedipus complex is the super-ego which represents the barrier *against* incestuous and murderous instincts, repudiating Oedipus with the aid of the whole social order and morality and religion. Yet the myth, like other myths, lives on, imaginatively ascribing to gods and heroes our own primordial desires and their fulfilments after most human beings have been obliged to renounce them.

Freud supported his emphasis on incest by deducing from Charles Darwin a primeval situation of the bull-ape sons banding against their father's monopoly of the females. As this reconstruction of the past ceased to find favour, the corollary of incest-guilt likewise proved unacceptable. Freud was also challenged by Malinowski (1922), one of the first anthropologists to test how psychoanalytical theories applied to primitive societies in the field. Malinowski concluded that the matrilineal society of the Trobriand islanders in Melanesia shows no signs of the Oedipus complex, thus contradicting Freud's view of this as a basic absolute in human development: the child's rivalry with the father, whether of sexual origin or not, only occurs in cultures with a strong patriarchal authority.

In other words, Freud had discovered one of myth's important aspects—its link with dreams and with other manifestations of the unconscious mind—and like so many sorts of mythologist, magnified this, with special attention to Oedipus, into a general explanation of myth and life alike. Many of his fellow psychoanalysts, in their various ways, have subscribed to this general estimate of his discoveries. Jung (page 151) saw special value in the infantile fixation postulated by Freud (and added the term 'Electra complex' for the affection of girls for their fathers), but made the whole process more symbolic, the mother representing the unattainable, and the father the inner check. Otto Rank, believing with others that Oedipus' blinding was a substitute for castration (page 115), elaborated also upon the idea that he had wanted to solve man's origin and destiny by returning into his mother's womb. Fromm shifted the emphasis from incest (which seemed to him a secondary element) to the rebellion of the son against the father's patriarchal authority, contesting Freud's conviction that the conflict is wholly sexual and seeing the 'complex' rather as a struggle for freedom against social obstacles (page 152). Adler classified the Oedipus complex as one of *many* attitudes that appear in the life of a child— and particularly of a pampered child, over-indulged and isolated by its mother. Karen Horney, too, doubted the intensity which Freud claimed for these inclinations towards father and mother (pointing out, incidentally, that the acceptance of his doctrine was inclined to make parents forget the need for real warmth and sincerity). Melanie Klein offered the further critical comment that aggressive feelings towards the mother come first, before hatred of the father.

While Oedipus was still in the hands of the analysts, his complex was delineated, with an infusion of mysticism, by Hugo von Hoffmansthal; and his passion, egotism and insufficiency received operatic treatment in Stravinsky's *Oedipus Rex*. Described as frigid when it first appeared, but now found moving by many, this work is encased in a ritualistic frame starker than the humanism of heroic opera. Its music, too, is more disturbing in its savagery and wider in its range, suggesting at times the incantations of Christian liturgy and implications of Christian theology: man is dominated but may find his own redemption, and light comes to Oedipus when he loses his eyes.

When this opera was first being performed, the story was simultaneously receiving a very different treatment from French dramatists. Not that Greek mythology had been neglected in the nineteenth century; 582 French imitations, translations or adaptations of classical originals sprang from *le rêve hellenique* between 1840 and 1900. But many twentieth-century tragedies are more thoughtful. Few of the best, however, deal with contemporary reality: myth is what seems most fitted to illuminate the poetry, simplicity and heroism of the human condition, and if, as these writers are sometimes blamed for doing, they invoke the myths to give authority to their own obsessions, there are millennial precedents for this. Myth also makes it possible to dispense with realistic detail and to experiment with the supernatural. The psychoanalysts had recently found a new suggestiveness in mythology, and had provided reasons, in the Euripidean tradition (page 267), for a measure of debunking. Nevertheless, to us, said Sartre, 'a play should not seem too familiar. Violent and brief, it must remain a rite . . . severe, austere, moral, mythic and ceremonial', which falls in with the needs 'of a people exhausted but tense' disdaining to invent new forms or to arouse curiosity by new stories, yet searching, by reconstruction and recreation of what was old, for new principles.

The whole of antiquity has been rifled afresh to these ends, and subjected to many juxtapositions of sublime and trivial. But Oedipus and his daughter Antigone (page 238) have been the key figures, and their lives have provided the chosen norms of human life. In general the influence of fate, or heaven, as blind external force is, in Nietzschean spirit, denied. André Gide, especially, refused to submit to this 'tyranny', emancipating the human race to act according to its own will and inner necessity. His *Oedipe*, written in 1930 and published two years later, is terse, dry, intellectualized and written to shock. The characters are corrupt and proud, motives are vicious, and there is the familiar Gidean antithesis between Oedipus who, although a petulant little man, believes in progress and happiness, and the woman whose association with him he feels has stunted his development, the bigoted and priest-ridden Jocasta.

Jean Cocteau, too, found in Sophocles' plays 'the bone', the dramatic necessity, which he demanded. He saw his own swiftly moving *Antigone* (1922) and *Oedipe Roi* (1925) as merely sketches and abridgements, photographs from an aeroplane. But, after speaking the prologue and interludes of Stravinsky's opera, Cocteau reverted to the story of Oedipus in his *Infernal Machine* (1934), with a *décor* by Bérard who sees the bed of incest as a sacrificial pyre. Here is not to be found the usual minimization of fate, for the machine of the title is a divine piece of apparatus for the mathematical destruction of a human being. As the play proceeds, with its numerous well-timed dramatic and psychological tricks, this Oedipus has no chance against the overwhelming divine intervention which Cocteau provides. In an allegory of relentless determinism, Oedipus is a gambler who, forced to abandon his brash conviction that the uglier sayings of the gods can somehow be got round, realizes he is trapped. This acceptance gives him a new and bitter sobriety, 'which makes this king of cards, in the hands of the cruel gods, a man at last'. Here Cocteau is nearer to Voltaire or Shaw than to Freud. In 1942 he reverted to the theme once again, in his 'lyrical tragedy' *Oedipus Rex*, set to music, dance and mime by Maurice Thiriet, and first performed in 1962.

A Scottish poet in whose mind Oedipus played a dominant part was Edwin Muir.

> I have wrought and thought in darkness,
> And stand here now, an innocent mark of shame,
> That so men's guilt might be made manifest
> In such a walking riddle—their guilt and mine.
> For I've but acted out this fable. I have judged
> Myself, obedient to the gods' high judgement,
> And seen myself with their pure eyes, have learnt
> That all must bear a portion of the wrong
> That is driven deep into our fathomless hearts
> Past sight or thought; that, bearing it, we may ease
> The immortal burden of the gods who keep
> Our natural steps and the earth and skies from harm.

4 Oedipus at Colonus

Nevertheless, the fatal deeds which have so stirred psychoanalysts, and the fate of King Oedipus at the end of the play of that name, are not his end; and Sophocles' contemplation of him, with reference to general problems of human suffering, is only half-complete without the sequel which he wrote at the end of his life (406 BC), the *Oedipus at Colonus*. In this cryptic drama the blinded Oedipus goes to an Athenian sanctuary with the consent of Theseus, and then to an awe-inspiring death, and to heaven.

> Because his sufferings were great, unmerited and untold,
> Let some just god relieve him from distress!

I pray you, even Death, offspring of Earth and Hell,
To let the descent be clear
As Oedipus goes down among the ghosts
On those dim fields of underground that all men living
    fear.
Eternal sleep, let Oedipus sleep well![20]

The prayer is answered. Until then, he has not changed—unless his character has gained in strength. Heroically enduring, he three times proclaims his innocence: Sophocles seems to be upholding the importance of motive in judging conduct. This imaginative play is filled with a complex, violent rhythm of extremes. The contrasts of innocence and pollution, wretchedness and power, weakness and strength, hatred and devotion, hope and anxiety, are reflected by an episodic structure of successive movements. Yet finally all these contrasting notes are merged amid a sublime reconciliation, in which the ways of heaven are, not indeed justified (for Sophocles does not usually justify them), but made less wholly daunting to man; though they are still solemn and mysterious.

This development of the myth is hard for us to place in perspective, because we know of no theological equivalent to the demi-god, or semi-deified hero, which the dying Oedipus becomes. The mythical heroes—according to Hesiod their lives had been one of the Five Ages of Mankind[21] (page 126)—were powerful in death. Necromancy (page 92) led on to their posthumous invocation to help the living, and before long this practice had become very frequent: the passions of the living Oedipus seem to forecast his power to help and hurt when he is dead. Heroes of the past came back in visions at feasts and marched with armies, and after the fashion of the gods of the earth (though with different procedures) they were worshipped under the ground; just as in Palestine too there was a strong mortuary cult—severely condemned by the Hebrew prophets who instead taught departure to Sheol, far beneath the earth.[22] Like tombs in Palestine, the royal graves of Mycenae became places of worship, and conversely other shrines in Greece were wrongly believed to be ancient graves. In many temples, too, were shown the relics of legendary heroes and heroines, regarded with reverence or, in later and more cynical days, with amusement. The supposed tusks of the Calydonian boar slain by Meleager (page 393) were removed by Augustus from Tegea to his gardens at Rome, and a swan's egg, like the one laid by Leda to give birth to Helen, was hung with ribbons from the ceiling of a temple at Sparta.

These, however, are frivolities in total contrast with Sophocles' solemn revelation of what these demonic figures from the past still meant to Greek religion. They transcended the gulf between men and gods, and how this could happen is illustrated by the story of Oedipus, whom the gods had struck down but now lifted up. Here is not the shaken old man cut down to size whom Euripides was to present, but a hero regenerated through suffering, endurance and death. Just as Oedipus in life had possessed an awe-inspiring grandeur and more than human passion, a heroic quality already linking him with divinity, so his death also was more marvellous and terrible than any man's.

> What fate took Oedipus no living soul
> On earth, save only Theseus, can declare.

> Either the gods took him, or the earth
> In good will opened up its lightless caves.
> For with no lamentations was his passing,
> Nor sad with painful sickness, but most like
> A miracle. And if my words seem mad,
> I ask no grace of those who think them so.[23]

His final resting-place is the grave of the beneficent yet awesome Eumenides (page 194), and this play is comparable to the *Eumenides* of Aeschylus as Sophocles' drama of atonement and absolution. The comparison is maintained by the Athenian *milieu* of the event. Attempts made by Creon and Polynices to reclaim Oedipus for Thebes are frustrated (though in alternative versions he has not left that city), and his death and burial are placed at Colonus on the outskirts of Athens—or, according to other accounts, in Athens itself, where his grave was later shown in the precinct of the

Eumenides between the Acropolis and the Areopagus. There was an ancient local legend that only the kings of Athens, and when they were abolished the officials who succeeded to some of their duties, knew the exact spot. The transfiguration, the working out of god's purpose, belongs to Athens and its national hero Theseus (page 391), and Sophocles hymns his city at the contemporary height of its brilliance on sea and on land, before the Peloponnesian War brought it down.

> Last and grandest praise I sing
> To Athens, nurse of men,
> For her great pride and for the splendour
> Destiny has conferred on her . . .
>
> That lover of our land I praise again,
> Who found our horsemen fit
> For first bestowal of the curb and bit,
> To discipline the stallion in his prime;
> And strokes to which our oarsmen sing,
> Well-fitted, oak and men,
> Whose long sea-oars in wondrous rhyme
> Flash from the salt foam, following
> The hundred-footed sea-wind and the gull.[24]

Omitting such elements of patriotism, T. S. Eliot based much of his play *The Elder Statesman* (1958) upon Sophocles' *Oedipus at Colonus*. But as Claverton in this version reaches his last resting-place, he finds ghosts more implacable than the easily propitiated Eumenides of Sophocles, until he is able to accept responsibility for the influence he has exerted on others; and then he goes serenely to his death.

CHAPTER 8

ANTIGONE

>*◀◀◀●●●●●●▶▶▶*

1 The Story of the ANTIGONE *Told by Sophocles*

OUT OF the Theban palace—formerly the home of their father Oedipus—Antigone and her sister Ismene appear. Thebes has recently been besieged by an Argive army led by the Seven; their chief was the girls' exiled brother Polynices, whose brother Eteocles had driven him out of the city in order that he himself might be sole king. The two men have killed one another in single combat, but the invaders were thrown back, and now Antigone reveals to her sister a fateful edict pronounced by their uncle King Creon. For Creon has decreed that only Eteocles should receive honourable burial. The corpse of Polynices, on the other hand, since he has shown himself the enemy of his country, is to be thrown out and left lying in the plain, a prey for the birds. The penalty for anyone who attempts to bury him is death.

Antigone tells her sister she is determined to disobey this impious order, and appeals to Ismene to help her. But Ismene does not dare to agree, and Antigone casts her off—'since apparently the laws of the gods mean nothing to you'. The chorus of Theban elders enter and tell the story of the war, naming Polynices as the aggressor and describing how he and his brother met in duel and fell. Creon appears and informs the elders of his edict, declaring it a reward for patriotism and a penalty for treason. His hearers acquiesce—

238

For you can make such rulings as you will
About the living and about the dead . . .
What other order would you give us, then?
CREON: Not to take sides with any who disobey.
CHORUS: No fool is fool as far as loving death.[1]

Nevertheless, a guard now arrives with the news that some uniden-
tified person has already carried out funeral rites for Polynices, by
performing the symbolic act of sprinkling dust upon his body.
Creon dismisses the guard with threats of a horrible fate if he does
not find those who have committed this treasonable deed. But the
action prompts the elders to meditate upon man's daring and
inventiveness and resource, which bring him triumph if he obeys
divine and human laws, but ruin if he disregards them.

Words also, and thought as rapid as air,
He fashions to his good use; statecraft is his,
And his the skill that deflects the arrows of snow,
The spears of winter rain. From every wind
He has made himself secure—from all but one:
In the late wind of death he cannot stand.

O clear intelligence, force beyond all measure!
O fate of man, working both good and evil!
When the laws are kept, how proudly his city stands!
When the laws are broken, what of his city then?
Never may the anarchic man find rest at my hearth,
Never be it said that my thoughts are his thoughts.[2]

But they break off in distress as Antigone herself is led in by the
guard. Interrogated by Creon, she answers that she knew of his
decree, but had nevertheless paid burial honours to her brother
Polynices because she believed that no human law can rise above
the laws of heaven. Compared to these, she declares, her death is of
no importance. Creon swears that she shall indeed die a dreadful
death. Ismene, whom he likewise suspects, is now brought in, and
begs to die with her sister who refuses her plea, however, as 'unjust'.

Ismene then urges Creon to reprieve Antigone, but fails, even when she appeals to Antigone's betrothal to his own son Haemon. Creon sends the sisters into the palace as prisoners, denouncing both of them. The elders speak of the grim fate which has cursed the royal house of Thebes, one generation after another. But any greatness in human life, they add, brings doom, and the victims of those tricked by hope know nothing until they have walked into the flames.

Haemon enters, to plead with his father Creon for the life of his destined bride. He argues with restraint, and shows solicitousness for his father's position. But after receiving angry and stinging rebukes in reply, he goes away, telling Creon they will never see each other again. The king then discloses to the chorus what kind of death he has decided for Antigone.

> To take her where the foot of man comes not.
> There shall I hide her in a hollowed cave
> Living, and leave her just so much to eat
> As clears the city from the guilt of death.[3]

The elders, however, choose this moment to celebrate the power of love, and to stress that none can resist it: for love was what caused this present quarrel between kinsmen. When Antigone is taken out by Creon's servants, on their way to the tomb, the chorus declare that her death will bring her renown. She compares her fate to that of Niobe, daughter of Tantalus, who, after Apollo and Artemis had killed all her children, was turned to stone from weeping. But the elders attribute her end to her own overboldness, which has dashed her heavily against the lofty pedestal of Justice.

> You showed respect for the dead.
> So we for you: but power
> Is not to be thwarted so.
> Your self-sufficiency has brought you down.[4]

As Creon returns and orders her to be immured forthwith, Antigone asserts her belief in the loving welcome she will find from her father, mother and brother beyond the grave. 'The wise,' she says, 'will know my choice was right'—for even children or a husband could have been replaced, but never her brother, for whom she had performed this final service. She cries out asking what divine justice she has disobeyed, and which of the gods she can call her ally: for it is they who will judge whether she or the other side are wrong. Antigone is sent away, and the chorus, thinking of her rocky tomb, sing of Danaë who was immured by her father Acrisius of Argos but visited by Zeus in golden rain; of Lycurgus who raged at Dionysus and was pent in a rock-walled prison; and of Cleopatra—daughter of Boreas, and wife of Thracian Phineus—whom Idothea, taken by her husband in her place, so hated that she put out the eyes of Cleopatra's two sons.

Led in by a boy, the old, blind prophet Tiresias has an urgent warning for the king. The omens show that the gods are angry with Thebes, and the king's edict is the cause of this taint.

> All of the altars of the town are choked
> With leavings of the dogs and birds; their feast
> Was on that fated, fallen Polynices.
> So the gods will have no offering from us,
> Not prayer, nor flame of sacrifice. The birds
> Will not cry out a sound I can distinguish,
> Gorged with the greasy blood of that dead man . . .
> Yield to the dead![5]

Creon furiously refuses to abandon his plan, charging Tiresias with complicity in a plot fomented by seditious Thebans. This goads the prophet into declaring that Creon shall pay with his own son's life for his double sin: the detention of the dead among the living, and the imprisonment of the living among the dead. He leaves, but Creon is shaken, for he, like the chorus, has never known a prophecy of Tiresias to be wrong.

So the king decides to give way. He sets out with his servants for the plain, to bury the dead and set his niece free, while the elders pray joyfully that Dionysus may come with healing power to his beloved Thebes.

But one of his companions soon returns with a report, which is heard by the king's wife Eurydice. After burning the remains of

Polynices, Creon has found Antigone dead, by her own hand. Haemon was embracing her corpse, and his father appealed to him to come away.

> The boy looked at him with his angry eyes,
> Spat in his face and spoke no further word.
> He drew his sword, but as his father ran,
> He missed his aim. Then the unhappy boy,
> In anger at himself, leant on the blade.[6]

Eurydice passes silently into the house, and Creon enters with attendants carrying Haemon's body on a bier. As the king laments, a messenger announces that Eurydice has stabbed herself beside the altar, her last words a curse upon Creon the slayer of her children. Creon prays frantically to die, but the elders can only tell him that no mortal escapes the doom prepared for him, and that great words by proud men are punished by great blows.

2   Who is Right and Who is Wrong?

In the *Seven Against Thebes* following upon his lost *Oedipus*, Aeschylus had told the story of the strife of Eteocles and Polynices.

> Seven captains at seven gates
> Yielded their clanging arms to the god
> That bends the battle-line and breaks it.
> These two only, brothers in blood,
> Face to face in matchless rage,
> Mirroring each the other's death,
> Clashed in long combat.[7]

Aeschylus' drama was stark tragedy unrelieved by any effort towards moral justification. But one of the two brothers, Eteocles, is the earliest clearly drawn tragic hero: a man weighed down by a double load, responsibility for his city's well-being and awareness that his own grim destiny is about to be fulfilled. In Sophocles' play (*c.* 442–1 BC: we do not know if it won the prize of its year or what other tragedies were performed at the same time), the brothers are shadowy figures, for it is upon their sister Antigone that attention is centred. She had appeared in a scene spuriously included in Aeschylus' *Seven*, but her story had not been told by Homer or the lyric poets, and may be derived from some little-known local tradition. On another occasion, in the *Oedipus at Colonus* written not far from forty years later, Sophocles tells of the love that Oedipus had borne Antigone,[8] as she also loved him; yet she fails to sway his will,[9] although by means of her love she has mitigated his suffering. At the end of the *Oedipus at Colonus*, he entrusts his daughters to the Athenian Theseus, who gives them a safe conduct back to Thebes.[10]

The *Antigone* tells of the sequel. But it does not refer to what has gone before, for more rapidly than any other Greek tragedy it plunges into its own theme, in a tense opening that leads straight to catastrophe. In certain of Sophocles' other plays, for example the *Ajax* and the *Trachinian Women*, the speeches are sometimes argumentative and non-dramatic, soliloquies which develop a thesis of their own rather than the story of the myth. In the *Antigone* however the speeches, although elaborate and tending to abstraction —as the heroine, for example, appeals to her principles—are generally relevant to the character of their speaker and the remorseless development of the action. Many attempts have been made to read into what is said references to current philosophy and thought, as well as to the dangerously immoral statecraft of the day that would, before long, make its contribution to the downfall of Athens. Topical allusions have likewise been seen in choral pronouncements such as the Ode to Man (page 239)—a meditation on the precariousness of happiness and order which could be regarded as a humanist manifesto. Sophocles was well aware of the sophistical 'new thinking' which pervades Euripides (page 263), but his severe, heroic trend is to resist such undermining ways.

The myth is made into a bitter and disastrous clash between two passionately held principles. The clash involves individual human destinies, but also provides a test case with widely reverberating repercussions. The theme is collision between individuals and their political rulers—between private conscience and public authority. The protagonists also debate the competing claims of the divine law upon which the individual relies, and of those human laws with which the politician opposes her. The divine law is expressed, not in direct divine intervention, but in the existence of an inner moral standard. For Antigone, like many Greeks, appealed to 'unwritten laws', which represent something more universal than any particular law existing at any particular place or time. Heraclitus had written of a 'common law' rooted in nature,[11] and Antigone too claims super-human sanction for a natural law, the violator of which is inescapably punished.[12] At the bitter end, Creon admits this[13] (and Socrates was later quoted as repeating that the consequence was inevitable).[14] Pericles, early in the Peloponnesian War, was to speak of unwritten laws in the Funeral Speech ascribed to him by Thucydides (431 BC);[15] and Aristotle wrote of a universal law of Nature, and of 'the unwritten principles which may be said to be universally recognized'.[16] The conception was to have a long and varied future in the natural law of the Stoics which so greatly influenced the legal systems of Rome.

Antigone proclaims the eternity and validity of this code.

> Your edict, King, was strong,
> But all your strength is weakness itself against
> The immortal unrecorded laws of God.
> They are not merely now. They were, and shall be,
> Operative for ever, beyond man utterly.

> I knew I must die, even without your decree:
> I am only mortal. And if I must die
> Now, before it is my time to die,
> Surely this is no hardship: can anyone
> Living, as I live, with evil all about me,
> Think Death less than a friend? This death of mine
> Is of no importance; but if I had left my brother
> Lying in death unburied, I should have suffered.
> Now I do not.[17]

Her action is based not on general principles only, but on intense love and loyalty for her brother. These sentiments are expressed, at one point, in almost incoherent self-communing,[18] which seemed to nineteenth-century critics to imply an unromantic neglect for another and quite different obligation of Antigone—namely, her relationship with Haemon, who loved her and was to marry her (there is a ghastly tragic irony in her belief that he is unfaithful). These lines have shocked more than one critic into supposing them spurious. But if they are confused it is only because, wearily fumbling in the darkness, she is none the less instinctively certain, without the need for logical arguments, that she is right.

Shocking, too, is the manner in which, within the span of a hundred lines, Antigone and her sister Ismene are torn helplessly apart.

ISMENE: We are only women,
We cannot fight with men, Antigone!
The law is strong, we must give in to the law
In this thing, and in worse. I beg the dead
To forgive me, but I am helpless! I must yield
To those in authority. And I think it is dangerous
    business
To be always meddling.

ANTIGONE: If that is what you think,
I should not want you, even if you asked to come.
You have made your choice, you can be what you want
    to be.
But I will bury him; and if I must die,
I say that this crime is holy. I shall lie down
With him in death, and I shall be as dear
To him as he to me.
                         It is the dead,
Not the living, who make the longest demands:
We die for ever . . .
                         You may do as you like,
Since apparently the laws of the gods mean nothing
    to you.[19]

Such harshness in Antigone is not intended, as some have thought, as part of a 'tragic flaw' in her character (page 223) which strikes her down. The chorus, recalling her family's doom, are justified in finding her stubborn like her father;[20] but this is because she is acting, though no one understands her, for a principle and a passion. The test case takes an extreme form. Although the correctness of burial rites was still of great importance to the Greeks—as they had been in Homer's time—the circumstances here are technical and ritualistic. The principle is reduced to its barest terms—the sprinkling of a little dust upon the body (though tourists to Thebes were later shown 'Antigone's drag', where she dragged the body to the pyre). And then her *repetition* of this homage, whether necessary in religion or not, stresses the conservative, almost mystic deliberateness of her actions.

It has been protested that the martyr for a great and universal cause is not an appropriate central figure for a tragedy. But was this how Sophocles regarded Antigone? As the play swiftly takes its course, we see her courage, her voluntary almost ferocious self-sacrifice coming from an inner necessity, with no reward but the cold comfort of knowing that she did right, and that posterity would understand this: a true Sophoclean hero whose grandeur appears in her destruction. Whether she *ought* to have performed her deed or not the dramatist does not say. At all events, her deed brought no one happiness. But we should not expect Sophocles to point to easy rewards for goodness. Not he, but Euripides (in a play or plays that are lost) introduced a happy ending, in which the contestants were reconciled by Dionysus.

The ways in which mistakes receive their retribution are sometimes mysterious in tragedy (page 224). But this does not apply to the *Antigone*, which displays in detail how Creon paid the penalty for his own wrongful decisions. For, whether Antigone was perfect or not, Creon was at fault. This brother of Jocasta is given quite different roles in Sophocles' three Theban plays. His position in the *Antigone* is so conspicuous that he almost deserves a place in its title, for when Antigone has disappeared it is on Creon's fate that our attention is focused. This is one of a number of Greek plays in which the unity lies in the action, and in contrasted characters, rather than in the dominance of a single personality. Yet although Creon, speaking for the world, the state and expediency, has a respectable, reasonable, and therefore important case, his conception of duty is lower than Antigone's: they use the same terms to mean different things, and she has the better of him. Moreover, because his conception is not high enough, it leads him, not only into offences against common humanity, but into impiety. It was flouting the underworld gods (by creating a dangerous border-line magical state) to consign Antigone to her tomb while she was alive. Besides, these divinities had already been defrauded of Polynices, since in view of his unburied state the formal making over of his corpse to the powers beneath the earth could not take place—the ghost of one unburied could not secure admission to Hades. The gods above, too, were polluted by corpses left in their realm. All this was Creon's doing. Furthermore, he is made by Sophocles (though not by Euripides) to arrogate to himself the punishment of a woman who was under the guardianship of another, that is to say of his own son Haemon to whom she is betrothed. Haemon provides the link between the two parts of the play, because both Antigone and Creon love him.

Creon has a powerful sense of order, but with that special, classic *hubris* which makes important men do wrong (page 187) he tries to correct a moral standard over which he has no control. Perhaps he was the sort of totalitarian democrat whom Sophocles distrusted, whereas Antigone pleads the conservative cause of the great families threatened by the state. In any case, what Creon saw as justice was, in Sophocles' view, pride; and, in addition, his was the fatal error, characteristic of such persons, of accusing others of faults which are really his own.

But after the deaths of Antigone and Haemon he says, 'Alas, I have learned.' We can scarcely, in the end, withhold part of our sympathy from Creon. Nor, presumably, could the poet's audiences; although on reflection they may not have seen, in Sophocles' version of the myth, that the playwright retained much faith in worldly or national justice.

Hegel, studying Sophocles' Antigone and Creon, saw in them the logic of history, in which both are wrong and both are right. Shelley, however, declared that 'some of us have, in a prior existence, been in love with an Antigone, and that makes us find no full content in any mortal tie' (1811); to him her act was the noble violation of a prejudiced society's laws.

During the Second World War, Anouilh followed Gide, Giraudoux, and Cocteau in calling upon classical mythology to give permanence and universality to his dramatic ideas. Cocteau had written his *Antigone* in 1922, but it was in the days of enemy occupation (1942-3), when the air was full of seductive rationalizations, that Anouilh turned in his play of the same name to this same classic embodiment of refusal; though he was for some years erroneously accused of collaborationist intentions, because of the eloquent persuasiveness of Creon's arguments that power must necessarily involve compromise, and that someone always has to accept responsibility. Anouilh's Creon is the peacemaker, in contrast to the interpretation of Berthold Brecht who made Antigone into a pacifist repelled by Creon's belligerence. The Antigone of Anouilh is very far from a pacifist. Like his other heroines, she wants to live on terms so absolute and unreasonable that the world cannot find a place for her. She will not learn from experience or cease to ask too much of life: 'I am not here to understand, I am here to say *no*.'

She stands for the purity of youthful, intransigent idealism and personal conscience. But Anouilh pessimistically knows how these qualities are misunderstood, and how such misunderstandings reveal the ugliness of the world in which society's sluggish corruption will cramp the fulfilment of her ideals. Anouilh's Antigone, says Sartre, is not a 'character' in the sense that the between-the-wars theatre was a theatre of characters. She represents a naked will, a free choice; she shows how man is 'hurled into a life already complete which yet is his own enterprise and in which he can never have a second chance; where he must play his cards and take risks whatever the cost'. At a time when there was a demand for new codes of values, Antigone, invoking no divine standards or interventions, rejects the old codes; she is the Outsider, who did it 'for no one: *for myself*'.

Berthold Brecht's *Antigone* (1948) consists of Hölderlin's translation of Sophocles with new passages added, and a prologue set in 1945 Berlin. A more recent English version by Christopher Logue (1961) has inspired the comment that of all classical heroines Antigone seems to be the one with most to say to the present generation. But of Creon this playwright gives a new interpretation. The king is here a ruthless revolutionary commissar, claiming his entitlement to exploit the corpse of Polynices—as a bourgeois court of law would not be entitled to—on grounds not only of *Realpolitik*, but of Marxist historical necessity.

PART V

HERACLES AND DIONYSUS

CHAPTER 9

HERACLES WHO CONQUERS DEATH

〓〓〓〓〓〓❯◗❤❤❤❤❤❤❤❤◖❮〓〓〓〓〓〓

1   The Story of the ALCESTIS *Told by Euripides*

IN FRONT of the house of King Admetus at Pherae, Apollo tells how, in return for the kindness shown him while he served as the king's herdsman—a penance sent him by Zeus for killing the Cyclopes—he has saved Admetus from death, to which the king had been sentenced by Artemis for forgetting to sacrifice to her at his wedding feast.

But Admetus would only be saved on the condition that someone else shall die in his place. No one but his wife Alcestis was willing to sacrifice herself for Admetus, and she lies within the house, breathing her last. For Death (Thanatos) is approaching—and now arrives, to demand why Apollo is present in a house of mourning. Apollo pleads in vain for the life of Alcestis, but declares that there will soon come one more powerful than Death, who will rob him of his prey. But Death, unmoved, goes in to do his work. The chorus of citizens of Pherae lament that Alcestis is beyond all saving. Only Asclepius could have saved her—if he had not died himself:

> If the eyes
> Of Phoebus' son were opened
> Still, if he could have come
> And left the dark chambers,
> The gates of Hades.

> He upraised those who were stricken
> Down, until from the hand of God
> The flown bolt of thunder hit him.[1]

A maid comes out of the house and tells of the noble sadness of Alcestis when she understood that her day of death was near.

> This is what Admetus and the house are losing. Had
> He died, he would have lost her, but in this escape
> He will keep the pain. It will not ever go away.[2]

The citizens of Pherae pray to Zeus and Apollo for help, denying that marriage brings more pleasure than woe. Now Alcestis is brought out of the house on a couch, supported by her husband. As she bids him farewell, Admetus declares he will never marry or rejoice again, and would willingly have gone beneath the earth to bring her back. Her little boy, too, grieves for her; and she is carried inside the house to die, while the men of Pherae declare that, at Sparta and Athens alike, poets will sing in her honour.

> Ah! That I had the power
> To bring you back to the light
> From the dark halls of Hades,
> And from the waves of Cocytus
> With the oar of the river of hell!
> O, you only,
> O dearest of women,
> You only dared give your life
> For the life of your lord in Hades!
> Light rest the earth above you,
> O woman.
> If your lord choose another bridal-bed
> He shall be hateful to me
> As to your own children.[3]

Heracles enters, on his way towards Thrace to fetch the wild horses of Diomede as one of the labours he must perform for Eurystheus of Tiryns. When he asks his friend Admetus why he is mourning, the visitor is led to suppose, by evasive answers, that the dead woman is someone other than Alcestis. Nevertheless, Heracles wants to leave at once, fearing that his presence must be inconvenient at such a time. But Admetus, not wishing to be thought inhospitable, insists that the guest should stay. The citizens praise their king's hospitality, and his richness in flocks, which even Apollo himself has tended.

Admetus comes out with the funeral procession, and is met by his father Pheres with offerings for Alcestis' tomb. Admetus rejects his sympathy and gifts, and reviles both his father and his mother, since both are so old, for having refused to die for him. Pheres defends himself—with a reminder that Admetus still has Alcestis' brother Acastus to reckon with. Cursing his parents, Admetus leaves with the body.

The servant who has been looking after Heracles appears, and complains of the coarse, drunken manners of their distinguished visitor. Heracles, somewhat fuddled, comes on to the stage, and rebukes the servant for his melancholy expression. But the man replies by letting him know that it is Alcestis who is dead. Shocked— and remorseful for his own behaviour—Heracles declares that he will repay Admetus for his kindness by bringing back Alcestis from the grave: he will find black-robed Death drinking a death-draught from the victims slain beside her tomb, and will wrestle with him until Death yields up his victim. As Heracles goes, Admetus and the chorus arrive and exchange lamentations. He cries that his wife's fate is more fortunate than his own, and the men of Pherae tell of the terrible power of Necessity, against whom even Orpheus and Apollo have no herbs or drugs—without her, Zeus himself cannot fulfil his will.

But now Heracles returns, leading a veiled woman by the hand. Apologizing for his untimely appearance as guest he asks Admetus if this woman, whom he has won as a prize at certain games, may stay at Pherae until he himself returns from Thrace. Though her head is covered, the woman reminds Admetus of Alcestis, and he is deeply distressed by this reminder of his dead wife. But Heracles makes him take her hand in his, and reveals that she is Alcestis whom he has rescued from the grave; though she cannot speak to her

husband, he adds, until on the third day her obligations to the gods
of the underworld will have been washed away.

> So now
> Take her and lead her inside, and for the rest of time,
> Admetus, be just. Treat your guests as they deserve.[4]

Admetus presses him in vain to stay, and orders general rejoicing.

> For now we shall make our life again, and it will be
> A better one. I was lucky. That I cannot deny.[5]

2 *A New Look at the Myths*

The *Alcestis* was performed in 438 BC, when Euripides was in his
mid-forties. Its place in the programme was not that of a tragedy;
it was acted as the fourth of four dramas, in the terminal position
usually reserved for a satyr-play (page 173). The *Alcestis* was not
quite that, yet it was described in ancient times as 'rather of the
satyric order': no ordinary tragedy, the work is a disconcerting and
somewhat fantastic mixture of tragic and comic, such as Euripides
quite often attempts. But in the *Alcestis* these two genres are brought
together in so unassimilated a form that dramatic unity is strained—
although this is part of the piquancy which makes the play appeal
to modern audiences.

The myth is a composite one, comprising the folk-tales of a
bride's sacrifice for her husband and of the hero's successful
encounter with death. Alcestis is the heroine of another story also—
one of those in which extraordinary tasks are performed by wooers
(page 394), in this case by Admetus who had Apollo to help him.
The present theme, of her self-sacrificing love for Admetus, had
already been handled, probably as a satyr-play, by one of the earliest
Attic dramatists Phrynichus.

In this myth Artemis, who had condemned Admetus to death, is a
deity of the lower world akin to Hecate or Persephone (to whose
agency, in some versions, the restoration of Alcestis was due).
Artemis is also the patron goddess of Pherae, where her sacred

prehistoric tomb was shown, and where there were no doubt annual rites corresponding with the myth (page 158). Pherae was strategically placed near the south-eastern end of the Thessalian plain. At certain epochs, and especially when it owned the port of Pagasae, this town controlled the export of corn from Thessaly, a land which was as rich in grain as in horses and cattle; for example, a generation or two after Euripides' time, Pherae itself was to have a brief period of far-reaching authority, under its king Jason. In the sixth century BC the Thessalians had been among the leaders of Greece, and they had also possessed an important prehistoric culture, of which these myths and folk-tales are probably an echo.

'If I wrote on this theme as an illustration of the husband-wife relationship,' Jean-Paul Sartre once remarked, 'my version would imply the whole story of female emancipation': the woman chooses the tragic course when her husband has refused to face death—and when she returns, she becomes the powerful partner, because Admetus will always be sneered at. Euripides does not deduce this final turn of events. Yet his play is, in other respects, a lesson in sex-equality, for this was a subject dear to Euripides' heart, and the *Alcestis* is one of a group of his dramas dominated by problems of married life and by women experiencing various strong emotions—here, self-sacrificing wifely love. Some have seen the present heroine as frigid, anti-social, humourless—'that frightful figure, the thoroughly good woman'. But that does not do justice to this un-theatrical, direct, instinctively feminine, domestic heroine, uttering not just conventionally high-minded but poignant words:

Admetus, Admetus . . .
You see what is happening to me now . . . .

    Yet this is no small thing,
For me to die. I am young, these years have been
  pleasant.
Your father and mother, who failed you,
Might have died for you, and it would have been noble:

For they had no other son, nor any hope
Of children after you. They might have saved you,
And you and I could have lived out all of our days,
And you would not be left alone now
With these poor children...

But I suppose some god
Managed this thing to turn out as it has—
And so let it be.[6]

To return to Sartre's proposed ending, everyone is *not*—society
being what it is—going to sneer at her husband. Yet what does
Euripides think of this man who allows his wife to sacrifice herself?
Admetus is a good man, with all the conventional virtues such as
nobility and hospitality—which had far greater moral significance
than now. He is a typical product of his class, and Heracles thinks
him a fine fellow. But we can say, without anachronistic calls upon
Teutonic or Christian chivalry, that Admetus was *meant* to seem
insensitive and selfish—unconsciously, like Torvand Helmer in
Ibsen's *Doll's House*. Euripides characteristically unveils the weak
spot in the myth, which is the flaw in Admetus' character. Yet such
tragedy as is to be found in this world of fantasy lies in the clash
between these unheroic qualities and his very real misery at the loss
of his beloved wife, who is dying for him—and who may, in the end,
be 'happier' than he is.

Woman, whoever you are, you are like Alcestis—
Did you know it?—the same height, the same bearing—

Heracles, Heracles!
For God's sake, take her away!
I am beaten: do not stand here torturing me!
I look at her, and it is Alcestis that I see!
I look at her, and my heart splits, my
Heart is an agony of weeping: Go,
Take her, go!

I think that for the first time I know what unhappiness is.[7]

The story has often been imitated; indeed the first Renaissance attempt at tragedy in the ancient style, Trissino's *Sofonisba* (1515), was written under its influence. The *Alcestis* was the subject of operas by Handel and Gluck, and plays by Alfieri and Herder. A version by Wieland was strongly criticised by Goethe who compared its false sentimentality unfavourably with the realism of Euripides. To Robert Browning, the Greek play was 'that strangest, saddest, sweetest song', and in his retelling of the myth (*Balaustion's Adventure*, 1871) he forecasts, with more specific optimism than Euripides, the change of character which these events would produce in Admetus:

> Renovated now—
> Able to do now all herself had done,
> Risen to the height of her.

Thornton Wilder's *Alcestiade* became the libretto of an opera. T. S. Eliot, who has written his plays within the framework supplied by Greek drama (page 198), used the *Alcestis* as 'a point of departure' for *The Cocktail Party* (1949), as he used another tragi-comedy of Euripides, the *Ion*, for *The Confidential Clerk* (1953). In *The Cocktail Party* Lavinia, who 'returns' (though not from the dead), has shown little of the generosity of Alcestis; but she, as well as her husband Edward, are compelled (like Admetus) to undergo moral introspection. The mysterious, god-like Reilly is inclined, like Heracles, to drink and sing in the house of 'death'—which is here not death, but a failure of life. For this is Greek drama with Christianity and psychiatry added:

> It is a serious matter
> To bring someone back from the dead . . .
> Ah, but we die to each other daily.

The interest in human character, which is so manifest in the

Alcestis, was one of Euripides' peculiar contributions to tragedy. At the height of Athenian imperialism, society's values were being called in question, and the experience of the individual soul was receiving ever more attention. Euripides knows the stinging gales that try to beat the individual down, and he feels compassion with man's strivings to rise above the deadly circumstances that encompass him. Pity and fear, said Aristotle, are the emotions properly stimulated by tragedy (page 227), and pity aroused by undeserved misfortune seemed to him to make the best plays. To Aristotle, then, the most tragic of poets was Euripides, who is the first exponent of pity and demonstrator of its validity. The idea was in the air, for an Altar of Pity was erected in the Athenian market-place only a decade or two after the *Alcestis* was written. Yet Euripides was under no illusion concerning the difficulties that this quality imposed. As Orestes says in his *Electra*:

> Uneducated men are pitiless,
> But we who are educated pity much. And we pay
> A high price for being intelligent. Wisdom hurts.[8]

In the *Alcestis* there is a rather queer happy ending, but many of Euripides' other plays reveal an utterly tragic viewpoint with no consolation or comfort for the unmerited afflictions that abound. Man is the helpless victim either of injustice or of irresponsible natural powers, and the blind or demonic forces which cause the chaos of events reveal no moral meaning or rational pattern. All but the earliest plays of Euripides handle their mythical themes against the background of the Peloponnesian War (431–404 BC), in which Athens suffered grievously, deteriorated sharply in moral standards, and went down in defeat. Veering between grim realism and unfocused *Weltschmerz*, the dramatist saw the miseries in his myths as shocking but true. Yet he remained a humanitarian amid the senseless horrors of war.

> How are ye blind,
> Ye treaders down of cities, ye that cast
> Temples to desolation and lay waste

Tombs, the untrodden sanctuaries where lie
The ancient dead; yourselves so soon to die!⁹*

Accordingly, the heroes of the Trojan War are often scarcely more
attractive in Euripides than they are in *Troilus and Cressida*. Agamemnon, in the *Iphigenia at Aulis*, is feeble and contemptible.
Achilles is a pampered, boastful youth who dreads a scene, and
Menelaus is constantly satirized as uxorious, degraded, and self-
centred. They are very unlike the gently noble personages of
Goethe's *Iphigenie*. Among Euripides' women, too, are many
notorious horrors; the high-souled Alcestis is a rarity beside the
hate-consumed maniac Medea, and the no less murderous sex-
starved Electra.

Euripides' leading characters, and particularly the women, are
endowed with psychological interest, at whatever expense of greatness. In the centre of the myths, as he retells them, are man and
woman, and towards the end of a play, before a divine solution is
provided (page 268), their strong feelings are climactically displayed.
And yet the humanity of these characters seems curiously diluted by
the sophistic arguments which rage—making Euripides an historically
significant child of the age which also produced Socrates, as well as
natural philosophers and many professional hair-splitters. Thus in
the *Alcestis*, the quarrel between Admetus and his father Pheres is
conducted with remorseless home truths on both sides. 'Does your
father really owe you his life?' asks Pheres.

That is no law of the Greeks, my father told me of no
    such law.

Dear boy, listen:
For happiness or unhappiness, every man is born for
    himself.
I gave you all you deserved, slaves, subjects, money,
And you'll soon have my lands, as I had them from my
    father.
Then how have I cheated you? How have I hurt you?

* For an alternative translation of this passage, see above, page 68.

Die for you—?
Don't you die for me, and I'll not die for you!
You love the daylight: do you think your father does
    not?
Our stay in the world below will be long enough.
Life, I take it, is short: it is none the less
    agreeable.
And as for dying—
Well, when it came to dying, did you not
Shudder away from it? Are you dead now?
Or did you not shove off the burden on your pretty wife?
'Coward!' You call me a coward? You,
Less brave than the girl who died for you? A
    cautious hero!

But you know best:
A gallant road you've found to immortality!
Marry wife after wife, first making sure that they'll
    die for you—
That's all . . .

God, these young men! How they pray for life![10]

This is unromantic; yet it adds a new topicality to the myth. For Euripides has a clinical eye for the seamy side of the contemporary scene, the coldly calculating, profit-and-loss attitude that was abroad. All Greek tragedians show something of a lawyer's spirit; their stage is a court-room (just as the court-room itself is the scene of many a play and film today). Everyone is judged, and Euripides uses mythology to frame displays of unscrupulous, quasi-forensic advocacy.

    Like Socrates, he was a little early for his time, since he won few prizes before his death and it was the young who loved him best. Later thinkers have either, like Goethe, regarded Euripides as supreme, or have denounced him as a wrecker of classical poetry. Schlegel and Nietzsche declared that the logic of his plays coils round itself and bites its own tail. Nietzsche also attacks him as an incorrigible moralist; and it is true that Euripides seeks to persuade, infusing into the myths a new, contemporary, didactic morality. After its prosy realism, the lyric passages—which were accompanied, it seems, by music of the latest and most original kind[11]—provide, as in Ibsen, a strangely contrasted beauty and relief.

No one is more aware than Euripides of the sweet dangers lurking in the Athenian love of disputations, which he so fully shared. 'The art of over-subtle words,' Phaedra calls it in the *Hippolytus*,[12] and in the *Bacchae* the same conservative distrust is voiced by Tiresias.

> We do not trifle with divinity.
> No, we are the heirs of customs and traditions
> hallowed by age and handed down to us
> by our fathers. No quibbling logic can topple *them*,
> whatever subtleties this clever age invents.[13]

Characters of Sophocles had said much the same, but Euripides was playing with fire, for he was far more tempted to recast the myths into just this disputatious shape. By his contriving, the myths are brought down to the new and colder light of earth, and in the give-and-take of argument less holds are barred than hitherto.

For a long time now, in intellectual and moralizing circles, there had been criticism of Homer and Hesiod for depicting the gods as imperfect and immoral.

The average early Greek must have accepted the myths as the traditional history of his race—if not right in every detail, at least substantially true—since people had been telling them for centuries past. And this, no doubt, continued to be the view of many. But the gradual growth of philosophical thinking, in which at first myth and rationality remained side by side (page 110) as they still do in most people's thoughts today, introduced more astringent doctrines. Stesichorus of Himera explained that Homer was wrong in his facts (page 49), and then Pythagoras of Samos, if reported correctly, consigned the two poets to Hades for their lies about the gods.[14] His contemporary, Xenophanes of Colophon (born *c.* 570 BC), refused to believe that there could be deities performing actions which, if human beings had performed them, would be regarded as disgraceful.

> Homer and Hesiod fathered on the gods' divinity
> All deeds most blameful and shameful that here on
>   earth there be—
> Yea, thieving and deceiving and adultery.[15]

Xenophanes maintained that this error arose from the fallacious idea that the gods must be like ourselves (page 62).

> If oxen, or lions, or horses had hands like men,
>   they too,
> If they could fashion pictures or statues they could
>   hew,
> They would shape in their own image each face and
>   form divine—
> Horses' gods like horses, like kine the gods of kine.
> 'Snub-nosed are the Immortals, and black', the
>   Ethiops say;
> But 'No,' the Thracians answer, 'red-haired, with
>   eyes of grey.'[16]

But surely, Xenophanes said—as contemporary Hebrews were also saying—there is one god, and he is not fashioned in the likeness of man.

Next, in the fifth century, Pindar struck a clear distinction between myths that were true and those that were false. Odysseus for example, he says, won more fame than he deserved, because of Homer.

> On his falsehood and his winged cunning
> A majesty lies. Art tricks and deceives us with tales,
> And blind is the heart of the multitude of men.[17]

And men can only 'trust to time and the future to sort out the true from the false'.[18]

This, then, was the task set themselves by compilers and researchers such as Hecataeus of Miletus (*c.* 500 BC), forerunners of the great historians, when they attempted to expurgate and systematise. The historians themselves approached the problem from different points of view dictated by their own tastes. Herodotus wanted, if possible, to save the picturesque myths, yet added the comment that, although he was bound to say the things that were said, he was not bound to believe them[19]—but 'anything may happen'.[20] Thucydides, on the other hand, while in fact accepting many mythical traditions as historical, was fully prepared in principle to recognize a myth as unauthentic and unacceptable.

And so the way was clear for the complete scepticism of Euripides' contemporary, Critias, who after the downfall of Athens in 404 led an extreme right-wing régime in the city until his murder in the following year. From his tragedy the *Sisyphus*, there survives a long fragment offering a thoroughgoing rationalization of men's belief in the gods.

'There was a time when the life of man was disordered, and like that of wild beasts controlled by brute strength. There was then no reward for the good nor any punishment for the bad. Next, men conceived the idea of imposing laws as instruments of punishment, so that justice may be sole ruler and hold violence in check. If any erred, he was punished. Then, since the laws only prevented the commission of deeds of *open* violence, men continued to commit secret crimes. At this point it is my belief that some far-seeing and resolute man saw the need for a deterrent which would have effect even when *secret* deeds were done or contemplated. So he introduced the idea of divinity, of a god always active and vigorous, hearing and seeing with his mind . . . all that men say or do.'[21]

This pointed the way to other explanations of the myths. Epicureans agreed that such stories were fabrications to bolster authority; while Euhemerus of Messene (*c.* 300 BC) maintained—to the subsequent satisfaction of Christians—that the 'gods' were men of past epochs whose deeds had attracted worshippers to them: deriving the

Artemis-Actaeon myth (page 141), for example, from the story of some young man who had been ruined by the expense of maintaining his pack of hounds. In like fashion Vico (d. 1736) attempted to reduce culture-heroes to class symbols of society, and Herbert Spencer maintained that the veneration of gods had arisen from people's fear of ghosts.

The interpretation of Critias was very far from the attitude of Aeschylus and Sophocles; to the ideas of Euripides it was closer, but there was still a difference between them. Euripides leaves the gods as identifiable units, yet not as gods in any traditional sense. Heracles in the *Alcestis* is a disconcerting mixture of superhuman power and low comedy, Apollo in the *Ion* is a dishonest though not ill-natured seducer, Dionysus in the *Bacchae* (page 284) personifies a psychological force which deeply affects the human condition. As ethics rather than theology, religion interests Euripides very much. But his attitude to it is one of inquiry and on many occasions his characters echo his own manifest questionings about the nature of the gods. For example Heracles, in spite of his drunken boorishness in the *Alcestis*, repeats in the play named after himself Xenophanes' assertion that the gods cannot do wrong.

> I cannot think gods do adultery.
> Nay, I have ever scorned, and ever shall,
> To dream a god can bind a god with chains,
> Or one be born by Fate another's master.
> For God, if God indeed, has need of nothing.
> These are but poets' old unhappy tales.[22]

And in the same play, Theseus contests a conventional view when he denies that a mortal can pollute the gods.[23]

Can it be supposed, however, we read from a fragment of the *Melanippe*,[24] that the gods bother to keep a record of every man's deeds? Yet the answer seems to be that for God to neglect human beings would be inconsistent with his nature. But then again the chorus of the *Electra* speaks like Critias in hazarding that stories which terrify men are useful to ensure their worship of the gods,[25] and another passage, from the lost *Bellerophon*, contains the familiar cry that the prevalence of evil proves no gods exist.

> Doth some one say that there be gods above?
> There are not; no, there are not. Let no fool,
> Led by the old false fable, thus deceive you.
> Look at the facts themselves, yielding my words
> No undue credence: for I say that kings
> Kill, rob, break oaths, lay cities waste by fraud,
> And doing thus are happier than those
> Who live calm pious lives day after day . . .
>   All divinity
> Is built up from our good and evil luck.[26]

In the *Hecuba* the herald Talthybius is moved by the aged queen's sorrows to replace the gods by this Luck or Chance[27]—the preferred divinity of the centuries that lay immediately ahead (page 227).

Euripides, though expressing his plays in mythological terms, rejected the myths as a true picture of the gods: they are a shadowy stream on which we drift.[28] Yet he found them indispensable as the means for presenting problems that troubled him. He welcomed in them—well-known and obscure tales alike—a framework capable of carrying his new and sensational remodellings of values and motives and characters. His alleged 'sin' against the myth was to inject new life into the old stories, as has been often done before and since. By invigorating them with contemporary, fifth-century tensions and everyday problems, he made them tragic all over again.

What did he believe himself? Many contemporaries regarded this destroyer of illusions as impious, like his friend and admirer Socrates; and this may have been partly why, near the end of his life, the playwright went to live far away from Athens, in Macedonia. But he was not so much impious as a disbeliever in easy or complete solutions. It was, after all, in the best tradition to show the difficulty in this flawed world of justifying the 'actions of the gods', especially in doubtful particular cases when it was painfully hard for their human victims to understand what they ought to do. But Euripides, thinking of newer contests of right and wrong than the old divine vengeances, made the problem more harrowing than ever before. For he approached it as a student rather than a pious believer; his treatment of the myths was that of a restless thinker—not untypical of contemporary intellectuals—who refused to settle down to any single system of belief.

The consequent discordance, or irresolution, of his thought is revealed by a strange feature of certain plays, the god or goddess who intervenes at the end, the 'deus ex machina' who cuts all knots. This divine solvent is for the devout and for those who prefer a happy ending, whereas the less conventionally-minded could supply a less happy conclusion for themselves if they stop reading, or watching, the play at the point where the divinity appears. Thus the solution of the *Alcestis* is provided by the superhuman intervention of Heracles. In this case, however, the 'deus ex machina' is not purely Euripidean, since he is derived from earlier folk-tales and is therefore an already-existing feature of the plot—though Euripides makes a rather eerie use of the tradition. But the *Electra*, the *Hippolytus*, the *Andromache* and the *Orestes* end with epiphanies of a more mechanical nature. These devices introduce new thoughts, and possess a strange and often poignant beauty of their own; but they terminate the action so abruptly, and in a fashion so far removed from a logical modern 'curtain', that a whiff of schizophrenia is left in the air.

For Euripides was a difficult man. A poet, George Seferis (d. 1971), has written about his thoughts and the legends of his life.

> He lived and grew old between the burning of Troy
> And the hard labour in Sicilian quarries.
>
> He was fond of rocky caves along the beach;
> Liked pictures of the sea;
> The veins of man he saw as it were a net
> Made by the gods for trapping us like beasts.
> This net he tried to pierce.
> He was difficult in every way. His friends were few.
> The time arrived and he was torn to pieces by dogs.

3   *The Harrowing of Hell*

The principal comic element in the *Alcestis* (page 256) is provided
by so exalted a figure as Heracles. He is jovial and powerful and
generous, a rough and cheerfully stoic hero. But he does not escape
the ironical disenchantment of the poet, and he is summed up thus
by the servant who looked after him.

> I have known all sorts of foreigners who have come in
> from all over the world here to Admetus' house,
> and I have served them dinner, but I never yet
> have had a guest as bad as this to entertain.
> In the first place, he could see the master was in
>   mourning,
> but inconsiderately came in anyway.
> Then, he refused to understand the situation
> and be content with anything we could provide,
> but when we failed to bring him something, demanded it,
> and took a cup with ivy on it in both hands
> and drank the wine of our dark mother, straight, until
> the flame of the wine went all through him, and heated
>   him,
> and then he wreathed branches of myrtle on his head
> and howled, off key.[29]

And the god himself, the buffoon-like strong man provoking laughter
tempered by awe who occurs so frequently in the folk-tales of the
world, has given us some gems of philosophical pastiche.

> There you are, friend: straight from a first class
>   authority.
> Ponder, rejoice and have a drink.
> Today is today. Tomorrow will be
> Tomorrow. And so on.[30]

Euripides is modernizing an old joke. There was traditional sanction
—reflected in early epic parodies, the *Margites* and the *Battle of
Frogs and Mice*—for this jocular treatment of the beloved *starker*

Hans, with his vices (regarded as pardonable) of gluttony, quick temper and lecherousness.

Though Heracles was sometimes worshipped as a god, perhaps he had once lived upon the earth, for his name 'Hera's glory' is human, and in the *Odyssey* his shade was in Tartarus. He is a hero (page 235) rather than a god, and hero-tales are a distinct branch of myth (or, some might say, not myths at all). His successive triumphs over brute force, later treated as vindications of truth and justice, are embodied in the tales of the Twelve Labours: a conglomerate collection, many of them characteristic of the tasks set to mythical candidates for kingship and for the hand of the king's daughter. He performed the Labours at the orders of Eurystheus of Argos—or, according to the *Alcestis*, of neighbouring Tiryns, the fortress of which Heracles if he ever lived was perhaps the prince. These deeds were celebrated in major epic poems, which are now lost. We learn also of the *Exploits of Heracles* by Pisander of Rhodes in the sixth century BC, and of another version by Herodotus' cousin Panyassis of Halicarnassus a century later. In early visual art, too, Heracles was the most popular of the heroes. A New York amphora shows his slaying of the centaur Nessus in *c.* 660 BC, and before the sixth century he was depicted by Attic, Argive, Corinthian and Spartan artists, as well as at Thebes, which sought to take over his saga as its own. The fifth-century metopes on the Temple of Zeus at Olympia portrayed his labours as symbolizing the obstacles which man must overcome if he is to realize his powers at their greatest, and the sophist Prodicus of Ceos was praised by Plato for showing Heracles as one who had chosen the hard path of right action, in preference to a life of ease.

Six of the labours of Heracles tell of triumphs in his own Peloponnesian area: his conquests of the Nemean lion (Stesichorus already dresses him in a lion's skin), the Hydra of Lerna (a favourite theme of sixth-century art), the boar of Erymanthus, the hind of Ceryneia, and the birds of Stymphalus; and the cleansing of the stables of Augeas at Elis. Then there was the slaying of the Cretan bull, the capture of the horses of Diomede in Thrace (to which Heracles is on his way in the *Alcestis*), and the seizing of the girdle of Hippolyte, queen of the Amazons. Finally there are three Labours which relate to the climax of Heracles' achievements, the conquest of Death. Far away in the west (and his cult was strong in Sicily and south Italy) he slays the triple-bodied monster Geryon; at the world's end he takes the golden apples of the Hesperides, which Gaea (Earth) had given Hera as a wedding-present; and he goes down to Hades and steals the watchdog Cerberus. These three tales are elaborations of a story that Heracles once encountered Hades and defeated him: the tradition, mentioned in the *Iliad*,[31] which provides the *Alcestis* with its theme.

For Admetus' sake
We must bring Alcestis back to her house from the dead.
I will follow the black god,
Old Thanatos, to her tomb: for there
I shall find him drinking the blood of the lustral victims.
And I will wrestle with Death,
I will crack his charnel body between my arms
Until he yields her up.
But if he is gone,
If he leaves the blood of offering untasted,
I will go down to the sad streets of the Dead,
To Persephone and the dim Lord of Hell, and there
Beg for her life.
And I
Will bring Alcestis back to the good sunlight,
Back to my friend who welcomed me to his house
In spite of his loss.[32]

This Harrowing of Hell was an ancient story. It had been a main subject of the Sumerian Gilgamesh poems (page 95). In that collection (as in the Mesopotamian visual arts also) there are killings of lions and the giant-dragon Humbaba and other beasts, as well as many other scenes to which the labours of Heracles are akin. There are also wrestlings with death and with the underworld, which it was the prime purpose first of Enkidu (who fails) and then of Gilgamesh to overcome. How these stories came westward may be suggested, in part, by Egyptian reports (noted by Here-dotus) that the home of Heracles was Phoenicia; and there is much on the same subject in the literature of Phoenician Ugarit (page 49).

Then, in the ancient world, there are many and varied Harrowers of Hell—Heracles, Theseus, Dionysus, Orpheus and Aeneas (pages 310, 328); and so on to Cuchulain in Ireland, to Arthur, Gwydion and Amathaon in Britain, and to Ogier le Danois in Brittany. The idea recurred in fourteenth-century miracle plays of York, Chester, Wakefield and Coventry, and in the epic of Langland. Expressed in terms of the rescue of Adam and Eve, its sanction was often the apocryphal *Gospel of Nicodemus*, an appendix of the *Acts of Pilate*: 'remove, O princes, your gates, and be ye lift up ye doors of Hell, and the King of Glory shall come in'—the scene is shown on one of the south windows of King's College Chapel at Cambridge. In Shakespeare's latest plays, again, although mythology involving religious language and doctrine is avoided, there are many variations upon the theme of the dead returning to life; many characters reappear as if from death to life, and in the *Pericles* Thaisa is literally recovered from the dead.

The supreme rescuer, to the Greeks, was Heracles, whose 'Lives' came to resemble the Gospel portraits of Christ. Though Euripides, in imperfectly serious vein, makes the rescue of Alcestis a mere incident in the hero's exploits, the Harrowing of Hell was thought of as the greatest and hardest of his labours. It was because of such triumphs that Heracles rose to heaven (page 235).

> It was Heracles, Alcmene's son, who scaled Olympus,
>   who knew
> all earth, and sounded the deeply veiled abyss of the
>   grey sea
> to make easy the passage for sailors.
> Now he dwells in bliss and magnificence beside
> the lord of the aegis, honoured and beloved among
>   immortals, with Hebe to wife,
> master in a house of gold and son-in-law to Hera.

To him beside the Electran gate his citizens have
    dedicated a feast
and the freshly built circle of altars; there we feed
the fires for his eight bronze-armoured sons who died,
sons that Megara bore him, Creon's* daughter.
In their honour the flames rise up at sunset to shine
    night-long
and beat the air with billows of fragrant smoke.[33]

Heracles partook of divinity; and Pindar proclaims why this is.

If men are brave, or wise, it is by the divinity
in them. How else could Heracles'
hands have shaken the club against the trident,
when by Pylos' gate Posidon stood over against him,
and Phoebus strode on him with the silver bow in his
    hands poised?
neither the death-god Hades rested the staff
wherewith he marshals mortal bodies, of men perished,
down the hollow street.[34]

And so Heracles became the exemplar of Euhemerus' doctrines that
all gods had really once been men (page 265), and phenomena such
as Roman emperor-worship were deduced from the same idea.

    Although Euripides, as part of his complex approach to the
Olympians, chooses to show us a hero who is partly comic, his great
play *Heracles* displays a figure wholly tragic. For his mighty strength
is ruined by the madness which has come upon him after returning
from Hades. He has slain his own children, and plans to slay himself:
from which he is dissuaded by Theseus of Athens. Sophocles, too,
follows this same familiar Greek pattern of showing that no one is
all-powerful: the Heracles of his *Trachinian Women*, also, is
fatally attacked by the poisoned robe given him by his wife Deianira,
who believed that its spell was not poisonous but would win back
his affection.

---

* An earlier king of Thebes than the Creon who was Jocasta's brother (page 246);
though the two are sometimes confused.

Such themes enabled dramatists to make tragic material out of Heracles. But to later generations he was rather the fighting superman. Hellenistic sculptors liked to display his baroque, bulging muscles; and in the Renaissance he provided favourite subjects for Michelangelo, Pollaiuolo and many others, including, particularly, the modellers of exquisite bronze statuettes, such as Andrea Briosco (Riccio) of Padua.

CHAPTER 10

DIONYSUS WHO GIVES ECSTASY

1   The Story of the BACCHAE *Told by Euripides*

DISGUISED in human form the god Dionysus, son of Zeus, stands before the royal palace at Thebes, beside the grave of his mother Semele—slain by lightning, because she slept with Zeus and Hera was jealous. Dionysus is back from his triumphant progress through Asia, where he established his dances, mysteries and rites. He has come to refute the slander of his mother's sisters, including Agave of whom King Pentheus of Thebes is the son. For these women have denied that Zeus was Dionysus' father, and because of this they have been stung with frenzy and made to wander upon Mount Cithaeron, crazed, in Dionysus' service. Pentheus, too, has refused to acknowledge the divinity of Dionysus, and the god declares that Pentheus, like every other man in Thebes, will be forced to recognize that he is god indeed.

The chorus of Maenads—Asian women who have followed Dionysus—enter and pronounce a litany to the god. They warn the uninitiated to depart, and praise devotees for their good fortune. The miraculous birth of the god is described, and then the strange costume and ivy-crowns of his worship, and the wands and dances and music—

> the strict beat of the taut hide
> And the squeal of the wailing flute . . .

He drops to the earth from the running packs.
He wears the holy fawn-skin. He hunts the wild
    goat and kills it.

He delights in the raw flesh . . .
With milk the earth flows! It flows with wine!
It runs with the nectar of bees!
Like frankincense in its fragrance
Is the blaze of the torch he bears.
Flames float out from his trailing wand.[1]

The old blind prophet Tiresias enters*, and then the aged Cadmus,
Pentheus' father; both are in the costume of the god and dedicated
to dance with the Maenads in his name. But King Pentheus, who
now appears, is greatly angered to learn that the women of
Thebes have gone to honour the newly arrived stranger upon the
mountain.

I am told a foreigner has come to Thebes
from Lydia, one of those charlatan magicians,
with long yellow curls smelling of perfumes,
with flushed cheeks and the spells of Aphrodite
in his eyes. His days and nights he spends
with women and girls, dangling before them the joys
of initiation in his mysteries.
But let me bring him underneath that roof
and I'll stop his pounding with his wand and tossing
his head. By god, I'll have his head cut off![2]

His wrath is increased at seeing Cadmus and Tiresias preparing to
follow the women to the hills. But they warn him to be wise, and
Cadmus recalls the dreadful death of his cousin Actaeon, torn to
pieces by his own hands because he boasted himself a greater hunter
than Artemis. The women of Asia call upon the goddess Holiness
to note the impiety of Pentheus' words against Dionysus.

---

* Although these events belong to an earlier mythical generation than Oedipus (page
215), Tiresias is already of advanced age.

> These blessings he gave:
> Laughter to the flute
> And the loosing of cares
> When the shining wine is spilled
> At the feast of the gods,
> And the wine-bowl casts its sleep
> On feasters crowned with ivy.[3]

They urge Dionysus to lead them to Cyprus, island of Aphrodite, and to Pieria, haunt of the Muses, and to Olympus; and they tell how he hates the overwise who reject the happy life.

> But what the common people do,
> The things that simple men believe,
> I too believe and do.[4]

A servant enters with Dionysus, who has been arrested. The king interrogates the god about his alleged Mysteries, and then bids him be led away and imprisoned in the royal stable. The women attack Thebes for rejecting the worship of Dionysus, and Pentheus for chaining their comrade. They demand vengeance, and beg the god come from one of his haunts as rescuer.

A voice is heard from within announcing that it is a god who speaks: there is earthquake and thunder, and lightning glows round Semele's tomb. Dionysus enters and finds the Maenads prostrate in reverence and fear. Without revealing who he is, he tells how he escaped from the bemused Pentheus, and how 'the god' shattered the palace with fire.

Pentheus now enters, declaring his anger because Dionysus has escaped. He is told, by a messenger, of the strange dances and orgies led by Autonoe, Agave and Ino upon the mountain.

> We fled
> And barely missed being torn to pieces by the women.

> You could have seen a single woman with bare hands
> Tear a fat calf, still bellowing with fright,
> In two, while others clawed the heifers to pieces . . .

Scraps smeared with blood hung from the fir-trees.
   Whoever this god may be,
Sire, welcome him to Thebes![5]

Pentheus, however, resolves to arm all the men and march against the women in the hills. But as the king's wits thicken, Dionysus persuades him to go alone disguised as a woman. The god promises Pentheus that all will be well—but informs the chorus that this is the clothing the king must wear to Hades when his own mother shall have butchered him, and he shall be dead: and thus he shall come to know Dionysus, most terrible yet most gentle of gods. The Asian women discourse on the excitement of midnight Dionysiac revels, and reflect that the gods move slowly but, in the end, punish those who disregard them. Then, as Dionysus and Pentheus set out together, the chorus pray that the spirits of madness and justice may bring disaster upon the unbelieving king who has rebelled against the god and his mother Semele. To Dionysus they cry:

> Cast your noose about this man who hunts
> Your Bacchae! Bring him down, trampled
> Underfoot by the murderous herd of your Maenads![6]

The king is already half-raving, and soon a messenger enters to tell that he is dead. He had climbed into a fir-tree to watch the women dancing; but led by his own mother Agave they tore him down.

> She was foaming at the mouth, and her crazed eyes
> rolling with frenzy. She was mad, stark mad,
> possessed by Bacchus. Ignoring his cries of pity,
> she seized his left arm at the wrist. Then, planting
> her foot upon his chest, she pulled, wrenching away
> the arm at the shoulder—not by her own strength,
> for the god had put inhuman power in her hands.
> Ino, meanwhile, on the other side, was scratching off
> his flesh. Then Autonoe and the whole horde
> of Bacchae swarmed upon him. Shouts everywhere,
> he screaming with what little breath was left,
> they shrieking in triumph. One tore off an arm,

another a foot still warm in its shoe. His ribs
were clawed clean of flesh, and every hand
was smeared with blood as they played ball with scraps
of Pentheus' body.[7]

As the chorus exult, Agave arrives daubed with her son's blood and
carrying a spear on which his head is impaled—she believes it is the
head of a wild lion that she has killed. But after Cadmus has come
with men bearing the torn fragments of the body in a bier, she
returns to her senses, and is horror-struck.

Her lamentations, and those of the old man, are cut short by the
appearance of Dionysus himself. Justifying his vengeance upon the
man who has blasphemed against him, he ordains that Agave and the
other women who have killed Pentheus must go into exile; and so
must Cadmus and his wife Harmonia, daughter of Ares, who are
both destined to be transformed into snakes. Cadmus and Agave say
a grief-stricken farewell to each other, and the chorus have the last
word.

> The gods have many shapes.
> The gods bring many things
> to their accomplishment.
> And what was most expected
> has not been accomplished.
> But god has found his way
> for what no man expected.
> So ends the play.[8]

2 *The Irresistible Irrational*

This is one of Euripides' latest plays, written over thirty years after
the *Alcestis*. Yet unlike other productions of the same time, the
Bacchae is cast in the strictest mould of early drama, and is, indeed,
the most formal of all Greek tragedies that have survived. Its excitement is enhanced by the tension between the strange, savage myth
and the classical severity of its presentation—by the contrast of a
more than usual state of emotion, as Coleridge put it, with more than
usual order.

279

TABLE 6

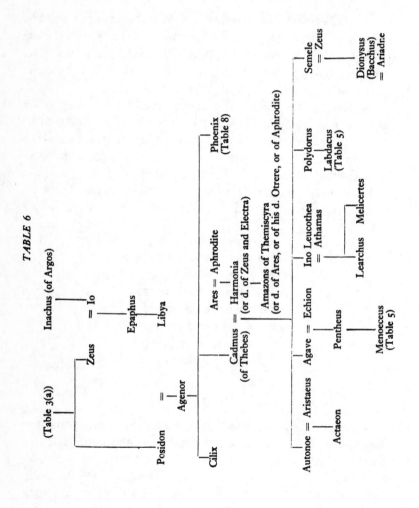

The magnificent choral odes recall Aeschylus by their prominent role in the action. Although full of colour, sympathy with nature, and wild movement, they are almost liturgical in the measured rhythms through which they reveal the mystery and holiness of religion. It is possible to guess at many links between these odes and what we may suppose to have been the ancient ritual pattern of Dionysus' worship.[9] For these hymn-like poems surely reflect a close interweaving of myth and ritual (page 159), and indeed the whole play reveals similarities, in structure and language, to a ritual paean written for Dionysiac festivals by one Philodamus of Scarphe.[10] The *Bacchae* piously recalls Attic tragedy's Dionysiac origins and the institution of the Athenian Dionysia as a playwrights' festival (page 176). Dionysus, seen in the *Bacchae* as the Master of Illusions who could make the world seem what it is not, was indeed the spirit of the theatre.

Although not many plays about the god have survived, his career may have formed the oldest of dramatic subjects. The first tragedian Thespis is said to have written a *Pentheus*, and Aeschylus wrote a lost trilogy on Pentheus' fellow-recusant Lycurgus (page 241), as well as four or five other plays in which Dionysus was a central figure. Dramatist, actors and audiences all partook to some degree in the Dionysiac excitement of tragedy (page 174), and their interrelation in the *Bacchae* must have been peculiarly intense because of its subject and its disturbingly swift, taut violence.

Pentheus is a tragic figure, as infatuated as an Aeschylean victim. Taking him from the folk-lore in which he and other Guy Fawkeses were doomed for refusing Dionysus, Euripides shows him as an ordinary well-meaning man faced with a problem beyond his strength and understanding, and destroyed by the lack of imagination with which he presumes to deny the god. Pentheus means 'grief-stricken', and his doom comes from failure to recognize the irresistible nature of the infectious Dionysus-guided impulse to escape from the repressions that so dangerously exist below conventional consciousness. The earlier ages of Greece had been full of collective hysterias for which the worship of the mighty liberator Dionysus provided ritual outlet, promising freedom where Apollo promised security.

This freedom ranged from simple country pleasures to the intoxi-cated, bloody rending of animals and—it was reported from Thrace, up on the hills—the tearing also of human beings, limb from limb.

On the gems and seals of Minoan Crete there are already monsters serving, as satyrs, a young male god who is Master of Animals—god of vegetation and wild life, like Attis and Adonis—and the name of Dionysus (not necessarily the god) appears on a tablet soon after 1300 BC. In the *Bacchae* is repeated the tale of his journey through 'all Asia'. The Phrygians in Asia Minor had originally come from Thrace, which was known as Dionysus' home, and it was probably from one or both of those lands that the savagely orgiastic element in his worship swept over archaic Greece, institutionalized, not in a central religion such as that of Eleusinian Demeter (page 148), but in numerous local cults and private groups. When the Olympic deities failed to satisfy, this god of wine and frenzy provided more thrilling fare. He is no god for Homer, for Homer did not dwell much on the poor, and it is they who became Dionysus' followers. That is why, when in the seventh and sixth centuries BC 'tyrants' controlled many cities, the worship of Dionysus flourished, and choral dances were introduced in his honour (page 176). For the poor were the tyrants' following too.

There were, in those days, bloody scenes of the tearing of flesh because the life-blood of animals was needed to renew the blood of man. This supreme exaltation and repulsion is passed over rapidly by Euripides. Yet the eaters of raw flesh are referred to as late as 276 BC in the regulations of Dionysus' cult at Miletus. Probably this eating of the warm, bleeding gobbets was an eating of the god himself, the 'noble bull' as he was called in an ancient hymn at Elis, who was assimilated by his worshippers through these wild sacraments. They identified him with Zagreus, who was devoured by the Titans to be born again (in very un-Homeric fashion) amid the flames of Semele's death; and it was from this tale, incorporated in the Orphic literature, that there emanated doctrines of future life and reincarnation (page 313). The worshipper who performed the rite was *at one with the god* ('entheos'), expressing an idea of mystic communion—in contrast with the view, so often expressed in Greek literature, that there is a sharp gulf between human and divine (page 185).

So this early Dionysiac ritual was a cathartic that took man out of himself and purged his irrational impulses, or directed them into this special channel. These were times when the religious sanction had become guilt instead of shame (page 188), and some of the Greeks, their old clan solidarities weakened, were finding it difficult to bear their new burdens of individual responsibility. Dionysus was rightly called Lysios, the loosener; his cult of excess was the reverse side of the sense of sin which, in the same epoch, took strong hold. In his unrestrained rites, stimulated by his product of wine (which poets also claimed as a source of their inspiration (page 174)), was to be found that ecstacy, a taking out of oneself or possession, which anthropologists and psychologists have noted in many societies. The natural affinities of this orgiastic element seem to be with the ancient Mediterranean fertility cults (page 146) rather than with the less emotional Olympian religion. On Minoan and Mycenaean rings we can see frenzied dances by the ancestors of these Maenads whose raging mania in honour of the god is described in the *Bacchae*. In the same play are references to the snake-handling which is shown on vases, recorded in fourth century BC Macedonia, mentioned in the Gospel according to St Mark;[11] and which still forms part of the ecstatic rattlesnake cult of the Holiness Church in Kentucky.

Throughout history there have been periodic mass-waves of neurotic, often quasi-religious hysteria. Though archaic Greece was their special stamping-ground, Herodotus still tells of them,[12] the Romans were afraid of such outbreaks—with specific reference to Dionysiac cults[13]—and in our own century there have been recurrences, for example at Yenisehir on the Dardanelles (1909–11), and in Japan (1944–5).

The Greeks, choosing to turn these tendencies into institutional channels, officially recognized the ecstatic wine-religion at Delphi, Corinth, Sparta and Athens. The aim of these cults was to discourage even more primitive rites—as Orphic writers (page 312), too, sought to discipline their aspirants' raptures. Thus, in the more civilized areas at least, cannibalism and ritual murder had probably come to an end before the fifth century began—recurring only in emergencies such as the Persian war, when at Athens itself Themistocles sacrificed three Persian youths to Dionysus the eater of raw flesh (Omestes). In the same desire to institutionalize ecstasy the Moslem sage Jelal al Din Rumi proclaimed, in the thirteenth century, that 'he who knows the power of the dances dwells in God', and the Whirling Dervishes perpetuate this ecstatic tradition. But at Aissouan in Algeria, a mystical sect still recalls the *Bacchae* by tearing a live sheep to pieces and devouring it raw.

We cannot tell how far the ecstatic cult of Dionysus survived in Greece at Euripides' own time. It has been thought significant that he wrote or completed the *Bacchae* in semi-Hellenized Macedonia, where he died (*c.* 406 BC). But this may not have influenced Euripides decisively in his choice of theme, since analogous orgiastic worships —such as that of the god Sabazius—had been introduced to his own city of Athens by slaves and foreigners, and were making headway at this date. Euripides' other later plays likewise show an increasing interest in mysticism and ecstasy. But the *Bacchae*, by its treatment of the myth of Dionysus, sums up the whole theme of emotionalism as a factor in social as well as individual life: those 'things utterly non-human and non-moral,' in the words of Gilbert Murray, 'which bring man bliss or tear his life to shreds without a break in their own serenity'.

Sometimes the mysterious stranger in the *Bacchae* has been interpreted as a young eastern follower of Dionysus. But surely he is the powerful god himself. Dionysus is the spirit of unthinking, physical enjoyment, of the instinctive group-personality, of anti-intellectual energy. In him, as E. R. Dodds said in his fine book *The Greeks and the Irrational*, are mingled joy and horror, insight and madness, innocent gaiety and dark cruelty. We ignore at our peril the demand of the human spirit for Dionysiac experience. Faced with this imperative, Pentheus makes a tragic decision and suffers the classic reversal of fortune. First we had blamed him as unimaginative, but then we are sorry for his dreadful fate (as we are sorry for the fate of that other victim of repression in Somerset

Maugham's play *Rain*). For all the savage emotion of the play, Euripides is stating for us fully and objectively both the beauties of religious self-abandonment and its dangers. As André Gide remarked, 'he takes sides no more than does Ibsen. He is content to illuminate and develop the conflict between natural forces and the soul that claims to escape their damnation.' And perhaps the reason why, in this final vision of man's tragic condition, the dramatist expresses the dilemma so fairly, lies in the conflicts of his own soul.

Dionysus had returned to favour because Greek rationalism needed an antidote. His cult inspired not only the poetry of Euripides but the mysticism of Plato, to whom it suggested that assimilation to God was the purpose of philosophy. Their contemporary, the comic dramatist Aristophanes, laughed Dionysus off in the *Frogs* as an effeminate debauchee, the most cowardly of the gods. But in later, Hellenistic, Greece the cult of this punisher of unbelievers and rewarder of the faithful gained enormous popularity as the setting for Mysteries: Dionysus is the distinctive deity of Macedonian and Greek expansion into oriental lands. Then under imperial Rome his worship, depicted on thousands of sarcophagi, became a prosperous, materialistic hope for comfort and jollity in the next world—and more urgent religions eclipsed it.

Dionysus captivated the Renaissance. The poetry of Lorenzo the Magnificent is best known for his chorus to Bacchus and Ariadne, *How beautiful is youth*, later adopted by Fascism. Donatello's David is partly Dionysiac, Michelangelo's Bacchus (1496) almost Euripidean in its startlingly equivocal impact (to Shelley the statue seemed a shocking mistake). Then Titian's full-blooded Bacchanals (1518–23)—less alarming than some of his other mythological paintings—give place to Caravaggio's Bacchus (*c.* 1596), a plump coarse Roman youth studied with a new firm assurance and variety of modelling; and to Annibale Carracci's Triumph of Bacchus and Ariadne (1597–1604), in which the motifs of the ancient sarcophagi are galvanized into boisterous exuberance.

Nineteenth-century Germany witnessed a more formidable Bacchic revival. In *Bread and Wine* (1801) the deranged Hölderlin interpreted Dionysus and Christ as one, the last god on earth, the sunset radiance of the gods. Heine too came under Dionysus' sway— responding first light-heartedly, and then with tragic intent, to the ambiguous master-magician of pleasure and pain, beauty and cruelty. Nietzsche's *Birth of Tragedy* (1872) displayed still more vividly the god's allurement to Germanic minds. To him the powers of Dionysus shatter the bonds of the individual, invade and pull down and melt his identity—as they melted Nietzsche's, for he finally identified himself with the destroyer. Germanic Hellenism, already vigorous (page 52), had acquired a more perilous, dissonant element; the recreation of tragic myths through Wagner was at hand, and also the anti-humanist catastrophes which it is possible that Nietzsche unwittingly helped to bring about.

PART VI

HEROIC SEARCHERS

CHAPTER 11

THE QUEST FOR THE GOLDEN FLEECE

———————⫷⫸⫷⫸⫷⫸———————

1 The Story of the ARGONAUTICA *Told by Apollonius*

THE POEM celebrates the heroes who, in search of the Golden
Fleece, sailed the Argo through the Straits between the dark Rocks,
and into the Black Sea. Pelias of Iolcus sent them on their quest.
For an oracle had told that king that his death would be caused by a
man wearing one sandal; and Jason appeared before him with one
sandal missing, which he had lost in the river Anaurus. So Pelias
dispatched Jason on a perilous adventure, to fetch back from King
Aeetes of Aea in Colchis the Fleece which Phrixus had once given
Aeetes in exchange for his daughter in marriage.

Jason's ship *Argo* was built by Argus, under the direction of
Athene. The heroes who joined its crew included Orpheus, who with
the music of his voice enchanted even rocks and streams; Admetus
of Pherae, Mopsus and Idmon the soothsayers, Telamon and Peleus
the sons of Aeacus, Tiphys the helmsman, Heracles and his squire
Hylas, Castor and Polydeuces, Meleager, Laocoon, Zetes and Calais
(children of the North Wind, Boreas), and many others. The people
of the place called them Minyans, since most of them were descended
from the daughters of Minyas. Heracles was offered the headship of
the expedition, but refused, and Jason was made its leader.

The voyage started from Pagasae, the harbour of Iolcus. All the
gods looked down from heaven that day, seeing the *Argo* start with
its noble-spirited crew, the finest seamen of their time. Chiron the

289

Centaur also came to watch, and so did his wife (the Naiad Chariclo), carrying the infant Achilles whom she held up for his father Peleus to see as he went on his journey.

Passing the mountains of Pelion, Ossa, Olympus and then Athos they came to the island of Lemnos, where Hypsipyle reigned over a population of women only, since they had killed their husbands for bringing home Thracian girls as booty. The Lemnian women welcomed the Argonauts, who stayed and lived with them for a time. But then the travellers passed on to Samothrace, where at Orpheus' suggestion they were initiated into the secret rites and mysteries of the island. Passing through the Hellespont, they were hospitably received on the peninsula ruled by King Cyzicus, whom Heracles and his companions delivered from the six-armed earth-born giants who were his foes. But when the Argonauts were blown back to this coast by adverse winds, the inhabitants failed to recognize their visitors, taking them for invaders; and in the fighting Cyzicus was killed. His wife Clite killed herself, and the tears shed for her by the woodland nymphs turned into the fountain which bears her name.

After twelve days of bad weather they proceeded on their journey, but Heracles' oar broke and the *Argo* had to put in at Cius. Hylas went off to fetch water for their supper, and came to a fountain inhabited by Naiads, who were so taken by his beauty that they pulled him into the water to be their companion. Heracles searched and raged in vain, and at last the *Argo* had to leave without them both.

Their next stop was among the Bebryces, a savage Bithynian people whose King Amycus, son of Posidon, insisted that no visitors should leave his country without a boxing-match. After a hard struggle Polydeuces beat and slew him, and the Argonauts fought off the Bebryces and celebrated their victory. On the next day, they sailed up the Bosphorus, navigating a huge wave, and came to land upon its European shore. Here lived blind King Phineus, a prophet whom Zeus had punished for irreverence by giving him a sightless, lingering old age. He was also haunted by Harpies, who snatched away all the food that was placed before him and befouled any remaining scraps with their loathsome stench. Zetes and Calais flew after the swooping monsters until Iris called them off. 'Sons of Boreas, you may not touch the Harpies with your swords: they are the hounds of almighty Zeus. But I myself will swear that never again shall they come near to Phineus.' In his gratitude the old man showed the Argonauts how to reach Colchis.

They needed his advice very soon after they left, for he had warned them of the dark Clashing Rocks, and of the need to take with them a dove to send between the rugged cliffs ahead of the ship. As they launched the dove on its journey, 'once more the Rocks met face to face with a resounding crash, flinging a great cloud of spray into the air. The sea gave a terrific roar and the broad sky rang again. Caverns underneath the crags bellowed as the sea came surging in. A great wave broke against the cliffs and the white foam swept high above them. *Argo* spun round as the flood reached her. But the dove got through, unscathed but for the tips of her tailfeathers, which were nipped off by the Rocks.'[1] The narrows opened again, and they rowed through—only to be held up by the swirling tide just at the danger-point. 'This was the moment when Athene intervened. Holding on to the hard rock with her left hand, she pushed the ship through with the other; and *Argo* clove the air like a winged arrow, though even so the Rocks, clashing in their accustomed way, sheared off the tip of the mascot on the stern. When the men had thus got through unhurt, Athene soared up to Olympus. But the Rocks were now rooted for ever in one spot close to one another.'

After this escape the Argonauts sailed through the Euxine (Black) Sea, along the coast of Asia Minor. At the lonely island of Thynias they had a vision of Apollo, and at Orpheus' bidding dedicated this place to the god. As they continued eastwards, the *Argo* made harbour at dawn by Cape Acherusia, which is near the icy Cavern of Hades. Here Idmon was lost, killed by a boar, and Tiphys: two monuments still mark the place. But at dawn on the twelfth day they sailed on, with Ancaeus replacing Tiphys at the helm. After paying honour to the tomb of Sthenelus who had fought with Heracles against the Amazons, 'they landed on the coast where Zeus himself had once given a home to Sinope, daughter of Asopus, granting her the boon of virginity. He was trapped by his own promise. In his passion for the girl he had solemnly sworn to fulfil her dearest wish, whatever that might be, and she very cleverly had said, "I wish to remain a virgin." By the same ruse she outwitted Apollo when he made love to her—and the river-god Halys as well. Men fared no better than the gods; this woman never was possessed by any lover'.[3]

At the mouth of the river Thermodon, with its ninety-six branches, they ran ashore, but cast off with a north-wester in time to avoid the aggressive Amazons of Themiscyra, daughters of Ares and Harmonia. The *Argo* next sailed past the lands of the Chalybes, who dig for iron (with never a holiday) in a black atmosphere of soot and smoke, and the Mossynoeci in the *mossynes* or wooden houses upon their Sacred Mountain. 'These people have their own ideas of what is right and proper. What we as a rule do openly in town or market-place they do at home; and what we do in the privacy of our houses they do out of doors in the open street, and nobody thinks the worse of them. Even the sexual act puts no one to the blush in this community. On the contrary, like swine in the fields, they lie down on the ground in promiscuous intercourse and are not at all disconcerted by the presence of others. Then again, their king sits in the loftiest hut of all to dispense justice to his numerous subjects. But if the poor man happens to make a mistake in his findings, they lock him up and give him nothing to eat for the rest of the day.'[3]

A day of rowing now brought them nearly abreast of the Isle of Ares. Here they were attacked by a shower of pointed feathers from the War-god's birds, but they withstood the onslaught by locking their shields over their heads and making an intimidating din. On the day of their arrival at the island they encountered the four sons of Phrixus, the man who had given the Golden Fleece to King Aeetes of Colchis. His sons had remained at Colchis, but now after their father's death they were returning to Orchomenus in the hope of recovering the rich possessions of their family. Invited to go with Jason and the others on their quest, the sons of Phrixus were at first horrified by its boldness, for they knew that Aeetes could be a deadly and relentless enemy. But finally they were reassured, and sailed on with the Argonauts.

As the last recess of the Euxine Sea opened up, the travellers caught sight of the high crags of Caucasus, and of Prometheus chained to its rocks with an eagle devouring his liver. And now they came to the mouth of the Phasis, and rowed some way upstream. Then, after Jason had poured a libation to Earth, to the gods of the land, and to the spirits of its famous sons, they put into the bank, hiding their ship in a bed of reeds.

So that the love of Medea, daughter of King Aeetes, might help Jason bring back the Golden Fleece to Iolcus, the goddesses Hera and Athene sought the help of Aphrodite; and she bribed her son Eros (with a ball of golden hoops) to shoot an arrow into Medea's heart. When the Argonauts, after passing through the marvels of Aeetes' courtyards, arrived at the royal palace, Eros was there; and he lodged his arrow in the heart of Medea, kindling the flame of love.

Aeetes received the Argonauts badly, and before he would part with the Fleece imposed on Jason a terrible test: to plough a field with wild fire-belching oxen. Next, the ground was to be sown with the teeth of a monstrous serpent, and the armed men who would spring up from them must be defeated and destroyed. When Jason had failed, Aeetes planned to burn the invaders, ship and all. But Medea, feverish with love, chose a magic ointment from among her many healing or deadly drugs and charms. A man who anointed himself with this, if he then propitiated Hecate (Brimo) with a midnight sacrifice, became invulnerable. The ointment was named after Prometheus, for it came from a yellow-flowering plant that had sprung from the blood-like ichor in his veins.

Leaving the city and its streets, Medea drove across the plain to the shrine of Hecate, of whom she was priestess. She sang and danced with her maids, distracted by her longing to see Jason, but telling the girls that the drug she had prepared for him was a fatal one. He came, and they confronted one another with love in their hearts, and exchanged all their inmost thoughts. Jason begged her to help him, and she gazed into his face. 'How to begin, she did not know; she longed so much to tell him everything at once. But with the charm she did not hesitate; she drew it out from her sweet-scented girdle and he took it in his hands with joy. She revelled in his need of her and would have poured out all her soul to him as well, so captivating was the light of love that streamed from Jason's golden head and held her gleaming eyes. Her heart was warmed and melted like the dew on roses under the morning sun.'⁴

And so, while he rubbed the magic ointment on his body and armour, Medea revealed to him how he must make sacrifice to the goddess Hecate. Unharmed by the oxen's fiery breath, he ploughed and sowed the field. Warriors sprang up, but he hurled a boulder which started a fight among them and helped him to kill them all.

But Medea was filled with agonizing fears, for she knew that her father would learn of her help to Jason. 'How I wish, Jason,' she cried, 'that the sea had been the end of you!' Yet she fled from her home and ran barefoot through the alleys, making for the temple along roads that, as witches do, she had often searched for corpses or lethal roots. Joining the Argonauts in their camp, while it was still dark she led Jason to the sacred wood.

There, by her arts, his quest was fulfilled. Chanting a spell, she dipped a fresh spring of juniper in her magic brew, and sprinkled the eyes of the giant serpent which guarded the Golden Fleece; and Jason snatched the Fleece from the oak on which it hung. 'Lord Jason held up the great Fleece in his arms. The shimmering wool threw a fiery glow on his fair cheeks and forehead; and he rejoiced in it, glad as a girl who catches on her silken gown the lovely light of the full moon as it climbs the sky and looks into her attic room.'⁵

The Argonauts now started home, pursued by a Colchian fleet but assisted by Hera, who wanted Medea to reach Iolcus with all speed and bring doom to the house of Pelias. At the mouth of the Danube they found they had been outstripped by part of the Colchian navy under Medea's brother Apsyrtus. But, while she deceived Apsyrtus with a pretence of parleying, Jason set upon his force and killed him. Medea's silvery veil and dress were painted red with blood, and the Fury saw what had been done.

Then Jason and his companions embarked and sailed up the Danube, never pausing till they reached the sacred Isle of Amber, the innermost of all the Amber Islands at the mouth of Eridanus (Po). Sailing southwards through the Adriatic, the Argonauts were driven north again by Zeus, angry at Apsyrtus' death; and they turned into the river, sailing up its stream as far as ships could sail.

'They reached the outfall of that deep lake where Phaethon, struck in the breast and half-consumed by a blazing thunderbolt, fell into the water from the chariot of the Sun. His wounded body smoulders to this day and sends up clouds of steam. Even the light-winged birds that try to fly across the water fail to reach the other side and with a helpless flutter plunge into the heat. All around, the Daughters of the Sun, encased in tall poplars, utter their sad and unavailing plaint. Shining drops of amber fall from their eyes on to the sands and are dried there by the sun. But when the wailing wind stirs the dark waters of the lake to rise above the beach, all the tears that have collected there are swept by the overflow into the river. The Celts, however, have another tale about these amber drops that are carried down the current. They say they are the many tears that Apollo shed for his son Asclepius when he visited the sacred people of the North. Apollo was banished from the bright sky by his father Zeus, whom he blamed for having killed Asclepius his son.'[6] From there they made their way from the Po to the Rhone, and so by its mouth to the Tyrrhenian sea, to Elba, and to Aeaea island of Circe, sister of King Aeetes.

'A number of creatures whose ill-assorted limbs declared them to be neither man nor beast had gathered round Circe like a great flock of sheep following their shepherd from the fold. Nondescript monsters such as these, fitted with miscellaneous limbs, were once produced spontaneously by Earth out of the primeval mud, when she had not yet solidified under a rainless sky and was deriving no moisture from the blazing sun. But Time, combining this with that, brought the animal creation into order.'[7] The Argonauts made for Circe's hearth and sat as suppliants, and dared not look her in the face. So Circe knew that there had been a murder, and performed propitiatory rites. But then, although she was not told that the dead man was her nephew, she drove them from her threshold.

Hera bade Iris calm the winds for the Argonauts, and told Thetis to keep them from disaster. Accordingly they were preserved from the Sirens on Anthemoessa, and escaped Scylla and Charybdis and the Wandering Rocks; and they came to Sicilian waters and then to the Phaeacian island of Corcyra. The Colchians caught up with them and demanded the return of the terrified Medea to her father. But the Phaeacian king Alcinous, after his wife Arete had warned him against the excessive severity of fathers to their daughters, decided that Medea should not be separated from Jason if they were man and wife. And so, within a sacred cave upon the island, they were wedded, and the shining Golden Fleece was spread upon their marriage-bed.

But when the *Argo* left Corcyra, it was caught by a northerly gale and swept southwards for nine days and nights into the Syrtian gulf of Libya, full of shoals and sand, silent and lifeless. There, while searching desperately for fresh water, the Argonauts came to the sacred Garden of Atlas and to the Hesperides, whose golden apples had been stolen by Heracles on the day before; and they found the spring which he had struck from a neighbouring rock. Without one of their party Mopsus, who had been killed by a snake, they embarked again, and Triton emerged from the depths as their guide. At Dicte in Crete, Medea by her magic overcame the bronze giant Talus. Then they sped northwards, stopping at the isle of Anaphe— and themselves creating another island, Thera, from a clod of earth which (obeying a dream) they threw into the sea. Their last stop was at Aegina, and from there they sailed peacefully homewards, and with joyful hearts at last stepped ashore at Pagasae.

2   *Alexandrians and Victorians*

At first sight we are back in the *Odyssey*'s epic world of travel and adventure and quest. And indeed the Argonautic legend is as old as the *Odyssey*, since this speaks of the 'celebrated *Argo*'[8] which Jason with Hera's help brought through the Wandering Rocks* when homeward (not outward) bound from Aea, the land of Aeetes. *Odyssey* and *Argonautica* alike are great conglomerations of myths and folk-tales, familiar and obscure (page 84). There are innumer-

* These rocks, in western waters, were sometimes confused with the Clashing Rocks, or Symplegades, at the north end of the Bosphorus (page 291).

able stories like Jason's, in which the hero is sent on a dangerous journey to get rid of him, and, when he arrives at his destination, is confronted with tasks and helped in them by the daughter of the ferocious local ruler; the Norse *Mastermaid* and Gaelic *Battle of the Birds* are related to the same themes. Aea is 'the land', the magic country 'east of the sun and west of the moon'.

But this land is located in the Black Sea (Colchis) and the heroes who visit it reflect the seamen who in the Minoan and Mycenaean Bronze Age (page 33) sailed those waters. Every Greek city later claimed an Argonaut to justify its trading rights in the Black Sea, so there are several, irreconcilable, lists of the crew. But its nucleus—the people whom Pindar calls the Argonauts[9]—are the mysterious, semi-historical Minyans. Of this people two main branches existed, one inhabiting Boeotian Orchomenus[10]—a leading Mycenaean city of which Minyas, hero of a lost epic, was the legendary founder—and the other, Iolcus in Thessaly which was the *Argo*'s home. These Minyans were the people round whom the earliest Argonautic sagas were centred.

However, the story may then have been elaborated elsewhere—perhaps at Miletus on the western coast of Asia Minor, which had a large Black Sea trade and claimed as its founder the member of a family tracing descent from Minyas. The return journey of the Argonauts had several different versions—it was either through 'Oceanus', or by the way they had come (page 290), or by the fantastic route (through the Danube to the Rhine and the Rhone) which is described in the present poem. For in the colonizing and exploring period of the seventh and early sixth centuries BC, many strange myths and adventures were added to the original story, and then in the classical period attempts were made to fuse them into a systematic whole. Such, for example, is the version told in the Fourth Pythian Ode of Pindar, the longest and most straightforward and ambitious of all his poems.

> In these sons of Gods Hera kindled
> That all-persuading sweet desire
> For the ship *Argo*, that none be left behind

To nurse at his mother's side a ventureless life,
But, even though he die,
Find in his own valour the fairest enchantment
With others young as he.[11]

In Pindar's Ode, as in Apollonius' epic, the journey culminated in
Jason's successful conclusion of his quest for the Golden Fleece
(page 289). This had belonged to the flying ram on which, by the
help of Hermes, Phrixus and Helle escaped from their father
Athamas and stepmother Ino at Orchomenus. Helle fell off and was
drowned in the Hellespont (Dardanelles), but Phrixus reached
Colchis, where the ram was sacrificed to Zeus and its fleece given to
the local king, Aeetes. Probably the fleece became golden in the story
because there was gold to be found at Colchis; but it was the sort of
magical treasure for which heroes go in search, and Aeetes had to
fight in its defence because the luck of his kingdom was bound up
with the possession of the fleece.

Already in ancient times the story suffered many rationalizations.
Strabo believed Jason was looking for gold, and explained that the
Colchians collected the dust from the river in fleecy skins.[12] According to the Byzantine Suidas, the fleece was a parchment book
explaining how to obtain gold by alchemy.

This final, historic version of the *Argonautica* has been described
as a mixture of science, history, and fiction. Or rather it is fiction
infused with the romantic and scholarly interests of a new age. In
spite of the epic framework of quest and adventure, the clear
Homeric air of the extrovert ballad has turned into a cloudier
atmosphere, a different sort of magic, set amid treachery and
intrigue. Apollonius was born in *c.* 295 BC, many centuries after
Homer and more than a hundred years after the leading Attic
tragedians. The civilization of the Creek city states had lost its
nerve, and then, under Alexander the Great and the monarchs who
divided his inheritance, had lost its substance too. One of these
successor states was the kingdom of the Ptolemies in Egypt, and in
their realm Greek literature and mythology took, yet again, a new
and active turn.

This retelling of the myths at Alexandria was marked by close attention, at worst to pretty sentimentality, at best to authentic personal feeling. The new Romantic Epic was above all the creation of Apollonius, the Alexandrian (though he was called Rhodian after the city that received him) who wrote the *Argonautica*. His poem was framed as an epic not too far short of traditional length (5,835 lines long), and traditional in its structure; but it breathed the new spirit of the age. However, this novel sort of long mythological poem met with powerful opposition, led by Callimachus who equated a big book with a big nuisance. Callimachus, who had taught Apollonius but later served under him in the library at Alexandria, remarked that there was no future in poems like the *Argonautica*, because 'another has the laurels already'. Yet, in spite of Apollonius' many affectations, that does not quite do justice to the sort of humanism which he employed the epic form, and mythical subject, to convey.

This was an individualistic time. In the huge kingdoms of the near east, the old city-state patriotisms lacked urgency and reality, whereas the new centres of power were too remote to focus people's emotions. So they turned inwards upon themselves and their personal concerns; and Apollonius infuses the traditional myths with something unfamiliar to the world's poetry—romantic love. His Medea's character has a psychological subtlety far from the simple extroversion of a Homeric heroine, and sometimes reminiscent of Euripides. If that dramatist's *Andromeda* had survived, we might have found in it more than a touch of romantic love. As it is, this seems characteristic of the later epoch in which Apollonius lived, and of his native Alexandria at this time of its greatest cultural achievements.

Unlike perhaps his *Andromeda*, Euripides' play the *Medea*, telling how she slew their children when Jason preferred the king of Corinth's daughter to herself, had agreed with the general classical condemnation of self-willed passionate love between man and woman. But now they face each other in a changing world, romantic as well as classical, which Apollonius, here the forerunner of Virgil (page 333), depicts with a true and delicate feeling for nature.

Without voice, without murmur, they stood there
    face to face,
As oaks or towering pine-trees stand rooted in their
    place,
Side by side, unmoving, high up among the hills,
When winds are hushed—but, sudden, a gust through
    their branches thrills
And they whisper with infinite voices. So now before
    Love's gale
Those two were doomed, in a moment, to tell their
    whole hearts' tale.[13]

Yet the character of Medea was not easy for Apollonius to draw, for as well as a young girl in love she is a dangerous witch—while Jason, who attains success only through her magic, is admitted to be an unresourceful hero, one of the first of many ordinary men to play the hero's part in European literature.

But is Apollonius retells the myth romantically, he also does so with a great regard for its learned, archaeological content. For one important aspect of the elaborate Alexandrian scholarship was this antiquarianism, and on numerous occasions Apollonius seeks to explain his stories 'aetiologically' by some ancient custom or conjectured derivation or rationalization (page 122). Herein he and his contemporaries were forerunners of one of the principal schools of modern mythological research. This, initiated by men such as C. A. Lobeck (1781–1860) and encouraged by the rise of anthropology since the 1870's (page 82), makes a point of looking for the sources of a story, seeking to determine its date and the place of its origin, and linking it—by archaeological or other means—to further evidence in the fields of comparative religion, economics and social life. Thus in Britain Andrew Lang, Sir James Frazer and Jane Harrison ransacked these stories for primitive survivals. Their approach, though superseded at many points, was sound in principle since the myths, though hard to fit into chronological patterns, always reproduce some point of tradition which could (if we knew the key!) be rescued from the distortions with which time has encrusted it. So this historical, anthropological method, though tempting as a quarry for puzzle-merchants, is justifiable, and probably at least as hopeful as any other.

But it is a difficult task to pursue; indeed the job, though somewhat further ahead than in the days of Apollonius, has nevertheless scarcely begun. For early Greece contained many diverse racial, religious and social elements and, as the pioneer K. O. Müller (1797–1840) appreciated, we have to assess and interpret these before we can assess and interpret the myths to which they gave birth. But unfortunately we have little real access—except from the internal evidence of the myths themselves—to the minds and cultures of the early Greeks; archaeology cannot yet provide even an approximate tabulation or time-table of the early tribal movements in the country, and can do less still to reconstruct the rituals and beliefs which the migrants distributed. Meanwhile, in searching for the origins of myths, we can only avoid sweeping theories and look at each story on its merits. Since this is such a technical, fragmentary and largely unrealized process, I have preferred in the present book to see the myths through the eyes of the great ancient writers whom they inspired—though that, of course, means that the stories come to us at an advanced stage in their life-histories (page xx).

Apollonius, for example, is a latecomer to the theme of the *Argonautica*. Yet even he was very far from the *last* to deal with this eternal story. Ovid, for example, in his studies of distressed female psychology entitled the *Heroides*, enters into the feelings first of Hypsipyle[14] (page 290) and then of Medea, after their successive abandonments by Jason. Then the Roman epic poet Valerius Flaccus wrote an *Argonautica* in eight books during the later first century AD.

About the fame of the tale in the Renaissance, Spenser can tell:

> Therein all the famous history
> Of Jason and Medaea was ywritt; . . .
> His goodly conquest of the golden fleece . . .
> The wondred *Argo*, which in venturous peece
> First through the Euxine seas bore all the flowr of
> Greece.

The nature of this story again gave it prominence in the nineteenth century's romantic revival of Hellenism—the age when Leigh Hunt (1818) spoke of myths as 'elevations of the external world and of accomplished humanity to the highest pitch of the graceful, and embodied essences of all the grand and lovely qualities of nature'. Leigh Hunt is saying that is how Shakespeare saw Greek mythology, but he is really interpreting the views of his own time. Thus Grillparzer, in his fine *Golden Fleece* (1820), carried the German-Greek tradition a step farther from Goethe (page 52) into a territory where the myths are employed primarily for their own sake, as pure poetry. From there it was an easy step to their use as pure entertainment, and for children at that. And so almost simultaneously in the early eighteen-fifties, two men wrote, for the American and British markets, best-selling versions of the Argo's voyage and other stories, which are still circulating widely to this day. The American was Nathanael Hawthorne of Salem in Massachusetts, and his book the *Tanglewood Tales* (1851). A whimsical but captivating story-teller, he writes that 'these immortal fables are legitimate subjects for every age to clothe with its own garniture of manners and sentiment, and to imbue with its own morality'. Such adjustments of Greek mythology to a new age are in keeping with an ancient tradition; though his own treatment, the American adds, is Gothic more than Greek. Yet it also reflects that dream of lost potency and innocence, of lost Arcadia and Eden, which runs through so many of Hawthorne's works.

Meanwhile, in England, Charles Kingsley published the *Heroes* (1855). They are about Perseus, about Theseus and above all about the Argonauts. In these brisk, antiseptic narratives there is no trace of any Germanic furore about the myths. Jolly good hero-worshipping yarns, without esoteric overtones or significances, Kingsley's versions exactly caught the popular British attitude; although perhaps to say that 'while they (the Greeks were young and simple) they loved fairy-tales, as you do now' seems a little patronizing, to his subject if not to his youthful readers, for there is nothing very young or simple about the *Agamemnon* (or the Minotaur). Kingsley's retellings of the myths, however, are designed to bring out a moral he found in them: do right, and God—of whom Zeus had been 'some dim remembrance'—will help you. Next to the medieval romances, he said, 'there are no fairy-tales like these old Greek ones, for beauty and wisdom and truth, and for making children love noble deeds and trust in God to help them through'. Accordingly, as G. K. Chesterton remarked later, 'little children ought to learn nothing but legends. They are the beginnings of all sound morals and manners'.

Hawthorne and Kingsley have introduced Greek myths to generation after generation of English-speaking children. This has been much to the children's advantage. But to the adult study and appreciation of this mythology, in all its varied strength, the achievement has been of dubious benefit. For what most people know about the Argonauts, and other such mythical figures, has come filtered through these two writers and their followers—and it represents a singularly small proportion of what is truly significant in the tradition. Besides, although every age has recast the myths in its own image, the nineteenth-century's recastings are among the most drastic of all; though the success of its two chief exponents in this field shows that the stories had lost none of their inspiring force.

Within the next decade the theme of the Argonauts had reappeared as the framework for the longest single mythological tale in modern English poetry, *The Life and Death of Jason* by William Morris, 7,500 lines long. Its broad, clear narrative moves freely and smoothly, in a restrainedly medieval spirit, and with little drama until the end. The comment of the author himself is illuminating. 'If a chap can't compose an epic poem while he's weaving tapestry, he had better shut up, he'll never do any good at all.'

CHAPTER 12

THE QUEST FOR A LOST WIFE

===•••••••••===

1   The story of ORPHEUS AND EURYDICE *Told by Virgil*

THIS IS the story told in the latter part of Virgil's fourth *Georgic*.

When the bees of the shepherd Aristaeus died of pest and hunger,
he left his home in the Vale of Tempe and came to his mother,
Cyrene goddess of the sea, to ask why he had been visited by such
misfortunes. She, surrounded by her nymphs, ordered the waters to
be parted so that he might come to her, and then she bade him go to
the sea-green soothsayer Proteus, 'who lives in the Carpathian sea and
drives through the ocean in his chariot drawn by fishes and two-
footed steeds'.

> Him we nymphs and ancient Nereus hold
> In honour, for he knows all
> That is, that has been, and all that is about to be—
> Knows all by the god Neptune's grace, whose herd of
>   monsters
> And hideous seals he pastures in meadows submarine.
> This seer, my son, you must bind in fetters before
>   he'll tell you
> The whole truth of your bees' sickness and put things
>   right.
> Except to violence he yields not one word of advice;
>   entreaties
> Have no effect: you must seize him,

304

But when you have him fast in a handhold and fettered,
then
With the guise and visage of various wild beasts he'll
keep you guessing:
Suddenly he'll turn into a bristling bear, a black tiger,
A laminated dragon or lioness tawny-necked,
Or go up in a shrill burst of flame and thus from his
fetters
Escape, or give you the slip gliding off in a trickle
of water.
But the more he transforms himself,
The tighter, my son, you must strain the shackles
that bind his body,
Until at last it changes back to the first likeness
You saw at the start when his eyes were closing down
in sleep.[1]

And so when Cyrene, to give her son great strength, had bathed him in ambrosia, he sought out Proteus in his cavern; and, as the seals and the other watery creatures gambolled round, attacked him as he slept. After transforming himself into all manner of shapes in vain, Proteus asked his attacker what he wanted. But Aristaeus replied that the seer already knew—for there was no deceiving Proteus—that he had come to seek an oracle to remedy his misfortunes.

Then Proteus explained that Aristaeus was followed by the anger of an unhappy god, Orpheus, and must expiate a grave offence. For Aristaeus had pursued Eurydice, the wife of Orpheus, along a river-bank, and she had been killed by the bite of a snake. As all her comrades, and all the countryside of Thrace, lamented her fate, Orpheus had sung of her to his lyre upon the lonely shore. Then he had gone through the jaws of Taenarus down into the underworld to seek her out. His singing had held all Tartarus spell-bound, and Death's very home was shaken to hear that song; the Furies and three-mouthed Cerberus had been lulled, and Ixion's wheel had ceased to turn. Orpheus began to retrace his steps towards the upper world, followed by Eurydice. But forgetting that Proserpina had laid down the condition that he must not look behind him, he stopped, and looked back. In that moment all his labour was wasted.

> Pardonable, you'd say, but Death can never pardon.
> He halts. Eurydice, his own, is now on the lip of
> Daylight. Alas! he forgot. His purpose broke.
>   He looked back.
> His labour was lost, the pact he had made with the
>   merciless king
> Annulled. Three times did thunder peal over the
>   pools of Avernus.
> 'Who,' she cried, 'has doomed me to misery, who has
>   doomed us? . . .'
>
> Thus she spoke: and at once from his sight, like a
>   wisp of smoke
> Thinned into air, was gone.
> Wildly he grasped at shadows, wanting to say much
>   more,
> But she did not see him; nor would the ferryman of
>   the Inferno
> Let him again cross the fen that lay between them.[2]

Already, death-cold, Eurydice was on Charon's boat.

For seven months Orpheus wept beneath a cliff by the river Strymon, and deep in icy caverns, as he roamed the northern snows of Tanais; his lamentation fascinated even the tigers, and even oak-trees. No love, no wedding-song could move him, and the women of the Cicones, during their sacred, midnight orgies in honour of Bacchus, punished him for his neglect by tearing him apart. They strewed his flesh over the land, and hurled his severed head in the river Hebrus. As it was swept along by the waters, the head called out 'Eurydice', and the river-banks echoed the name.

When Proteus had finished speaking, he plunged into the sea again. Aristaeus was startled by the tale, but his mother Cyrene said that it explained why his bees were destroyed by the Wood-Nymphs; for they had been Eurydice's companions. She bade her son offer the Nymphs sacrifices and homage. He must slay four splendid bulls and four heifers, and leave the bodies, drained of blood, beside four altars. Then, nine days later, after sacrificing poppies of Lethe to Orpheus and killing a black ewe, he must revisit the grove, and appease Eurydice by the slaughter of a calf.

He did as she had ordained, and when on the ninth day he came back to the grove, he saw a portent. From the broken, putrid flanks of the oxen a great stream of bees was buzzing and swarming up to the bending boughs of a tree, upon which they fastened to hang in clusters.

Before Virgil wrote these *Georgics*, his first collection of poems the *Eclogues* (*c.* 42–37 BC) had adapted to Rome, among other themes, a set of Greek pastoral or bucolic myths, relating to rural matters, and dealing with such topics as shepherds' singing contests and mutual bantering, laments for rustic lovers, and the like. This bucolic genre had been developed into a branch of Greek literature by Theocritus in the third century BC. Although Theocritus lived first, perhaps, at Cos and then at Alexandria—where he supported the crusade of Callimachus for short poems (page 299)—he had been born at Syracuse, and it is to Sicily that the origin of these shepherd myths belongs. Tradition, however, came to associate them with the singing competitions of rustic Arcadia, in Greece itself, and Virgil blends references to that countryside with allusions to the region of his native north Italian Mantua as well.

In the hands of Theocritus and Virgil the simplicity of this sort of poetry is elaborate and refined. Yet it may well go back to the unaffected songs sung (and accompanied on the pipes) by the herdsmen themselves, as they still are in many parts of the Mediterranean area today. The traditional founder of this branch of mythology and poetry was the shepherd Daphnis, who, blinded by a nymph (or Aphrodite) for rejecting her or being unfaithful, spent the rest of his life—until Hermes took him to heaven—making sad songs about his own fate (unless it was his companions who made the songs about him). But Daphnis, Corydon, Thyrsis, Amaryllis and the rest were introduced to Greek literary circles, with subtle humour, by

Theocritus and then, in more ethereal and enigmatic fashion, were adopted by 'the Virgilian pastoral, that frail and impossible beauty,' as George Gordon described it, 'so foolish in foolish hands, but capable of such elegance, such tenderness and capricious grace.'

The pastoral took Rome by storm. During the Renaissance, and particularly in the seventeenth century, it came into its own again. Milton infused *Lycidas*, *L'Allegro*, *Il Penseroso* and *Comus* with a good deal of this spirit, and Poussin, in his picture 'Et in Arcadia ego' (1630), sums up in an autumnal enchanted mood, recalling his Ovidian scenes (page 383) but with deeper underlying emotion, this blissful uncorrupted Arcadia, tempered by regret at the brevity of human life. Twenty years later, Poussin's repainting of the theme is stiller and more spacious, enfolded in a sad, comforting Virgilian evening light. But the future course of the pastoral tradition was to lead to the superficiality of the Petit Trianon, to shepherdesses of Dresden china—and to extensive adaptation of this imagery in a number of works by André Gide.

Virgil's second work, the four *Georgics*, took seven years to complete (*c.* 36–29 BC), being published shortly after Augustus' defeat of Antony and Cleopatra at Actium. The name of the work, in Greek, refers to farming, and it was a patriotic aim of Virgil to bring the spirit of Hesiod's *Works and Days* (page 108) to the Latin language and to Roman audiences. 'The best poem of the best poet,' according to Dryden—and Montaigne had thought it the most highly finished work of all poetry—the *Georgics* are a collection of poems to the Roman homeland, and to Italy, not long united and now a word with profound emotional associations. This is the spirit in which Virgil, dedicated to the farmer's hard work which was the basis of Italy's triumphs, adapts and transforms into a wholly new splendour the material of Alexandrian didactic poets, adding something of the philosophical manner of his own older contemporary Lucretius, and even drawing upon a recent prose treatise on country life by Varro.

The first *Georgic* deals with crops, the second with fruit-trees (particularly the vine and olive), the third with farm animals, and the fourth with bee-keeping. This played a larger part than now because sugar was not yet employed, except for medicinal purposes, and honey was eaten when we should eat butter. In the first part of the fourth book Virgil tells of the struggles and ambitions of the bees, a microcosm of human endeavour.

> Illustrious of wing, through the battle-line the
>   monarchs
> Move, vast passions agitating their little breasts,
> Obstinate not to give in till superior weight of numbers
> Has forced one side or the other to turn their backs in
>   flight.[3]

But then the poet turns from this account to tell how the mythical Aristaeus loses his bees, and, appealing to his mother the water-nymph Cyrene, is instructed to seek out Proteus the Old Man of the Sea, and hear his prophecy. Some ancient critics believed this story to be a later addition—inserted to replace praises of Virgil's friend Gallus, because Gallus, first governor of Egypt after its conquest from Cleopatra, had fallen into disgrace with Augustus and lost his life. But this suggestion is almost certainly wrong. The miniature epic of Aristaeus with two shorter stories (Proteus and Orpheus) within its folds, is not only the most satisfying of many brilliant insets in the poem, but a fitting, if surprising, climax.

Aristaeus was the foster-brother of Jupiter, in relation to whom he was worshipped in Arcadia,[4] though the cult originated in Thessaly. He was the legendary protector of cattle and fruit-trees. He was also, according to a Hesiodic poem, the shepherd who has seen the Muses, and has been endowed by them with herds to guard, and with the arts of healing and foretelling.[5] Pindar recounts the love of Apollo for Aristaeus' mother Cyrene, and how the centaur Chiron prophesied her son's birth, and how he was born in Libya;[6] and the tale is briefly told by Apollonius.[7] The scene of Aristaeus' visit to his mother beneath the ocean is modelled upon the *Iliad*[8] and perhaps also upon the lyric poet Bacchylides of Ceos. According to an alternative version, he is the son of Melissa (= bee), and is fed by her upon nectar and ambrosia.

The strange story of a new swarm of bees being born from a

carcass reproduces a widespread belief in the ancient world[9] and, indeed, until the seventeenth century. In fact, far from being generated by carrion, bees detest it; but drone flies do not, and perhaps the superstition arises from the clouds of drones that surround a carcass. The details speak of stinking corruption. Yet all the same this strange story, as Jules Michelet said, is 'a song full of immortality, which, in the mystery of Nature's transformations, embodies our highest hope—that death is not a death, but the beginning of a new life'.

As in the *Odyssey*[10] Idothea, the daughter of Proteus, advised Menelaus to seek out her father, so in the *Georgics* Cyrene bids her son go to Proteus. In the Homeric poem Proteus served Posidon in Egypt, and in Euripides' *Helen* he was the virtuous king of Egypt who kept her safe. Egypt was much in the minds of Romans when the *Georgics* were published, for the country had just been incorporated into the Roman empire (page 309). Yet whereas in the *Odyssey* the seer had satisfied all the requests of Menelaus, here his intervention is a riddlingly imperfect fulfilment of Cyrene's assurance;[11] and this is one of the reasons why the poem remains enigmatic. Francis Bacon found particular fascination in the myth of Proteus, in whom his love for allegory (page 423) fancifully detected an analogy to nature or matter, imprisoned and handcuffed by mechanical arts, and so made more tractable and ready to yield evidence—such are 'the vexations of art!'

At all events the tale which Proteus tells *contributes* to Aristaeus' solution; and the prophet's authoritative pronouncement on the sin—his pursuit of Eurydice—gives added richness and impressiveness to the elaborate tale. It is fitting, too, that we hear the myth of Orpheus from no ordinary mouth. For this 106-line climax within a climax is the story of the supreme singer and patron of poetry—Orpheus whom the hero of the Aeneid was to meet before all others in the Underworld (page 328). This tale of Orpheus, the culmination of the *Georgics*, is a fusion of ancient traditions, folk-tales, romances and, perhaps, semi-historical memories. When Orpheus looked back, Eurydice was lost to him. The earliest known mention of a wife of Orpheus is in Plato's *Symposium*, where he recovers only her phantom.[12] In a long fragment by the third-century BC Alexandrian writer Hermesianax, to whom (as to his master Philetas of Cos) Orpheus was a central figure, his wife is called Argiope. The name of Eurydice the 'wide-judging' (perhaps originally a synonym of Persephone-Proserpina) is first found in the Alexandrian *Lament for Bion*, in which she was successfully restored to life. This had apparently been the earliest version. If so, the account of the failure of Orpheus' quest was introduced later, as an instance of the widespread folk-tale motif of punishment for curiosity (page 417).

But then some poet, unknown to us, saw the myth as symbolizing the futility of seeking to outwit death. The final version seemed to Virgil, as to the Alexandrians before him, the best and most pathetic of all accounts of love. It reproduces a folk-tale current from Thrace to North America and Japan, the story of the man who went to the other world to fetch his wife and (usually) lost her, because he broke some taboo. Ancient and widespread, too, is the idea that men must always avert their eyes from gods or ghosts of the underworld. The gods had warned Orpheus; and even the lord of song was not so powerful as their warning. The power of song was mighty and it could almost call back the dead—but not quite. For song belongs to the human heart, and even the loving human heart is of less avail than death.

2   The Holy Orphic Books

Probably there was an early, lost *Descent of Orpheus to the Underworld*. Such *Descents*, in the eastern Mediterranean world at least, and perhaps among the North American Indians also, have a source in common with the Sumerian epic of Gilgamesh (page 94). There were Greek versions in poems and on vase-paintings, relating to many heroes from Odysseus onwards—though he, according to the main tale, went rather to the ends of the world (pages 74, 92). These adventurous journeys were undertaken in order to search for the dead and interrogate them for revelations of the afterlife; Plato sees such descents as temporary absences of the soul from its human frame. Stories of this kind are common to all agricultural peoples, since the vegetation and crops depended upon the under-world deities, whose other task it was to keep the souls of the dead. Earth is the mother, and the dead return to her (page 146).

St Paul, too, claimed to have travelled beyond the grave. 'Descents' are still told of, and believed today, in Siberia, Mongolia and Tibet where there are *shamans*—in descent from the Sibyls (page 340) or the Delphic Pythia (page 139) or others like them—held to possess an occult control over nature, which they can use to harm or benefit their fellow-men. The Siberian *shaman* wears a feather-coat identifying himself with the dead, who in the Gilgamesh epic have birds' feathers. Assyrian priests wore them too, and Virgil compares the ghosts to thronging birds.

But this myth of the other world, in relation to Orpheus, is only one aspect of the impact made by 'Orphic' tales upon beliefs regarding the afterlife. For the name of Orpheus had also been attached to a collection of religious movements or tendencies which reached their climax in the sixth century BC. He was held to have been a human prophet and teacher and a religious founder; though whether this is true, or if he existed at all, we shall never know. He was said to have come from Thrace, and his rites were linked or identified with those of the Thracian god Dionysus-Bacchus (although later the adherents of the two were at variance). For alongside the tearing apart of Orpheus himself (the subject of Aeschylus' play the *Bassarae*), the Orphics adopted the myth of the child Dionysus' dismembering by the Titans (page 282). Orpheus was also united, especially at Delphi, with Apollo, of whom he may originally have been a satellite; though they came to be contrasted, both laid stress on purification and righteousness. So Orpheus combined both the Apolline and Dionysiac tendencies in Greek religion.

About the Orphic holy books, from which Plato quoted verses, there is much uncertainty. These extensive religious poems presumably included accounts of the life, death and miracles of Orpheus. But what else did they contain? And were some or all of them written (as was conjectured in ancient times) by a pious forger, Onomacritus, in sixth-century Athens? Or perhaps they were the work of a South Italian devotee. For Orphism is close, so close as to be sometimes almost indistinguishable from it, to the ascetic mystery-religion and way of life established in southern Italy during the later sixth century by Pythagoras. Golden tablets subscribing to such beliefs have been found in that country (as well as in Crete), and after Rome's capture, in 209 BC, of Tarentum (Taras)—the home of the Pythagorean school—there was a fresh burst of interest among cosmologically minded Romans.

The most original feature of Orphic doctrine was its much increased emphasis on the judgements and rewards awaiting mankind in the afterlife. The Mysteries of Demeter at Eleusis had long conveyed a similar message (page 148). But that was an established, centralized festival, whereas the Orphics ranged far and wide in small and scattered units, proclaiming in the name of Orpheus the way of salvation,[14] which was also ensured by the sale of indulgences and by every kind of charm and incantation. The specific belief of Orphism was that the soul of man was a fallen god or demon impatient of its imprisonment in an alien body, and due for a cycle of perpetual re-embodiment on earth; and that this 'sorrowful wheel'—for in the archaic age life was scorned—could only be escaped by initiation and (since the ethical content of religion was growing) by righteousness.

Six centuries later, in the *Aeneid*, Virgil amalgamates such doctrines with the Stoic idea (already expressed in the fourth *Georgic*)[15] of a universal spirit from which all animate creatures possess a spark. Human life is a struggle, and the prize of victory—the other face of death—is the coming, through rebirth, to a blissful afterlife. Anacreon of Teos, in the sixth century BC, had expressed all men's horror of the gloomy pit, that Tartarus already located beneath the earth in the *Theogony* (page 127).

> I have gone grey at the temples,
> yes, my head is white, there's nothing
> of the grace of youth that's left me,
> and my teeth are like an old man's.
> Life is lovely. But the lifetime
> that remains for me is little.

> For this cause I mourn. The terrors
> of the Dark Pit never leave me.
> For the house of Death is deep down
> underneath; the downward journey
> to be feared, for once I go there
> I know well there's no returning.[16]

And the most famous painter of antiquity, Polygnotus of Thasos, painted at Delphi, in the following century, many elaborations upon the punishments to be undergone in Hades.[17] His contemporary, Pindar, on the other hand, told of the blessings that awaited him who was saved. With sun shining for evermore,

> The good men
> have life without labour . . .
> Beside the high gods
> they who had joy in keeping faith lead a life
> without tears. The rest look on a blank face of evil.
>
> But they who endure thrice over
> in the world beyond to keep their souls from all sin
> have gone God's way to the tower of Cronus; there
> winds sweep from the Ocean
> across the Island of the Blessed.[18]

So *this* place is not in the underworld but still at the ends of the world, like the goal of Odysseus' journey (page 92). Yet Pindar also wrote of a blessed place beneath the earth.

> For them, when it is night here,
> The strong sun is shining below.
> In fields of scarlet roses lies their city,
> Shadowy with frankincense
> And heavy with golden fruit.[19]

Such hopes and beliefs naturally engendered the further ideas that dying may be a blessed release, that death is 'swallowed up in victory', and that the best preparation for this awaited conclusion is an ascetic life, the root of Puritanism.

The Virgilian poems represent, in ancient times, one of the profoundest attempts to construct Orphism into a necessarily non-logical, only partially coherent, but profoundly moving view of the afterlife.

3   *The Poetic Expression of Myth*

Even divested of the elements which made it the nucleus of religions, the myth of Orpheus is of outstanding significance to its poet, and to poets. For in Orpheus the power of poetry reached its zenith; he is the father of song.[20] To Virgil, as to many a Greek writer, the myth of Orpheus is the myth of the power of *carmen*, the symbol of the poet's incantatory power. Many poets had sought to obtain prestige for their work by using the name of a greater than themselves. The name of Orpheus, in particular, was often used, since he had both the dignity of remote antiquity and the cachet of a mystery-making magician.

Moreover, Orpheus enchants not only human beings but the rest of animate life.

> Over his head
> Birds without number are flying. Fishes leap around
> Out of the deep blue waters, won by the tuneful sound.[21]

Even inanimate things, such as oaks (even stones), are brought under a measure of control. Such scenes were dramatized, Varro tells us, by rich Romans who produced Orphic enchantments, to lyre and trumpet, in their parks. This idea of inanimate objects controlled by the magic of song is considered by Elizabeth Sewell: 'poetry has power not merely over words and hence over thoughts, but also in some way over natural objects and their behaviour.' She uses the myth as a prime symbol of the ancient struggle to evolve a poetical, mythological way of thinking about change and the processes and organisms of life. Not only Virgil, but Shakespeare in the floral fantasies of the *Winter's Tale*, and Marlowe, and more directly and didactically Goethe (page 378) and Erasmus Darwin, have sought to span the gulf between poetry and science by such attempts to develop a poetical and mythical expression of biological realities.

Miss Sewell calls her book *The Orphic Voice*, but is her theme, or the whole of it, truly inherent in the myth of Orpheus? Or is this not rather another instance of the modern employment of myth as a suggestive framework or vehicle for a pattern of thought which was not in it from the beginning?

Miss Sewell makes a point more directly applicable to the myth of Orpheus when she stresses its introspective self-consciousness. 'In the Orpheus story, myth is looking at itself. This is the reflection of myth in its own mirror . . . Orpheus is poetry thinking about itself.' That is why the poet feels the story so deeply. Both statements made by Miss Sewell are true, but by identifying Orpheus and his tale first with self-conscious myth and then with self-conscious poetry, she is referring to two different, though interacting, things. Myth and poetry are interwoven but not completely synonymous; for example poetry cannot really be translated, whereas the mythical value of myth remains preserved, even in the worst translation (page xx). In primitive communities, myths are told less often in song (the ancestor of poetry) than in simple prose, and when song became the medium, it selected and emphasized in order to present a single or limited aspect of the myth. Besides, myth implies, if not belief, at least a background and atmosphere of past beliefs, whereas poetry, in the words of Kant, is 'entirely indifferent to the existence or non-existence of its subject.' The imagination of the myth-maker has been fairly described as the less controlled half-sister of the imagination of the artist or poet, rather as magic is the half-sister (or bastard sister) of applied science.

Yet the association of myth and poetry remains extremely intimate. To poetry, in which reality is experienced on several planes at once, 'the use of recurrent themes is,' as T. S. Eliot said, 'as natural as it is to music'. Myths, because they dealt with the supernatural, very soon inspired songs and owed their orderly presentation to this medium, while song used myth to give itself a new dimension related to the unseen. Throughout the centuries, therefore, many (perhaps most?) poets have gained strength and even originality by drawing upon the accumulated artistic, mythological heritage. Tradition, according to this classical idea, dominates, yet does not hamper.

Instead it provides a framework, a basis of tales and events appealing to the great human affections, which enables and encourages the poet to find himself—in the image of the mythical situation he can concentrate his emotions, or set them in perspective.

Dante (*Paradiso* XXXIII), Byron in *Manfred*, Wordsworth in *The Prelude*, have given their various expressions to this inextricable link between poetry and myth: so has Shelley, whose *Triumph of Life* sees in mythology a liberation from the 'curse which binds us to be subjected to the accident of surrounding impressions'. Even in our own century, when such an attitude is far from universal, Edwin Muir, Ezra Pound and Robert Graves thought that if a poet is to transcend his time he must enter imaginatively into the world of the prime classical myths. And if poetry needs these myths (no less than it needs, for example, metaphor), they in their turn need poetry, 'because a myth is not a myth until it is imaginatively expressed—and it needs to be expressed in poetry before its profoundest reserves of significance can be tapped'.

To the Greeks above all poetry seemed inseparable from myth. What enchanted and moved them, thus forming the basis and fit subjects for their poetic tradition,[22] was the memory of mythical or legendary deeds attributed to supermen of old. An idealizing influence upon the early Greeks, myth found its natural vehicle in poetry, of which the very origins were derived from ballads in praise of the heroes. As time went on the myths, far from becoming the decayed remnants which our own eighteenth century made of them, were loaded by the Greeks with ever more significance and emotional power, derived from the accumulated expression of one poetic imagination after another.

Oscar Wilde, in *The Burden of Itys*, wrote of

> all those tales imperishably stored
> In little Grecian urns, freightage more rich
> Than any gaudy galleon of Spain
> Bare from the Indies ever.

But this gives rather too static an impression, for as Aristotle says 'when telling a tale all men add something to it, because that increases the pleasure'.[23] For this reason, as well as because of faulty memories, patriotic propaganda, mistaken aetiologies (page 122) and the like, there are bewilderingly numerous interpretations of every story: the myths are not frozen, but continuously prompt the exploration of fresh areas of thought and feeling, the weaving and re-weaving of a never completed or completable pattern. Moreover, there are almost as many different *versions* as there are interpretations. Rarely does a single writer supply a full account of any tale, and the seeker after origins desiring to analyse, arrange and classify will often find genuine, ancient material in the least promising and latest authors. Often Callimachus, or Ovid, or the Byzantine Tzetzes give versions earlier in origin than those recorded by poets five hundred or a thousand years before them.

Indeed, the fullest of all mythological handbooks in prose is the *Library* (*Bibliotheca*) bearing the name of Apollodorus, perhaps of the first or second century AD (Diodorus the Sicilian, in the first century BC, had made use of a similar work which is now lost). But to read the uncritical, inartistic Greek prose of Apollodorus is a deadening experience, far indeed from all that Orpheus stands for. It is the task of today's researcher into myths to look at both sides of this question: to match with one another both brands of ancient writer about mythology, the prosaic analyst and the dynamic poet. Without the former, we only have the finished masterpieces, which inevitably distract their admirers from the origins that the archaeologist and anthropologist are obliged to seek (page xx)—distract them so much that Vico (page 424) and Herder even argued the whole corpus of myths to be a product of poets; it remained for Heyne (Christian Gottlob) to distinguish between the myth and its poetic expression. As for the poets of later times, from the Renaissance until today, though they have often brilliantly refashioned Greek myths after their own images, they are less well equipped to offer scholarly explanations of the same stories' origins; and when this is attempted, as in Robert Graves' *White Goddess*, the result is rather to add new myths to old ones.

This special link between Greek poetry and myth has peculiar significance because the role of poetry in Greek society so far

exceeded its part in modern life. Poetry continued without inter-
mission (and even, to a lesser extent, in the Roman world) as the
medium through which great issues were discussed and clarified.
Aristotle points out its advantages for this purpose over history.
The one describes what has happened, the other what might happen.
Hence poetry is the more philosophical and serious of the two, for
poetry speaks of what is universal, history of what is particular.[24]
The distinction was not clear-cut, for the heroic myths were regarded
as containing a core of historical truth (page 34)—such as is present,
for example, in Shakespeare's historical plays. Yet the myths were also
elevated and universalized by their poetical embodiment, and thereby
took a share in poetry's eminent position in society. As a vehicle for
religion and an ideal stratum of history, as material for painting and
sculpture, this mythology represented a body of experience superior
to any other. The number of predicaments in which human beings
can become involved fall into not too many categories. A widespread
human instinct, therefore, prompts the conversion of stories or
events or places or persons into instinctive centres of reference,
which, since the world is too much with us, take the form of myths.

The Orpheus story looks inwards upon the literary creators and
recreators of those myths, reminding us that poets have always
striven to create a mythical world that shall be a symbol for the
world of actual existence. A few, such as Byron and Rimbaud, have
even completed their myths by living them. Most have written about
them, or painted them, instead. 'There is no doubt about it,' remarked
Thomas Mann, 'the moment when the story-teller acquires the
mythical way of looking at things marks a new beginning in his life.
It means a peculiar intensification of his artistic mood, a fresh
serenity in his powers of perception and creation.' And this usually
comes rather late in life. Another novelist who used mythical
material to grasp at the permanent relations of things was Hermann
Broch. It was Broch's view (1945) that mythical novels come into
being at periods of dislocation, like the present time, which call for a
new coherence. The popularity of Herman Melville today (page 211)
points in the same direction; so, in more general terms, does the
steadily increasing critical interest in the literary uses of myth. As the

straightforward naturalism of the 1950's declined, dramatists, too, have often returned to the classical mythology (pages 59, 198, 212, 248). 'I am always looking for myths,' Sartre is quoted as saying (1961)—'in other words, for subjects so sublimated that they are recognizable to everyone, without recourse to minute psychological details'. And it is to the classical stories that he is referring.

Yet, even if we know a little more about the origins of their mythology than the Greeks themselves knew, we are naturally, in other respects, far less at home with this sort of material than they were. For one thing, we have for centuries been living in a civilization that is allegedly based on Christian, not pagan, traditions and values. We also live in a scientific age. Besides, the fact that our poetry and our visual arts no longer work in close association with each other means that myths, which used to be presented simultaneously in both media, have much less chance to make an impact upon us. In Greece, at least from the seventh century BC if not before (page 39), the poet and visual artist worked on the same mythological material and enjoyed comparable prestige and influence over the minds of men. Daedalus is an emblem of that prestige (page 385). So is Pygmalion of Cyprus, who loved a beautiful statue which Venus brought to life to become his bride; Ovid said he had made the statue himself. And so this story (adapted by Shaw to the version popular today in the musical play *My Fair Lady*) reminded the Greeks of an earlier and even more imposing function of art when the artist aimed at rivalling creation itself.

The literary and visual arts served a single end: when the poet varied, explained and embroidered a myth, the visual artist could do the same, for Greeks expected him to and, as Bernard Berenson observed, 'art flowers and ripens upon this humus of minds open to such stories'. Thus the first free-standing sculptured figures (attributed to Daedalus himself)* represent attempts to depict a *mythical* situation. India on the other hand is an example of a country in which epic and drama led to no such association or parallel development with the visual artists. But in the whole history of western art

---

* From the mid-seventh century BC, the Greek 'treaty-port' of Naucratis on the Nile acted as a channel for the transmission of Egyptian sculptural techniques and other ideas.

there has been continual interaction, and at certain times of outstanding artistic achievement, such as the sixteenth century, this has—as in ancient times—taken the form of a preference by sculptors and painters for classical myth. Today, the harnessing together of poetry and visual art does not exist to nearly the same extent. Indeed, except for a few men such as Picasso, Braque and Kokoschka (page 323), artists do not often draw upon the classical myths. The impact neither of poetry nor of mythology, today, is generally reinforced by visual means.

Not, however, that a devotion by artists to myth would nowadays do much to reinstate mythology as an integral part of society. For, whereas neither poetry nor art enjoy the public interest and repute of Greek or even Graeco-Roman times, art even more than poetry has ceased to make much impact upon public taste. There are a few *chic* names, and there are more books and exhibitions about art than ever before, but art has become alien from the community's most cherished habits and preoccupations. As Edgar Wind has remarked, 'an immunity to art enables us to glide along the surfaces of many different artistic experiences without getting involved in any'. The mythological experience is one of them. It may conceivably be communicated to us *either* through Greek literature (even in translation) *or* through the Greek visual arts; or we may gain a vivid, though non-Greek, whiff of it from the varied idioms of Titian, or Claude, or Picasso. But in ancient times the impact of this experience was powerful indeed, for not only were the myths still present and lived with, but they were potently and simultaneously transmitted by the related talents of poetry and visual arts alike.

Throughout the centuries since then until quite recently, poet, painter and sculptor have remained united in their devotion to mythological themes. But it is the poets, in particular, who have agreed with Virgil that Orpheus is their symbol, and have used his name and myth to talk about their art. Ovid, in his *Metamorphoses* (page 375), gives greater prominence to Orpheus than to any other single figure in the work.[25] He is at the hinge of the whole book; Ovid uses the story of Eurydice to claim a lofty value for love, but he also dwells particularly upon Orpheus' death, which Virgil had only told briefly. The fate of Orpheus was to be torn apart by Maenads, either because he had neglected to honour Dionysus or because he taught homosexuality. His severed head floated down the Hebrus, and came finally to Lesbos.

Even in the Catacombs, Orpheus is to be seen singing; the Christians identified him with the Prince of Peace in Isaiah. Dante allegorized the story; Politian in the fifteenth century made it into a tragic drama; and to Henryson (1415–1500) Eurydice is 'goddes infernall' and 'quene of fary'. The Venetian painters dwelt on various aspects of the myth. To Shakespeare, too, the power of music and poetry was a civilizing and pacifying force symbolized by Orpheus.

> Therefore the poet
> Did feign that Orpheus drew trees, stories and floods;
> Since nought so stockish, hard and full of rage,
> But music for the time doth change his nature.

And in him every poet triumphs and suffers. To Milton also Orpheus was a central figure. In *l'Allegro* he calls for soft Lydian airs:

> Untwisting all the chains that tie
> The hidden soul of harmony,
> That Orpheus' self may have his head,
> From golden slumber, on a bed
> Of heaped Elysian flowers, and hear
> Such strains as would have won the ear
> Of Pluto to have quite set free
> His half-regained Eurydice.

Then, in the resonant rhetoric of *Paradise Lost*, he tells of Orpheus' death, and of the might of his song.

Orpheus and Eurydice, familiar from Offenbach, have provided an operatic theme ever since the first of extant operas, Peri and Caccini's *Euridice* of 1600, written for the marriage of Henri IV. But it was Gluck (1714–8) whose treatment of the same theme wedded drama to a more truthful and dignified kind of music, with tension or pathos well contrived by his librettist Calzabigi. The notes of Novalis (d. 1801) for his unfinished novel *Heinrich von Ofterdingen* show that he proposed to identify his hero's death with that of Orpheus. Goethe, in his difficult *Orpheus* (1817), saw him as an oracle darkly revealing the processes of time and change. In Wordsworth's *Power of Music* (1806), he is a street-fiddler in Oxford Street, with New Testament overtones. To Shelley in *Prometheus Unbound*,

> Language is a perpetual Orphic song
> Which rules with Daedal harmony a throng
> Of thoughts and forms which else senseless and
> shapeless were.

Rainer Maria Rilke enjoyed a special power of reliving myths and infusing them with a new, personal meaning; and the story of Orpheus, in particular, is one which provides the framework for many of his private symbols. His *Orpheus, Eurydice, Hermes* (1904) is unusual because it is with Eurydice, not Orpheus, that the poet seems to identify himself—abdicating from human relations, and celebrating the rejection of fertility that is death. The twenty-six poems that form the first part of Rilke's fifty-five *Sonnets to Orpheus* (1922), comprising an extraordinary, climactic lyrical spasm, are addressed to Orpheus whose music breaks down rigid forms of nature, lending them new rhythms and dimensions. About twelve of the poems deal with the Orphic legend in the closer sense, and of these the first and last tell his story. The final poem recounts his death and destruction, but also declares that his influence does not die.

> Though they destroyed you at last and revenge had its
> will,
> Sound of you lingered in lions and rocks you were
> first to
> Enthral, in the trees and the birds. You are singing
> there still.

Oscar Kokoschka, too, has been thinking of Orpheus since 1913 at least. During a personal crisis after he was wounded in the

First World War, he wrote the play *Orpheus and Eurydice* which has been performed at Vienna (attracting great attention) in 1961. The décor is by the author—a significant versatility in the recreation of a myth. Orpheus descends to Hades for Eurydice, but Eurydice must return there: for she expects Pluto's child, who will incarnate creative regeneration. In this strongly emotional view of the basic sex-war, woman is permanent, linked with the growth of the earth; man (although our civilization is dominated by him) is impermanent and restless, his love for woman leading only to sorrow and death. A more positive attitude to Orpheus inspired the dramatically surging figures carved in wood (1935, 1949) by Ossip Zadkine (born in Smolensk), a sculptor who prefers the basic classical myths as the subjects for his seething, unexpected imagery. His interpretation of Orpheus may be contrasted with the calm, graceful vitality of the same mythical figure in the hands of Carl Milles.

The *Eurydice* of Anouilh (1941) on the other hand—the first of his war-time plays—symbolizes the dreariness of life, with all the elements of Greek tragic inevitability. The love of a penniless musician's young son for the daughter of an insignificant actress can only be saved (as there is a mysterious Hermes to show) if, metaphorically, the young man does not turn his eyes upon this love. But he insists on knowing the truth of her life—the theme which Proust had worked out in so much detail—and he is doomed by the irreconcilability of her banal, futile everyday makeshifts with the ideal picture in his mind. Yet Anouilh is on the side of Eurydice—one of his typical heroines as Harold Hobson said, 'all simple, all kind, all frail, all with a curious stamp of soiled purity'. In Cocteau's surrealist but poetic extravaganza *Orphée*, the medium of the cinema, including trick photography, is mobilized to reinvigorate the same myth. The poet is torn to pieces because, in the poetry competition, he submits a coarse joke. Death, on which the film (like its sequel *Testament d'Orphée*) is a meditation, is its most imposing figure. 'We are in the supernatural,' concludes Cocteau, 'up to our necks'.

CHAPTER 13

THE QUEST FOR A NEW HOME

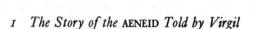

I   The Story of the AENEID *Told by Virgil*

I SING of arms and the man who, fated to be an exile, was the first to sail from the land of Troy and reach the coast of Lavinium in Italy. He suffered greatly on sea and land because of the anger of Juno, and he endured much in warfare, before he could build a city and instal his gods in Latium. From him came the Latin race, the lords of Alba Longa, and the lofty city of Rome.

Carthage, the home of settlers from Tyre, was loved by Juno above all other lands, and even above Samos. But at the siege of Troy her love for Argos had made her an enemy of the Trojans, and now, knowing that men of Trojan descent were fated one day to overthrow Carthage, she sent storms to scatter Aeneas' remnant from the siege—those whom even Achilles had not been able to kill—all over the ocean. For as Aeneas was sailing from Sicily towards the Italian shore, the goddess persuaded Aeolus, lord of the winds, to raise a tempest and scatter his fleet, which was driven near the perilous coast of Africa. Neptune, however, felt the upheaval and calmed the waters. Three of the Trojan ships were sunk, but the rest came safely to different points of the shore. Next day, Aeneas journeyed inland, accompanied by Achates, and reached the city of Carthage. Encountering on the way his mother Venus, who had learnt from Jupiter of Rome's great destiny, he was informed by her that the new settlement's ruler was Dido: she had fled from her native Tyre after the murder of her husband Sychaeus. The queen gave Aeneas a hospitable welcome, and Venus sent Cupid to make her fall in love with him.

At a banquet that night Dido invited her visitor to describe the fall of Troy and his wanderings. He began by telling of the wooden horse, devised by Epeus the Greek, which the Trojans were deceived into accepting in their town; and of the ill-omened death of the Trojan priest Laocoon, strangled by huge red-crested snakes. Then Aeneas recalled the last night of his city, when the Greek soldiers descended from the horse's hollow belly and opened the gates to their army, which had secretly returned from Tenedos.

> They were young and angry, like wolves, marauders in
>   black mist, whom hunger
> Drives blindly on; whose whelps, abandoned, wait them
> Dry-jawed . . .

> Who could explain that night's destruction, equal
> Its agony with tears?

> Everywhere sorrow,
> Everywhere panic, everywhere the image
> Of death, made manifold.[1]

Aeneas told how at the bidding of Venus he made his escape from the burning city, taking his wife Creusa, his father Anchises, his son Ascanius (Iulus), and his household gods. He and his father and son escaped, but in the turmoil he became separated from Creusa. Searching for her, he met her ghost, for she was already dead—and her wraith disclosed that he was destined to settle in the land of the west.

Aeneas went on to speak of his wanderings since that day. Warned away from Thrace by the voice of his murdered relative Polydorus, he and his men had visited Delos, where the oracle of Apollo bade them 'seek their ancient mother'. They tried to stay in Crete but were attacked by a plague, and Aeneas was warned by his household gods in a dream that Italy, not Crete, was to be his destination. Storm-driven to the islands of the Strophades, they were attacked by Harpies and landed on the shores of Epirus. Here Priam's son Helenus had settled, become king, and married Andromache, whose ravisher Achilles' son Pyrrhus (Neoptolemus) had died. Helenus bade them make for Italy, consulting the Sibyl at Cumae and conciliating Juno.

And then Aeneas concluded his story to Dido with an account of their journeyings along the coast of Sicily, past the perils of the Cyclops, to the western extremity of the island. There, at Drepanum, ruled by his kinsman Acestes who hospitably received them, Aeneas' father Anchises had died.

The Carthaginian queen confided to her sister Anna that, although she had sworn never to marry again, she was falling more and more deeply under Aeneas' spell. When a storm burst upon the two of them as they were out hunting, they sheltered in a cave, and made love.

> And the mountain nymphs wail high their incantations:
> First day of death, first cause of evil.[2]

Venus had persuaded Juno to consent to the match so that the two goddesses should be at peace. But Jupiter sent Mercury to warn Aeneas that it was not his destiny to remain in Africa, and that he must leave Dido at once. Aeneas planned to depart in secret, but the queen discovered his intentions and desperately begged him to stay.

> And good Aeneas, longing
> To ease her grief with comfort, to say something
> To turn her pain and hurt away, sighs often,
> His heart being moved by this great love most deeply,
> And still—the gods give orders, he obeys them.
> He goes back to the fleet.[3]

And so Dido killed herself; and as he sailed away, Aeneas saw her funeral pyre.

He returned to Drepanum, and celebrated the anniversary of his father's death with funeral games. While these were taking place, the Trojan women, at Juno's instigation, burnt four of his ships. But he himself, leaving some of his men behind as settlers, sailed on. However, Venus and Neptune had made a pact that one man must pay with his life for the safety of the rest, and his pilot Palinurus, sleeping at the helm, fell overboard and was drowned.

Aeneas now landed in Italy and sought out the Sibyl of Cumae, who in a prophetic trance foretold that he would fight wars in Italy for the sake of a foreign bride. He begged her for admission to the Underworld, so that he might again see his father face to face, and she told him how this could be done.

> By night, by day, the portals of dark Dis
> Stand open: it is easy, the descending
> Down to Avernus. But to climb again,
> To trace the footsteps back to the air above,
> There lies the task, the toil. A few, beloved
> By Jupiter, descended from the gods,
> A few, in whom exalting virtue burned,
> Have been permitted.[4]

The Sibyl told Aeneas to seek out and pluck the Golden Bough which would admit him to the Underworld. She also bade him bury a dead comrade whom he would find; and on leaving the cave, he saw and buried the body of Misenus, drowned for challenging the gods with the music of his horn. Then Aeneas plucked the Golden Bough, and after sacrificing to the gods of the Underworld descended with the Sibyl into an opening of the earth beside Lake Avernus. They went on their way, 'walking in the darkness, with the shadows round them and night's loneliness above them, through Pluto's substanceless Empire, and past its homes where there is no life within; as men walk through a wood under a fitful moon's ungenerous light when Jupiter has hidden the sky in shade and a black night has stolen the colour from the world.'[5] They passed a giant elm tree—the home of False Dreams—and the ghosts of many monsters.

> From here, the road turns off to Acheron,
> River of Hell; here, thick with muddy whirling,

Cocytus boils with sand. Charon is here,
The guardian of these mingling waters, Charon
Uncouth and filthy, on whose chin the hair
Is a tangled mat, whose eyes protrude, are burning;
Whose dirty cloak is knotted at the shoulder.
He poles a boat, tends to the sail unaided,
Ferrying bodies in his rust-hued vessel.
Old, but a god's senility is awful
In its raw greenness.

To the bank come thronging
Mothers and men, bodies of great-souled heroes,
Their life-time over, boys, unwedded maidens,
Young men whose fathers saw their pyres burning,
Thick as the forest leaves that fall in autumn
With early frost, thick as the birds to landfall
From over the seas, when the chill of the year
    compels them
To sunlight. There they stand, a host, imploring
To be taken over first. Their hands, in longing,
Reach out for the farther shore. But the gloomy
    boatman
Makes choice among them, taking some, and keeping
Others far back from the stream's edge.[6]

When Aeneas and the Sibyl had crossed the stream, they heard the
loud wailing of those who had died in infancy. They also passed the
ghosts of men who had been condemned on a false accusation,
and others who had killed themselves. Then, in the Fields of Mourning, they came upon those who had died because of the cruelties of
love; among them was Dido. Her unjust fate brought pity to
Aeneas' heart. But he and the Sibyl passed on, and entered the
Secluded Fields thronged by war heroes. From there, he saw beneath
him, encircled by the burning river Phlegethon, great battlements.
These were the prison-walls, the Sibyl told him, for those whom
heaven had condemned to eternal punishment.

Finally they came to the Elysian Fields. There, after seeing Orpheus, Aeneas met the spirit of Anchises, his father. Anchises revealed to him the workings of the universe, and the purifications through which men could be admitted to Elysium. From this Land of Joy, though 'each of us finds the world of death which is fitted to himself', some, after a thousand years, would be sent back to earth, deprived by a draught from Lethe of all memory of what they had been before. Among these would be Aeneas' own descendants; whom Anchises now showed him, in a pageant of Roman history culminating in Augustus and Augustus' nephew Marcellus, cut off in his youth.

And so Aeneas and the Sibyl departed from the Underworld. They went out by one of the Twin Gates of Sleep—not by the Gate of Horn, which provides a path for shadows that are true, but by the Gate of Ivory, through which the spirits send visions that are false in the light of day. Rejoining his comrades, Aeneas coasted along to Caieta, and then into the Tiber's mouth.

Latinus, ruler of Latium, had a daughter Lavinia, whom the oracle of his father Faunus, at Albunea's spring, had warned him he must marry to a stranger. Turnus, prince of the Rutulians, had claimed Lavinia's hand, but Latinus now knew that her bridegroom must be Aeneas. His queen, Amata, however, still favoured Turnus; and Juno, through the Fury Allecto, caused war against Aeneas to break out by making Ascanius unknowingly kill a pet stag. The people of Latinus and their allies rose against the Trojan invaders, and Latinus was compelled to declare them his enemies.

Aeneas was visited in a dream by father Tiber, who bade him seek the help of Evander the Arcadian, ruler of the Palatine Hill at Rome. When this message was confirmed the next morning (as the dream had foretold) by the sight of a white sow with a white litter, Aeneas made for the site of Rome. He found Evander celebrating the festival of Hercules, and learnt from him how the hero-god had slain the monster Cacus on the Aventine Hill. Evander took Aeneas on a journey round the hallowed sites of Rome; and they saw the thick Capitoline wood which Romulus was to make a sanctuary.

From there
They went to the Tarpeian house, and a place
Golden as we now know it, once a thicket,
Once brush and briar, and now our Capitol.
Even then men trembled, fearful of a presence
Haunting this wood, this rock. 'A god lives here,'
Evander said, 'What god, we are not certain,
But certainly a god. Sometimes my people
Think they have seen, it may be, Jove himself
Clashing the darkening shield, massing the storm-cloud.[7]

As night came, they went in to Evander's humble dwelling.

Venus persuaded her husband Vulcan to make celestial armour for Aeneas, including a shield engraved with a prophetic series of scenes from Roman history, down to the battle of Actium. During the absence of Aeneas, however, Juno had sent Iris to warn Turnus that his chance was at hand. Turnus attacked the Trojan camp, and set the ships on fire. But at the request of the goddess Cybele, from whose holy mountain of Ida their timbers had come, Neptune transformed the vessels into nymphs of the sea.

In accordance with instructions left by Aeneas, the Trojans stayed behind their walls. But during the night Nisus and his youthful comrade Euryalus left the place secretly in order to reach Aeneas and tell him what had happened. Among the Rutulians, lying in drunken disarray, they did great carnage, but were finally tracked down and slain. On the following day Turnus renewed the attack, and even broke inside the ramparts, but he was cut off, and retreated with difficulty.

At a Council of the Gods, Juno and Venus debated angrily about the war, but Jupiter decreed that the issue must be left to Fate. As the fighting continued, Aeneas gained the reinforcement of an Etruscan army which had revolted from its brutal King Mezentius, whom Aeneas now killed in a duel. But first the young son of Evander, Pallas, had met his death at the hands of Turnus.

> Ah, mind of man, so ignorant of fate, of what shall befall him,

So weak to preserve moderation when riding the crest
    of good fortune!
For Turnus a time is coming when he'd give anything
To have left Pallas unharmed, and will loathe this
    day and the spoils
It brought him.

Today had been his baptism in war, today his end;
Still, he had left behind him a trail of Italian dead.[8]

The dead were buried, under truce. But a decision, prompted by the Latin Drances, to settle the war by single combat between Aeneas and Turnus came to nothing against Turnus' advice to try another battle. On the Latin side, the Amazonian heroine Camilla performed feats of great valour, but lost her life. As Diana's companion Opis cries,

You lived alone in the wild wood, you served Diana and
    carried
Our quiver upon your shoulder; but none of this
    saved you now.
Still, your mistress has seen that you shall not be
    left dishonoured
In death's last hour . . .

Whoever it was that wounded and desecrated your body
Shall get the death he deserves.[9]

The Latins withdrew in disorder into their city, but Turnus roared out defiance like a lion.

   Another truce now resulted in Turnus' acceptance of the duel with Aeneas. His sister the nymph Juturna prompted the Rutulians to violate the agreement, and to wound Aeneas treacherously with an arrow. But Venus caused his wound to be healed, and Queen Amata, believing that Turnus was already dead, hanged herself. After Jupiter had conciliated Juno with a decree that Trojans and Latins would become united, the two heroes fought. Turnus was struck down, and, as he died, begged that his body might be returned to his old father. Aeneas might have weakened—but he saw on Turnus' body the bright-studded belt of Pallas. Then, with a shout of vengeance, he struck the fatal blow.

2 *Nationalism and Guilt*

Virgil's last and greatest work was this *Aeneid*, which was all but complete at the time of his death at Brundisium (19 BC). Its preservation, according to tradition, was ensured—against the poet's dying wish—by Augustus.

The *Iliad* and the *Odyssey* had fixed for ever the form, metre and structure of ancient epic poetry. Centuries later, Alexandrians such as Apollonius Rhodius had infused the Greek epic with a new, romantic element (page 299); and Virgil, too, marries epic with romance. But shortly after Apollonius, the Romans had launched out upon their own epic tradition, starting (as far as we know) with Livius Andronicus' translation of the *Odyssey*. Very soon, however, there developed a national epic, embodying the nation's conception of its own past history. This idea came naturally to the Romans, who tended to think of the prime function of literature as patriotic. Naevius, from Campania (*c.* 270–201 BC)—using a native metre, the Saturnian—chose a subject from the recent past, the First Punic War (*Bellum Poenicum*), in which he probably interpreted the Trojan legend as the preface to Rome's struggle with Carthage. Ennius of Rudiae in Calabria (b. 239 BC) adapted the Homeric metre to write a Latin verse chronicle, the *Annals*, containing passages of crude and rugged grandeur. Then, in the first century BC, Lucretius wrote a long philosophical poem *On the Nature of Things* (*De Rerum Natura*).

For his *Aeneid* Virgil drew upon all these and many other poems besides, and yet it is a work of outstanding originality. In a sense, the poem consists of an *Odyssey* of travel followed by an *Iliad* of war. But there is an enormous gulf between the ballad-like, orally transmitted Homeric epics and the complex, contrapuntal profundities of the Virgilian poem.

The story of Dido's love for Aeneas, and of his departure from her, is the climax of romantic epic and of Virgil's sensibility. Aeneas returns her love, but this is patriotic as well as romantic myth, and his individual freedom is less than his allegiance to a cause. Destiny is calling him to Italy; and Italy is doomed to be Carthage's enemy. So he must go and, in harrowing scenes reminiscent of the conflicts of Greek tragedy, she kills herself.

> Even thus was the hero belaboured for long with
>   every kind of
> Pleading, and his great heart thrilled through and
>   through with the pain of it.
> Resolute, though, was his mind; unavailing rolled
>   her tears.
> But the hapless Dido, frightened out of her wits by
>   her destiny,
> Prayed for death: she would gaze no more on the
>   dome of daylight.[10]

Yet Virgil does not explicitly say whose were the tears that rolled unavailingly: and for many centuries it has been disputed whether it was Dido or Aeneas who wept.

Tragic, too, is the fate of Aeneas' enemy, the Latin warrior Turnus.

> As Turnus saw the Latins failing, broken,
> With Mars against them, and all eyes upon him
> Awaiting the fulfilment of his promise,
> He burned with wrath, implacable, and lifted
> His spirit high, as in the fields of Carthage
> A lion, sorely sounded by the hunters,
> Fights harder for the hurt, the happier for it,
> And the mane rises on the neck and shoulders,
> And the jaws break off the weapon, and the bloody
>   mouth
> Roars out defiance; even so in Turnus
> The violent spirit raged.[11]

Turnus resists the invaders, but is doomed to lose his promised bride Lavinia to Aeneas, and to die at his enemy's hand. Fate overrides strong manhood, as well as strong love. But the sympathetic tenderness which the poet feels for the victims of destiny and power is heard in—

> the Virgilian cry,
> The sense of tears in mortal things.

Such, in the words of Matthew Arnold's *Palladium*, is the human sympathy of the poet who, more than any other, expresses the bitter sweetness of mortal triumphs—seeing that they mean the sorrow of another.

So nobly, it has been said, are Turnus and Dido depicted, in Virgil's myth, that the character of Aeneas is insipid by comparison: they are man and woman, but he is only the servant of Fate. Yet that is not the poet's point of view. Aeneas represents his ideal of the good man, the man who presses on regardless of life's buffers and obstacles. This was the ideal put forward by Zeno of Citium, founder of the Stoics (*c.* 300 BC); and it was the finest of moral exemplars before Christianity. There is, moreover, a dramatic development of Aeneas' character: he has his weaknesses and only gradually, with the aid of Providence, overcomes them. Meanwhile, Aeneas feels all the sorrow in what he has to do. There is a new and terrible sophistication about this knowledge that right must be done despite misgivings, and the height of poignancy is reached when Turnus has to die.

> Turnus is down, on hands and knees, huge Turnus
> Struck to the earth. Groaning, the stunned Rutulians
> Rise to their feet, and the whole hill resounds,
> The wooded heights give echo. A suppliant, beaten,
> Humbled at last, his hands reach out, his voice
> Is low in pleading:— 'I have deserved it, surely,
> And I do not beg off. Use the advantage.
> But if a parent's grief has any power
> To touch the spirit, I pray you, pity Daunus

(I would Anchises), send him back my body.
You have won; I am beaten, and these hands go out
In supplication: everyone has seen it.
No more. I have lost Lavinia. Let hatred
Proceed no farther.'
Fierce in his arms, with darting glance, Aeneas
Paused for a moment, and he might have weakened—
For the words had moved him—when high on the
    shoulder
He saw the belt of Pallas, slain by Turnus;
Saw Pallas on the ground, and Turnus wearing
That belt with the bright studs, of evil omen
Not only to Pallas now, a sad reminder,
A deadly provocation. Terrible
In wrath, Aeneas cries:— 'Clad in this treasure,
This trophy of a comrade, can you cherish
Hope that my hands would let you go? Now Pallas,
Pallas exacts his vengeance, and the blow
Is Pallas, making sacrifice!' He struck
Before he finished speaking: the blade went deep
And Turnus' limbs were cold in death. The spirit
Went with a moan indignant to the shadows.[12]

And yet, for all this desperate tragedy, the fate of Turnus is only
incidental to Virgil's principal concern. For the poet's pathos and
Stoicism alike are harnessed to Roman nationalism; his main theme
is the preparation for the founding of Rome by Aeneas' descendants.

The poet's chosen hero Aeneas, King Anchises' son (fairly prominent in the *Iliad*) who escaped from the conflagration of Troy, had
figured actively in Greek myth since Stesichorus, not long after 600
BC, traced his wanderings as far as Sicily. Either the same poet or,
more probably, a later writer made Aeneas the founder of Capua in
Campania. An early sixth-century coin of the Macedonian city
Aeneia shows that this town too considered him its founder; and
statuettes from Etruscan Veii, perhaps of the next century, show him
carrying his father from the ruins of Troy. Greek writers of the

fifth and fourth centuries linked him with Rome, which according to the historian Timaeus (*c.* 356–260 BC) was founded in 814 BC (the *Theogony* had known of a King Latinus living at the end of the 'gulf of sacred isles');[13] the amended date later preferred was 753.

But either date left a gap of centuries between the traditional time of the Trojan War (*c.* 1200 BC) and the establishment of the city. So in this intervening period the Roman mythologists, taking over the awkward hiatus from the Greeks, gave themselves free play, peopling the gap with mythical ancestors fabricated by their own leading families. By about 300 BC there was an accepted tradition that the Trojans had landed in Latium, and Timaeus was shown their relics in the Temple of Venus at Lavinium—a town which Aeneas was supposed to have founded as a forerunner of Rome.

These Trojan traditions were eagerly welcomed or invented, since the Roman desire to follow and equal Greek literature demanded that the foundation of the state should be based on a theme from the Greek epic cycle. Yet Rome's tradition of wars against Greece required that it should take Troy's side in the Trojan War—for indeed its Greek enemy King Pyrrhus of Epirus, early in the third century BC, had declared himself the descendant of Achilles. Aenean traditions were strengthened at Rome in the first Punic War, when the Romans were pleased to find common origins with the Aeneas-founded communities of Sicily, with which they were allied. At the time when Virgil wrote, the latest of Rome's enemies had again been a Greek: Queen Cleopatra of Egypt, regarded as the epitome of un-Roman-ness. Her conqueror was Virgil's friend and patron Augustus, whose future glory is disclosed to Aeneas, in the sixth book of the *Aeneid*, by his father Anchises.

> One promise you have heard
> Over and over: here is its fulfilment,
> The son of a god, Augustus Caesar, founder
> Of a new age of gold, in lands where Saturn*
> Ruled long ago; he will extend his empire

* Saturn (Cronus) was believed to have ruled Italy ('Saturnia') in its primitive Golden Age.

Beyond the Indies, beyond the normal measure
Of years and constellations, where high Atlas
Turns on his shoulders the star-studded world.[14]

Aeneas is not, indeed, the replica of Augustus, but is very clearly his
forerunner. There were tough features about Augustus' rule, which
cannot have commended themselves to the sensitive Virgil. Yet both
belonged to a generation which after decades of civil war needed
peace more than anything else, and men were prepared to acclaim
the bringer of peace although he brought also a limitation of personal
freedom. Even Homer's attitude to war had at times been less than
enthusiastic (page 55); Virgil is war-weary, and sees the miseries and
frustrations of battle. Even the death of Aeneas' wholly evil foe,
Mezentius, is a cause for no exultation. Virgil suffers from a malaise,
or from a national guilt about war, and interprets his myths accordingly.

He has dominated western culture. In ancient times he soon became
not only a linguistic and spiritual model, but an oracle, and medieval
thought at every level was dominated by his fabulous repute, as
superhuman sage and magician as well as poet—the reteller of myths
himself became a myth. This was partly because his fourth *Eclogue*,
in which he foretold the millennium, seemed to Christians a
messianic prophecy. But the fate of Dido was what distracted
Augustine from weeping over his own sins; and Chaucer, too, in
his *Legend of Dido*, dwelt on the tragedy of Aeneas' broken vows.

Dante was guided by Virgil to the Underworld, as the Cumaean
Sibyl had guided Aeneas; and the Sibyl was given supreme artistic
expression by Michelangelo in his figure on the ceiling of the Sistine
Chapel (1510–11), which displays his unequalled knowledge of the
human body, at rest as in movement, and was the admiration of
Goethe, Reynolds and Fuseli. Three years later Raphael painted the
Sibyls in S. Maria della Pace in Rome, and there are Cumaean and
Tiburtine Sibyls by Veronese at S. Sebastiano in Venice.

Milton, who attained international renown as a Latin poet,
remade English poetry in a Latin mould so as to reproduce, in

Paradise Lost, the sonorous, complex rhythmical patterns of the *Aeneid*. Like Virgil too, and like Tasso in his *Jerusalem Delivered* and Camoens in his *Lusiad*, Milton makes a divinely sponsored cause the true protagonist of his epic—and he extends Virgil's prophetic, mythological treatment of history to the bounds of all time and creation. His relation to Virgil is like Virgil's to his own forerunners: Milton's multitudinous debts to Virgil are the very means by which he achieves originality, blending tradition and inspiration in powerful union.

The same seventeenth century witnessed one of the supreme interpretations of the *Aeneid* in the visual field also. Though Claude could not read the poem—knowing its contents through translations, conversations and the work of earlier artists—a wondering love for the Virgilian country-side round Rome and Naples was what inspired his painting. In these serene yet moving compositions, the Aenean golden age (as well as the pastoral utopia of the *Eclogues*) lives again, in the heat of the noon, the glow of evening, and the cool that follows the dawn. In contrast to the logical, heroic landscapes of Poussin (page 308), Claude suffused the deeds of Aeneas with a nostalgic tone of changing lights and mingling associations, a poetry that breathes a new classicism of France.

3 The Two Gates of Sleep

The myths of the *Aeneid* are devoted to religion as well as nationalism. Virgil calls Aeneas *pius*, which means dedicated to his family and his country, and in harmony with the will of Providence. The poet was lovingly attentive to the tales of the gods and especially to the old traditions (scarcely myths, page 347) of native Italian cult. But he was at heart a monotheist who believed—as the Stoics did— in the rule of the world by an omnipotent deity who was also Fate; and, if he had lived longer, he was to have passed on to philosophy.

The turning point of the *Aeneid* comes in the sixth of its twelve books, when Aeneas has landed in Italy. His wanderings, though not his troubles, are at an end, and he is granted initiation into his new heritage. Lake Avernus, where he is allowed in the company of the

Sibyl to penetrate into the Underworld, lies in the centre of a volcanic country, the Phlegraean plain—named after Macedonian Phlegra, where the giants were struck by lightning when they fought against the gods. Near by was Cumae, the most ancient of Greek colonies in Italy. Founded in the eighth century BC—though tradition took it back three centuries earlier—this city was the nucleus and diffusing agent of Greek civilization in the Italian peninsula.

The shores of Lake Avernus had, in Virgil's time, been made into a naval harbour, and many ancient substructures (some of them visible today) had no doubt come to light, suggesting speculations about the past. Oldest of all, not far from these dark, mephitic waters, was the Cumaean oracle, for the Greek colonists were said to have found a necromantic holy place already there when they came.[15] Its priestesses the Sibyls—whose predecessors' bones and mummies were displayed at Cumae—were ministers of Apollo and Hecate, trance-experiencing, possessed ecstatics like the Delphic Pythia and Siberian *shamans* (pages 139, 140). There were many frenzied women described as Sibyls in different places, and generally their shrines were associated with the earth and with caverns. There was believed to have been a Sibyl at Erythrae in Ionia before the Trojan War, and Heraclitus (*c.* 500 BC) tells of the Sibyl who 'with raving lips uttering things mirthless, unadorned and unscented, reaches over a thousand years with her voice, thanks to the god in her'.[16] In an older tradition than Virgil's, Aeneas consulted the Sibyl of Marpessus not far from Troy. But the *Aeneid* reflects the belief that in early times one or more of these tranced prophetesses came to Italy. The most famous was here in Campania, the country where Virgil spent the greater part of his adult life, mostly at Neapolis (Naples) and Nola where Augustus had given him residences. Ten miles west of Naples were Lake Avernus and Cumae, where reigned the Sibyl in her subterranean shrine (now uncovered) beneath Apollo's temple.

The prophecies of Sibyls, written on leaves, contributed largely to the Books of Sibylline oracles which were held in awe among Romans. Their initial collection was ascribed to King Tarquinius Priscus—whose name stands for the period of Etruscan rule at Rome (page 364)—and the oracles were lodged in a stone box within the Temple of Jupiter, Juno and Minerva (page 366). They were under the control of a committee of fifteen men, but could only be consulted at the Senate's command. These records were destroyed when the temple was burnt down in 83 BC, but seven years later a new collection of oracles (including much Graeco-Jewish material) was made and deposited within the rebuilt temple. In these disturbed years of the failing Republic, when prophecies abounded and religion and astrology attracted keen interest, the Sibylline Books received much attention; and finally Augustus, after editing their contents, transferred them to the new temple of his patron god Apollo on the Palatine Hill. Consultations of the oracles continued until AD 365. Exactly two centuries later the Sibyl's cave was destroyed by the Byzantine general Narses.

The descent of Aeneas to the Underworld, while belonging to a widespread pattern, especially resembles a Journey after Death in the myth of Malekula in the Melanesian New Hebrides, a tale which anthropologists such as Leo Frobenius and Adolf Jensen plausibly regard as sharing an ultimate common source with the Graeco-Roman tradition (page 82). At Malekula, as here, the journey starts in a cave near the sea-shore, with a female companion, a maze or labyrinth at the outset of the quest, and a ferryman. In both cases a bough or wand is necessary as a talisman; at Malekula it is called *ne-row*, in Virgil it is the Golden Bough.

> In a dark tree there hides
> A bough, all golden, leaf and pliant stem,
> Sacred to Proserpine. This all the grove
> Protects, and shadows cover it with darkness.
> Until this bough, this bloom of light, is found,
> No one receives his passport to the darkness,
> Whose queen requires this tribute. In succession,
> After the bough is plucked, another grows,
> Gold-green with the same metal. Raise the eyes,
> Look up, reach up the hand, and it will follow

With ease, if fate is calling; otherwise,
No power, no steel, can loose it.[17]

Such a bough, widely paralleled in other cultures, has already
appeared in the Gilgamesh epic (page 94); its gold foil is reminiscent
of Minoan and Mycenaean work, and of the golden tablets of
Pythagoreans in Italy (page 313). Virgil's bough is compared, or
identified, with the mistletoe[18] which is famous for its magic powers
in European folk-lore—the mistletoe which stands for life in the
midst of death, and wards death off, being allegedly indestructible
by fire or water.[19]

An ancient commentator identifies this bough with another,
plucked in the grove (*nemus*) at Aricia beside Lake Nemi, which
inspired the title of Sir James Frazer's *Golden Bough*. This sacred
grove of Diana at Aricia, though it had no myth (the Romans, by a
false etymology, provided one), possessed a sinister rite, based on
the ideas of ritual regicide which, originating somewhere between the
Caspian Sea and the Persian Gulf, spread west, south-east, and south-
west through Arabia and Africa. Every aspirant to the priesthood
of Diana was a runaway slave: who, after breaking a certain branch
as a challenge, struck down his predecessor—'the priest who slew
the slayer and shall himself be slain'. The scene beside the Alban
Hills, luminously serene in contrast with its bloody past, is rendered
in a picture by J. M. W. Turner (1775–1851)—a wonderful attempt to
set within the Aenean framework, and to display in his own curving
rhythms, the warmth and glitter, the high key of colour, which made
such an impression upon the painter when he first visited Italy.

However, whatever the relation between Virgil's bough and that
of Nemi, the *function* of the former was distinct: it was associated
with the rites of Proserpina, and provided a key to the Underworld.

In the *Odyssey* as it has come down to us, there had been an
inconsistency. The account of Odysseus' visit to the land of the dead
(page 92) does not explain how, since he remained beside the
trench and did not go down to Hades, he could have seen the
criminals suffering punishment in the Underworld. Virgil does not
cause Aeneas to enter this region of pain, but makes the Sibyl

describe it to him. It is his father Anchises, on the other hand, who foretells to him the glories of the future: when Aeneas has overcome the horrors and dangers that encompass his route, Anchises reveals to him a prophetic vision. Odysseus, having called up Tiresias from the dead, had heard from him of his own voyage home and his future fate. But Aeneas learns from Anchises not only of the wars and adventures awaiting himself in Latium, but also of the coming glories of Rome which his line is to found.

> There will be a son of Mars; his mother
> Is Ilia, and his name is Romulus,
> Assaracus' descendant. On his helmet
> See, even now, twin plumes; his father's honour
> Confers distinction on him for the world.
> Under his auspices Rome, that glorious city,
> Will bound her power by earth, her pride by heaven,
> Happy in hero sons, one wall surrounding
> Her seven hills; even as Cybele riding
> Through Phrygian cities wears her crown of towers,
> Rejoicing in her offspring and embracing
> A hundred children of the gods, her children,
> Celestials, all of them, at home in heaven.
> Turn the eyes now this way; behold the Romans,
> Your very own! These are Iulus' children,
> The race to come.[20]

And the climax is the advent of Augustus (page 337).

To Aeneas are also disclosed the mysteries of the universe. These are conveyed in an account, already foreshadowed in the fourth *Georgic* (page 308), blending Orphism and Stoicism with folk-tales and myths gathered from a variety of sources. Like many people today, Virgil combines, and does not wholly reconcile, a Stoic belief in predestination and the Orphic conviction of immortality as a reward for virtue. But he is writing poetry, not theology.

Virgil's Underworld myth, and his own mind, would yield some of their secrets if we could understand the Two Gates of Sleep, through one of which—the Gate of Ivory—Aeneas reascended, at the end of this sixth book of the *Aeneid*, to the upper air.

In the *Odyssey* Penelope, after telling her dream of an eagle killing twenty geese (page 76), had said that dreams are not necessarily fulfilled. For there are two gates of unsubstantial dreams: the one is wrought in horn and the other in ivory. 'Those then that have come through the sawn ivory are vain' (the Greek verb *elephairontai*, 'are vain', has the same sound as *elephas*, ivory), 'and bring messages that are not fulfilled. But they that have come forth through the carven horn attain true fulfilment' (the verb *krainousi*, 'attain fulfilment', resembles *keras*, horn). 'But I think not that my strange dream came thence: welcome would it be for me and my son were it so.'[21] Virgil adapts the *Odyssey*, as he adopts much else too, in order to express his own poetic conceptions. 'There are twin Gates of Sleep,' he says, 'of which one is said to be of horn, allowing an easy exit for shadows which are true (*veris umbris*). The other is all of shining white ivory, perfectly made; but the Spirits send visions which are false (*falsa insomnia*) in the light of day (or, by a variant translation, "send false visions to the light of day"). And Anchises, having spoken, now escorted his son and the Sibyl on their way, and let him depart through the Gate of Ivory.'[22]

Avoiding a perfunctory return to the upper air by the route which had taken Aeneas and the Sibyl on their downward journey to the lower world, Virgil uses the Homeric imagery. But he alters it. In the first place, he does not retain the Greek play upon words. Secondly the Gates are of Sleep not Dreams; and presumably this was not merely to make the line scan. Thirdly, 'true shadows'—ghosts, spirits—not 'dreams that attain true fulfilment', are what come through the Gate of Horn. Fourthly—and this is the feature that has proved enigmatic ever since the Aeneid was written—the poet decides to send back his hero through the Gate of Ivory, though this is reserved for 'false visions'. According to common belief, false dreams appeared before, and true dreams after, midnight; thus the fact that Aeneas came out by the Ivory Gate could be intended to show (for some reason unknown, or no particular reason) that his journey ended before midnight. Yet no student of Virgil's rich subtlety of expression, operating simultaneously at several different levels of meaning, will be satisfied that there is nothing more to be said. One suggestion is that whereas the 'true shadows' are ghosts of the dead—realities in Hades at least—the 'false visions' are not real inhabitants of the world of shades, but visions of one's waking hours. For ghosts, that is to say, the correct passage out of the Underworld is by the Gate of Horn set aside for 'true shadows', but Aeneas and the Sibyl are *living* and must therefore pass through the Gate of Ivory, connected with wakefulness and life.

Yet Virgil seems to say something more than this. Why, departing from the *Odyssey* in this respect, has he decided to relate the Gates of Sleep to the Underworld? 'I awoke from sleep', says Cicero, too, at the end of his comparable account of the other world in the *Dream of Scipio*;[23] and there are Biblical analogies.[24] By sending Aeneas out by the Gates of Sleep the poet seems to be saying, as Plato said before him (page 208), that truths about such deep matters as the afterlife can only be formulated in terms of myth expressed in dream and vision. 'For Shakespeare also,' as Sir Frank Fletcher remarks, 'there was a moment when the last word of philosophy seemed to be that "We are such stuff as dreams are made on".' It is also possible that Virgil, in abandoning the Greek play upon words, has introduced another of his own. Things seen (the gate of horn, *cornu*, representing the eye with its horny tissue the *cornea*) are perhaps more to be trusted than things reported and unverifiable (the ivory gate being the teeth). And, indeed, even if this is thought to be straining at the evidence, the choice of the gate of false visions for the reascent of Aeneas and the Sibyl could suggest that they, and all they stand for, have not the same degree of truth as is granted even to 'real' spirits. Has Aeneas only seen insubstantial pictures?

If so, the poet is saying that the fabric of his story is poetic imagination. We have, it seems, reached a time when myth, in the hands of one of its greatest interpreters, is admitted (though in cryptic language) to lack the historical or Biblical validity attributed to it by the early Greeks (page 34). Virgil is a good deal more of a religious believer than, say, Euripides. But he uses the old stories as symbols and illustrations of his religion, not as its fundamentalist justifications. He does not any longer 'live' the myths as the myth-making communities had lived them (page 160), and he creates, through these riddling words, the sort of distinction between mythical and non-mythical elements in religion that Bultmann, in our own day and in prose, has sought to establish in Christianity (page 156).

When Virgil wanted to express his religion in non-mythical terms, he was guided by the *Hymn to Zeus*, which Cleanthes of Assus, one of Zeno's successors as leader of the Stoics, had written in the third century BC.

> For from these we are born, and alone of living things
> That move on earth are we created in God's image.
> So will I praise thee, ever singing of thy might,
> By whom the whole wide firmament of heaven is swayed
> And guided in its wheeling journey round this earth
> In glad submission to thee: for in thine unconquered
> hands
> Thou hast a mighty servant, the thunderbolt of heaven
> Wrought with a double edge and of never-dying fire,
> A pulse of life beating through all created things
> That walk in thy ways; and with this thou dost direct
> Thy Omnipresent Word that moves through all creation
> And mingles with the sun and the company of the stars.[25]

This is the belief which Virgil quotes in the fourth *Georgic* and again in the sixth book of the *Aeneid*; and he repeats it with a personal conviction.

> For God (they hold) pervades
> All lands, the widespread seas, the abysms of unplumbed
> sky;
> From whom flocks, herds, men, every creature in his kind
> Derive at birth the slight, precarious breath of life.[26]

Wordsworth was moved by Anchises' philosophic vision to voice a feeling of transcendence,

a sense sublime
Of something far more deeply infused.

And Tennyson, too, declares his view of nature in an invocation to Virgil.

Thou that seest Universal
Nature moved by Universal Mind;
Thou majestic in thy sadness
At the doubtful doom of human kind.

Not only does this religious position go back to the Greeks, but, elsewhere in the sixth book of the *Aeneid*, when the poet wishes to express his religion in mythological terms the myths that he employs are Greek. For the Romans themselves, unlike the Greeks, were not a myth-making people. But Virgil and his contemporaries cared for local Italian folk-lore and religion (page 339) and the rise of Rome to greatness, and under Greek influence they clothed these themes in mythological form. Yet in early days they were far less ready than the Greeks to visualize gods in human shape (page 62); their own antiquarian of the first century BC, Varro, estimates that there was an initial period of more than 170 years when Rome 'worshipped gods without statues'[27]—and no doubt without temples also.

Virgil tries to put into words the meaning Romans gave to *religio*,[28] an awe of certain unpersonalized objects and phenomena which they endowed with a vague supernatural force. This 'dynamistic' attitude to religion, paralleled in the Polynesian and Melanesian concept of *mana*, came to the Romans at least as early as, perhaps earlier than, the 'animistic' belief—leading to anthropomorphism—that such objects and occurrences had a sort of life analogous to that of human souls. The personalization of gods developed gradually, as Rome formed contacts in the eighth century BC with Cumae and other Greek colonies, and with the Etruscans who were themselves influenced by Greece. But the old ideas remained strong, and the ordinary Italian still found the gods less substantial than the something holy or uncanny in a stream, or cave, or tree, or stone.

The Latin word for this conception, at least in historical times, is *numen* (later identified with the Greek *daemon*)—that which effects everything beyond the ordinary power of human beings, or outside the common processes of nature. 'You too have *numen*,' says Ovid to a boundary-stone.[29] Oak-trees or strange stones such as meteorites, which might later be regarded as holy to Jupiter, at first *were* Jupiter.

Such conceptions remained active at Rome, together with a lot more magic and taboo which survived even into imperial days. And yet this anti-mythological reluctance to see the gods as human, until Greek influence overcame the feeling and gave them temples, need not be regarded as merely backward. To Warde Fowler, for example, the 'old Roman *numen* was a far nobler mental conception than the miserable images of Graeco-Roman full-blown gods and goddesses reclining on their couches and seeming to dine like human citizens'. When an early Roman propitiated the gods, he was meticulous about their definite and limited functions, but incurious about their vague unindividualized personalities. Accordingly, no indigenous mythology comparable to that of the Greeks ever arose—until Greek promptings, satisfying nationalist needs, brought one into being.

But if the Romans were not 'religious' in that sense, they were very religious in another. Men who thought about the Roman Republic, such as Varro or the historian Polybius of Megalopolis (*c.* 203–120 BC), agreed that Roman power was due to piety. Indeed early Roman thought, of which so much lived on, is little but religion; the basic concepts, however, of that religion are not myth, but the family and its 'natural' extension the state (page 353).

CHAPTER 14

THE QUEST FOR A ROMAN PAST

=====♦♦♦♦♦♦♦♦♦♦=====

1   The Story of Romulus Told by Livy[1]

LIVY TELLS how Aeneas, after defeating Turnus and the Rutulians, united his own Trojan followers with the Latins, and founded the town of Lavinium; and when he died, his son Ascanius (or Iulus) left Lavinium to establish a new settlement at Alba Longa. There the family ruled for a number of generations, until strife arose between twin brothers, Numitor and Amulius. Amulius, the younger of the two, drove out Numitor, seized the throne, and imposed upon his niece Rhea Silvia perpetual chastity as a Vestal Virgin. But she was raped—it was said by the god Mars—and gave birth to twin sons, Romulus and Remus. The king imprisoned her and ordered the boys to be drowned. But the men told to do the deed left them on the edge of the flooded Tiber, at the spot where the Ruminal fig-tree now stands. There a she-wolf, coming down from the hills to quench her thirst, heard them crying and fed them with her own milk; and the king's herdsman, Faustulus, found her licking the babies. Faustulus took them to his hut and gave them to his wife Larentia to nurse. And so they grew up, and as they became strong enough, they began to attack robbers and divide the stolen goods with their friends the shepherds.

The Palatine Hill was already the scene of the annual Lupercal festival, at which young men ran about naked and engaged in various horse-play. As Romulus and Remus were attending the festival, brigands, infuriated by the loss of their plunder to the brothers, laid a trap for them. Romulus escaped, but Remus was captured and delivered to King Amulius. The brigands complained that the youths had been leading raids upon the lands of the king's brother, Numitor; and to Numitor Remus was handed over.

But now the truth about the boys' birth gradually came out, and the young men murdered Amulius and saluted Numitor as King. They also planned to establish a new settlement, for the surplus population of Alba Longa, upon the place where they had been left to drown as babies and had been subsequently brought up. But 'unhappily the brothers' plans for the future were marred by the same curse which had divided their grandfather and Amulius—jealousy and ambition. A disgraceful quarrel arose from a matter in itself trivial. As the brothers were twins and all question of seniority was thereby precluded, they determined to ask the tutelary gods of the country-side to declare by augury which of them should govern the new town once it was founded, and give his name to it. For this purpose Romulus took the Palatine Hill and Remus the Aventine as their respective stations from which to observe the auspices. Remus, the story goes, was the first to receive a sign—six vultures; and no sooner was this made known to the people than double the number of birds appeared to Romulus. The followers of each promptly saluted their master as king, one side basing its claim upon priority, the other upon number. Angry words ensued, followed all too soon by blows, and in the course of the affray Remus was killed.

'There is another story, a commoner one, according to which Remus, by way of jeering at his brother, jumped over the half-built walls of the new settlement, whereupon Romulus killed him in a fit of rage, adding the threat, "So perish whoever else shall overleap my battlements!"

'This, then, was how Romulus obtained the sole power. The newly built city was called by its founder's name.'²

Romulus fortified the Palatine, sacrificed to the gods—using the ritual of Alba, except in the worship of Hercules where he followed Greek rites—and gave his subjects laws. With an eye to the future, he sought to increase the population by establishing a sanctuary for fugitives on the slopes of the Capitoline Hill. He also created a hundred senators or 'fathers' (*patres*), whose descendants were to be called patricians.

But a serious shortage of women meant that Rome's new strength was not likely to last for more than one generation. Romulus sent envoys to many states to propose marriage alliances, but the fear and contempt in which the new community was held gave these proposals a uniformly bad reception. However, the king now planned a new move, to coincide with the annual festival of the Consualia in honour of Neptune. For this occasion large crowds flocked to Rome. Not only were the neighbouring Latin townships represented, but the Sabines came too, with their wives and children; and they were lavishly entertained and shown round the city. But when the festival began, all the able bodied male inhabitants of Rome rushed through the crowd and seized the young women who were among the visitors. Most of the girls were taken by whoever first got hold of them, but some especially beautiful ones were reserved for themselves by leading senators, who sent gangs to fetch them. The festival broke up in panic, and the girls' parents, shouting curses and prayers, had to depart.

The abducted women, too, were furious and fearful for the future, but Romulus went from one to another with reassurances. Promising that they would enjoy all the privileges of married Romans, and suggesting that children, when they came, would form a bond with their new husbands, 'he urged them to forget their wrath and give their hearts to those to whom chance had given their bodies. Often, he said, a sense of injury yields in the end to affection; and their husbands would treat them all the more kindly in that they would try, each one of them, not only to fulfil their own part of the bargain, but also to make up to their wives for the homes and parents they had lost. The men, too, played their part: they spoke honied words and vowed that it was passionate love which had prompted their offence. No plea can better touch a woman's heart. The women in course of time lost their resentment.'[3]

But their parents were far from resigned, and the communities thus despoiled of their women sent armies to attack Rome. The

Latins were beaten back; but then the Sabines employed a ruse. Spurius Tarpeius, the commander of the Roman citadel, had a daughter Tarpeia. This girl, 'when she had gone outside the walls to fetch water for a sacrifice, was bribed by Tatius, the king of the Sabines, to admit a party of his soldiers into the fortress. Once inside, the men crushed her to death under their shields, to make it look as if they had taken the place by storm—or, it may be, to show by harsh example that there must be no trusting a traitor.

'There is also a story that this girl demanded as the price of her services "what they had on their shield-arms". Now the Sabines in those days used to wear on their left arms heavy gold bracelets and fine jewelled rings—so they kept their bargain: paying, however, not, as the girl hoped, with golden bracelets, but with their shields. Some say that after bargaining for what they "had on their left arms" she did actually demand their shields, and being proved a traitor was killed, as it were, by the very coin that paid her.'[4]

After occupying the citadel, the Sabines moved down to meet the advancing Romans. These were headed by Romulus, who vowed a temple to Jupiter the Stayer of Flight if his men could stand firm. The Sabine commander Mettus Curtius narrowly saved himself from sinking into a swamp, and the battle was continuing on the low ground when the Sabine women, the original cause of the quarrel, decisively intervened. With hair streaming and clothes rent, they thrust themselves in a body between the combatants, and appealed to them to stop fighting. The effect of this appeal was powerful and instantaneous, and a moment later the rival commanders stepped forward to make peace.

And they did more than this; for the two states were henceforth united under a single government, with Rome as its capital city.

2 Patriotic Foundation-myth

Augustus and the Roman traditions which he cherished were honoured not only by poets, such as Virgil and Horace, but by historians as well. Foremost among these was Livy of Patavium (Padua), who spent forty years writing a history of Rome from the earliest times down to his own day. Nearly 107 out of his 142 books are lost, including the portions relating to contemporary events. But the first books are among those that have survived. Dealing with legendary events, these blend history, archaeology, folk-tale and myth. Livy's work is a Virgilian evocation of the city's traditional origins, and the two men must have influenced one another.

The Roman religion of family and state fostered the nationalist legends which served for a mythology (page 348). When Herbert Spencer (1820–1903) explained myths as glorified ancestral legends, and ancestor worship as the source and origin of religion, he was right, not entirely for the Greeks, but for the Romans—whose reverence for their ancestors (like that of the Chinese) was the core of their religious and social life.

These early books are among the most stimulating of all Livy's work. For his gifts are essentially of this romantic and poetic character; he is an artist undertaking, in rich, clear, vivid language, an unprecedented eight-century-long reconstruction of Rome's national greatness, with much attention to the mythology in which its early days were concealed. Here is epic poetry in prose—as far as Livy is concerned, Shelley was right in saying 'the distinction between poets and prose-writers is a vulgar error'. Like other writers in this strain, Livy adheres to the widespread ancient custom of seeing history through the eyes of a moralist. Indeed, though he aims at telling the truth, his main purpose is to draw moral lessons from the mythical or historical past for the needs of the present—and for the glorification of Rome, of Italy (from whose frontiers he came), and indirectly of Augustus.

Nevertheless, writing when nearly thirty years of civil war were only just over, and the world was not used to the Augustan peace (page 338), Livy sees the early Romans in a roseate light by comparison with his own contemporaries. Yet he begins his history with an apology for going back to these legendary times, which bring him pleasant relief from the anxieties of his own epoch—and the anxieties of attempting to describe it. Besides, the ancient legends, as he and Virgil and the contemporary Greek writer Dionysius of Halicarnassus interpreted them, illustrated the greatness of the human soul which, under Providence supervising the glory of Rome, mastered events. A critical use of sources seemed less important and, though Livy's sources were numerous and varied, he did not use them scientifically. Plausibility, however, is aimed at, and the aberrations and anachronisms of earlier Roman annalists are toned down, so that the artistic unity of his story is complete.

R. M. Ogilvie has compared Livy with Sir Walter Scott, who hoped his own works were 'wise and manly'. Both were amateur enthusiasts, creators more than critics. Moreover, the contemporary appreciation with which both were rewarded is eclipsed in our own age, which hesitates to acclaim men so unreservedly as heroes; though Livy is now again attracting researchers into Roman ideas. The times of his high renown were the later Middle Ages, and the prelude and height of the Italian Renaissance. Dante, who had only read Livy's semi-mythological first four books, pronounced him infallible. Petrarch, who knew twenty-nine books of Livy and even outdid him in idealizing the early Romans, believed the new Rome should adopt the ancient Republic's constitution; and there is much of the Roman historian in Petrarch's humanistic ideals of *virtù* and *fama*, linking success with merit and popular acclaim, and stressing the value and rewards of individual effort.

Machiavelli too devoted an important work to Livy's early books. In these *Discorsi sopra la Prima Deca di Tito Livio* (1516–19) he singles out the figure of Romulus, who inherited political chaos not, like Caesar, to deepen this chaos, but to rebuild ordered government in its place. In Machiavelli's *Prince*, too, Romulus is one of the noble exemplars, like Cyrus, Moses and Theseus, who have found and taken the opportunity to raise their peoples from the morass where they had been floundering before. Renaissance thinkers, seeking for heroes, preferred Livy to Tacitus—though Erasmus, perhaps frowning on the cult, omitted him from his reading list for schools. To the French Revolution, however, Livy's account of the origins of the Republic was a favourite work of reference and study.

The miraculous preservation of Romulus and Remus is a widespread theme of folk-lore. Their cradle was at first floating, like that of Sargon on the Euphrates, with its partial Biblical parallel of

Moses laid beside the Nile.[5] The rescuing of the exposed child has already appeared in the story of Oedipus (page 220), and many folk-tales recount the suckling of such children by animals; Nereus was fed by a bitch, and Pelias by a mare. As for Romulus and Remus, they were suckled by the she-wolf sacred to their father Mars.

Macaulay retold the Livian tale as the poetry which it nearly is (page 371).

> Raging beast and raging flood
>   Alike have spared the prey;
> And today the dead are living;
>   The lost are found today.
>
> The troubled river knew them,
>   And smoothed his yellow foam,
> And gently rocked the cradle
>   That bore the fate of Rome.
> The ravening she-wolf knew them,
>   And licked them o'er and o'er,
> And gave them of her own fierce milk,
>   Rich with raw flesh and gore.

Greek influence has contributed to the story (the begetting of children by gods is Greek) and even to the nomenclature. Rome, though certain of its hills were inhabited from the second millennium BC if not earlier, became a unified city—as archaeologists have shown—from *c.* 575–550 BC, not from the eighth century as in Roman tradition (page 337). In the fifth century, or thereabouts, the Greeks invented 'Romus' (Rhomos) as a typical eponymous city-founder. In Italy, the form Romulus became current—'the Roman', just as Siculus is one form of Sicanus, 'the Sicilian'. When the Greeks heard of Romulus, they differentiated him from Romus: thus Timaeus writes of Romulus and Romus, the sons of Latinus, and of Aeneas' daughter Rome. This tradition was on the analogy of other legends which told of twins; or perhaps the twins here stood for the amalgamation of two different communities or represented some ancient indigenous pair, like Cacus (page 330) and Caca, such as quite often appeared in Italian religion and folk-lore. But for some reason, in Italy, the second of the twin sons of Rhea Silvia by Mars became, not Romus, but Remus—possibly a back-formation from a family name such as Reminius, or from a place-name like Remona or Remuria (part of the Aventine Hill), or maybe derived from Roma in the same way as the Greek Kerkyra (Corfu) became Corcyra. The story of the death of Remus was clearly introduced to

TABLE 7

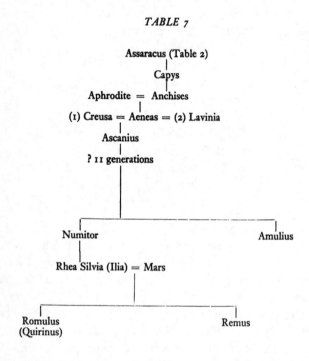

Assaracus (Table 2)
|
Capys
|
Aphrodite = Anchises
|
(1) Creusa = Aeneas = (2) Lavinia
|
Ascanius
|
? 11 generations

Numitor   Amulius
|
Rhea Silvia (Ilia) = Mars

Romulus   Remus
(Quirinus)

point the moral that aggression against the new foundation would be punished. But the implied rivalry of Palatine and Aventine also seems to recall occasions in the fourth and possibly even fifth century BC when the plebeians were in revolt on the Aventine and 'seceded' from the central power at Rome. Later, the fratricide was considered an ominous anticipation of the civil wars that racked the late Republic.

As for the suckling of the twins by the she-wolf, the Roman family of the Ogulnii dedicated a statue of this scene in 296 BC; or perhaps they added effigies of the twins to an older statue of a she-wolf. A bronze group of the event stands in the Capitoline Museum today, though of this only the wolf is ancient (*c.* 500 BC)—the figure originally had, as far as we are aware, no connection with the Romulus and Remus myth, and the present infants are Renaissance additions. The story of the twins was told in the third century BC by the Roman annalist Fabius Pictor, who was reported to have learnt it from an unknown Greek. In his own days, said Fabius, the Romans still sang 'ancestral hymns' about the brothers—not as swineherds or cowherds but 'such that men might well guess them to be of the blood of kings and gods'. The tale had become even more famous in the antiquarian-minded first century BC,[6] when an anonymous 'Constitution of Romulus' circulated. And it was especially appropriate for Livy, writing under Augustus, who was envisaged as the second Romulus and had, at first, supposedly thought of calling himself Romulus before finally preferring the less regal and fratricidal 'Augustus'.

To complete the literary amplification of the story, the Romans, in this as in other myths, mobilized traditions of local topography, and especially names of forgotten meaning which could be given aetiological explanations (page 121), such as the Lupercal grotto (believed to come from *lupus*, wolf) and the Ruminal fig-tree (from a word meaning 'to suckle'?—but perhaps really a corruption of 'Romularis'). The foster-parents, too, Faustulus (a by-form of the god Faunus, believed rightly or wrongly to come from *favere* and mean the favoured) and Acca Larentia, are ancient local deities personalized under Greek influence. Speaking of the foster-mother, Livy quotes a sceptical rationalization of the whole myth. 'Some think,' he says, 'that the origin of this fable was the fact that Larentia was a common whore and was called she-wolf (*lupa*) by the shepherds.' Nevertheless, even in Livy's own time there was a thatched hut of great antiquity, called the hut of Romulus, upon the Palatine Hill (it twice caught fire under Augustus),[7] though the same honour was also claimed for a prehistoric hut upon the Capitol.[8] Upon the

Palatine, too, have been discovered traces and foundations of primitive buildings going back to the ninth and eighth centuries BC.

According to the tradition followed by Livy, Romulus shared power with a co-monarch Titus Tatius, king of the Sabines, who ruled jointly with him and died, leaving Romulus as sole ruler. Livy[9] follows a tradition that one of the original three centuries of 'knights', the Titienses, was named after Tatius (the others were the Ramnenses, 'named after Romulus', and the Luceres). This link was already doubted by the first century BC, and many now regard all three names as foreign importations from Etruria. Besides, the joint monarchy itself looks suspiciously like a later invention, on the analogy of the Roman Republic with its two consuls. Tatius seems to be merely 'tata' or 'daddy'. But his rule with Romulus is put in this story to explain the historical fact that the Romans were the descendants not only of a Latin community settled on the Palatine, but also of Sabine communities on other hills later incorporated in the city—the Viminal, Quirinal and Esquiline.

Just as the introduction of the dual monarchy stood for the Latin and Sabine strands in the Roman community, so the preceding story of the Rape of the Sabines—so favoured a subject for artists such as Giovanni Bologna, Rubens, Poussin, and the sculptor Girardon—symbolizes the union of these two elements. The forcible nature of the union also represents an attempt to explain a feature of the Roman marriage; for the ceremony traditionally included a reference to capture, suggesting an element of coercion. By the same token the story is seen patriotically from the point of view of the Latins, rather than the Sabines, since the union is presented as a conquest of the latter by the former. (However, no conquest of Sabines by Latins has hitherto been confirmed by excavators. As far as can be judged, the inhabitants on the various hills joined one another by gradual and peaceable means, presumably through intermarriage.)

After the Romans had seized the women, the return of the Sabine warriors to the attack is made the occasion of some further aetiological stories. The name of a pool in the Forum, the Lacus Curtius, is explained by the Sabine champion Mettius Curtius, and by the plunge of his horse into the marsh that was there, from which he was only rescued with difficulty. But the variability of such stories is suggested by Livy's later provision of a different and more famous myth to explain the pool's name: a cavity suddenly opened at the place, and Mettius Curtius, on horseback, leapt into the yawning gulf.[10]

Shortly before these events, we have the story of Tarpeia, which exists in numerous versions widely varying in detail. In historical times, part of the Capitoline Hill was still known as the Tarpeian Mount, and upon its summit was the Tarpeian rock or cliff—now identified by archaeologists—from which criminals were hurled to their deaths. There was also an ancient grave known as the tomb of Tarpeia, who was a deity of a near-by spring or rock, or of the hill itself. Similar stories of the bribed and traitorous maiden had long been known, for example at Megara (where Minos drowned Scylla, seduced by Cretan gold bracelets), and at Lesbos, Pedasus, Naxos and Ephesus. The same theme of corruption by riches occurs in Scandinavian folk-lore. Its patriotic moral in the Roman version is obvious enough, and Tarpeia's figure, enveloped in heaps of shields, appears on coins of Augustus.[11]

Salomon Reinach believed the myth to have originated from ancient beliefs concerning the dangerous magic inherent in trophies or enemy spoils. For such spoils of war were taboo. 'Alone of all offerings to heaven,' says Plutarch, 'they are left to the mercies of moth and rust.' They could only be brought back into use in the utmost crisis; even contact was perilous, for they were infected with evil, and must be left alone. They could be hung in buildings, or thrown into water, or destroyed by fire, or piled up: Caesar tells of the Gauls heaping spoils on the ground.[12] The presence of such an ancient pile on the Capitoline would provide just the right material for the adaptation of this Greek, moralizing, patriotic tale. But unfortunately we cannot say that such a mound of arms actually existed on the right spot!

The tale of Tarpeia's treachery suggests that the Capitoline Hill and its citadel once belonged, at least for a time, to the Sabines.

'Tarpeia', 'Tarpeius' could well be a Sabine pronunciation of words recalling Rome's sixth-century BC Etruscan rulers, namely 'Tarquinia', 'Tarquinius'. For the Sabines belonged to the Umbro-Sabellian group of peoples who used 'p' where the Latins used 'q' (a parallel phenomenon is found amongst the Celts), saying 'Pompilius', for example, instead of 'Quinquilius'. If this is so, then the name of Tarpeia, in spite of its Sabine associations, dates from the period of Etruscan domination: of which something will be said next. She is called by Livy the daughter of Spurius Tarpeius, the commander of the Roman citadel, and this may be an echo of the time when Tarquins were kings of Rome.

3   The Stories of Tarquin and Horatius Told by Livy[13]

Livy describes how Tarquin the Proud, the last king of Rome, came to the throne by the murder of his predecessor, Servius Tullius. Tarquin refused the dead man burial, executed his supporters and surrounded himself with a personal bodyguard. In personal control of Rome's foreign policy, without consulting the Senate he formed many connections with noblemen from Latin towns. When, on one occasion, he was late for a meeting of the Latin League at the Grove of Ferentina, and was criticized for this unpunctuality by Turnus Herdonius of Aricia, he had Herdonius killed, and used the incident as a pretext to revise Rome's treaty with the Latins.

A distinguished war-leader himself, Tarquin is recorded as opening hostilities against the Volscians, and thus inaugurating a two-hundred-years' war against this mountain people. He also fought the people of Gabii, twelve miles from Rome. When his operations against that town proved unsuccessful, he sent his youngest son, Sextus, to the place, in the assumed character of a refugee from his father's cruelty. Sextus, we are told, ingratiated himself with the leaders of Gabii, and on the grounds that his father lacked support at home, persuaded them to resume the fighting. This went well for Gabii, where Sextus gained such popularity that he finally felt ready to embark on his treacherous plan.

'At last he was able to feel that he had the town, as it were, in his pocket, and was ready for anything. Accordingly, he sent a confidential messenger to Rome, to ask his father what step he should next take, his power in Gabii being, by God's grace, by this time absolute. Tarquin, I suppose, was not sure of the messenger's good faith: in any case, he said not a word in reply to his question, but with a thoughtful air went out into the garden. The man followed him, and Tarquin, strolling up and down in silence, began knocking off poppyheads with his stick. The messenger at last wearied of putting his question and waiting for the reply, so he returned to Gabii supposing his mission to have failed. He told Sextus what he had said and what he had seen his father do: the king, he declared, whether from anger, or hatred, or natural arrogance, had not uttered a single word. Sextus realized that though his father had not spoken, he had, by his action, indirectly expressed his meaning clearly enough. So he proceeded at once to act upon his murderous instructions.'[14] The leaders of Gabii were executed, assassinated or sent into exile, and the town passed into Tarquin's hands.

At Rome, the king embarked on great building activities, including the completion of Jupiter's temple upon the Capitoline Hill. But while many such plans were under way, a sinister omen occurred at the palace: a snake slid out from a crack in a wooden pillar. In order to discover what this portended, the king dispatched his two eldest sons, Titus and Arruns, to consult the Delphic oracle. They were accompanied by the king's nephew Lucius Junius Brutus, who had posed as a half-wit to avoid the king's murderous inclinations. When they had reached Delphi and carried out the king's instructions, Titus and Arruns could not refrain from putting another question to the oracle: who would be the next king of Rome? The answer was, 'the man who shall be the first to kiss his mother'. The king's sons decided to say nothing of this to their brother Sextus who had been left at Rome, but drew lots between each other to decide which of the two of them, on their return, should be the first to give their mother a kiss. But Brutus, pretending to trip, fell flat on his face, and his lips touched the earth—the mother of all living things.

361

Back home, they found the Romans besieging Ardea, the capital of the Rutulians. The officers, especially the young princes, whiled away the time in lavish entertainments. One day they and a certain Collatinus were drinking in Sextus' quarters when the conversation turned to the subject of wives. Each praised his own, but Collatinus suggested a way of proving the incomparable superiority of his Lucretia. He proposed that they should all ride straight to Rome and see how their wives were behaving. Off they rode, and found the other ladies enjoying themselves with young men at a party. Lucretia, on the other hand, was quietly seated in her home in Collatia, with her maids around her, industriously spinning by lamplight. Collatinus, in delight, asked his friends to dinner, and it was then that Sextus Tarquinius decided to seduce Lucretia. A few days later he rode again to Collatinus' house, but failed by every plea and threat to win her compliance. But if she continued to reject him, he declared, he would kill her, and also kill a slave whose naked body he would place by her side, so that all would think the slave had been her lover. By this threat, Tarquin overcame her resistance. Then he returned to Ardea.

Lucretia summoned her husband and her father, bidding each of them bring a trusted friend: they brought Brutus and a certain Valerius respectively. She told them what had happened, and demanded that they should avenge her. Then she stabbed herself, and died. Brutus swore he would pursue Tarquin and all his house, and would never again allow them or any other man to be king at Rome. The others joined him. Lucretia's funeral roused the people of Collatia, and with Brutus in the lead they marched on Rome. In the Forum, he spoke eloquently of the Tarquins and their crimes, and the people demanded the king's abdication and exile. Tarquin started back from Ardea to restore order, but found the gates of Rome closed against him. On receiving this rebuff, he fled into exile with his two elder sons to Caere in Etruria. Sextus went instead to Gabii, where he was assassinated.

Kings had ruled at Rome for two hundred and forty-four years, and Tarquin's reign had lasted for twenty-five. He and his family now took refuge with Lars Porsena, king of Clusium in Etruria, and urged him defend his fellow Etruscans and the principle of monarchy by restoring the Tarquin dynasty at Rome. There, however, two consuls to rule the city were elected by popular vote; and the first to hold this Republican office were Brutus and Collatinus. The new government granted the populace a number of concessions to secure their loyalty.

On the approach of the Etruscan army, however, the Romans outside the city had to abandon their farms, and move within the walls. The most vulnerable point was the Tiber's wooden bridge, and upon this the invaders, after a successful surprise attack upon the Janiculum Hill on its right bank, concentrated their forces. The routed Romans fled before them on to the bridge. The soldier who was guarding it, Horatius Cocles, tried to persuade them to stand and fight with him. Two companions, Spurius Lartius and Titus Herminius, joined him and with their help he staved off the first onslaught. But soon, as those who were demolishing the bridge called them to come, Horatius made Lartius and Herminius leave him and save themselves. Now Horatius stood alone, and held the Etruscans at bay. Before they could overcome his resistance, the bridge, safely demolished, crashed to its fall, and with a prayer to Father Tiber he plunged fully armed into its stream and swam through a rain of missiles to safety.

4 History in Legend

According to Roman legend, the kings who followed Romulus were Numa Pompilius, Tullus Hostilius, Ancus Marcius, Tarquinius Priscus, Servius Tullius and finally Tarquinius Superbus (the Proud); the two hundred and forty-four years ascribed to the whole period of monarchic rule was placed between the years 753 and 510 BC. How far are these tales history and how far are they myth? 'The clash,' it has been said, 'of the over-credulous and the over-sceptical must continue for the benefit of the resulting golden mean.' The contents and chronology of many tales about the kings in Livy are fictitious; for these stories include arbitrary guesses based on etymology and topography, and indeed, even when they contain a nucleus of history, are often placed (for reasons of patriotic or family pride) several hundred years earlier than they belong. Yet the Roman tradition that the city was originally governed by kings is plausible. And it is corroborated by state offices which, surviving for a millennium longer, retained the word *rex*—namely the *rex sacrorum*, a priestly official, and the *interrex* who was appointed to fill gaps between consuls.

As for the individual kings, however, certain of these may be wholly or nine-tenths mythical—our oldest surviving account of them, though it goes back to sources of uncertain date, is only of the first century BC[15]. Numa is a classic Prince of Peace, as familiar a folk-lore figure as his predecessor Romulus the Prince of War; and Tullus Hostilius and Ancus Marcus look like artificial duplicates of the same process. For Ancus, like Numa, is a culture-hero and originator of customs—and perhaps owes his insertion in the list to the Republican clan of the Marcii. These were a great family from the fourth century BC onwards, and the fact that Caesar's mother was a Marcia may partly account for the prominence of Ancus in Augustan writers such as Livy. Tullus, however, was probably an historical figure: first because there were no distinguished early Hostilii to have fabricated him, since the clan were not famous before the second century BC, and secondly because the House where the Senate is first known to have had its meetings (long before we hear of that family) bore the same name, the Curia Hostilia.

The two Tarquins, however, unmistakably represent a period of Etruscan rule at Rome. This was a time when the development of Rome was enriched and accelerated by the civilization of Etruria. The country of plain, hills and dense forests beyond the Tiber's right bank contained its loosely federated city states, later twelve in number; and these states, ruled by kings during the period of their greatest power, possessed an elaborate, individual art, excelling in filigreed, granulated jewellery. The revealed religion in which the Etruscans believed was a fear-ridden, ritualistic business requiring vast cities of corridor- and chamber-tombs for the dead. They loved bloodthirsty Games, feasting and music. Their language—though its inscriptions are largely incomprehensible to us—was evidently non-Indo-European. Their art shows influences from the near and middle east. But these reached them (from Syria) through Greek traders and colonists, especially those in Campania.

The Etruscans become identifiable shortly before 700 BC as a separate civilization, occupied in trade, industry and agriculture, but particularly in piracy and war. They made great use of horses, introducing the chariot to Italy. Etruscan strength came from the working of metals: the copper of Tuscany and the iron of Elba were perhaps what had tempted them to settle, and the whole of northern Etruria became a region of mines. Hesiod mentions them (p. 103).

In the sixth century BC the Etruscan city-states rose to the climax of their power, dominating Italy from the Po valley to Campania. During this period, not long after the Latin-Sabine union, an Etruscan dynasty conquered and ruled Rome, making it the most prosperous city in the whole area. The Tarquins, part-legend and part-history, stand for this epoch of Etruscan domination over Rome. The first of the two kings of that name Tarquinius Priscus, says Livy, was born at Tarquinii in Etruria; and *Tarchon* was the name of a great family at Etruscan Caere, close to Rome. Livy also mentions that Priscus' name at birth was Lucumo,[16] which seems to correspond to *Lauchme*, the Etruscan chieftains' title of rank or office. At Vulci, north-west of Caere, inscriptions on wall-paintings record the name *Cneve Tarchunies Rumach*. Would this, in Latin, not be Cnaeus Tarquinius Romanus, a Tarquin who was a 'Roman' or king of Rome?

For there is ample evidence of a period of Etruscan rule in the city. Although never truly a city of the Etruscans, Rome owed to their dominant families much of its government, religion, town-planning, technology and ceremonial. These debts have left early graves on the Palatine and Esquiline Hills, a tradition of Etruscan connections with the Caelian Hill,[17] and a Black Stone—discovered in the Forum—suggesting links with near-by Veii in Etruria. Livy also indicates specific Roman institutions that came from that country—the 'curule' chair, purple-bordered toga, lictors;[18] not to speak of drains, urban architecture, divination by entrails, and perhaps the name of the city itself. There was also, at Rome, an Etruscan road, the *Vicus Tuscus*, leading from the western end of the Forum down to the bridge: 'Tuscus' either because it led *to* Etruria, or because this was an Etruscan quarter.

The régime of the Etruscans at Rome coincided with, and caused, the city's rise to grandeur. The traditional date of Tarquinius Priscus (616–579 BC) is close to the time when, as archaeological material shows, Rome first became a large, grand, prosperous city with monumental architecture (*c.* 575–550). Surrounded by earth-works and including as its common market-place the former marsh-land of the Forum, the town could now assert itself against powerful Etruscan-ruled neighbours, likewise of mixed population, such as Veii. Later in the century, Rome's grandeur culminated in the Etruscan-built temple of Jupiter (with Juno and Minerva) upon the Capitoline Hill, the largest temple in Italy.

Livy's story, however, is that Tarquinius Priscus was not himself an Etruscan, but was the son of Demaratus of Corinth, who 'had been forced by political troubles to leave Greece and happened to settle in Tarquinii'. Corinth was at this time in the grip of an auto-cratic dynasty the Cypselids (*c.* 657–585 BC), from whom the important trading families could well have fled. Livy's contemporary Dionysius of Halicarnassus adds that Demaratus was accompanied by *fictores*, image-makers, Eucheir and Eugrammus, and this story corresponds with the archaeological evidence. For from the seventh century BC onwards Etruria was flooded with the 'orientalizing' vases (page 50) for which at this time Corinth was famous; and masses of local Etruscan copies were made. Corinthian craftsmen and potters are likely enough to have settled in Etruria, and indeed, a Greek settlement is known to have been established at Pyrgi, the port of Caere. This then is one way in which Roman myth and legend operate. There is no need to accept Livy's dramatic embroiderings as historical fact, or even to believe that one of the kings was actually of Greek origin, but the tale does rightly reflect, not only Etruscan domination at Rome, but Greek influence in Etruria.

Very probably there was more than one Tarquin at Rome, but the symmetrically balanced 'good' Priscus and 'bad' Superbus look like myth. In the absence of a detailed tradition, something had to be done to separate the 'bringer of prosperity' from 'the defeated tyrant'. The latter, Superbus, is endowed with all the traditional features of the Greek tyrant type—bodyguard, organization of forced labour for public works, distribution of corn to win public support.

Another complication is the insertion in the king-list, between the two Tarquins, of Servius Tullius. To him are attributed stories— divine interventions, omens and the like—recalling Romulus and indicating the role of 'second founder'. Servius was credited with the first stone wall round Rome, of which portions still exist, and his traditional treaty with the Latin League was known to Livy's contemporaries; he was also said to have built a temple to the Latin goddess Diana on the Aventine, which was not yet inside the wall. For such reasons, although Livy reports varied accounts of his origins,[19] Servius was believed to have been a Roman or a Latin. But the antiquarian emperor Claudius (AD 41–54) identified him with an Etruscan hero Mastarna[20] (perhaps this is a title, not a name), who figures on the wall paintings at Vulci as successor to a *Tarchunies* whom he had slain (page 365). Claudius evidently believed (whether rightly or wrongly we cannot say) that the monarchy, having once become Etruscan, had remained Etruscan until its end.

Servius Tullius is said to have done what Greek reformers did, and transferred the Roman tribal system from a kinship basis to a geographical system, thus giving more power to the rising middle-class (like the 'hoplite revolutions' in Greece) and less to the aristocracy. Although such a royal reformer *may* have existed, the career of Servius, as described, sounds like a fabricated precedent for the plebeian democratic agitations of the fourth century BC.

Servius was of mysterious origins, perhaps the son of a slave (*serva*); and his destiny became apparent by a miracle (flames were seen burning round his head)—these being phenomena which have surrounded reforming autocrats since the days of Sargon in the third millennium BC (page 220).

Of the expulsion of the kings, who stood, despite their achievements, for the horrors of un-Republicanism, Livy tells a myth-encrusted story. But this must contain a nucleus of historical truth. For at some point the kings *did* give way (suddenly or by gradual stages), not to a democracy as often in Greece, but to an aristocratically-based government by annually appointed pairs of consuls. Moreover, excavations confirm that, not far from the traditional expulsion date (510 BC), Rome did cut itself off from Etruria. The city seems temporarily to have returned to a parochial, isolated, perhaps semi-civilized existence, with no outlets for export and a consequent series of famines. These, preserved by the historical record, were what caused the Romans to develop war and aggression as national industries. We know independently that Etruscan control of western Italy was weakening at just about this time. Aristodemus, leader of the Greek settlement at Cumae (page 340), is said to have repulsed the Etruscans in 524 BC, and to have overcome them again at Aricia in about 505; in 474 a Greek fleet from Syracuse defeated an Etruscan naval attack on Cumae.

What happened at Rome can scarcely now, through the tangle of patriotic myth, be reconstructed. The fact that one of the alleged first consuls was called Tarquinius (Collatinus)[21] *might* suggest that an Etruscan monarch stayed on for a spell with reduced powers. Indeed there may even, for a time, have been an intermediate stage of a non-hereditary early monarchy with circumscribed functions. Little help is obtained from the other consul's name, Junius (Lucius Junius Brutus), since this looks like an interpolation of the fourth century BC, inserted at the instance of Junii who were prominent at that time. They were a plebeian clan, and therefore all the more in need of early and distinguished ancestries, since foreign or insignificant origins could not be admitted. The family of the defender of the bridge however, the Horatii, were authentically one of the houses that led Rome in its post-regal days. The name of Marcus Horatius, whom a variant tradition included among the first consuls (Livy makes his tenure slightly later), is associated with the dedication of the Capitoline temple (page 366), and with Rome's earliest treaty with Carthage. The family's role is reflected, first, in a duel between the Horatii and Curiatii—invented to explain an obscure piece of ritual—and then by the fight of Horatius Cocles (one-eyed) to defend the bridge. This story (first known to us, in the third century BC, from Callimachus[22]) is likewise aetiological, for opposite the Sublician Bridge was an ancient statue of a lame one-eyed man. This represented Vulcan, one-eyed as the sun-god and lame like Hephaestus (or because the sculptor could not represent legs). But the statue's meaning was forgotten, and the patriotic tale of Horatius Cocles, exemplar of Roman epic prowess, grew up as an explanation of its origin.

The wooden (Sublician) bridge, of which the foundations are still visible, is attributed by Livy to Ancus Marcius (seventh century BC) but was probably not constructed until the Tarquin period, when the link with Etruria became vital. Rome owed much to the bridge, as the lowest land-crossing—like London's—of an important navigable river; the Fidenae ford, ten miles higher, had been captured by Veii. The Sublician Bridge was, even in historical times, surrounded by elaborate taboos which recall that *Pontifex*, 'priest', originally meant bridge-maker; and certain of these taboos, for instance those forbidding the use of iron nails, recall the days when the bridge was first made and was made of wood.

The enemy of Horatius Cocles and of Rome, in Livy's version, was Lars Porsena, king of Clusium in Etruria.[23] Pliny said he was king not of Clusium but of Vulci, and another view is that he ruled neither of these but Rome's threatening neighbour, Veii. 'Porsen(n)a' may well be an Etruscan title explained by the Romans as a name, like Mastarna (page 367) with whom some identify him. Perhaps Porsena, in historical fact, was not in league with the Tarquins but overthrew them—not repelled, as in Livy's nationalist version, but temporarily recapturing Rome. Indeed the town, with its command of the river ford, may well have changed hands several times, like other border-fortresses such as Newcastle or Carlisle in the Middle Ages.

And so various tales of Horatius at the bridge grew up, recurring, we are told, as a typical specimen theme in Roman funeral oratory.[24] Used only occasionally by painters—such as the Genoese Bernardo Strozzi (1581–1644)—the myth was immortalized more than two centuries later in the free adaptation of Macaulay, to whom it seemed (and he makes it seem to us) the most stirring of heroic sagas.

> Lars Porsena of Clusium,
>   By the Nine Gods he swore
> That the great house of Tarquin
>   Should suffer wrong no more.
> By the Nine Gods he swore it,
>   And named a trysting day,
> And bade his messengers ride forth,
>   East and west and south and north,
> To summon his array . . .
>
> And nearer fast and nearer
>   Doth the red whirlwind come;
> And louder still and still more loud,
> From underneath that rolling cloud,
> Is heard the trumpet's war-note proud,
>   The trampling, and the hum.
> And plainly and more plainly
>   Now through the gloom appears,
> Far to left and far to right,
> In broken gleams of dark-blue light,
> The long array of helmets bright,
>   The long array of spears . . .

And then, imagines Macaulay, came Sextus Tarquinius:

> Yet one man for one moment
>   Stood out before the crowd;
> Well known was he to all the Three,
>   And they gave him greeting loud,
> 'Now welcome, welcome, Sextus!
>   Now welcome to thy home!
> Why dost thou stay, and turn away?
>   Here lies the road to Rome.'

> Thrice looked he at the city;
>   Thrice looked he at the dead;
> And thrice came on in fury,
>   And thrice turned back in dread:
> And, white with fear and hatred,
>   Scowled at the narrow way,
> Where, wallowing in a pool of blood,
>   The bravest Tuscans lay.

Macaulay's vigorous, cut-and-thrust, ballad-style narrative, charging the antique names and places with a powerful emotional throb owing something to Walter Scott—but stressing civic patriotism rather than Scott's feudal loyalties—took the public by storm from 1842 onwards, and acquainted generation after generation with the legends of the Roman Republic; rather as Hawthorne and Kingsley, a decade later, gave popular currency to Greek myth also (page 302).

As a prelude to the tale, Livy has recounted how Lucretia, belonging to a clan represented by Brutus' successor as consul, killed herself because she could not bear the dishonour of her rape by Sextus Tarquinius. She is one of many women who play a dramatic, though very broadly characterized, part in these pages. The fate of this classic Fair Maid and model of virtuous fidelity was the chosen theme for many Venetian masterpieces. There is the strange strength of Titian's old age, a lofty mood of farewell, in his renderings of Tarquin and Lucretia; another Titian subject, utilized also for a characteristically different treatment by Veronese, is Lucretia stabbing herself. Her rape by Tarquin appealed particularly to Tintoretto who, employing for his mythological paintings of the 1550's a decorative, narrative objectivity absent from his other works, found in Livy's story a vehicle for the saying he inscribed on his studio wall, 'Michelangelo's design and Titian's colour'; the combination of Venetian richness and harmony with suffering, restless movement and chiaroscuro. In Tintoretto's renderings of this theme of Tarquin and Lucretia the relation of her nude body to draperies and window points ahead to Courbet.

This, too—like the story of Venus and her beloved Adonis, killed by a boar—was one of the myths chosen by Shakespeare as the subject of a poem, *The Rape of Lucrece:*

> What could he see but mightily he noted?
> What could he note but strongly he desired?
> What he beheld, on that he firmly doted,
> And in his will his wilful eye he tired.
> With more than admiration he admired
>   Her azure veins, her alabaster skin,
>   Her coral lips, her snow-white dimpled chin . . .

> Wrapped and confounded in a thousand fears,
> Like to a new-killed bird she trembling lies;
> She dares not look; yet, winking, there appears
> Quick-shifting antics, ugly in her eyes:
> Such shadows are the weak brain's forgeries;
>   Who, angry that the eyes fly from their lights,
>   In darkness daunts them with more dreadful sights.

PART VII

THE THOUSAND FACES OF LOVE

CHAPTER 15

OVID

═══════►◖◗◖◗◖◗◖◗◄═══════

1   Changes of Shape

OVID OF Sulmo (Sulmona) in the Apennines belongs to a generation which, at its more gilded levels, was both tired of Augustan
imperialism and too sophisticated for the strong personal feeling
with which Propertius had infused a diction rich in myths. The new
young men were more interested in psychology—especially feminine
psychology—than their elders, whose emotional climate they found
stifling. In smart, glittering elegiac couplets Ovid wrote the *Loves*
(*Amores*); the *Heroines* (*Heroides*), poetic letters by mythological
figures—mostly by women to their absent husbands and lovers;
the *Art of Love* and *Remedies of Love*, cynically pretending to be
scientific discussions of the subject; the *Fasti*, a calendar of the
Roman year; and, after his exile to Tomis on the Black Sea by
Augustus (for 'a poem and a mistake'), the *Lamentations* (*Tristia*)
and *Letters from the Black Sea* (*Epistulae ex Ponto*). All these poems
exhibit Ovid's prime talent, which was the narration of mythology;
his light, brilliant verse lent itself perfectly to such story-telling.

But his greatest repository of the myths is his long poem the
Metamorphoses. This poem, which Ovid knew to be his most
important work, consists of fifty longer and two hundred shorter
stories, written in the hexameters of Homer and Virgil, though the
metre is handled with quite a new raciness. These stories have one
thing in common. They are all (even if sometimes the link is far-

375

fetched) tales of magic changes of shape; they are about people, mostly mythical, transformed into animals, or birds, or trees, or flowers, or stones.

Metamorphosis haunts most folk-lore. All over the world stories have been invented to account for a name which sounds, or a natural object which looks, like something else. In early religion, as W. F. Otto observed: 'the divine river is this water, which I see flowing by me, hear rippling and can scoop up with my hand; but just as the primitive group consists of men, who can also be eagles or the like, so the river is at the same time a bull, and more than that, a creature in human shape'. Man and god, man and beast, man and plant, are interchangeable, as it seemed also to our own ancestors until a few centuries ago; for 'these examples and reasons', said Reginald Scot in his *Discoverie of Witchcraft* (1584), 'might put us in doubt that every asse, woolfe, or cat that we see were a man, a woman or a child'.

In Greece, such tales of magical changes of shape were a frequent theme from Homer onwards. Then in Hellenistic Alexandria (page 300) learned and experimental poets, though infinitely removed from such beliefs, wrote antiquarian collections of metamorphoses, harking back to early versified catalogues. Ovid retains their scholarship and their variety, but adds his own rapid, champagne-like genius. Metamorphosis, he says, is a very condition of the soul —which, according to Pythagoras, itself transfers its dwelling from beasts into human bodies and back again (page 313), like pliant wax that changes its shape but yet is still itself.[1]

> For spirits, freed from mortal laws, with ease
> Assume what sexes and what shape they please.

Accordingly, Ovid justifies his theme as the keynote of all natural development; and he has been hailed as one of the poet-founders of evolution as an attitude of mind. In the same spirit, he gives a decidedly aetiological turn to many stories, making them into explanations of natural as well as man-made phenomena—though the explanations are often tacked on afterwards, rather than true reasons for the tale's existence (page 122).

Vastly diverse are the myths in the *Metamorphoses*, embracing satire or parody, sentimental fable, 'pseudo-history', anthropology, antiquarianism, patriotic propaganda, moral legend, humorous anecdote, heroic saga, rhetorical fireworks, and romantic or macabre melodrama. 'The poem,' says Patrick Wilkinson, 'is baroque in conception, with its huge extent of ceaseless movement . . . its fantasy, its conceits and shocks, its penchant for the grotesque and its blend of humour and grandiosity.' And yet over-elaboration is avoided, first because this heterogeneous material is welded into a fabulous, Arabian Nights unity, and secondly because Ovid 'plays it straight', telling his stories with an impassive pseudo-naïveté which forms a telling part of his gift.

Ovid did not, like some of the Alexandrians, make heavy weather of his remarkable knowledge and memory. He had always felt the contradictory tugs of the real and mythical worlds. 'It is hard to believe,' said Harold Nicolson, 'that a man so convivial, urban and disrespectful can have approached these myths with any reverence.' But the deference that Ovid shows is rather to the hearts and fallible souls of human beings. In spite of the lightness which, it has been said, looks at passion in terms of Don Giovanni rather than Euripides (for all his debts to Euripidean psychology), Ovid sees everything with the eyes of the loved one or the lover—and particularly, of the *girl* who is involved and in distress; the love of woman for man is treated as no less poignant than man's love for woman.

The gods receive on the whole less sympathy, as might be expected from the poet who, in *The Art of Love*, echoed the ancient view (page 265): 'it is expedient that there should be gods, and in accordance with expediency let us suppose that there are gods'.[32]

A Roman academic critic, Quintilian, criticized Ovid as too clever by half. Yet the poet's stories, his wit and his grace—particularly in the *Metamorphoses*—have dominated the literary world for many generations. Medieval romantic love evolved not only from reverence for the Virgin Mary and the ascetic ideal, but also from the amorous picturesqueness, the quick response to feeling and to nature, of Ovid. Seventy-seven copies of his works have been noted in twelfth-century library catalogues, as against seventy-two of Virgil (and not half as many of any other poet). Dante placed him among the 'four great shades'; and then by his imaginative, inexhaustible store of word-pictures, Ovid became the master and model of Renaissance poets and painters, and of the English Elizabethan Age. The *Metamorphoses* were famous in the translation of Arthur Golding (1565–7). Golding is a little on the defensive as a popularizer of pagan immoral tales, but from his version came the mythological allusions with which Shakespeare abounds, and Milton's many detailed echoes.

But perhaps the supreme exponent of Ovid was the painter Nicholas Poussin. Devoting for more than a decade (*c.* 1629–42) his rich, harmonious clarity to rationalizing Annibale Carracci's and Domenichino's experiments in classical landscapes, Poussin, before passing to a more earnest Stoic classicism, created a personal, elegiac interpretation not only of Virgil's shepherds and shepherd-esses (page 308) but particularly of Ovid. 'No modern picture,' said Sir Joshua Reynolds, 'so much resembles the paintings of the ancients as do those of Poussin.' Yet a comparison in terms of this sort is always misleading, for the authors of antiquity are never 'resembled' by the artists of later ages who have used them to inspire their own talents. The versions of Poussin, for example, though warm with the colours he learnt from Titian, are more softly melancholy and disillusioned than his sparkling literary model.

The Ovidian manner was understood by Dryden, and prolonged into the eighteenth century by the facility and dexterity of Prior and Pope. Goethe liked Ovid more than any other poet, and his mind was early permeated by the *Metamorphoses*. For 'everything in life,' he said, 'is metamorphosis, in plants and in animals, up to and including mankind as well' (1815). And he himself had already written his *Metamorphoses of Plants* in prose and verse (1798), and his poem *Metamorphoses of Animals* (1806), with the same sort of scientific bent as Erasmus Darwin was devoting to verse in England. To the Victorian age, however, Ovid's brand of *chic* seemed heartless; the myths had become hackneyed, and the place for psychology was now the novel.

But in a new epoch, Rainer Maria Rilke (page 323), un-Ovidian though were his feelings and circumstances alike, read Ovid's poem admiringly in a French translation and became preoccupied with the whole concept of metamorphosis—*Wandlung, Verwandlung, Wendung*—which he enjoins upon himself as a norm of his own development (1914). Similarly Spengler's cyclic view of world history reflected 'the image of a perennial configuration and trans-figuration', and André Malraux, in his *Metamorphosis of the Gods*, works out a similar principle, on rather more fluid lines, for the arts: in which one kind of sacred image 'continues and at the same time destroys' its predecessor.

2 *Loves Sad and Heavy*

Ovid tells the story of Pyramus and Thisbe, who lived next door to one another in Babylon.[3] Pyramus was the most handsome man, and Thisbe the most beautiful girl, in all the East. They became friends and then began to love each other, but their parents forbade them to marry. They could only exchange loving words through a chink in the wall between their two houses, and when they said good night, each kissed a different side of the wall.

One day, however, they formed a plan to meet at night, outside the city at the tomb of Ninus.

> And lest in open country they pursue
> Divergent paths and fail to meet, a tree
> At Ninus' tomb their meeting-place should be:
> There, near a spring, a lofty mulberry made
> With clustering snow-white fruits a friendly shade.[4]

Night came, and Thisbe reached the appointed place. But, as she waited, the light of the moon revealed a lioness, fresh from the kill, coming to quench its thirst in the spring. Thisbe, terrified, fled into a cave, dropping her cloak: which the lioness, returning to the woods from the spring, found and ripped to pieces with its bloody jaws.

A little later, Pyramus came out of the city. When he saw the footprints of the animal and the blood-stained coat, he cried out that this meant Thisbe was dead. He himself was to blame for making her come to such a dangerous place; he too would die. So saying, he plunged his sword into his side, and the blood spouted out over the mulberry trees, dyeing its berries dark red.

And now Thisbe, though still afraid, came back from her hiding-place, anxious not to disappoint her lover. At first she did not recognize the tree because of its changed colour. But soon she saw the body of Pyramus. On hearing her call his name, he opened his eyes for a moment. But then he closed them again, for ever. So upon his sword, still warm from his own blood, Thisbe cast herself too. In accordance with her dying wish, the remains of the two lovers rest together in a single urn. And henceforward the mulberry fruit, when ripe, is always dark red.

The setting of the tale of Pyramus and Thisbe is Babylon, and from that region no doubt came the story, a forerunner of the Arabian Nights. Such romances may have reached Ovid through late Greek writers of Syrian Antioch. The fact that both lovers have the names of rivers in Cilicia suggest that the story was in origin, or at some stage of its travels, a myth of the loves of river-deities in this south-eastern area of Asia Minor.

But it comes to us first from Ovid, and the human, exciting, romantic, miniature tragedy which he tells has fascinated many writers after him. Pyramus and Thisbe were favourites of the Middle Ages, for example in twelfth-century France. Then Dante employs the concluding scene as a simile.

> As at Thisbe's name the eye
> Of Pyramus was opened (when life ebbed
> Fast from his veins), and took one parting glance,
> While vermeil dyed the mulberry; thus I turned
> To my sage guide, relenting, when I heard
> The name that springs for ever in my breast.

Chaucer closely follows Ovid's version in his *Legend of Good Women*; but John Metham, in *Amoryus and Cleopes* (1448–9), prefers to give the tragedy a cheerful ending, in which the lovers, revived by the prayer of a hermit, are baptized and married, and live happily ever after. There are countless other versions of the story, with un-Ovidian trimmings, and one of them—perhaps the Sonnet in *A Handfull of Pleasant Delights* (1566, enlarged 1584)—is burlesqued by Shakespeare in the last Act of *A Midsummer Night's Dream*. In *The Merchant of Venice*, too, Jessica says:

> In such a night
> Did Thisbe fearfully o'ertrip the dew,
> And saw the lion's shadow ere himself,
> And ran dismayed away.

King James I wrote a lyric invoking the example of Pyramus, as well as Leander (page 425), and Abraham Cowley retold this *Tragical History* at the age of ten, publishing his version five years later (1633). Goethe compared Ovid's tale to Romeo and Juliet.

Ovid begins the story of Narcissus and Echo[5] by telling how, when the nymph Liriope—ravished by the river-god Cephisus—gave birth to Narcissus, the prophet Tiresias was asked if the baby would live to a ripe old age. He replied: 'if he never knows himself'; and the prophecy came true in this way. When Narcissus, a beautiful youth of sixteen, was driving deer into his nets, he was seen by the nymph Echo, who cannot herself speak first yet cannot remain silent when others speak. She longed to address Narcissus, but when he called to his companions, from whom he was separated, she could only repeat the ends of his sentences. Echo wasted away with love, until finally only her voice remained. And now she hides in the woods and cannot be seen, but her voice is alive and can be heard by anyone.

However, one of the youths whose love Narcissus had likewise mocked made a plea to heaven that Narcissus, too, might fall in love, and be unable to gain the object of his passion. This prayer was heard by the goddess Nemesis.

There was a lucid spring, gleaming like silver,
Which neither shepherds nor the mountain goats
Nor other herds had touched: no savage beast
Nor bird had troubled it, nor falling branch.
Around, the grass which the spring water fed,
And woods which kept the place from burning sun.
Here once the boy, tired with hunting and heat,
Stretched out to rest, charmed by the lovely spring.
He strove to quench his thirst, but other thirst
Was born—he was bewitched by his own beauty:
Loving a bodiless dream, and a body's shadow.
He saw himself with wonder, motionless
Poised, like a statue carved of Parian stone . . .
Now he desired himself and loved his lover,
And sued his suitor, kindling his own flames.[6]

What Narcissus loved was but a shadow, yet he gazed upon this and could not leave the place. Distraught since he knew that he and his reflection must die together, he pined away; while Echo, though still angered by him, grieved and repeated his lamentations. Upon the grass beside the waters he died, and she and his sisters, the nymphs of the spring, mourned for him. The pyre, the torches and the bier were made ready, but the body of Narcissus was nowhere to be seen. In its place, they found a flower, yellow-centred, and with white petals.

Euripides' lost *Andromeda* had introduced a novel solo by Androm-eda, in which her laments were repeated by an echo. As far as we know, Ovid was the first to bring Echo and Narcissus together. The story has lent itself irresistibly to symbolists, allegorists and moralists. How far their interpretations are latent in Ovid's *tour de force* may be questioned, though he was well enough aware that a tale like this has many implications. The image of Narcissus mirrors man's idle hopes and disappointments—and an echo's evanescence again comments on the human condition. In later Roman times, the story, with a new lesson that the soul finds no satisfaction in the body, much influenced the Neo-Platonists.[7]

In the later Middle Ages the fate of Narcissus, along with the tale of Pyramus and Thisbe (page 379), was more popular than any other story. In *Ovide Moralisé* (early fourteenth century), Echo receives approbation as the embodiment of virtue, and the fragmentary thirteenth-century *Roman de la Rose* translated by Chaucer contains the tale.

> This is the mirour perilous
> In which the proude Narcisus
> Saw al his face fair and bright.

Boccaccio saw Echo as true fame, spurned by those who look instead in the waters of worldly delight; and to Marsilio Ficino (1433–99) Narcissus, like Orpheus, stands for mankind's idle pursuit of the unreal.

Caravaggio painted him (*c.* 1599–1600) in sharp contrasts of shadows and lighter tones far from the more frigid accuracy of his academic contemporaries. This great designer and innovator—variously called the inventor of modern painting, pioneer of social realism, rebel against the counter-reformation—shows, straight from life, a moody, difficult youth crouching over the pool, his good looks cast back by the water in an ungracious grimace. Here 'life and love,' said Roger Hinks, 'are two mirrors, facing each other, reflecting nothing'; though Caravaggio—like Ovid in this, for all his disclaimer of debts to the antique—is sympathetic to fallible humanity. A more devoted Ovidian, Poussin (page 308), painted no less than four versions, showing what different feelings the story can evoke. One of his pictures has been called an illustration, another a more picturesque dramatic interpretation, the third a requiem, and the fourth a stimulus to serious intellectual reaction. Milton, on the other hand, surprisingly used Ovid's story, with selections and exclusions, for his delineation of Eve.

After a Platonic study by André Gide, the *Traité de Narcisse* (1891)—discussing the fusion of man's moral and aesthetic natures into a new principle of art—the name of Narcissus has become famous again as the psychoanalyst's word for the self-adoration and self-absorption which makes a man or woman dead to the whole external world. The term Narcissism, describing this attitude, originated with Havelock Ellis (1898), and was more narrowly defined by Näcke (1899) as a person's treatment of his or her own body as the sexual object. Freud devoted a detailed study to the theme (1914), with special reference to the personality of Leonardo da Vinci—now 'analysed' again, in so far as this can be done, by K. R. Eissler.

Paul Valéry, himself the most self-conscious of artists, has written two versions of his three *Fragments du Narcisse* in which the philosophizing soul, recalling Dante, not only contemplates the truth but also contemplates, with love, its own contemplation and the beauty thereof. A nymph tells Narcissus, 'your crime is to ignore all the hearts around you'. But Narcissus chooses to reject the populous, impure world in favour of purity: which may mean nonentity, yet the introspective mind is determined to preserve itself intact from worldly fragmentation. Valéry returned to the story in his *Narcissus Cantata* (1939). 'Beloved body,' declares Narcissus to himself, 'I abandon myself to your power alone; the calm water draws me in the direction of my outstretched arms. To this pure intoxication I offer no resistance.'

Rainer Maria Rilke, in the last year of his life (1926), translated Valéry's *Fragments*, after himself writing two poems about the same myth (1913, 1922). This theme, representing the opposition between life and art, became (like the story of Orpheus, page 323) one of the integral symbols of his poetry—and of his life, with its self-centred denial of the loved one.

> There is no lover for him there. Down below
> Is but the calm of toppled-over stones,
> And I can see the sadness I present.
> Was this my magic in the light of her eyes?

Rilke's obsession with Narcissus is related to his preoccupation with the imagery of mirrors: 'no one,' he says to them, 'has yet distilled with patient knowledge your fugitive essence.' Through mirrors the artist, like many a gazer in folk-tales, projects himself into another dimension, overcoming his personal inhibitions and creating his own ideal, opposed though it may be to socially acceptable standards.

Ovid's story of Daedalus and Icarus is the tale of a loving father's tragic loss of his son.[8]

Daedalus was a great craftsman and inventor who, exiled from Athens, had gone to Crete in order to construct the labyrinth for King Minos. When his task was finished, Daedalus petitioned the king to be allowed to go home; and this being refused, he planned to make the journey all the same—by way of the sky. 'Minos possesses the earth and the seas; but he does not control the air, and that is the way we shall go if Jupiter pardons the enterprise.' So Daedalus carried out this strange, ill-omened project, putting feathers, linen fastenings and wax together to fulfil his purpose.

His son Icarus, as he watched and touched the machine with joy, was told he was to try it out himself, flying behind his father at a moderate height. They set out; and Icarus, in his exhilaration, became more and more daring. They had passed Samos, and Delos sacred to Apollo, and Naxos and Paros, when the boy began to go too high. The wax, too close to the sun, melted. From the heights of heaven Icarus gazed down in terror into the sea, and down into its depths he plunged, his screams cut short as the waters engulfed him. His father cried out to him, but only saw the feathers floating on the surface. Where his son fell, is called the Icarian Sea.

The arch-craftsman Daedalus was identified by a later rationalist as the sculptor who (no doubt to illustrate a myth, page 320) first separated the legs of his statues. But he is an ancient culture-hero almost of the calibre of Prometheus, for he sought to rival creation itself, thus incurring the tragic fault of self-confidence and the disasters that this brings (page 187).

The Fall of Icarus inspired Peter Brueghel the elder (*c.* 1525–69) to a startlingly personal interpretation in which fisherman, shepherd and ploughman continue their tasks unheeding, within a wide landscape, as a tiny, insignificant figure of Icarus strikes the water. Brueghel, gazing at the human drama with a rough, realistic philosophy which sought the universal through the particular, saw the story of Daedalus within a framework of indifferent nature—and indifferent human beings, detached and apathetic in their eternally humble lives, for no plough stops, the proverb says, for a man who dies. Here is a classic instance of a myth directly inspiring an interpretation which is, nevertheless, original and not based on any previous version of the story.

James Joyce invoked Daedalus in the last lines of the *Portrait of the Artist as a Young Man*, and Stephen Daedalus in *Ulysses* is a partial self-identification—the explorer of unknown arts which the author himself wished to explore on imagination's wings. J. B. S. Haldane's optimistic *Daedalus or Science and the Future* was answered by Bertrand Russell's pessimistic *Icarus or the Future of Science* (1924): 'I fear that the same fate may overtake the populations whom modern men of science have taught to fly.' Lauro de Bosis translated his own Sophoclean tragedy *Icaro* into unusual reality by flying over Rome, to be shot down as he scattered anti-fascist pamphlets (1931).

Michael Ayrton is a modern painter and sculptor who has concentrated on this myth, with its relevance to modern astronauts, and on the personal experience of Icarus: his fall proved his mortality (and his father's), yet it achieved something—for they had at least flown.

The labyrinth which Daedalus had been ordered to construct by Minos was to house the Minotaur, offspring of a bestial love. Ovid tells how Minos' wife Pasiphae had fallen in love with a white bull with a black spot between his horns; and from their union, brought about with the help of a wooden cow made by Daedalus, she had given birth to this monster, half-bull, half-man.[9] To hide away the horror, Minos employed Daedalus to build the labyrinth with its innumerable maze-like passages, and the Minotaur was consigned to its depths.

The palace blazed with trophies; but within
Was scandal dark and hideous fruit of sin,
The household shame, full-grown and foul to see,
The illicit half-and-half monstrosity.
To rid his roof of such a stain, the king
Commissioned Daedalus to house the thing;
And he, the world-famed architect, designed
A multiplex of courts and cloisters blind
Where misdirections led, in mazes long,
The cheated eye circuitously wrong.[10]

The Minotaur was fed every nine years on the blood of Athenian youths and maidens. Twice this tribute was paid, but the third time Theseus, son of Aegeus king of Athens*, volunteered as one of the seven young men who were sent to Crete. Ariadne, daughter of Minos, gave him a ball of thread to unwind when he entered the labyrinth. He slew the Minotaur and, by winding the thread up again, found his way back to the entrance of the labyrinth and escaped.

The great mythological cycles of the Greeks, as M. P. Nilsson showed, are all closely connected with Minoan and Mycenaean sites. Minos, who became monarch and judge of the dead, is also the generic name for the kings of Crete during their Minoan sea-empire of the second millennium BC. He is described as the son of Zeus and Europa, and his wife Pasiphae, whose name means 'all-shining' (or 'she who gives light to all'), need not be regarded, as she sometimes is, as a moon-goddess, since her father is identified with the Sun; probably both the kings and the queens of Minoan Crete had been regarded as partly divine. Pasiphae was also worshipped in Laconia, and Athens, too, had a ritual which, although not associated with her name, may have a bearing on the Minotaur myth: each year an Athenian woman was 'married', in a building called the cattle-stall, to the bull-god Dionysus (page 282).

When the kingship of Crete was disputed after Asterius' death,

* According to another belief, Theseus was the son of Neptune (Posidon) (*see* page 391).

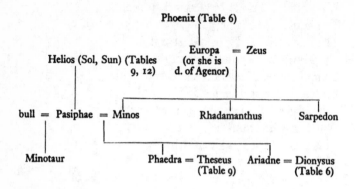

Minos prayed to Posidon to send a bull from the sea for him to sacrifice. Posidon did so, thus confirming Minos' claim. But the bull was so handsome that Minos did not kill it after all; and that is why, by Posidon's arrangement, Pasiphae fell in love with the animal. The product of this love, the Minotaur, is one of a series of monsters who appear on Cretan seals, mostly as demonic attendants, but no doubt also symbolizing the worship of the bull—for which there is a strong evidence in Crete. The beast, who embodied the virile principle, is seen leaping, as he had been shown in artifacts of the Indus civilization at Harappa in the third millennium BC. We are shown him fighting, too, or being sacrificed. On some of the Cretan seal-stones a man's face and head are covered by a bull's mask, and the theme is repeated on coins of the fifth century BC.

Perhaps the survival of such art-forms was enough, in itself, to explain the invention of the Minotaur. Or does the immolation of young Athenians to the monster go back to actual human sacrifices such as were offered to the Phoenician Baal-Moloch, who is likewise bull-headed? Or were the 'victims' only trainees for the bull-ring? Or was it not a Minotaur at all, but a real Cretan king, wearing a ritual bull's mask, that a real Theseus slew? It was also believed that Theseus collected ships secretly on the mainland, at his birthplace Troezen, and then set sail, destroyed the Cretan fleet and captured unwalled Cnossus. Here, perhaps, is an echo of the events which caused the Minoan civilization's downfall (page 33): perhaps this variant of the combat myth (page 131) reflects a successful invasion of Crete from the mainland.

The monstrous and forbidden love of Pasiphae for her bull appealed to the poets of Hellenistic Alexandria, with their taste for the out-of-the-way and macabre. Such themes again interested the *fin de siécle* poets of the 1890's, and then Montherlant, whose *Pasiphaé* (1928) was illustrated by Matisse (1944) and Cocteau (1948). But the modern artist who has made the Minotaur his own is Pablo Picasso, who combines understanding of classical myth with a hereditary passion for bull-fighting. His work of the early 1930's, including the Skira edition of Ovid's *Metamorphoses*, reveals obsession with the monster as symbol of brutish, untamed strength amid the haunting imminence of catastrophe. The equivocal beast— amorous, savage or blind—appears in drawings and engravings in various media (pastel, gouache, indian ink, coloured crayon). His *Minotauromachia*, at New York, plays on the double theme of violence and truth, light and darkness, menace and hope. To Picasso, the Minotaurs have almost become what angels had been to El Greco. Yet to Picasso there is no straightforward religious solution; there is an attempt to comprehend life in all its oscillations from gracefulness to horror.

The labyrinth (the word is not Greek) in which the monster is confined may represent a cave, although it has also been compared to the actual labyrinthine structure of the palace at Cnossus. Herodotus describes a labyrinth at Cnossus and another at Crocodilopolis (Arsinoe Ptolemais, now Hawara) in the Fayum.[11] Virgil locates a painted representation of a similar maze near the entrance to the Underworld (page 328). But the labyrinth also recalls the mazes marked out as ritual dancing patterns in many countries from Wales to north-east Russia, almost always in connection with a cavern. Possibly, although this is not certain, such mazes are already identifiable in the intricate passages and signs of Palaeolithic sanctuaries.

As for their symbolism, 'both the winding path,' said G. R. Levy, 'and the rope or clue, appear in European tales of entry into an actual or subjective spiral maze'. This labyrinthine path, found in medieval churchyards, relates to the life after death and gives initiation, on terms, to the mysteries of the dead. The clue, Theseus' thread, is like the fatal spindle of Sleeping Beauty, and the ball of wool which the kitten unwinds before Alice goes through the Looking Glass.

3 Loves Triumphant

Ovid's Cretan stories have told of Daedalus' loss of his son, and of the monstrous progeny of Pasiphae's bestial love. They continue with the relations of a woman, Ariadne, first with a man and then with a god.[12] The immediate outcome of her help to Theseus, which enabled him to kill the Minotaur, was disaster for herself. She abandoned her family, and left with him for Naxos: but while she slept upon its shore, Theseus returned to Athens (at the sight of his black sails his father drowned himself).

She awoke, and wandered distractedly along the beach, ungirt, barefooted, her golden hair streaming. Crying out to her faithless lover, she desperately asked what would become of her. But as she wept, there was suddenly a sound of cymbals and frenzied drumbeats, and she was afraid. Silenus appeared on his humpbacked donkey, chasing the Bacchanals and toppling to the ground, urged on by Satyrs; and Bacchus (Dionysus) himself came into sight, holding the golden reins of his tiger-drawn chariot, festooned with clusters of grapes. Ariadne forgot everything, including Theseus, and three times she tried to flee but could not. The god declared to her that she was to be his wife, and that he would be more faithful than her former lover. 'Your wedding present is the sky itself!' he proclaimed, and taking the crown that she wore upon her head he changed its gems to gleaming fires and set it in the heaven as a constellation. When he had spoken, he leapt down from his chariot, and clasped her to him. And they departed together.

Minos did not pursue Ariadne and Theseus—a fact which worried the ancient commentators and caused Plutarch, for example, in his monograph on Theseus, to suggest some strange rationalizations.[13]

And then at Naxos Theseus deserted Ariadne, thus becoming not, as so often, the model of gay and spontaneous lovers, but instead the prototype of Victorian cads and bounders who unchivalrously abandon their obligations. But probably in the original form of the story, as in a classic kind of folk-tale, he forgot her, owing to some charm or the breaking of a taboo. And so he moved on to his luminous future as king of Athens and unifier of Attica, the special hero of the Athenians who early appropriated him as their own. They saw in him the embodiment of merciful human justice, who gave sanctuary to Oedipus (page 234), as opposed to the executants of destinies dealt out by the gods.

Nevertheless, Theseus' foreign relations as king struck a different note. He fought the Amazons—taking their queen Hippolyte as his trophy—and fought also the Centaurs in support of his friend Pirithous the Lapith, whom he then helped to invade the lower world in an endeavour to carry off Persephone. Unlike Pirithous, he escaped from Hades—according to the most usual version of the story—and carried off Helen instead (very young at the time), thus subjecting Attica to an invasion by her brothers Castor and Polydeuces. The myths or legends of Theseus, in our own century, have attracted André Gide and Robert Graves, and now Marie Renault.

TABLE 9

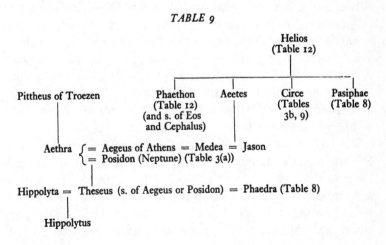

The origins of his earlier love, Ariadne, are suggested by a tablet from Cnossus which mentions her as 'lady of the Labyrinth' to whom offerings of money were made, perhaps as a goddess of the Underworld. Ariadne's distress at the desertion of Theseus was pictured in a long, elaborately mythological poem by Catullus (LXIV) and in a poem of Ovid's *Heroides*—where she says how well she understands that even the Minotaur's horns could not penetrate her faithless lover's breast. In the House of the Tragic Poet at Pompeii there is a picture, probably from a Greek original, of Theseus embarking and Ariadne gazing after him from the top of a cliff.

Ovid's version of the arrival of Bacchus-Dionysus, coming from his eastern travels (page 275), has been called as fresh and colourful as Titian's famous picture of the scene, though in treatment Ovid is perhaps closer to the rendering of Rubens. But the painters had also seen the sarcophagi on which, during the later centuries of the Roman empire, the same theme figured in endless repetition, as an earnest of the immortal life which human beings could win (page 285).

According to Ovid[14] the beautiful Atalanta, daughter of King Schoeneus of Boeotia, could run faster than any man. When she asked an oracle whom she should marry, the reply was: 'a husband is not for you; avoid having one! And yet you will not be able to avoid this, and though still living you will then cease to be yourself.' Alarmed by these words, Atalanta repelled all her many suitors, insisting that no one could have her unless he had first beaten her in a race; and that any who insisted on competing, but were outstripped by her, would have to die.

Yet even on those conditions many were eager to try their fate. Hippomenes, on the other hand, regarded this as a mad risk, and came to the race as a spectator only. But when he saw Atlanta getting ready to run, and still more when he saw her running, he fell passionately in love with her and, in spite of the fate of defeated contestants, resolved that he too would compete for such a prize.

The girl admired his looks and regarded him with a softer expression than usual. However, she could not resist a general demand that the race must take place.

Hippomenes prayed to Venus that, since his love came from her, she should give him help, and she did so by passing him three golden apples which she happened to have in her hand, plucked from a golden apple-tree beside her temple at Tamasus in Cyprus. The race started, and although Atalanta ran as slowly as she could she drew easily ahead. But when Hippomenes threw one of Venus' golden apples in front of the maiden as she ran, she stopped to pick it up. This enabled Hippomenes to catch her; but not for long, since she soon passed him again—so he threw the second apple, with the same result as before.

Now they were on the last lap, and Venus describes what happened.

> And then, to keep her longer from the course,
> To the field's edge he threw, with all his force,
> The glittering gold. At first the girl seemed slow
> To follow after, but I made her go,
> And, as she took it, added to its weight,
> By loss of speed to make her yet more late.
> And, lest my long-drawn tale as slowly run,
> The girl was beaten, and her hand was won.[15]

Later, because Hippomenes forgot to offer Venus grateful incense, and profanely made love to Atalanta in a temple of the mother-goddess Cybele, they were both turned by Cybele into the lions who draw her chariot. Venus and Cybele here become the neglected and vengeful goddesses of many folk-tales.

There are two stories of Atalanta. The other—the subject of a lost play by Euripides—tells how, after failures by Jason, Pirithous and others, she was the first to wound the monstrous boar of Calydon in Aetolia. The beast was then dispatched by Meleager who gave her the head and hide as trophy.[16] Ovid treats the heroines of the two tales as the same person, though whether this identification was his own, or inherited by him, cannot be determined. Claimed both by Arcadian Tegea and by Boeotia, Atalanta may well be a by-form of the divine huntress Artemis, who in the Calydonian story had sent the boar because King Oeneus had omitted her harvest offering.

In other versions of the myth, the suitor's name is not Hippomenes but Milanion. Propertius, whose elegies are thickly encrusted with mythology, gives the tale as a parallel to his own devotion to Cynthia, with Milanion as the stock example of a patient lover. Theocritus,[17] like Ovid, calls the runner Hippomenes. The story is the folk-tale of many trying and failing for the hand of the fair princess. The Dyaks of Borneo still very recently—if not today—had to cut off heads to win their brides. But the Greeks have adapted this familiar theme to their love of races and competitions. The present version is a curious variant in which the princess herself runs and loses. Robert Graves makes the stimulating (but not, without further evidence, convincing) suggestion that the race was deduced from a pictorial representation of the doomed year-king, with golden apples in his hand, being chased to death by a goddess; and that the punishment of the lovers records an old ruling according to which members of the same totem clan—or kindred clans—might not marry one another, as the lamb and goat clans could not intermarry at Athens.

The race or its results were occasionally painted in later centuries, for example by Bon de Boullogne, but it is Atalanta's doings in Calydon, as part of Meleager's saga, that have received much more attention. Swinburne's *Atalanta in Calydon* stands high among his major achievements. Saturated in the classics, he describes his poem as 'pure Greek, and the first poem of the sort in modern times, combining lyric and dramatic work on the old principle'. Yet, although he used Ovid (as well as Apollodorus) for his main outline, Swinburne and his work are of course strikingly un-Greek as well as un-Ovidian in spirit, form and style.

Acrisius king of Argos would not, according to Ovid,[18] believe that Perseus, whom his daughter Danae had conceived of a shower of golden rain, was the son of Jupiter. But when he grew up Perseus roamed throughout the world and performed marvels, of which the most famous was the slaying of the snake-haired monster Medusa, one of the three Gorgons. Her hair had been beautiful once, but she had been ravished by Neptune—in the temple of Minerva who, in punishment, turned Medusa's locks into snakes. Guided to the Gorgon by the aged daughters of Phorcys—who shared one eye between them—Perseus passed through lands filled with the rigid shapes of animals and men, who had looked upon Medusa's face and been turned to stone. Perseus, on the other hand, gazed at her only in the reflection of his bronze shield, and this enabled him to overcome and slay her. He cut off her head, and as he flew with it over the sandy deserts of Libya, drops of blood fell from the wound. When they reached the ground, these drops became deadly snakes, with which Libya now abounds.

Perseus flew three times over the whole world. On the borders of the west, Atlas refused him hospitality, whereupon Perseus uncovered the head of Medusa and turned Atlas into a huge mountain upon which rests the sky and all its stars. Finally Perseus came to the Ethiopian kingdom of Cepheus, where he looked down and saw, with love at first sight, the king's beautiful daughter Andromeda. Though innocent of crime, she was chained to a rock, in order to expiate the words of her mother Queen Cassiope who had boasted of her own beauty and had offended the sea-goddesses. Accordingly, King Cepheus had been ordered by an oracle to sacrifice their child to a sea-monster sent by Neptune. When the dragon appeared out of the sea, and her father and mother lamenting clung to Andromeda, Perseus flew down to them and offered to save her if she would be his wife. They promised him their daughter, and a kingdom as dowry too. Perseus sped into the air, swooped down upon the monster and struck.

> Perseus, light-winged, evades his jaws, and where
> The shell-crustation gapes and leaves him bare,
> On back, on bony flanks, the sword-strokes hail,
> Or where the fish-flukes end the tapering tail.[19]

Finally the hero drove his sword three times into the creature's heart.

The king and queen welcomed Perseus as their son-in-law, but the wedding-feast was interrupted by the king's brother Phineus, who strode in declaring that Andromeda had been promised to himself, and that he had come to avenge her theft. Phineus hurled his great ashen spear at Perseus, and a general fight began. But Perseus, protected by Minerva, raised Medusa's head aloft. Two hundred of his enemies saw the Gorgon's face and were turned to stone, including at last, though he begged for mercy, Phineus.

By the same means, then, Perseus drove Acrisius' brother Proetus from the throne of Argos, which he had usurped; and killed the vindictive Polydectes, lord of Seriphos, for refusing to believe that Perseus had slain the Gorgon at all.

Perseus is described by Pindar as the arch-hero of Argos, where a mound allegedly contained the grave of his daughter and the head of Medusa. Argos in historical times means Mycenae in Mycenaean times, and of the latter city he was said to have been the founder. His story, told in early epics that are now lost, became pan-Hellenic; his name was early connected with many ancient monuments and natural objects (such as the rocks of Seriphos into which his enemies had been turned), and already in Hesiod's time the tale was well-known in central Greece.[20]

Furthermore, there is no Greek hero apart from Odysseus whose adventures are so extensively merged with the folk-tales of many other peoples. The deeds of Perseus, like those of Odysseus and Jason, circulated far and wide with the early navigators. His links however are not, as theirs were respectively, with the central Mediterranean or the Black Sea, but with the Levant. Perseus has been convincingly related to the Canaanite god Resheph—and with less certainty his story has been held to reflect a ritual pattern of human sacrifice.

He is primarily the slayer of the Gorgon, who had originally, perhaps, been the sort of nightmare apparition that reduces the dreamer to stony rigidity; and similar horrific masks were depicted on Greek shields and buildings in order to frighten enemies and ward off evil spirits. It was not until Alexandrian times that artists made her beautiful—and Perseus, in Ovid, says how beautiful she once had been. He, the flier upon winged sandals in his cap of darkness, using the bronze of his shield as a magic mirror, looks like a survival of archaic prophets and *shamans* (page 139).

TABLE 10

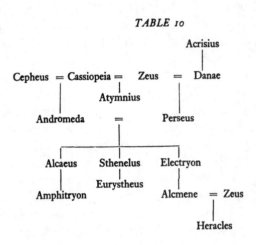

Perseus' conception by Danae from Jupiter's golden shower was regarded by Justin Martyr as a demon-inspired travesty of the Virgin Birth. But the scene attracted innumerable European painters, while Perseus himself is represented by Cellini's bronze statue in the Loggia dei Lanzi at Florence. The story lent itself to the allegorizing of Francis Bacon, who interpreted Perseus as a symbol of war and the fact that Perseus singled out for attack the only Gorgon who was mortal (as her sisters Sthenno and Euryale were not) as an indication that no wars should be attempted except those within one's power. This is one of the most fanciful of all the allegories suggested in Bacon's *Wisdom of the Ancients* (page 423).

Sigmund Freud's interpretation of Medusa's Head (1922) was posthumously published in 1940. To him, the head surmounted by snakes represents the female genitals crowned by hair. By analogy of dreams, that symbol's persistence in horrifying form—found in the myths of at least twenty-five peoples—relates to the widespread terror of castration (page 115) for which, in dreams, decapitation stands. Minerva-Athene, who according to another version herself killed Medusa (in battle with the giants), symbolizes these fears by wearing upon her breastplate the apotropaic Gorgon's head, which numbs her enemies with terror and repels desire. Thus, too, Iris Murdoch's novel *A Severed Head* (1961) discloses what primitive gulfs lie beneath our lives and civilizations; and one of her characters, Honor, is the Medusa who is struck down but triumphs, who repels but immobilizes.

The secondary episode in the story of Perseus, though it comes foremost to Ovid's dramatic imagination, is his rescuing of Andromeda from the dragon. This further version of the familiar combat myth (page 131) includes no less than forty variants, in which the 'dragon' ranges from several kings or rivals to two sorts of monsters and a mountain-giant. Ovid links his tale with the vaguely located 'Ethiopians', but the stories are generally associated with Palestine, or south-eastern Asia Minor. In particular, the traces of Andromeda's fetters, and the skeleton of the monster, were still pointed out in the first century AD near Joppa.[21] But the myth seems to originate from farther east or south, and to represent a mixture and elaboration of several middle-eastern variants. The Persian king Xerxes, like many people of his day, was using ancient myths for modern political ends when he quoted the union of Perseus (Argos) with Andromeda (the east) to enlist Argive friendship for his own cause in the Persian War.

Only fragments survive of the plays which Athenian tragedians devoted to the theme (such as the supposedly romantic *Andromeda* of Euripides, page 299), but its fascination for the great painters and sculptors of Europe is amply attested. A mature masterpiece of Titian (*c.* 1554) heightens the drama of the subject by his presentation of light and shade. Even if the mood of the ageing Titian was not, as Roger Fry said, specifically pagan, the painter felt the myths too freshly and experienced them too directly to echo the formal naturalistic conceptions of his contemporaries; and when in the 1550's he turned from portraits and religious subjects to mythology, his total mastery of this genre re-created the stories in an original idiom of colour and movement. Yet alongside the high seriousness of his approach to the myths is another element. The human nude is the central core of Renaissance humanist art, and the naked Andromeda of Titian is the object of lust, the woman beheld and desired by a man. This erotic aspect of his genius commended itself to King Philip II of Spain and I of England, who commissioned a series of Titian's mythological paintings, including this Perseus and Andromeda. Guido Reni, Rubens and Rembrandt returned to the theme, which later appealed, for different reasons, to the nineteenth-century romanticism of Burne-Jones and Charles Kingsley.

4 Pious Couples Rewarded

After Jupiter hurled down the Giants (or Titans) who had tried to climb to Olympus (page 127), Ovid[22] tells how Earth, drenched with their gore, breathed new life into this, creating from it human beings. But they too, like the Giants, were cruel, violent and contemptuous of the gods—true children of blood; and in particular Lycaon, king of Arcadia, had doubted the divinity of Jupiter when the god visited his land. So Jupiter resolved to destroy this human race also. In order, however, not to risk demolishing the universe with the fire of his thunderbolts, he decided to send torrents of rain and plunge mankind beneath the waters. Imprisoning the north wind and all other cloud-scattering gales, he released the south wind, while Iris drew up water to fill the clouds and Neptune, struck the earth with his trident. Rivers raced across the plains until every building was submerged, and the whole world was a shoreless ocean. Human beings and animals were swept away or died of hunger, and even the birds, exhausted, fell into the sea.

Only Deucalion, son of Prometheus, and his wife and cousin Pyrrha were able to survive in a little boat. Jupiter saved them because they were the best and most reverent of mankind.

When Jove beheld, among the thousands slain,
In all the world awash one man remain,
And of all women one surviving still,
Who both had served the gods and done no ill,
He loosed north winds, and, routing clouds and rain,
Showed earth to sky and sky to earth again.[23]

Neptune bade Triton blow on his conch and recall the floods and streams, and Deucalion and Pyrrha landed on one of the twin peaks of Parnassus. Their first action, after landing, was to offer prayers to the nymphs and deities of the mountain, and to Themis, who at that time kept the oracle.

As earth came back into view, Deucalion saw that it was an empty world, and tearfully told his wife how fortunate they were to have each other, but how precarious their hold on life still was. 'If only, by arts like my father's, I could create again the nations of the earth and breathe life, as he did, into the moulded clay! As it is, the human race depends upon us two.' They appealed for help to the oracle of Themis, who replied: 'Leave my temple, veil your heads, loosen your robes, and, as you go, throw behind you the bones of your great mother.' They were deeply perplexed until Deucalion interpreted their mother as the earth, and bones of their mother as the stones in the body of the earth. So they picked up stones, and threw them behind their backs; and the stones grew, and changed into the shapes of men and women. That is why we are a tough race, accustomed to hard work—we recall the origin from which we came.

Next, as the moisture remaining in the earth was warmed by the sun, the earth, growing warm again, gave birth to animals of many kinds, and brought forth innumerable forms of life. Some were creatures known before, and others were new and strange.

Deluge myths occur in thirty-four out of a specimen group of fifty among the world's mythologies. Almost all these stories reflect the idea of humanity returning to the water from which it had come (page 110)—with philosophical implications, sometimes, relating to the purification of sins. Then a new era and a new humanity are established, though often there are to be further cyclic alternations and periodical re-engulfings, such as lie behind Plato's myth of Atlantis. Psychoanalysts see the boat or ark as the precious contents of a mother's womb, floating in its amniotic fluid.

In the Pacific area, it is told that one shipwrecked man alone, or the offspring of a lunar animal (here lunar and deluge myths converge), escaped from the watery catastrophe—which had been caused by ritual shortcomings. Similarly, the disaster from which Noah was saved came about because 'the earth was corrupt before God, and full of violence'—like the world tainted, in the Deucalion story, by Lycaon's evil (which may go back to some savage ritual of Zeus 'Lycaeus', the Arcadian). But Noah landing on Mount Ararat—still, today, the objective of expeditions seeking the Ark—is closely paralleled, even down to the story of the birds let loose, by Sumerian and Babylonian deluge myths. A six-column tablet from Nippur, going back at least to the third millennium BC, tells the story, which some believe to have been recited at a great Autumn Festival. Floods were more important to Mesopotamia, and particularly to the cities of Sumeria in the south, than they were to Palestine. But it was the Hittite and Hurrian peoples (pages 34, 114), or their predecessors, which translated the Mesopotamian story and introduced the role of Ararat to the Palestinians. The Deucalion version, on the other hand, may perhaps enshrine memories of a post-Palaeolithic epoch in Greece itself, when central Thessaly became a lake.

In the inscription from Sumerian Nippur, the role of Noah was played by a hero called Ziusudra ('he saw life'). There are also independent Old Babylonian versions dating from early in the second millennium, in which the hero is the 'exceedingly wise' Atra(m)hasis. The relation of Noah's story to these renderings is much disputed; some regard Noah as their product, many believe that he comes instead from an ancient, independent source. At some stage, too, a version of the Flood was inserted in the Gilgamesh epic (page 94). Its best preserved tablet (in an Assyrian version) consists of more than three hundred surviving lines giving an account of the deluge by him who has been saved from it, Utnapishtim 'the far away'. Mount Nisir (whether Ararat or a mountain of north-eastern Iraq) is where

TABLE 11

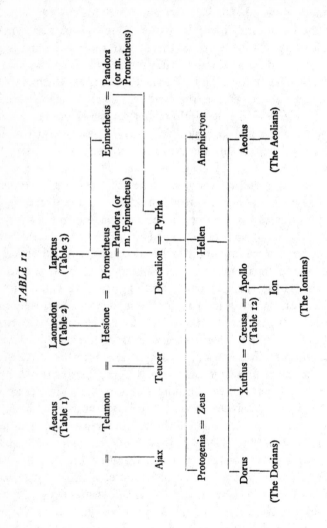

the boat lands, and the Sumerian city-state of Shurrupak (now Fara) on the Euphrates is the home of Utnapishtim.

What happened at the end differs in the various stories. In *Genesis* God promises Noah: 'while the earth remaineth, seedtime and harvest, and cold and heat, and summer and winter, and day and night shall not cease'. In the story of Utnapishtim, the rescued man thanked the gods with a sacrifice, to which, when they smelt its sweet savour, they gathered like flies. The tale of Deucalion, which reached Ovid through Pindar,[24] ends with the creation of the new human race, not from mud or clay as in later versions of the story of Prometheus (page 209), but from stones: probably because of the similarity between *laas* (stone) and *laos* (people). This is less solemn than the conclusion of *Genesis*, but more creative and hopeful than the Gilgamesh ending. The peoples of Mesopotamia had neither the humanism of the Greeks nor the Covenant of the Jews, and therefore perhaps, for all the splendour of their civilizations, lived out their lives in greater psychological insecurity.

And so from Deucalion and Pyrrha were descended the various branches of the Greeks.

On a mountain-side of Phrygia, tells Ovid,[25] there stand an oak-tree and a lime-tree with a low wall beside them; and near by is a marsh, which used to be habitable land, but is now the haunt of coots and diving birds.

Once Jupiter and Mercury came to this country, in human shape. To a thousand houses they went, looking for somewhere to rest, and every house was bolted and barred against them. But in the humble thatched cottage of the aged Philemon and Baucis they were kindly received; from this poor but contented old couple they received rustic hospitality.

> So when the gods came to this dwelling poor
> And stooping entered through the lowly door,
> Philemon brought a bench for them to sit;
> And bustling Baucis spread a rug on it,
> Stirred on the hearth the ashes scarce alive,

Yesterday's fire with bellows to revive;
Fed it with bark and puffed it into flame.
Chopped sticks, dry branches, from the roof the dame
Brought down, and broke and placed beneath the pot,
And next the cabbage, from the garden-plot
Picked by her husband, stripped. He with a fork
Reached and unhooked a smoky side of pork
From a blackened beam, and from this treasured spoil
Cut a small piece and put it on to boil.
Meanwhile they both beguiled the time with talk . . .
The gods lay down. Baucis the table laid,
Girt up and trembling. One leg of the three
Was short: a tile restored stability.
The top thus levelled she with mint did wipe,
Then set Minerva's olives clean and ripe,
Cherries of autumn-tide preserved in lees,
Endives and radishes and thick cream cheese,
And eggs cooked lightly on the gentle fire,
All served on earthenware. No metal higher
Than this the encrusted wine-bowl dignified
And beechwood beakers lined with wax inside.
Nor was it long before the hearth sent up
Its steaming dishes. Then they filled the cup
With wine of no great age. A little space
Was cleared, and these to nuts and plums gave place,
And wrinkled dates, and open baskets decked
With fragrant apples, purple grapes fresh-picked,
And last a honey-comb; but better still
Their kindly looks and bountiful goodwill.[26]

As the meal went on, the hosts noticed with amazement, mingled with fear, that every time the wine-bowl was emptied it filled up again of its own accord. Extending their hands in prayer, they asked to be forgiven for the simplicity of the meal. They still had a single goose, which acted as the watchdog of their little property, and this they now tried to catch for their divine guests. But successfully eluding them until they were exhausted, the bird finally went close to the gods themselves, as if to take refuge. Jupiter and Mercury declared that the bird should not be killed; and they added this further message. 'We are gods,' they said, 'and this inhospitable neighbourhood is going to be punished as it deserves. Both of you, however, will be spared. But you must leave your home, and come with us up the mountain near by.' Philemon and Baucis did as they were told. But when, near the top, they looked round, they saw the whole country-side covered with water, and only their own house still above its surface. As they watched, the little building changed before their eyes into a gleaming shrine.

Jupiter now told them that they could have any gift they liked; and they asked to be the priests of the two gods, and custodians of their temple. They also begged that the same hour might bring death to both of them. These prayers were granted—and at the end of their lives as Philemon and Baucis in extreme old age stood before the temple talking of old times, they were transformed into the two trees which the Asian peasants still show growing side by side.

The story is a Phrygian rendering of the Flood, of which the more familiar version of Deucalion and Pyrrha was also told by Ovid (page 399). There are many such tales of divine visits, resulting in favour to one hospitable person or family alone. Perhaps it was a local story of this visitation of Jupiter and Mercury which, in *The Acts of the Apostles*, caused the people of Lystra (in neighbouring Lycaonia) to identify Paul and Barnabas with the two gods.[27]

The myth of Philemon and Baucis is paralleled in variants 'The Poor Man and the Rich Man' collected by the Grimms. The two old people of the Greek version are granted their wish, as in *Les Trois Souhaits*; and the two trees into which they are turned recall Norse myths of the creation. Ovid borrows colouring from the Alexandrian poets (page 299), and this same realistic, sentimental *genre* was fashionable in contemporary statues and paintings of the poor, such as gnarled, aged fishermen and the like.

The story, with its moral that humility is one way of avoiding humiliation, is a simple, touching, understandable tale—and easily

Christianized, so that a medieval commentator could gloss that he who receives one poor man in the name of God receives God. But the seventeenth century witnessed the most important paintings of the theme, and especially of the Meal of the Gods, which had already attracted Bramantino and the Zuccari. Flemish, Dutch and German painters in particular liked this subject, notably Elsheimer whose version was used as a model for Rembrandt's Supper at Emmaus; and Rembrandt also drew and painted the classical subject itself, infusing Christian symbolism.

'I see Baucis and Philemon as perfectly before me,' said Dryden, 'as if some ancient painter had drawn them'; and he translated Ovid's tale.

> Meantime the beechen bowls went round, and still,
> Though often emptied, were observed to fill,
> Filled without hands, and of their own accord
> Ran without feet, and danced about the board.

The young Jonathan Swift (1708) used a village parson and his wife as models for another version of the theme, turning the couple into two old yew-trees: the gods are saints who

> Disguised in tattered habits, went
> To a small village down in Kent.

Goethe, more far-reachingly, used Philemon and Baucis in *Faust* (Part II) as representing a stage in man's struggle for salvation. But today Graham Hough, in his *Legends and Pastorals*, offers a more astringent commentary.

> Charmed with plain innocence of speckled eggs
> The strapping radiant guests ate up their crust,
> Returned the apple smiles, stretched out their legs,
> And at the spring washed off the morning's dust;
> Determined the poor house must be new built,
> Turned the thatched gable to a pediment,
> Left the old couple to a tedious cult
> Of virtue spoilt by knowing what it meant.

OVID

Well pleased, the tall companions took the road,
Aglow with high Olympian charity—
One to hunt Daphne panting through the wood
Until she froze into a laurel tree;
One, horned and dewlapped, by the randy sea
To tumble soft Europa's maidenhood.

CHAPTER 16

THE INVISIBLE LOVER

1 The Story of CUPID AND PSYCHE Told by Apuleius

ONCE UPON a time a king and queen had three very beautiful daughters, but much the most beautiful was the youngest, Psyche. People came from many lands to admire her, in the belief that she was Venus, or had succeeded her as goddess of love. This caused the rites of Venus to be neglected, and the goddess angrily bade her son Cupid wound Psyche so as to make her fall in love with some completely degraded creature. Venus then went on her way across the sea to her sacred island of Cyprus. But Psyche received no benefit from all the honours paid to her. Her sisters had married kings, yet no one courted Psyche, and she sat alone at home, feeling ill and miserable.

Her father, suspecting divine anger, inquired from the oracle of Apollo at Miletus where he might find a husband for her. The answer, however, came that Psyche's husband was no human being but a winged serpent of whom even Jupiter was afraid; she must put on black mourning and go to a mountain-top for her deathly marriage. To the accompaniment of funeral music and lamentation, she headed the procession like a woman going to her grave.

Sending away her parents, who shut themselves in their palace to grieve, Psyche climbed to the very top of the hill. A breeze came, and lifted her off the ground, and carried her down to a valley beneath, where she found herself laid upon a bed of flowery grass. After sleeping for a while there, she rose and walked beside a stream into the depths of a wood, and she came upon a palace so radiant with gold and gems and precious woods that she knew it was a god's. When she finally ventured to cross the threshold of this heavenly abode, Psyche found within its doors unbelievably valuable treasures, with no guard to watch over them.

But the voice of an unseen maidservant guided her to her bedroom and bathroom. 'First she found her bedroom and dozed off again for a while, then she went to the bath, where invisible hands undressed her, washed her, anointed her and dressed her again in her bridal costume. As she wandered out of the bathroom she noticed a semi-circular table with a comfortable chair in front of it; it was laid for a banquet, though there was nothing yet on it to eat or drink. She sat down expectantly—and at once nectarous wines and appetizing dishes appeared by magic, floating up to her of their own accord. She saw nobody at all, the waiters were mere voices, and when someone came in and sang and someone else accompanied him on the lyre, she saw neither of them, nor the lyre either. Then a whole invisible choir burst into song.[6]

'When this delightful banquet was over, Psyche thought it must be about time to go to bed, so she went to her bedroom again and undressed and lay awake for a long time. Towards midnight she heard a gentle whispering near her, and began to feel lonely and scared. Anything might happen in a vast uninhabited place like this, and she had fears for her chastity. But no, it was the whisper of her unknown husband.'[1] He came and lay with her, without being seen, and left before daybreak; and the next two nights he visited her again. Meanwhile Psyche's parents, joined by her sisters, were still lamenting her as lost, but her unseen husband warned her not to answer her sisters if she heard them mourning. When, however, she pleaded to be allowed their company, he reluctantly relented, but on the condition that she must not, however much they importuned her, try to find out what he looked like. So the West Wind brought her sisters to the palace, and Psyche, drawing upon her imagination, told them her husband was a handsome young man with his first beard, who liked hunting.

When they were alone with one another on their way back to their father's house, the elder sisters indulged in jealousy. One of them complained that her own husband was bald, feeble and miserly. The other grumbled that she was married to a man who suffered so badly from sciatica and gout that his wife was no more than a nurse, whose hands were ruined by his plasters and poultices. So they returned to their homes, full of malicious intentions; and now Psyche's husband again warned her of the danger from them, this time with the assurance that she was to have a baby by him— a god if she kept his secret, but only a mortal if she talked.

But next time she saw her sisters, Psyche was not sufficiently on her guard. She was very simple-minded and, forgetting what story she had told them before, invented a new one. She said that he was a middle-aged merchant from the next province, very rich, with slightly grizzled hair. Then, breaking the conversation off short, she loaded them with valuable presents and sent them away. As they rode home, the younger sister said: 'Now, what do you make of the monstrous lies she tells us? First the silly creature says that her husband is a very young man with a downy beard, and then she says that he's middle-aged with grizzled hair! Quick work, eh? You may depend upon it that the beast is either hiding something from us, or else she doesn't know herself what her husband looks like.' 'Whatever the truth may be,' said the elder sister, 'we must ruin her as soon as possible.'²

And so, correctly guessing the unwelcome prospect that Psyche's baby was destined to be a god, they deliberately frightened her by suggesting that her husband was a fiendish reptile. Accordingly, at their proposal, next time she was in bed with him she got up and took a lamp, and took also a carving knife to kill him. But by the light she saw he was Cupid himself in all his glory. She tried the point of one of his arrows, which pricked her, and the lamp she was carrying spilt a drop of burning oil upon his shoulder. He woke, and immediately departed from her, and flew to the top of a cypress-tree. After pausing there with a reproachful message, he soared up into the air and was gone.

After vainly trying to drown herself—the river set her ashore—

Psyche wandered off in aimless misery, and came to the city where one of her elder sisters lived. She told this woman what had happened, but deceitfully added: 'As he flew away, he said that he would have you in my place as his wife.' So, like Psyche before her, 'the sister jumped off the rock too, shouting confidently: "Here I come, Cupid, a woman worthy of your love. West Wind, convey your mistress to the Palace at once".' Then she took a head-long leap; but she never reached the valley, either dead or alive, because the rocks cut her to pieces as she fell and scattered her flesh and guts all over the mountain-side. So she got what she deserved, and the birds and beasts feasted on her remains.'[3] Soon afterwards the other sister met with the same fate.

Meanwhile, in his mother's celestial house, Cupid lay groaning with pain. Venus, who was bathing in the sea, was told of his affair by a sea-gull, and furiously complained to her step-mother Juno and Ceres about what had happened; but they, in fear of Cupid's arrows, tried to excuse him. Psyche, looking everywhere for her lover, came to their shrines for protection. But although they would have liked to help her, they dared not offend Venus. After announcing a reward for anyone who could find Psyche, Venus—through her servant Custom—soon tracked her down. After two of her other women, Anxiety and Sadness, had whipped the girl, the goddess leapt on her, tore her clothes to rags, pulled out handfuls of her hair, and shook her repeatedly.

Then she imposed a series of formidable tasks. First, before nightfall, Psyche must sort out an enormous heap of wheat, barley, millet, lentils, beans and the seeds of poppy and vetch. 'You look such a dreadful sight, slave,' said Venus, 'that the only way that you are ever likely to get a lover is by hard work'—and she flew off to a wedding-party, from which she returned at midnight, scented and slightly drunk. But Psyche, helped by an army of ants, had completed her task. She was then set a second and more dreadful task, of bringing Venus a piece of wool from some fiercely dangerous golden sheep on the bank of a stream. But this too, with the help of a green reed, she was able to achieve, and she brought Venus back a whole lap-full of the golden wool.

Yet even her performance of this second perilous task did not satisfy the goddess, who frowned and told her with a cruel smile: 'Someone has been helping you again, that's quite clear. But now I'll put your courage and prudence to a still severer test. Do you see the summit of that high mountain over there? You'll find that a dark-coloured stream cascades down its precipitous sides into a gorge below and then floods the Stygian marshes and feeds the hoarse River of Wailing. Here is a little jar. Go off at once and bring it back to me brimful of ice-cold water fetched from the very middle of the cascade where it bursts out of the rock.'4 Psyche was horrified by the fierce dragons guarding the stream, but Providence came to her aid and sent her Jupiter's eagle, which owed Cupid a debt of gratitude for helping him carry Ganymede to heaven to be Jupiter's cup-bearer. With critical words for Psyche's silly simplicity, the eagle took the jar and induced the stream to give up its water.

Declaring Psyche was a witch, Venus now bade her take a box down to the Underworld itself, and hand it to Proserpina, with the request that the queen should put a little of her beauty inside the box, and send it back for Venus; who had expended some of her own beauty in looking after her sick son, and needed further supplies for a theatre-party that evening. Psyche was now desperate, and went up a high tower, resolved to throw herself from its top and reach the Underworld by killing herself. But the tower broke into speech, and dissuaded her. 'Listen to me. The famous Greek city of Lace-daemon (Sparta) is not far from here. Go there at once and ask to be directed to Taenarus, which is rather an out-of-the-way place to find. It's on a peninsula to the south. Once you get there you'll find one of the ventilation holes of the Underworld. Put your head through it and you'll see a road running downhill, but there'll be no traffic on it. Climb through at once and the road will lead you straight to Pluto's palace. But don't forget to take with you two pieces of barley-bread soaked in honey water, one in each hand, and two coins in your mouth.

'When you have gone a good way along the road you'll meet a lame ass loaded with wood, and its lame driver will ask you to hand him some pieces of rope for tying up part of the load which the ass has dropped. Pass him by in silence. Then hurry forward until you reach the river of the dead, where Charon will at once ask you for his fee and ferry you across in his patched boat among crowds of ghosts. It seems that the God Avarice lives thereabouts, because neither Charon nor his great father Pluto does anything for nothing. (A poor man on the point of death is expected to have his passage-feed ready; but if he can't get hold of a coin, he isn't allowed to achieve true death, but must wander about disconsolately for ever on this side of Styx.) Anyhow, give the dirty ruffian one of your coins, but let him take it from your mouth not from your hand.

'While you are being ferried across the sluggish stream, the corpse of an old man will float by. He will raise a putrid hand and beg you to haul him into the boat. But you must be careful not to yield to any feeling of pity for him; that is forbidden. Once ashore, you will meet three women some distance away from the bank. They will be weaving cloth and will ask you to help them. To touch the cloth is also forbidden. All these apparitions, and others like them, are snares set for you by Venus; her object is to make you let go one of the sops you are carrying, and you must understand that the loss of even one of them would be fatal—it would prevent your return to this world. They are for you to give to Cerberus, the huge, fierce, formidable hound with three heads on three necks, all barking in unison, who terrifies the dead; though of course the dead have no need to be frightened by him because they are only shadows and he can't injure shadows.'⁵ After dealing with Cerberus, Psyche would be welcomed by Proserpina. But on her way back she must take care not to open or even look at the box. Its treasure was not for her.

All went well upon her dangerous quest, and she obeyed every instruction, until she was on her return journey and had left the Underworld behind. But then, out of a foolish desire to have some of the beauty for herself, she opened the box; and at once she fell down in a fatal sleep, as if she were dead.

But Cupid, now recovered, came to rouse and rescue her, and Psyche was able to rise to her feet and deliver Proserpina's present to Venus. Meanwhile her lover pleaded with Jupiter, who summoned the gods and goddesses to Council and told them Cupid had best stop roving and settle down with Psyche. Assuring Venus that this would be no disgrace for herself, he sent Mercury to bring Psyche up to heaven, and gave her a cup of nectar to make her immortal, and to keep Cupid, for all time, from flying away from her again.

Then Jupiter ordered a great wedding-banquet, at which, to the accompaniment of flute and pipe-music, the Muses chanted the marriage-hymn, and Apollo sang to his own lyre. And, as he sang, Venus performed a lively dance.

So Cupid and Psyche were married; and their child was a daughter called Pleasure.

2 Fairy-Story

Novelist, priest and popular philosopher, poet and devotee of Isis, lawyer and lecturer, the writer of this story Lucius Apuleius was born at Madaurus (Mdaourouch in Algeria) in about AD 123. This was an epoch when the Roman Empire was profoundly at peace—Gibbon thought it the happiest period of the world's history—but was convulsed by spiritual and magical movements and excitements. The equivocal Apuleius was accused of magic: we possess his *Apologia*, the exuberant *tour de force* with which he shadow-boxed against these charges.

The transformation of one 'Lucius' into an ass (a theme perhaps adapted from some lost Greek novel) is recounted in his book the *Metamorphoses*, of which the title consciously echoes Ovid (page 375). Apuleius' work has also been called *The Golden Ass*, at least from the time of St Augustine onwards. The book uniquely represents in Latin that 'last child of the Greek genius', the fictional genre which developed, from the first century BC onwards, into novels such as the *Ninus Romance*. But the *Golden Ass* is in a scintillatingly florid, fantastically un-Ciceronian Latin—and is the only Latin novel that has come down to us complete. Many and varied are the ribald, hair-raising or mystic short stories that it contains, rather as Dostoevsky in the *Brothers Karamazov* likewise diversifies and enriches his main action by varied tales and dreams.

The longest and most elaborate of Apuleius' stories is told in a robber's cave, by an old cook, to the young bride Charite while she is kidnapped and awaiting ransom. This is the tale of the Fairy Bridegroom, *Cupid and Psyche*. Strangely enough, there is no trace of this theme in Greek or Latin literature until Apuleius. Possibly he had before him a Greek version, which is now lost; or perhaps he himself introduced the names Cupid (Eros = love) with Psyche (the soul) into the fairy-story. Or rather, this is not a single fairy-story, but a huge conglomeration of fairy-stories and other folk-tales, many of them paralleled all over the world (page 82). Apuleius' capacity for story-telling has made him one of the most remarkable of all literary intermediaries with the anthropologist's world that lies only just below the surface of his narrative.

The very first words of *Cupid and Psyche* let us know, by their familiarity, that the sort of folk-tale with which we are concerned is the fairy-story. Fairy-stories are easier to recognize than to define. They need not necessarily be about fairies, and relatively few of them are. Nor should they be thought of solely in terms of those fluttering flower-sprites with antennae, devised for children who often so cordially dislike them. J. R. R. Tolkien sought to define the fairy-story as applying to Faerie, the Perilous Realm, powerful with magic of a peculiar mood and potency; magic designed to survey the depths of space and time, to hold communion with other living things, to give effect to visions of fantasy, and to resolve them by the Sudden Joyous Turn which consoles with a happy ending. 'In that land a man may (perhaps) count himself fortunate to have wandered, but its very richness and strangeness make dumb the traveller who would report it. And while he is there it is dangerous for him to ask too many questions . . .'

The *Odyssey* had contained many unforgettable fairy-stories (page 84), but not the most famous of them all—the Cinderella tale, usually with two elder sisters jealous of the youngest. This comes to the modern world through the *Cabinet des Fées* of Charles Perrault (1628-1703); but Apuleius had already given us a version in *Cupid and Psyche*. 'Once upon a time there lived a king and queen who had three very beautiful daughters.' Over nine hundred such stories have been collected in many lands—and particularly, though by no means exclusively, in countries where the youngest child is the most favoured. In Italian, Indian and Norse renderings the wife (as in Apuleius) is threatened by malevolent sisters. In a modern Greek variant they spread broken glass on the ledge of the window through which the eagle-husband enters the house. In Albania, Fatima is deserted by her sisters in a forest, but is looked after by thieves. In an Arab version the prince marries all three sisters, but the older ones do not keep their promises. They often, as here, offer insidious advice to their junior: in Mediterranean versions, for example, she is urged not to take the drink with which her husband drugs her, so that she may keep awake. Jealousy enters into the story in another way also, for Psyche suffers from the jealous persecution of her mother-in-law. Not only are bad relations with mother-in-law a familiar joke of west European low comedy, but peril at her hands is the theme of folk-tales from Australia, New Guinea, North America and Africa.

In a great area, including northern Asia as well as America, there are tales of a girl visited by her unseen lover; the two are often equated with the moon and the sun. Frequent, also, is the mystic prohibition which Psyche so disastrously disregards, upon the wife seeing her husband. In the words of Graham Hough,

> Where light was all forbidden
> My prying candle shone;
> Ah that he still lay hidden,
> My dark, my shining one.

In Grimm's 'Singing, Soaring Lark', as well as in other stories extending from Zululand to Wales, the veto is infringed as in Apuleius, and after many troubles the couple (of whom one, as here, is usually supernatural) are reunited. This prohibition recalls the customs of the Iroquois who, like the ancient Spartans, only go into their wives' huts under cover of darkness; while a Yoruba woman, traditionally, is prevented by modesty from seeing her husband's body at all. (Africans are often afraid of their women seeing some particular thing—not necessarily themselves—or the men will die.)

In the *Rig Veda*, on the other hand, it is Urvasi, a fairy, who visits Pururavas, a mortal man, and mysteriously declares: 'embrace me three times a day, but never against my will, and let me never see you without your royal garments; for this is the manner of women'.

Psyche, like the Ass in the *Metamorphoses* of which this story forms part, is a victim of curiosity. Cupid forbids her to 'answer any questions about him', which recalls the many stories in which the wife may not give her husband's name away. In Hindu and Ainu versions, this would kill him. Lohengrin orders Elsa not to divulge his identity; a Welsh fairy tells the heir of Corwrion not even to discover what her name is. The name is part of the personality, not to be revealed for fear of subjecting its possessor to another's control. These irrational taboos survive today in many people's sensitive feelings about the use, or peculiarity, of their names. This sort of veto can easily be rationalized and moralized into warnings about what happens to people who do not do as they are told, who are too curious, and do not keep their mouths shut—a stock theme, incidentally, of classical poetry (found in Simonides and Horace), easily traceable back to the need to avoid trouble in family and tribe. In particular there are many cautionary tales of wives' indiscretions, such as the Celtic 'Red and Black Bull of Norroway'. And yet, in citing world-wide resemblances, it must be stressed that every story, though the same, is different: in colouring, atmosphere, and individual details.

The declaration of Apuleius' oracle, that the husband was to be a snake or dragon (like the oracle which ordered Andromeda to be exposed to the dragon, page 395), and the consequent belief of the wicked sisters that this is what Cupid really was, may well go back to an earlier version in which the prince had, in fact, been transformed into one of the lower animals, from which he regained his shape at night. The Naga, or snake race, in India have a story of the serpent taking human form, but keeping its own forked tongue; again it was condemned to vanish if the wife asked questions. In other Indian (as well as Zulu) versions, the husband only *seems* to be a snake, because he is magically sewn into a snake skin, from which the girl rescues him. Keats' poem *Lamia* is adapted from a tale of a serpent-woman, going back to the Greek writer Philostratus 'the Athenian' who lived not long after Apuleius. Indeed serpents were in fashion at this time—a lecherous quack-prophet Alexander of Abonutichus in Asia Minor established oracles and mysteries round a snake which he claimed was a new incarnation of the health god Asclepius (Aesculapius). But snakes played a vast part in ancient folk-lore, and indeed, even today, there are snake-worshipping cults, for example in the southern United States (page 283).

The story of Cupid and Psyche is one which, like many folk-tales, is profoundly penetrated by the belief in intercourse between men and animals (page 376). Aboriginal Australians are 'of one flesh' with crows, crayfish and wallabies; and in *Puss in Boots*, too, the animals are friendly. Psyche, in common with a thousand others, has to surmount a series of labours, and she is helped by ants, who also (together with fishes and ravens) help the heroine in Grimm's 'White Snake'—and have been studied by Freud in relation to the insects who appear in dreams. In the collection of Indian stories of Somadeva Bhatta, it is bees who help the poor wood-cutter's daughter Tulisa—separated from the Prince of Snakes—to complete her task of collecting the scent of innumerable flowers; and it is squirrels who bring her jewels in exchange for seeds. Likewise, the Scottish folk-tale 'Nicht, Nought, Nothing' tells of fishes obeying the request of the giant's daughter, and draining the loch. Perhaps in an earlier version of the Cupid and Psyche story her lover helped her with her labours, as in the Swedish 'Wolf Prince'—the converse process to the winning of the Golden Fleece, in which Medea helps her lover Jason to accomplish the test he has been set (page 294).

3 *Allegory?*

Eros had already been named, nearly a thousand years earlier, as the all-powerful cosmic principle (page 110), and this was also the basis of Plato's discussions about love in the *Symposium* and the *Phaedrus*. Meanwhile the same god had been successively shown by sculptors as a handsome young athlete (Euripides endowed him with bow and arrows),[6] a boy, and the fat child of the sentimental Alexandrians.

During the same period, the human soul, little more than a bird or bat in Homer (page 94), had been elevated by the philosophers to a dematerialized divine being. The *Phaedrus* contains an inspired vision, or myth (page 208), of souls journeying in chariots. By Plato's time, artists had brought Eros and Psyche together: a relief at Istanbul shows them in quiet harmony. But then, in Hellenistic poetry and art, Eros (Cupid) turns on Psyche, and inflicts on her many tortures and labours. Paintings and gems show her prostrated at his feet in supplication, or she appears as a butterfly tormented by a boy, or as a girl wounded or in chains. The Greek poet most dedicated to Eros and Psyche is Meleager of Syrian Gadara, who in the first century BC wrote a series of exotic, graceful epigrams proclaiming the power of passion over the soul.

Here we have entered the realm of allegory: of stories and visual representations which mean, or are supposed to mean, something beyond what you see, something deceptively similar yet different, often of greater religious, moral or political importance. 'I dreamed and behold I saw'—though the unconscious or irrational levels of the mind may also throw off allegories of their own, with no clear relation to 'important' aims.

The ancient love of personifications lent itself readily to allegory and interpretations of allegory. There are traces of such deductions in Homer,[7] and Hesiod's description of Eros and other natural phenomena (page 105) in personified form suggests how, later on, thoroughgoing allegory could come about: indeed his whole cosmogony can be described as a sort of quasi-philosophical allegory. Explicit interpretations of the myths on these lines are at least as old as Theagenes (*c.* 525 BC), who regarded the Homeric battle of the gods as a war of the elements, Apollo representing fire, Posidon water, and Artemis the moon. Heraclitus, too, turned the myths into physical allegories. These early Ionian thinkers allegorized Homer because they thought they detected in what he said an important kind of truth—relating to the nature of the universe—which did not appear on the surface of these tales. This is true in so far as the themes of myths often suggest universal patterns of motivation and conduct, but not true in its supposition that these were already in the minds of their originators. The early allegorists, nevertheless, took the understandable, though unscientific, step of assuming that the mythographers had chosen to express abstract truths in the form of parables. And this attitude was further developed by thinkers of the fifth century.

Although Plato criticized their interpretations, he too felt that there was no abrupt division between mythical and physical explanations of phenomena. His own myths (pages 208, 419) are often allegorical; thus the Cave in his *Republic*[8] is an imaginative picture of human life and of what happens to the philosopher in its midst. Hellenistic Platonists and Stoics used allegory as a weapon for the preservation of traditional authority, and in the same way Jews and then Christians declared the Old Testament to contain hidden meanings as well as its surface truth.[9]

Though myth is by no means always allegory, allegory is nearly always myth. 'In the myth,' remarked Westcott, 'thought and form come into being together. In the allegory the thought is grasped first by itself, and is then arranged in a particular dress . . . The allegory is the conscious work of an individual fashioning the image of a truth which he has seized.' The ancients, when they adopted the allegorical method, did so from two motives—either because concrete stories (like the parables of Jesus) possessed greater attractive, persuasive power than abstractions, or because they believed that the myths contained a deep, instructive significance which had been deliberately hidden by the wisdom of the early sages in order to prevent the great truths from passing into minds unworthy to receive them.

The literatures of the world consist of an almost infinite series of nuances from plain mimesis and realism—that is to say, a situation in which the theme is dominant and imagery absent—all the way to that complete predominance of images which is allegory. But there are many gradations between these two extremes. First along the line from realism come writings in which there is some imagery, but it is superficial and external to the main ideas. Then come, for example, those plays of Shakespeare in which image and theme are elaborately fused, and works that personify cosmic events such as *Paradise Lost*, Hesiod's *Theogony*, and *Genesis*. Next are the free-style allegories of Ariosto, Goethe or Ibsen (and perhaps the symbolic revelations of Blake, which are however visions rather than allegories); and finally, complete and continuous allegories such as Spenser's *Faery Queene* or Bunyan's more explicit *Pilgrim's Progress*, or, in our own day, the paintings of Orozco and Beckmann which, in the most thoroughgoing way, translate abstractions into picture-language.

A tale in which the chief characters are personified by names such as Cupid and Psyche lent itself to any and all of these nuances of allegory, and such intentions of a great many kinds have been attributed to Apuleius. Yet the indications of allegory in his fairy-tale are not very extensive. All that can be said, on internal evidence, is that the protagonists are given these significant names, that Psyche suffers at the hands of Venus' slaves Custom, Anxiety and Sadness,[10] that Sobriety is an enemy of Venus,[11] that Psyche's child by Cupid is called Pleasure,[12] and that the animals who help her in her labours suggest the desire of all creation to stand well with love.

Apuleius was no doubt familiar with Meleager's mythology of Passion and the Soul, and being also an eminent Platonic scholar—for that is how St Augustine (of Thagaste near by) describes him[13]—understood the philosophical ramifications of this theme. Indeed the *Metamorphoses* as a whole, after their primary aim of entertainment, contain a religious purpose, including as they do—in contrast to badinage about Olympian ladies—a heartfelt eulogy of the Egyptian mother-goddess Isis, whose mystery religion led all other faiths in popularity at this time. The whole work may, at least to a subordinate degree, be regarded as a record of the journeys of the soul through carnal adventures into mystic peace. Accordingly, this same allegorical purpose may have been present in Apuleius' mind when he began work on that section of the *Metamorphoses* which tells the story of Cupid and Psyche. But if so, he soon forgot this intention, and allowed the folk-memories and his own brilliant narrative ability to take charge.

Not long afterwards, however, Plotinus (AD 205–269/70) and his Neoplatonists, in producing the completest philosophical system since Aristotle, gave a much more thoroughgoing interpretation to Apuleius' story, as symbolical of the human soul's quest for love. The age of allegory was well under way, and from now onwards, in literature of all sorts, even the most acute minds saw correspondences between sets of facts and ideas that seem to us unrelated. The Roman catacombs of Domitilla contain frescoes of Cupid and Psyche gathering flowers, and on pagan and early Christian sarcophagi alike Cupid appears as the soul's hope of future life and posthumous happiness. Sometimes the lovers are seen at work on the vintage, 'the true vine' first of Dionysiac funerary art and then of Christianity, from which Psyche plucks the grapes that represent the happy afterlife.

This is one of the points at which pagan myth merges into Christian symbolism. In art, as in literature, the early Christians were divided about classical mythology. Eusebius of Caesarea (c. AD 260–340) vaguely favours these traditions as forerunners of the Truth,[14] whereas many other Christians denounced them as a diabolically delusive counterpart of the old Testament. In the Renaissance, again, Pico della Mirandola (like Hölderlin two hundred years later) tends to the former interpretation that this was 'the theology of the ancients', while church reformers took a much severer view. Milton, again, saw the myths alternately as Satanic deceptions and mystic vehicles of the truth. W. E. Gladstone, however, was content to regard them as a degraded form of Revelation.

From the time of the early Fathers onwards the *Golden Ass* of Apuleius and his story of Cupid and Psyche figured prominently in such controversies. In the early Middle Ages even Virgil was scarcely regarded as a more powerful wonder-worker than Apuleius. His story of Cupid and Psyche was well known to Martianus Capella (c. AD 420) who, in a cumbersome Latin allegory, introduced the marriage of Philology and Mercury, in imitation of the wedding of Apuleius' lovers. At the end of the same century Fulgentius interpreted Psyche as lust, the wicked sisters as the Flesh and Free Will, and Cupid as both the Earthly and the Heavenly Love. After *c.* AD 800 there is a gap of two or three centuries in our knowledge of the *Metamorphoses*, our oldest manuscript (now in Florence) being of the eleventh century. From then onwards allegory proliferated even more intensely, as the universal vehicle of pious expression, 'the bone, muscle and nerves of serious literature'.

But it was in the Renaissance that Apuleius came into his own. Boccaccio did more than anyone else to make the *Cupid and Psyche* known—adding a long allegorical interpretation. There were many editions of the whole work from 1469 onwards, and Raphael decorated the Villa Farnesina with twelve scenes of the story. In the mid-sixteenth century, when a revival of mythography greatly influenced artists, translations abounded, including in England the bright but inexact version of William Adlington (1566). His rendering appealed to people's love of gay, ebullient story-telling, though the translator feels obliged to quote a higher aim: 'to utter and open the meaning of so sportful a jest . . . to the simple and ignorant, whereby they may not take the same as a thing only to jest and laugh at—but by the pleasantness thereof be rather induced to the knowledge of their present estate, and thereby transform themselves into the right and perfect shape of men.' Not long afterwards Francis Bacon, in the *Wisdom of the Ancients*, warned against 'the commodity of wit and discourse that is able to apply things well, yet so as was never meant by the first authors.' Nevertheless he himself, as keen a latter-day symbolist of 'pagan mysteries' as Botticelli or any other Renaissance Platonist, deduces from the myths an extraordinary abundance of 'concealed instruction and allegory', since 'parable has ever been a kind of ark, in which the most precious portions of the sciences were deposited' (just as Robert Graves, in the *White Goddess*, is one of those who uncode 'deliberately coded and jumbled' wisdom messages, claiming to recover forgotten events by the exercise of intuition or 'analeptic thought'). George Chapman too— echoing figures of late antiquity such as the Emperor Julian and Sallustius—wrote that 'learning hath delighted from her cradle to hide herself from the base and profane vulgar' (1614).

Then, after the *Grand Siècle* had made extensive use of the story

of Cupid and Psyche for dramatic rather than moralistic reasons—
the tale being retold by La Fontaine (1673) and innumerable
playwrights ranging from Molière and Calderon to the platitudinous
Thomas Shadwell—allegory and secret messages returned to favour
in the symbolic theory of Friedrich Creuzer (1810). According to
him, the priestly forerunners of the Greek and Latin writers had
possessed a dim, grandiose conception of monotheism and other
theological doctrines, and had set them forth in a series of symbols:
namely the myths, of which (as Giambattista Vico had already said)
the secret lessons about the human race and the world were later
misunderstood. Creuzer has been described as 'the first modern
scholar to reduce mythology to something else', and his theory,
followed by suggestions that myths were 'a disease of language'
(page 118), has been called the death-blow to their true study.

Soon afterwards, however, stories like that of Cupid and Psyche
began to recover, among the poets, from the discredit in which these
fantasies and the preceding Restoration banalities had deposited
them. 'I hope,' said Keats, 'I have not in too late a day touched the
beautiful mythology of Greece, and dulled its brightness.' Of all its
figures, to him, none was more brilliant than Psyche.

> O brightest! Though too late for antique vows,
>   Too, too late for the fond believing lyre,
> When holy were the haunted forest boughs,
>   Holy the air, the water, and the fire;
> Yet even in these days so far retired
>   From happy pieties, thy lucent fans
> Fluttering among the faint Olympians
>   I see and sing, by my own eyes inspired.

Elizabeth Barrett Browning and William Morris returned to the
theme, and so (admitting to seventeenth-century borrowings) did
Robert Bridges in his *Eros and Psyche* (1885); though he can scarcely
have been pleased to hear from Gerard Manley Hopkins that his
'Eros is little more than a winged Masher, but Psyche is a success,
a sweet little "body", rather than a "soul" '.

CHAPTER 17

HE DIED FOR LOVE

⫸⫷

1   The Story of HERO AND LEANDER Told by Musaeus

TELL, GODDESS, of the lamp, which was the confidant of secret loving, and of the youth who swam by night to wed across the sea; and of his dark marriage upon which no dawn ever shone.

Sestus and Abydus are divided by the sea, but Eros united them with an arrow which struck the fair Hero and Leander. Leander lived at Abydus, and Hero at Sestus, where she dwelt in a tower outside the town with one old servant. Hero ministered to Aphrodite and to her son Eros. Yet even so she did not avoid the boy's shafts, for at a festival of Adonis she met Leander, and they fell in love with one another. In the early evening twilight they stood, like beautiful shapes carved upon a relief, and Hero listened to Leander's pleas, and was persuaded. She told him of her home, and he vowed to swim to her by night; she must light a lamp to guide his journey.

They prayed for night to fall, and when it was dark and the lamp shone out, he came to her.

> His skin she bathed, and anointed his body fragrantly
> With oil of roses, to take away the harsh tang of the sea;
> Then in her bed, piled deep with rugs, laid him to
>   rest,
> Still breathing hard, and drew him with fond words
>   to her breast—

'Ah love so sorely tried as never lover yet,
O dear and sore-tried love, the bitter waves forget!
Forget the booming breakers, the harsh, fish-reeking
    brine,
And rest thy weary body within these arms of mine!'

He hearkened; then her girdle he loosened, and the
    will
Of glorious-hearted Cypris they turned them to fulfil.
A bridal it was where no man danced; no voice of
    minstrel praised
Hera, Queen of Wedlock; no marriage-hymn was raised.
Round *that* bride-bed no torches filled the night with
    flame,
No revellers light-footed whirling about them came,
Their bridal-song no father and well-loved mother led—
Nay, in Love's crowning hour 'twas Silence strewed
    their bed
And shut their marriage-chamber; 'twas Darkness
    decked the bride,
And night that gave them blessing.[1]

And so they made love through many summer nights.

But when winter came, and the sea grew stormy, Hero ought to have refrained from lighting her lamp. Yet love and destiny compelled her, and the fatal night arrived. Leander struggled with the waves, but his strength failed him—and Hero's lamp was blown out by the wind. When the grey morning dawned, he still had not reached her tower.

Everywhere over the sea's wide plains with straining
    eyes
She searched for sight of him, lest perchance his way
    was lost
When the light of her lamp was gone. And when she
    saw him dead,
Torn by the rocks and lying at her tower's foundation,

About her breast she tore the wondrous woven mantle
And from the sheer crag plunged in hurtling headlong
    fall
To find with her dead love a death among the waves,
And the joy of love together in life's last separation.[2]

2 *Autumnal Tint*

The story of Hero and Leander is found among the folk-tales of all
Europe, including the Ukraine—as well as in an Egyptian love-lyric
and in the Punjab. But this myth is a latecomer to extant classical
literature, its earliest known appearance being in the *Georgics* of
Virgil,[3] who may have taken the theme from some Alexandrian poet,
possibly Callimachus. Then the lovers are the subject of two
successive poems in Ovid's *Heroides*. The first contains Leander's
message to Hero, and descriptions of his journeys to her beneath the
light of the moon.

> The billows gleamed with her reflected light
> Which clear as day illumed the silent night.
> No sound, no murmur to my ears there came,
> Save where the surface rippled as I swam . . .[4]

Then Hero replies; she is impatient to enter the waves herself, were
it not that the fate of Helle (page 298) has shown that these waters
are even less safe for women than for men.[5]

A Greek epigrammatist is one of many other poets who returns
to the theme.

> Here it was once Leander crossed; here beats the
>   swelling
> Strait that brought a lover—and her he loved—
>   to dust,
> Here stands the ruined tower, that once was Hero's
>   dwelling,
> Where of old she kindled the lamp that failed
>   their trust.

> Here, in one grave together, they lie—still crying
>   in vain
> Against the wind that grudged them to each other's
>   arms again.[6]

The story is also depicted on frescoes at Pompeii, on a mosaic and a relief found at Zaghaouan in Tunisia, and on coins of Abydus and Sestus, the towns at the beginning and end of Leander's legendary journey.

The present poem of 340 lines was written in Greek by a certain Musaeus known as Grammaticus. He lived in the fifth or sixth century AD—when Rome had become an outpost of the Byzantine Empire or was beyond its borders; although Marlowe and Chapman, and Renaissance scholars such as Scaliger, believed that the poet had lived and written a millennium and a half earlier than his real date, and that he was the Musaeus who is recorded as a mythical pupil of Orpheus. Scaliger also called his poem finer than Homer. But Musaeus shows little or no similarity to Homer in theme or manner. This is a story of love, a gracefully proportioned miniature epic uniting classic form with sympathetic feeling; and, as its translator J. A. Symonds (1879) noted, 'with the warm autumnal tint of decadence'—such as may also be detected in a haunting fourth-century Latin hymn to Venus, the *Pervigilium Veneris*. Musaeus is nostalgic for young beauty and love, and his conceits do not spoil his firm clear brevity, a certain pathetic directness, an understanding of what it is to be lonely, and a knowledge of the sea's terrible grandeur.

In the thirteenth century the tale had become the Provencal story of Flamenca, part of the troubadours' repertory. It was also, for many centuries, the stock feature of a thousand chap-books. It appears in Dante's *Purgatorio*, and Chaucer planned to include 'Erro' in his Legend of Good Women. Bernardo Tasso's version inspired Juan Boscan's *Leandro y Hero* (1543), which established in Spain the genre of elaborate mythological poetry. In England, 'Leander and Heroes loue is in every man's mouth'—said Abraham Fraunce in 1592—reaching its most vivid expression in an expanded version, forming part of a longer poem, by Christopher Marlowe, one of the English poets who have made classical mythology their own. His version embodies and transcends all the greatest qualities (as well as exhibiting most of the vices) of the Italianate tradition. Marlowe infuses into Musaeus' quiet humanity something of the cynicism of Ovid.

> One is no number; maids are nothing, then,
> Without the sweet society of men.

But he also adds an exuberant voluptuousness which is his own, and which has earned the poem preference, for instance by Swinburne, over Shakespeare's less warm and passionate *Venus and Adonis*. Symonds, though he underestimates Musaeus' sophistication, compares Marlowe's melodious work to 'some radiant double rose, placed side by side with the wild briar whence it sprang by cultivation'. The poem by Marlowe was completed and published after his death by Chapman, who later translated, or rather expanded, Musaeus himself at a length of 1,600 lines. But a contemporary, Thomas Nashe, wrote a prose burlesque in his *Prayse of the Red Herring* (1599)—one of the first of many such travesties—in which Hero comes upon Leander 'sodden to haddock's meate'. Shakespeare repeatedly refers to the tale, and so do many other writers of the seventeenth and then of the eighteenth century. One suggests that the lover's adventures will soothe 'a modern Belle of Taste'. Goethe, in 1796, considered attempting a new poetic treatment of this sudden blazing up of love—instant fulfilment the only thought—and the tragic ending that followed.

In May 1810 Lord Byron swam from Sestus to Abydus, taking just over an hour. It is only one mile and a quarter, but a two-knot current compelled him to swim four. However, Leander, he pointed out, swam even in December: whereas

> For *me*, degenerate modern wretch,
>   Though in the genial month of May,
> My dripping limbs I faintly stretch,
>   And think I've done a feat today . . .

'Twere hard to say who fared the best:
    Sad mortals! thus the Gods still plague you!
He lost his labour, I my jest;
    For he was drowned, and I've the ague.

Yet three years later he chose the place to which he swam as the scene of his professedly escapist 'Turkish Tale', *The Bride of Abydos*.

A picture of Leander on a gem was the subject of a sonnet by Keats (1816–17), which shows his gift for the indirect description of a work of art. The timelessness of the tale also appealed to Leigh Hunt:

> I never think of poor Leander's fate
> And how he swam and how his bride sat late,
> And watched the dreadful dawning of the light,
> But as I would of two that died last night.
> So might they now have lived and so have died:
> The story's heart, to me, still beats against its
>   side.

And another in whose soul the pathetic story struck a chord was A. E. Housman:

> By Sestos town, in Hero's tower,
>   On Hero's heart Leander lies;
> The signal torch has burned its hour
>   And splutters as it dies.
> Beneath him in the nighted firth,
>   Between two continents, complain
> The seas he swam from earth to earth
>   And he must swim again.

A: GREECE

F. V. Botley

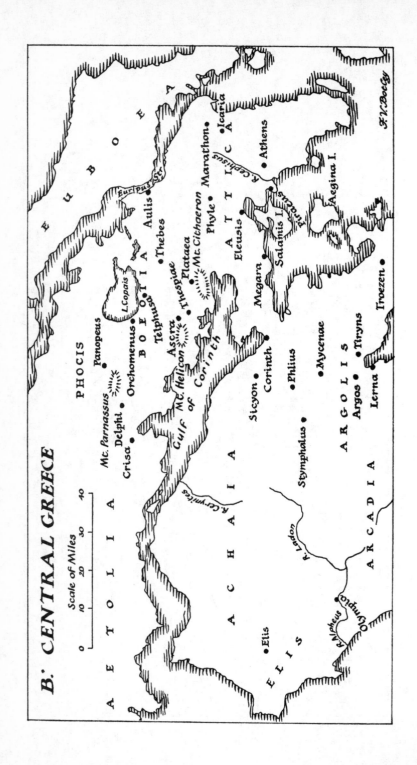

B. CENTRAL GREECE

Scale of Miles
0   10   20   30   40

AETOLIA

PHOCIS

Mt. Parnassus
Panopeus
Delphi
Crisa
Orchomenus
L.Copais
BOEOTIA
Aulis
Thebes
Telphusa
Ascra
Mt. Helicon
Thespiae
Plataea
Mt. Cichaeron
Gulf of Corinth
Corinth
Sicyon
Phlius

EUBOEA

Euripus Str.

Marathon
Phyle
Icaria
R. Cephisus
Athens
ATTICA
Eleusis
Megara
Salamis I.
Aegina I.
Troezen
Mycenae
Tiryns
Argos
Lerna
ARGOLIS

ACHAIA

Stymphalus
R. Ladon
R. Cerynites

ELIS
Elis

ARCADIA
R. Alpheus
Olympia

F.V. Bocly

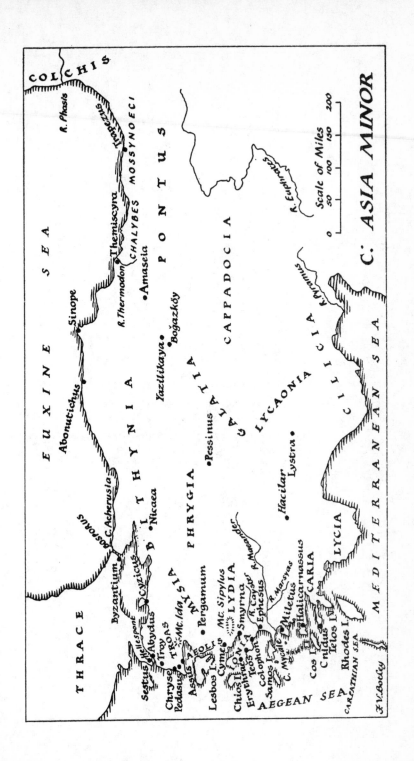

C. ASIA MINOR

COLCHIS

R. Phasis

EUXINE SEA

Trapezus

MOSSYNOECI

CHALYBES

Themiscyra

PONTUS

R. Thermodon

Amaseia

Sinope

Yazılıkaya

Boğazköy

CAPPADOCIA

Abonutichus

GALATIA

LYCAONIA

Pessinus

CILICIA

R. Pyramus

R. Euphrates

Scale of Miles
0   50   100 150 200

Bosporus

BITHYNIA

C. Acherusia

Nicaea

PHRYGIA

Hacilar

Lystra

Byzantium

Cyzicus

Mt. Ida

MYSIA

Sestus
Hellespont
Abydus
Troy
TROAS
Chryse
Pedasus
Assus
AEOLIS
Lesbos I.

Pergamum

Mt. Sipylus

Cyme

Smyrna

LYDIA

R. Maeander

Chios I.
IONIA
Erythrae
Teos
Colophon
Ephesus
Samos I.
Mycale
C. Trogilium
Miletus
R. Cayster
R. Marsyas
Halicarnassus
CARIA
Cos I.
Cnidus
Telos I.
Rhodes I.
CARPATHIAN SEA

LYCIA

MEDITERRANEAN SEA

THRACE

AEGEAN SEA

F. V. Bodley

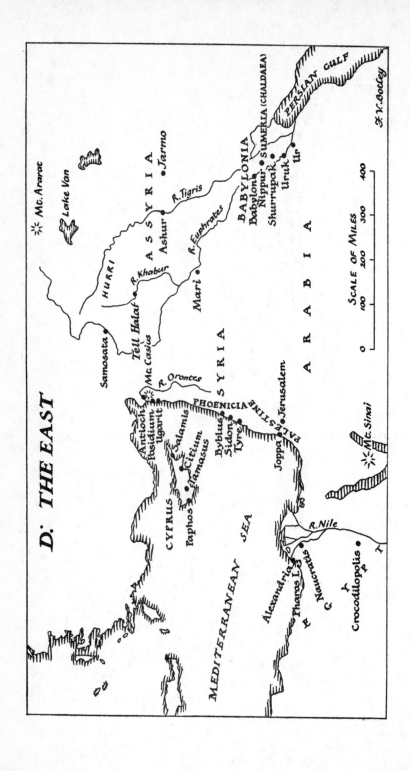

D: THE EAST

Mt. Ararat

Lake Van

HURRI

Samosata

Tell Halaf

Mt. Casius

R. Khabur

ASSYRIA

Ashur

R. Tigris

Jarmo

R. Euphrates

Mari

SYRIA

R. Orontes

Antioch
Posidium
Ugarit

PHOENICIA

Salamis
Citium
Tamasus

CYPRUS

Paphos

Byblus
Sidon
Tyre

PALESTINE

Jerusalem

Joppa

MEDITERRANEAN SEA

Alexandria

Pharos I.

Naucratis

R. Nile

Crocodilopolis

Mt. Sinai

ARABIA

BABYLONIA

Babylon
Nippur
Shurrupak

SUMERIA (CHALDAEA)

Uruk

Ur

PERSIAN GULF

SCALE OF MILES

0   100   200   300   400

F. V. Botley

E: ITALY AND NORTH AFRICA

Alps

R. Padus

Mantua

Patavium

ADRIATIC SEA

Apennines

ETRURIA

Clusium

ELBA I.

CORSICA

Tarquinii

R. Tiber

Rome

LATIUM

Sulmo

APULIA

Brundisium

Capua

CAMPANIA

Cumae

Neapolis

Tarentum

CALABRIA

SARDINIA

TYRRHENIAN

SEA

Himera

Drepanum

SICILY

Rhegium

Mt. Etna

Enna

Acragas

Syracuse

Carthage

Thagaste

Zaghaouan

Sicca Veneria

Madaurus

Scale of Miles

0   50   100   150   200

F.V. Botley

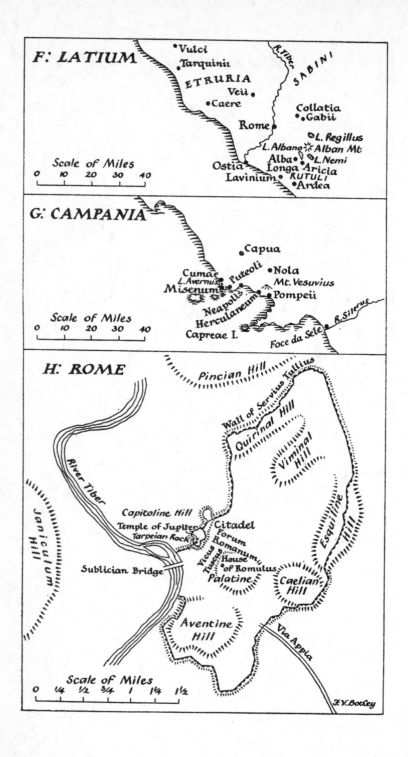

F: LATIUM

R.Tiber
Vulci
Tarquinii
SABINI
ETRURIA
Veii
Caere
Collatia
Gabii
Rome
L. Regillus
L. Albano • Alban Mt
L. Nemi
Alba
Ostia Longa Aricia
Lavinium RUTULI
Ardea

Scale of Miles
0 10 20 30 40

G: CAMPANIA

Capua
Cumae • Nola
L.Avernus Puteoli • Mt. Vesuvius
Misenum • Pompeii
Neapolis
Herculaneum
Capreae I. • R.Silerus
Foce da Sele

Scale of Miles
0 10 20 30 40

H: ROME

Pincian Hill
Wall of Servius Tullius
Quirinal Hill
Viminal Hill
River Tiber
Capitoline Hill
Temple of Jupiter Citadel
Tarpeian Rock Forum
Vicus Romanum Esquiline Hill
Sublician Bridge Tuscus House
of Romulus
Palatine Caelian Hill
Janiculum Hill
Aventine Hill
Via Appia

Scale of Miles
0 ¼ ½ ¾ 1 1¼ 1½

F.V.Botley

APPENDICES

SOME ADDITIONAL MYTHS

AEACUS, son of Zeus and the nymph Aegina, father of Telamon and Peleus. When the population of the island of Aegina died in a plague, Zeus turned ants (*Myrmekes*) into human beings to replace them. They were called Myrmidons, the name of the subjects of Peleus and Achilles.

AMPHION and ZETHUS, sons of Zeus and Antiope (the god's seduction of her was painted by Watteau and others), avenged her capture at Sicyon by Lycus of Thebes by having Lycus' wife Dirce dragged to death by a bull (the subject of the largest extant classical sculpture group, at Naples). Amphion and Zethus built the walls of Thebes, the stones being raised by Amphion's power as a harpist.

ARETHUSA, a nymph loved by the river god Alpheus and turned by Artemis into a fountain at Syracuse (Shelley's *Arethusa*). Portrayed on magnificent Syracusan coins.

ASCLEPIUS (Latin: *Aesculapius*), son of Apollo and Coronis, brought up by the Centaur Chiron, slain by Zeus for restoring to life Artemis' favourite Hippolytus; worshipped as god of medicine.

BELLEROPHON, son of Glaucus and grandson of Sisyphus, lived at the court of Proetus of Argos, whose wife Anteia loved him. Proetus sent Bellerophon to his father-in-law Iobates with a written request that Iobates should kill him. Bellerophon was therefore sent against the Chimaera (a monster with the head of a lion, the body of a goat and the tail of a dragon) which he slew with the help of the winged horse Pegasus. He then defeated the Amazons. But he became hated of the gods. The subject of a lost play of Euripides.

BUSIRIS, son of Posidon and king of Egypt, was accustomed to sacrifice visitors to Zeus; but he was slain by Heracles during the latter's quest for the golden apples of Hesperides.

CADMUS, son of Agenor of Tyre, brother (or according to another version uncle) of Europa, uncle of Minos. Founded Thebes by sowing dragon's teeth from which armed warriors arose. See also Ch. 10.

CASTOR and POLYDEUCES (*Pollux*), the Dioscuri, sons of Leda, the former (like Helen) by Zeus in the form of a swan, the latter by Tyndareus. Worshipped as protectors of seamen. Said to have led the Roman army at Lake Regillus (496 BC).

CECROPS, legendary ancestor or first king of the Athenians.

CLOTHO, LACHESIS and ATROPOS, the Fates (Moirai, Parcae), daughters of Night; or of Zeus and Themis.

CYBELE, the Asiatic Great Mother, worshipped especially at Pessinus in Galatia; identified by the Greeks with Rhea. Her youthful consort was Attis.

DAPHNE, river-nymph (Naiad), daughter of river Peneus (or Ladon), loved by Leucippus disguised as a woman (who was slain by the nymphs) and by Apollo, who at her request changed her into a bay-tree. The subject of many paintings.

DRYADS (or HAMADRYADS), the nymphs of trees.

EGERIA, Roman goddess of fountains and childbirth. Visited by King Numa Pompilius by night.

ENDYMION, the most beautiful of men, loved by Selene (the Moon). Father of Aetolus, the hero-founder of Aetolia. (Drayton's *Endimion and Phoebe* (1593), Keats's *Endymion* (1818).)

EOS (*Aurora*), goddess of dawn, sister of Helios (the Sun), daughter of Hyperion (the last of the Titans, dethroned by Apollo, the subject of a poem by Keats) and Thea. Loved by Tithonus, she bore him Memnon, for whose slaying by Achilles she shed tears in the form of dew.

ERECHTHEUS, legendary king of Athens, son of Gaea (Earth), was brought up by Athene. He sacrificed his daughter Chthonia, by consent of her mother Praxithea, in order to repel invasion by Eumolpus the Thracian, and was destroyed with his family by Posidon. The subject of tragedies by Euripides and Swinburne.

ERICHTHONIUS, often confused with Erechtheus, as whose grandson he is also sometimes regarded. Erichthonius is also said to be son of Hephaestus and Gaea (Earth). As a child he was placed by Athene in a chest and given to the three daughters of Cecrops. The two eldest, disobeying a prohibition against opening the chest, went mad (on seeing he had snakes for feet) and threw themselves from the Acropolis.

EUROPA, daughter of Agenor king of Tyre. Zeus in the form of a bull swam with her on his back to Crete, where she gave birth to Minos, Rhadamanthus and Sarpedon. Gauguin is one of many who have painted Europa and the bull.

GALATEA, a Nereid, loved by Acis whom, when his rival Polyphemus had crushed him under a rock, she transformed into a river—the theme of Gay's libretto for Handel's *Acis and Galatea*.

HERMAPHRODITUS, son of Hermes and Aphrodite, loved by the nymph Salmacis and merged with her as half-man, half-woman.

HESTIA (Vesta), daughter of Cronus and Rhea; goddess of the hearth, mentioned in all libations and prayer.

ION, son of Apollo and of Creusa daughter of Erechtheus; exposed in infancy and later (after his rescue by Hermes) accepted by Xuthus (wife of Creusa) as his own son, but menaced by Creusa (who believed him

Xuthus' bastard) until Athene intervened; ancestor of the Ionians. See Euripides' *Ion*.

IXION of Thessaly, after being excused by Zeus for murdering his father-in-law Eioneus, attempted the virtue of Hera, begetting the Centaurs (or their father) on a cloud which Zeus had made to resemble her. He was bound to an ever-turning wheel in the underworld.

LAOMEDON employed Apollo and Posidon to build the walls of Troy, but refused to pay them. He averted the sacrifice of his daughter Hesione to a sea-monster—sent by Posidon—by enrolling Heracles. Laomedon, however, then cheated Heracles, who captured Troy and gave Hesione to Telamon of Salamis.

LEDA, daughter of Thestius king of Aetolia, wife of Tyndareus, mother of the Dioscuri (see CASTOR), Helen and Clytemnestra. Her seduction by Zeus in the form of a swan, depicted by Michelangelo and many others, was one of W. B. Yeats' most important symbols.

> A shudder in the loins engenders there
> The broken wall, the burning roof and tower
> And Agamemnon dead.

MARSYAS, satyr-god of river in Phrygia, challenged Apollo to a contest on the flute, and on being judged loser by the Muses was tied by Apollo to a tree and flayed alive. A favourite theme of sculptors.

NAIADS, nymphs of springs, rivers and lakes.

NIOBE, daughter of Tantalus, mother of seven sons and seven daughters, boasted of her superiority on this account to Leto. So Leto's offspring Apollo and Artemis killed Niobe's children with arrows and their mother, weeping, turned into a column of stone on Mount Sipylus in Lydia.

OENONE, a nymph of Mount Ida loved by Paris before he met Helen. When wounded by Philoctetes he sought her help, too late. Tennyson's *Oenone* is her lament when Paris deserted her.

PAN, son of Zeus or Hermes, god of flocks and shepherds, invented the seven-reed pipe and named it after the nymph Syrinx who had turned into a reed in order to escape him.

PARIS, son of Priam. In addition to the stories told in Ch. 1, he had (according to a story unknown to Homer) caused the Trojan War by his Judgement (depicted by many painters, including Lucas Cranach and Renoir). At the wedding-feast of Peleus and Thetis, the goddesses Hera, Athene and Aphrodite all claimed a golden apple, inscribed 'for the most beautiful', which Eris (Strife) had thrown down. The decision was referred to Paris, the handsomest of men. Hera offered him greatness and Athene victory in war, but Paris awarded the apple to Aphrodite who offered him the loveliest woman; and with her help he carried off Helen. In late antiquity the story was interpreted as an elaborate allegory.

PHAEDRA, daughter of Minos and wife of Theseus, made unsuccessful advances to Hippolytus, son of Theseus and the Amazon Hippolyta, and hanged herself after writing a denunciation of Hippolytus as her seducer. Invoked by Theseus, Posidon sent a monster to frighten Hippolytus' horses so that he was dragged to death. The subject of plays by Euripides (*Hippolytus*), Seneca and Racine (1677).

PHAETHON, son of Helios (the Sun) and Clymene, drove his father's chariot, but the horses bolted. To prevent the earth from being burnt up, Zeus hurled a thunderbolt at Phaethon, and he fell into the Po. His sisters turned into poplars, and their tears became amber. Another Phaethon was the son of Eos and Cephalus.

PHILOCTETES, son of Poeas, inherited Heracles' bow and arrows, by which alone, as Helenus revealed, Troy could be taken. Healed by Machaon from a wound in the foot (inflicted by a snake in a shrine), Philoctetes was fetched back from Lemnos, and shot Paris with a poisoned arrow. The theme of a play by Sophocles.

PHILOMELA, daughter of Pandion of Athens, was seduced by her brother-in-law Tereus of Thrace, and avenged by her sister Procne, who killed her own son Itys and served up the flesh to her husband. Tereus was turned into a hoopoe, and Philomela and Procne into swallow and nightingale respectively (or vice versa).

PIRITHOUS, a Lapith, son by Zeus of Ixion's wife Dia. Pirithous' wedding-feast with Hippodamia was the scene of a battle between the Centaurs, who tried to carry her off, and the Lapithae. Theseus and he descended to Hades in an attempt to abduct Persephone.

PLEIADES, the seven daughters of Atlas and Pleione, were pursued by Orion, the Boeotian giant and hunter, and he and they were turned into constellations.

PROCRIS, daughter of Erechtheus, was jealous of her husband Cephalus (loved by Eos) and hid in a bush while he was hunting. Cephalus, thinking she was an animal, hurled his spear and killed her. Her death was painted by Piero de Cosimo and others.

PROCRUSTES of Eleusis used to lay visitors on a bed and, if this was too short for them, cut off their limbs accordingly; while if they were shorter than the bed, he stretched them until they fitted. He was killed by Theseus.

SCYLLA (1) daughter of Phorcys and Hecate; loved by Posidon and turned into a devouring monster (at the straits of Messina) by her rival the Nereid (sea-nymph) Amphitrite.

(2) daughter of Nisus king of Megara; in love with Minos of Crete who was besieging her city, she treacherously cut off her white-haired father's

TABLE 12

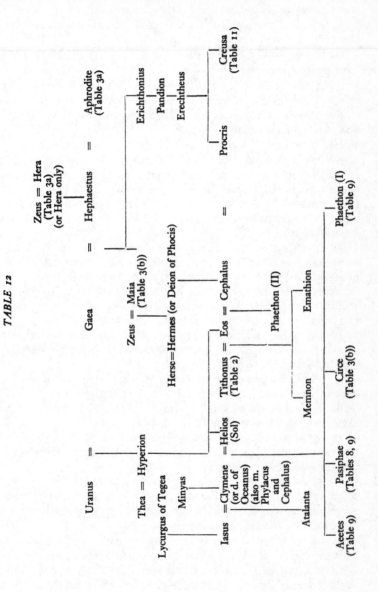

443

purple lock which guaranteed his safety. Megara fell, and Minos dragged her through the sea behind his ship. She was turned into a sea-bird, the *Ciris*, title of a Latin poem of unknown authorship. For her seduction by a bribe of gold bracelets, see above, page 359.

SILENUS, a Satyr (with horse's tail, or goat's legs), son of Hermes or Pan, companion of Dionysus.

SISYPHUS, king of Corinth, son of Aeolus, was the most cunning of human beings. But he was condemned for variously described misdeeds to roll a large stone eternally up a hill in Hades; when it reached the top, it always rolled down again.

TANTALUS, father of Pelops and Niobe. Either because he served his son's flesh to the gods, or because he stole their nectar or disclosed their secrets, he was condemned to eternal punishment in Hades. He sat for ever in a pool of water which receded when he tried to drink from it, under fruit branches which he could not reach; or his punishment was to have a huge boulder suspended over his head so that he could not enjoy the feast set before him.

TELEPHUS, son of Heracles and king of the Mysians. Wounded by Achilles, he was told by the Delphic oracle that the man who had inflicted the blow must heal him; and rust from Achilles' spear at Troy cured the wound. The subject of a (lost) play by Euripides, mocked for its realism by Aristophanes.

TEUCER, called this (= Trojan) because his mother Hesione was daughter of Laomedon. His father was Telamon, king of Salamis, and his half-brother Ajax. The greatest Greek archer before Troy, he was subsequently banished from his native city (as having caused his brother's death), and founded Salamis in Cyprus.

TITHONUS, son of Laomedon and brother of Priam. Eos (Dawn), whose son by him was Memnon, begged Zeus to make Tithonus immortal, but omitted to request eternal youth for him; so he shrivelled up and became a mere voice—or was turned into a grasshopper.

TITYUS, a giant, son of Gaea, killed by Apollo and Artemis for attempting to rape their mother Leto. He was condemned to lie bound in Hades, while two vultures tore at his liver.

VIRGINIA, daughter of a Roman centurion, who stabbed her to death rather than allow Appius Claudius, one of the ten ruling legislators (decemvirs), to assign her (for his own purposes) to one of his dependants. Retold by Petrarch and by Chaucer in the *Doctor's Tale*.

ZEPHYRUS, one of the winds, children (except Eurus) of Astraeus and Eos. Podarge (one of the Harpies) gave birth, by Zephyrus, to the horses of Achilles. Zephyrus (Favonius) is the West Wind, Boreas (Aquilo) the North (father of Zetes and Calais), Notus (Auster) the South, and Eurus the (unfavourable) East or South-east wind.

BIBLIOGRAPHY

Myth in General

J. Campbell and B. Moyers, *The Power of Myth* (1988), A. Cunningham (ed.), *The Theory of Myth* (1973), M. Detienne, *The Creation of Mythology* (1986), M. Detienne, L. Gernet, J. P. Vernant and P. Vidal-Nacquet, *Myth, Religion and Society: Structural Essays* (1982), F. W. Dillistone (ed.), *Myth and Symbol* (1966), R. L. Gordon (ed.), *Myth, Religion and Society* (1981), E. Leach (ed.), *The Structural Study of Myth and Totemism* (1967)*, C. Lévi-Strauss, 'The Structural Study of Myth' (1955) in *Studies in Anthropology, I* (1968), H. A. Murray (ed.), *Myth and Mythmakings* (1960), J. Puhvel, *Comparative Mythology* (1987), T. A. Sebeok, *Myth: A Symposium* (1955, 1958), J. B. Vickery (ed.), *Myth and Literature* (1966).

Greek Myth

A. Birchall and P. E. Corbett, *Greek Gods and Heroes* (1974), W. Burkert, *Structure and History in Greek Mythology and Ritual* (1982), P. Diel, *Symbolism in Greek Mythology* (1980), P. E. Easterling and J. V. Muir (ed.), *Greek Religion and Society* (1985), L. Gernet, *The Anthropology of Ancient Greece* (1981), M. Grant and J. Hazel, *Who's Who in Classical Mythology* (*Gods and Mortals in Classical Mythology* in U.S. eds.) (1973), R. Graves, *The Greek Myths* (1955), W. K. C. Guthrie, *The Greeks and Their Gods* (1968), S. C. Humphries, *Anthropology and the Greeks* (1978), G. S. Kirk, *Myth: Its Meaning and Functions in Ancient and Other Cultures* (1970, 1973), G. S. Kirk, *The Nature of Greek Myths* (1974), M. P. O. Morford and R. J. Lenardon, *Classical Mythology*, 2nd ed. (1977), S. G. Pembroke, *Myth*, in M. I. Finley (ed.), *The Legacy of Greece* (1981), F. Pfister, *Greek Gods and Heroes* (1961), H. J. Rose, *Handbook of Greek Mythology*, 6th ed. (1958), and later eds., M. Simpson, 'Myths and Cosmologies', (in M. Grant and R. Kitzinger, eds., *Civilization of the Ancient Mediterranean: Greece and Rome*, Vol. II, 1988, pp. 861–79). J. P. Vernant, *Myth and Society in Ancient Greece* (1980), J. P. Vernant, *Myth and Thought among the Greeks* (1983).

---

*See also W. G. Runciman, *British Journal of Sociology*, XX, 3, September 1969, pp. 259ff. against the structuralist approach to myth.

MYTHS OF THE GREEKS AND ROMANS

Part I (The Heroes of Homer)

C. R. Beye, *The Iliad, the Odyssey and the Epic Tradition* (1968), C. M. Bowra, *Homer* (1972), E. Bradford, *Ulysses Found* (1985), W. A. Camps, *An Introduction to Homer* (1980), R. Carpenter, *Folk-Tale, Fiction and Saga in the Homeric Epics* (1946), H. W. Clarke, *The Art of the Odyssey* (1967), H. W. Clarke (ed.), *The Twentieth Century Interpretations of the Odyssey* (1983), J. S. Clay, *The Wrath of Athena: Gods and Men in the Odyssey* (1983), B. C. Dietrich, *Death, Fate and the Gods* (1968), B. C. Fenik (ed.), *Homer: Tradition and Invention* (1978), J. H. Finley, *Homer's Odyssey* (1979), M. I. Finley, *The World of Odysseus*, 2nd ed. (1979), D. Frame, *The Myth of Return in Early Greek Epic* (1978), J. Griffin, *Homer on Life and Death* (1983), G. S. Kirk, *Homer and the Oral Tradition* (1976), G. S. Kirk, *The Songs of Homer* (1962), abridged as *Homer and the Epic* (1964), G. S. Kirk (ed.), *The Language and Background of Homer* (1964), A. B. Lord, *The Singer of Tales* (1961), J. V. Luce, *Homer and the Heroic Age* (1975), G. Nagy, *The Best of the Achaeans* (1979), D. L. Page, *History and the Homeric Iliad* (1960), J. Pollard, *Helen of Troy* (1965), J. M. Redfield, *Nature and Culture in the Iliad: The Tragedy of Hector* (1975), C. A. Rubino and C. W. Shelmerdine (ed.), *Approaches to Homer* (1983), K. Schefold, *Myth and Legend in Early Greek Art* (1966), S, L. Schein, *The Mortal Hero: An Introduction to Homer's Iliad* (1984), W. B. Stanford, *The Ulysses Theme* (1954, 1963), C. A. Trypanis, *The Homeric Epics* (1977), P. Vivante, *The Homeric Imagination* (1970), J. de Vries, *Heroic Songs and Heroic Legend* (1969), A. J. B. Wace and F. H. Stubbings, *A Companion to Homer* (1962), C. H. Whitman, *Homer and the Heroic Tradition* (1965), C. H. Whitman, *The Heroic Paradox* (1982).

Part II (Zeus, Apollo, Demeter)

Hesiod

A. R. Burn, *The World of Hesiod*, 2nd ed. (1967), R. M. Frazer, *The Poems of Hesiod* (1983), W. K. C. Guthrie, *In the Beginnings* (1957), G. S. Kirk, *Hesiod: The Theogony*, in *Hésiode et son influence* (*Entretiens sur l'antiquité classique* [Fondation Hardt], VII, 1962), P. Pucci, *Hesiod and the Language of Poetry* (1977), P. Walcot, *Hesiod and the Near East* (1966), M. L. West (ed.), *Hesiod: The Theogony* (1966), M. L. West (ed.) *Hesiod: Works and Days* (1978).

Homeric Hymns

J. Fontenrose, *Python: A Study of Delphic Myth* (1960), J. Godwin, *Mystery Religions in the Ancient World* (1981), E. O. James, *The Cult of the Mother Goddess* (1959), G. E. Mylonas, *Eleusis and the Eleusinian*

BIBLIOGRAPHY

Mysteries (1962), H. W. Parke and D. E. Wormell, *The Delphic Oracle*, 2nd ed. (1956), N. J. Richardson, *The Homeric Hymn to Demeter* (1974), C. A. Sowa, *Traditional Themes and the Homeric Hymns* (1984), R. A. Tomlinson, *Greek Sanctuaries* (1976), G. Zuntz, *Persephone* (1972).

Parts III to V (Myth in Greek Tragedy)

Tragedy in General

J. P. Guépin, *The Tragic Paradox: Myth and Ritual in Greek Tragedy* (1968), H. D. F. Kitto, *Greek Tragedy*, 3rd ed. (1961), R. Lattimore, *Story Patterns in Greek Tragedy* (1968), A. Lesky, *Greek Tragedy*, 3rd ed. (1968, 1983), M. C. Nussbaum, *The Fragility of Goodness: Luck and Ethics in Greek Tragedy and Philosophy* (1986), W. B. Stanford, *Greek Tragedy and the Emotions* (1983), O. Taplin, *Greek Tragedy in Action* (1978), J. P. Vernant and P. Vidal-Nacquet, *Tragedy and Myth in Ancient Greece* (1980), B. Vickers, *Towards Greek Tragedy* (1973).

Aeschylus

A. H. Ahrens, *The Plays of Aeschylus* (1966), M. Evans, *Wagner and Aeschylus: The Ring and the Oresteia* (1982), M. Gagarin, *Aeschylean Drama* (1976), L. Golden, *In Praise of Prometheus* (1967), S. Goldhill, *Language, Sexuality, Narrative, The Oresteia* (1984), M. Griffith, *The Authenticity of Prometheus Bound* (1977), J. Herington, *Aeschylus* (1986), A. Lebeck, *The Oresteia: A Study in Language and Structure* (1971), H. Lloyd-Jones, *The Justice of Zeus* (1971), B. Otis, *Cosmos and Tragedy: An Essay on the Meanings of Aeschylus* (1981), T. G. Rosenmeyer, *The Art of Aeschylus* (1982), H. W. Smyth, *Aeschylean Tragedy* (1969), R. P. Winnington-Ingram, *Studies in Aeschylus* (1983).

Sophocles

C. M. Bowra, *Sophoclean Tragedy* (1944), A. L. Brown (ed.), *Sophocles: Antigone* (1985), A. Cameron, *The Identity of Oedipus the King* (1968), L. Edmunds and A. Dundas (ed.), *Oedipus: A Folklore Casebook* (1983), G. F. Else, *The Madness of Antigone* (1976), A. Green, *The Tragic Effect: The Oedipus Complex in Tragedy* (1979), H. M. Harvey and E. D. Harvey, *Sophocles* (1978), J. C. Kamerbeek, *The Antigone* (1978), B. M. W. Knox, *Oedipus at Thebes* (1957), V. Lienieks, *The Plays of Sophocles* (1982), M. J. O'Brien, *Twentieth Century Interpretations of Oedipus Rex* (1968), D. Seale, *Vision and Statecraft in Sophocles* (1982), C. Segal, *Tragedy and Civilisation: An Interpretation of Sophocles* (1981), J. T. Sheppard, *The Wisdom of Sophocles* (1947), P. H. Vellacott, *Sophocles and Oedipus* (1971),

T. B. L. Webster, *An Introduction to Sophocles*, 2nd ed. (1969), R. P. Winnington-Ingram, *Sophocles: An Interpretation* (1980).

Euripides
D. J. Conacher, *Euripidean Drama: Myth, Theme and Structure* (1967), A. M. Dale (ed.), *Euripides: Alcestis* (1978), E. R. Dodds, *The Greeks and the Irrational* (1951), G. M. A. Grube, *The Drama of Euripides* (1941, 1964), C. Kerenyi, *Dionysus* (1976), P. McGinty, *Interpretation and Dionysus* (1978), W. F. Otto, *Dionysus: Myth and Cult* (1965), A. Pippin-Burnett, *Catastrophe Survived: Euripides' Plays of Mixed Reversal* (1985), T. G. Rosenmeyer, *The Masks of Tragedy* (1963), W. Sale, *Existentialism and Euripides* (1978), C. Segal, *Dionysiac Poetics and Euripides' Bacchae* (1982), E. M. Waith, *The Herculean Hero* (1962), R. P. Winnington-Ingram, *Euripides and Dionysus* (1948).

Part IV (Heroic Searches: Apollonius, Virgil, Livy)

Apollonius Rhodius
J. R. Bacon, *The Voyage of the Argo* (1925), C. R. Beye, *Epic and Romance in the Argonautica of Apollonius* (1982), M. Grant, *From Alexander to Cleopatra* (1982), D. M. Levin, *Apollonius' Argonautica Reexamined: Vol. I, The Neglected First and Second Books* (1971), J. W. Mackail, *Lectures on Greek Poetry*, 2nd ed. (1926).

Virgil
W. S. Anderson, *The Art of the Aeneid* (1969), W. A. Camps, *An Introduction to Virgil's Aeneid* (1969), R. J. Clark, *Catabasis and the Wisdom Tradition* (1979), J. Hamilton (ed.), *Virgil in a Cultural Tradition: Essays to Celebrate the Bimillennium* (1986), P. Hardie, *Virgil's Aeneid: Cosmos and Imperium* (1985), W. F. Jackson-Knight, *Cumaean Gates* (1936), W. R. Johnston, *Darkness Visible: A Study of Vergil's Aeneid* (1976), G. R. Levy, *The Gates of Horn* (1948), I. M. Linforth, *The Arts of Orpheus* (1941), C. Martindale (ed.), *Virgil and His Influence: Bimillennial Studies* (1984), A. G. McKay, *Vergil's Italy* (1970), R. C. Monti, *The Dido Episode and the Aeneid* (1981), B. Otis, *Virgil: A Study in Civilized Poetry* (1963), V. Pöschl, *The Art of Vergil: Image and Symbol in the Aeneid* (1962), M. C. J. Putnam, *Virgil's Poem of the Earth: Studies in the Georgics* (1979), K. Quinn, *Virgil's Aeneid: A Critical Description* (1968), J. Warden (ed.), *Orpheus: The Metamorphoses of a Myth* (1982), L. P. Wilkinson, *The Georgics of Virgil: A Critical Survey* (1969).

BIBLIOGRAPHY

Livy
D. Cox, *History and Myth* (1961), T. A. Dorey (ed.), *Livy* (1971),
E. Gjerstad, *Legends and Facts of Early Roman History* (1962), M. Grant,
Roman Myths (1971), M. Grant, *The Ancient Historians* (1970), T. J.
Luce, *Livy: The Composition of his History* (1977), R. M. Ogilvie, *Early
Rome and the Etruscans* (1976), P. G. Walsh, *Livy (Greece and Rome, New
Surveys 6)* (1974), P. G. Walsh, *Livy: His Historical Aims and Methods*
(1961).

Ovid
J. Barsby, *Ovid (Greece and Rome, New Surveys 12)* (1978), J. W. Binns
(ed.), *Ovid* (1973), W. Brewer, *Ovid's Metamorphoses in European Culture*
(1974), J. M. Fyler, *Chaucer and Ovid* (1979), G. K. Galinsky, *Ovid's
Metamorphoses* (1975), H. Jacobson, *Ovid's Heroides* (1974), R. Syme,
History in Ovid (1978), R. Whitaker, *Myth and Personal Experiences in
Roman Love Elegy* (1983), L. P. Wilkinson, *Ovid Recalled* (1955),
abridged as *Ovid Surveyed* (1962).

Apuleius
G. Anderson, *Ancient Fiction* (1984), J. G. Griffiths, *Apuleius of
Madauros: The Isis-Book* (1975), T. Hägg, *The Novel in Antiquity* (1983),
E. H. Haight, *Apuleius and His Influence* (1927, 1963), B. L. Hijmans and
R. T. van de Paardt, *Aspects of Apuleius' Golden Ass* (1978), B. E. Perry,
The Ancient Romances (1967), E. Rohde, *Psyche* (1925), A. Scobie, *Aspects
of the Ancient Romance and its Heritage* (1969), J. Tatum, *Apuleius and the
Golden Ass* (1979), P. G. Walsh, *The Roman Novel* (1970).

Musaeus
K. Kost, *Musaios: Hero und Leander* (1971), H. Livrea and P. Eleutheri,
Musaeus: Hero et Leander (1982).

Classical Myths in Later Times (in addition to books mentioned under
individual authors)
F. C. Blessington, *Paradise Lost and the Classical Epic* (1979), R. R.
Bolgar, *Classical Influences on European Culture: A.D. 500–1500* (1971),
R. R. Bolgar, *Classical Influences on European Culture: A.D. 1500–1700*
(1976), B. J. Bono, *Literary Transvaluation: From Vergilian Epic to
Shakespearean Tragicomedy* (1984), G. Braden, *The Classic and English
Renaissance Poetry* (1978), D. Bush, *Mythology and the Renaissance
Tradition* (1932), H. A. Clarke, *Ancient Myths in Modern Poets* (1910),
G. Highet, *The Classical Tradition* (1949, 1967), R. Jenkyns, *The
Victorians and Ancient Greece* (1980), F. Manuel, *The Eighteenth Century*

Confronts the Gods (1959), H. Rahner, Greek Myths and Christian Mystery (1963), J. Seznec, The Survival of the Pagan Gods (1953, 1961), J. A. K. Thomson, Classical Influences on English Poetry (1951), J. A. K. Thomson, The Classical Background of English Literature (1948), E. M. W. Tillyard, Some Mythical Elements in English Literature (1961), F. M. Turner, The Greek Heritage in Victorian Britain (1981).

Some Recent Books

T. J Sienkwicz, World Mythology (1996), M. A. Shapiro, Myth into Art (1994), Actes de VII Colloque du Centre des Recherches Mythologiques (Nanterre, 1992), C. Lévi-Strauss, Myth and Meanings (pb 1995), R. Stoneman, Greek Mythology (1991), A. R. Hope-Moncrieff, Myths and Legends of Ancient Greece (1995), J. Duchemin, Mythes Grecs et Sources Orientales (1995), C. Pengolase, Greek Myths and Mesopotamia (1994), M. W. Edwards, Homer: Poet of the Iliad (1987), R. J. Canko, Homer, Hesiod and the Hymns (1982), C. Segal, Tragedy and Civilisation (1981), R. W. Bushnell, Prophesying Tragedy (1988), E. Segal, ed, Readings in Greek Tragedy (1984), S. Ireland, Aeschylus (1986), M. L. West, Studies in Aeschylus (1990), R. G. A. Buxton, Sophocles (1984), H. Lloyd-Jones and N. Wilson, Sophocles (1990), C. Segal, Euripides and the Poetics of Sorrow (1993), R. C. Hunter, The Argonautica of Apollonius: Literary Studies (1993), J. Griffin, Virgil (1986), D. O. Ross, Virgil's Elements (1987), R. D. Williams, The Aeneid (1987), G. Williams, Techniques and Ideas in the Aeneid (1983), B. O. A. M. Lyne, Further Voices in Virgil's Aeneid (1987), F. Cairns, Virgil's Augustan Epic (1996), J. M. Bremmen and N. Horsfall, Roman Myth and Mythography (1987), S. Mack, Ovid (1988), J. Solodow, The World of Ovid's Metamorphoses (1988), J. Martindale, ed, Ovid Renewed (1988), P. Green, Ovid: The Erotic Poems (1982), T. Hughes, Tales from Ovid (1997), J. Tatum, ed, The Search for the Ancient Novel (1994), N. Holzberg, The Ancient Novel (1995)

CHAPTER NOTES[1]

[1] The quotations in the Foreword are from the following works. 'The intelligible forms . . .', from Coleridge, *The Piccolomini*, Act II, Scene IV, lines 123 ff; 'Dark, illimitable ocean . . .' from Milton, *Paradise Lost*, lines 891 ff; 'Ask not . . .' from Alexander Pope's adaptation of Horace, *Epistles* I, i, lines 13 f.

CHAPTER I: THE WRATH OF ACHILLES

1 *Iliad*, I, 1–7 (R. Graves)
2 Ibid, V, 87–88
3 Ibid. VIII, 553–65 (E. V. Rieu)
4 Ibid. XI, 628–41 (E. V. Rieu)
5 Ibid. XX, 490–503 (E. V. Rieu)
6 Ibid. VI, 168 f.
7 Strabo, I, ii, 9
8 *Odyssey*, VIII, 67, 254
9 Pind. *Isthm.* IV, 42
10 Pind. *Nem.* II, 1
11 *Il.* IV, 433–8 (E. V. Rieu)
12 Ibid. II, 455–73 (R. Lattimore)
13 Ibid. XI, 784
14 Eur. *Iph. Aul.* 800 f., 1346 f.
15 *Il.* I, 32
16 Ibid. IX, 315
17 Ibid. IX, 263 ff.
18 Ibid. XXIV, 568–70
19 Ibid. XIX, 375–91 (R. Lattimore)
20 Pind. *Isthm.* VIII, 125–31 (R. Lattimore)
21 *Il.* XIII, 803–5 (E. V. Rieu)
22 Ibid. XV, 610–14 (R. Lattimore)
23 Ibid. VI, 448–55
24 Ibid. VI, 520–5 (E. V. Rieu)
25 Ibid. X, 119–24 (E. V. Rieu)
26 *Od.* XI, 543–63
27 *Il.* X, 153–67 (E. V. Rieu)

28 Ibid. XXIII, 700–5
29 Ibid. III, 149–60 (R. Lattimore)
30 Eur. *Helen*, 31 ff; cf. Pl. *Phaedr.* 243a, Stesich. *fr.* 11
31 *Il.* I, 348–63; V, 860 f.; XVIII, 478–613; XXII, 69 (references owed to C. H. Gordon)
32 *Od.* V, 87–91; VII, 179; XIV, 78; XV, 148 f.; XVI, 11, 299
33 Ibid. XVII, 291–319
34 Ar. *Nic. Eth.* IV, 2, 20
35 Hes. *WD.* 159
36 *Nem.* VI, 4–7 (C. M. Bowra)
37 *Il.* XXIV, 46–9
38 Ibid. XVIII, 22–34 (E. V. Rieu)
39 Ibid. IX, 524–7; *Od.* 1, 279
40 *Il.* XVI, 734–50 (E. V. Rieu)
41 Ibid. XXII, 327–36 (R. Lattimore)
42 Ibid. XXIV, 15
43 Ibid. XXIII, 175–7 (E. V. Rieu)
44 Ibid. VI, 57–60 (E. V. Rieu)
45 Ibid. VI, 463–81 (R. Lattimore)
46 Xen. *Symp.* III, 5
47 *Wis.* XIII, 5, cf. *Rom.* 1, 20
48 Herod. I, 131
49 Ibid. II, 53
50 *Il.* VIII, 360–1
51 Ibid. VIII, 23–7 (R. Lattimore)

52 Ibid. XV, 14–22 (E. V. Rieu)
53 Soph. *fr.* 754 Nauck (C. M. Bowra)
54 *Il.* XXI, 424–6 (R. Lattimore)
55 Ibid. XVI, 114–23 (R. Lattimore)
56 Stasinus, *Cypria,* 11 *E.G.F.* ed. Kinkel p. 20, No. 1
57 Archil. *fr.* 58 Diehl, cf. *Il.* XXIV, 525 f.
58 *Il.* XIX, 91
59 Ibid. IX, 523
60 Eur. *Tro.* 95–97 (R. Lattimore)
61 *Il.* XIX, 410; XVI, 849
62 Archil. *fr.* 8 Diehl
63 *Il.* XXIV, 525–33 (E. V. Rieu)

CHAPTER 2 : ODYSSEUS

1 *Od.* V, 59–75 (R. Fitzgerald)
2 Ibid. VI, 76–80; 88–101; 116–19; 127–40 (R. Fitzgerald)
3 Ibid. VII, 211–14 (R. Fitzgerald)
4 Eur. *Tro.* 282–5 (R. Lattimore)
5 Str. I, 11
6 *Od.* VIII, 477–81 (E. V. Rieu)
7 Longinus, IX, 13
8 Soph. *Ant.*, 334
9 Ibid. XIX, 34 (lamp); 226–31 (brooch–clasp)
10 Ibid. VII, 84–94 (E. V. Rieu)
11 Ibid. XV, 48–55 (E. V. Rieu)
12 Ibid. XV, 82–5 (E. V. Rieu)
13 Ibid. XVIII, 143, 280
14 Ibid. XVII, 290–305, 326 f. (R. Fitzgerald)
15 Ibid. XVIII, 111
16 Ibid. XXII, 461–73 (E. V. Rieu)
17 Ibid. IV, 379
18 *Il.* V, 430, VIII, 30 f.
19 *Od.* VIII, 321–7 (E. V. Rieu)
20 Hes. *Theog.*, 1011–6
21 *Od.* XI, 15
22 Ibid. X, 506–15 (E. V. Rieu)
23 *Il.* VIII, 13–16, 481
24 Ibid. III, 279
25 *Od.* XI, 34–43 (E. V. Rieu)
26 Ibid. XI, 486–91 (E. V. Rieu)
27 Ibid. XI, 218–22 (C. M. Bowra; in hexameters)
28 Erinna *fr.* 2 Diehl (F. L. Lucas)
29 *Od.* IV, 561–9 (E. V. Rieu)

CHAPTER 3 : THE RISE OF ZEUS

1 Hes. *Theog.*, 124 f.
2 Hes. *WD.*, 763 f.
3 Pl. *Phaedr.*, 244a–245e; cf. *Od.* XXIII, 347–8
4 Hes. *Theog.*, 29–35 (R. Lattimore)
5 Ibid., 24–29 (R. Lattimore)
6 Hes. *WD.*, 100–4 (R. Lattimore)

7 Hes. *Theog.*, 24
8 Herod. II, 53
9 Pl. *Symp.*, 178b
10 Paus. IX, 31, 4
11 Hes. *Theog.*, 116
12 Ar. *Phys.* IV., 208b, 31
13 *Il.* XIV, 246
14 Procl. *ap.* Pl. *Tim.* Diehl III, 156a
15 Ar. *Met.* XIV, I, 4
16 Paus. IX, 27, 1
17 Hes. *Theog.*, 120–2 (R. Lattimore)
18 Soph. *Antig.*, 806, 856 f., *fr.* 855 Jebb; Eur. *Med.*, 627 f.
19 Soph. *Trach.*, 94 f.
20 Ar. *Met.*, XII, 6
21 Herod. II, 53
22 Hes. *Theog.*, 177–86 (R. Lattimore)
23 Ibid., 201
24 Lucr. I, 10 f.
25 Hes. *Theog.*, 203–6 (R. Lattimore)
26 Plut. *De Def. Or.* 420a
27 Timotheus, *fr.* 7 Diehl II (G. Highet)
28 Anon. *fr.* 464 Nauck (T. F. Higham)
29 Aesch. *Heliades*, *fr.* 73 Nauck (C. M. Bowra)
30 Hes. *WD.*, 3–8 (R. Lattimore)
31 Ibid., 267–9 (P. Green)
32 Archil., *fr.* 94 Diehl II (C. M. Bowra)
33 Hes. *Theog.*, 504 f.
34 *Exod.* XIX, 16–18
35 *Od.* XII, 127–30
36 Ar. *Met.* I, 11, 10
37 Lucian, *Prom.*, 14
38 Hes. *Theog.*, 513 f.
39 Hes. *WD.*, 77–82 (R. Lattimore)
40 Ibid., 373–5 (R. Lattimore)
41 Semonides, *fr.* 7 Diehl
42 Eur. *Hippol.* 616–24; *fr.* 1059
43 Eur. *Med.*, 419, 262–5, 408
44 Hes. *WD.*, 109
45 *Od.* VII, 59
46 Hes. *Theog.*, 678–84 (R. Lattimore)
47 Ibid., 824–34 (R. Lattimore)
48 Ibid., 853–67 (R. Lattimore)
49 *Il.* II, 783
50 Ibid. XIV, 315–28 (E. V. Rieu)
51 Arnob. *Contra Paganos*, IV, 22
52 Hes. *Theog.*, 943 f.

CHAPTER 4: APOLLO AND DEMETER

1 *Hom. Hymn* III, 2–4 (H. G. Evelyn-White)
2 *Il.* I, 472
3 Hes. *WD.*, 656
4 *Hom. Hymn* III, 172
5 Schol. Pind. *Nem.* II, 1
6 *Hom. Hymn* III, 6
7 Herod. I, 65, 6; VI, 86, 115
8 *Hom. Hymn* III, 147–61
9 Ibid. XXVII, 14
10 Ibid. III, 518
11 *Mark* XIII, 10–11, XVI, 17; *I Cor.* XII, *Eph.* V, 19
12 *Il.* XXI, 470 f.

13 *Hom. Hymn* XXVII, 5
14 Eur. *Bacch.*, 337 f.
15 Ov. *Met.* III, 138 f.
16 *Hom. Hymn* II, 12–14 (H. G. Evelyn-White)
17 Ibid., 401–3 (H. G. Evelyn-White)
18 Eur. *Bacch.*, 274
19 Pl. *Menex.* 238a
20 *Rig Veda* X, 18, 10
21 Aesch. *Cho.*, 127.; Paus. X, 12, 10
22 *Hom. Hymn* XXX, 1 f. (P. B. Shelley)

23 Ibid. II, 480–2
24 Pind. *Ol.* II, 66–70, and *frgs.* 131, 133 Farnell
25 Aristoph. *Ran.*, 154–8, 455–9
26 Isocr. *Paneg.*, 28–9
27 Lucian, *De Saltu*, 15
28 Themist. *ap.* Stob., Farnell 218h.
29 Hes. *Theog.*, 912–14
30 Alcman, *fr.* 1
31 *Lev.* IX, 12
32 *Lev.* XVII, 6
33 e.g. *Psalms* (New Year Festival); *Exodus* (Spring Festival)

CHAPTER 5: THE HOUSE OF AGAMEMNON

1 Aesch. *Agam.*, 239–41, 248 (A. Platt)
2 Ibid., 860–9 (R. Lattimore)
3 Ibid., 1216–20 (R. Lattimore)
4 Ibid., 1227–30 (R. Lattimore)
5 Ibid., 1382–92 (L. MacNeice)
6 Ibid., 1475–7 (P. Vellacott)
7 Ibid., 1672–3 (P. Vellacott)
8 Aesch. *Cho.*, 535–7 (R. Lattimore)
9 Ibid., 646–51 (R. Lattimore)
10 Ibid., 803, 826–31 (R. Lattimore)
11 Ibid., 883 (R. Lattimore)
12 Aesch. *Eum.*, 341–80 (R. Lattimore)
13 Ar. *Poet.* IV, 7a
14 Pollux, IV, 123
15 Herod. II, 42
16 Archil. *fr.* 4 Diehl; cf. Hor. *Ep.* I, 19, 1 ff.
17 Herod. I, 23 f., cf. Suid. s.v. Arion

18 Eur. *Or.* 338–44
19 Hom. *Od.* III, 304
20 Stesich. *ap.* Schol. Eur. *Or.*, 46; cf. Pind. *Pyth.* XI, 32
21 *Od.* III, 309 f.; cf. I, 35–43; IV, 512–37; XI, 397–434
22 Ath. VIII, 347e.
23 *Pyth.* XI, 18–25 (H. T. Wade-Gery & C. M. Bowra)
24 Aesch. *Ag.*, 160–5 (L. MacNeice)
25 Xenophanes, *fr.* 19 Diehl
26 Aesch. *Suppl.*, 1057–8
27 Ibid., 524 f., 574, 595
28 *Pyth.* VIII, 95–7 (H. T. Wade-Gery & C. M. Bowra)
29 Ibid. II, 49, cf. IX, 44
30 Aesch. *Ag.*, 70
31 Aesch. *PV.*, 515–18 cf.; Herod. I, 91; Simon., *fr.* 4, 20 Diehl
32 Aesch. *Eum.*, 1045 f.
33 Theogn., 133–42, 1075–8

34 Pind. *Nem.* VI, 1–7 (R. Lattimore)
35 *Phaedo*, 115a
36 Pind. *Pyth.* III, 81–4 (R. Lattimore)
37 Pind., *fr.* 41 Bergk
38 Theogn., 373–92
39 Alcman, *fr.* 1 Diehl II, 36–9
(G. Highet)
40 Solon, *fr.* 1 Diehl, 17–22 (R.
Lattimore)
41 *Hebr.* X, 31
42 Theogn., 153–4
43 Aesch. *Ag.*, 367–84 (R. Lattimore)
44 *Isaiah* X, 13
45 *Il.* IX, 512, cf. Hes. *WD.*, 214
46 Aesch. *Ag.*, 735, 1433, 1497
47 Aesch. *Cho.*, 313 cf. Antiphon,
Tetral., II, 2
48 Eur. *Bacch.*, 884 (W. Arrowsmith)
49 Aesch. *Niobe*, *fr.* 278a Mette
50 Aesch. *Ag.*, 1192
51 Aesch. *Pers.*, 747
52 *Od.* V., 118 f.
53 Aesch. *Ag.*, 750
54 Pl. *Rep.*, 379a–380c
55 Herod. VII, 134–7
56 Soph. *OC.*, 1224 f. (W. B.
Yeats)
57 Solon, *fr.* 1 Diehl, 69–70

58 Herod. VII, 101–4
59 Aesch. *Ag.*, 176–83 (L. Mac-
Neice)
60 Solon, *fr.* 1 Diehl, 29–32 (R.
Lattimore)
61 Aesch. *Ag.*, 737–49 (R. Lattimore)
62 Ibid., 1563–5 (R. Lattimore)
63 Ibid., 1018–21 (R. Lattimore)
64 Aesch. *Cho.*, 66–70, 72–5 (do.)
65 *Il.* XIX, 87
66 Ibid. XXI, 410–14
67 *Od.* XI, 280
68 Heraclit., *fr.* 22 B 94 Diels
69 Aesch. *Ag.*, 459–67 (L. Mac-
Neice)
70 Aesch. *Eum.*, 69–73 (G.
Thomson)
71 Ibid., 160–67 (R. Lattimore)
72 Ibid., 181–90 (R. Lattimore)
73 Ibid., 658–61 (G. Thomson)
74 Ibid., 685–90
75 Soph. *El.*, 110–20 (D. Grene)
76 Ibid., 530–3 (D. Grene)
77 Eur. *Or.*, 316 ff.
78 Ibid., 407 f.
79 Eur. *El.*, 839–43 (E. T. Vermeule)
80 Ibid., 1035–45 (E. T. Vermeule)
81 Ibid., 1105–10 (E. T. Vermeule)
82 Quint. X, i, 98

CHAPTER 6: PROMETHEUS

1 Aesch. *PV.*, 101–13 (R. Warner)
2 Ibid., 327–9 (P. Vellacott)
3 Ibid., 448–68 (R. Warner)
4 Ibid., 511–18 (P. Vellacott)

5 Ibid., 1071–9 (D. Grene)
6 Ibid., 553
7 Ibid. 168–77 (E. Hamilton)
8 Pind. *Isthm.* VIII, 30 f.

9 Apollod. II, v, 4, 11

10 Aesch. *Prom. Unbound, fr.* 199

11 Aesch. *PV*, 511–15

12 Ibid., 194 f.

13 *Ancient Near Eastern Texts* (2nd ed. J. B. Pritchard), 1955, p. 309, i, ii

14 Jer. XII, 1

15 Job X, 5; cf. XIII, 18

16 Eur. *Hipp.*, 1365

17 Aesch. *PV.*, 229–38 (R. Warner)

18 Aesch. *Suppl.* 93–5

19 cf. *Pap. Oxy.*, 2256, *fr.* 9a

20 Pseudo-Ar. *Mag. Mor.* XI, 6

21 Aesch. *PV.*, 771

22 Ibid., 520

23 Prob. *ap.* Virg. *Ecl.* VI, 43

24 *Rep.*, 377 ff., 388c.

25 *Phaedo*, 114d; cf. *Laws*, 682a; *Rep.*, 414, 607a.

26 *Prot.*, 320d-f.

27 Paus. X, 4, 4; Hor. *Carm.* I, xvi, 13 f.

CHAPTER 7: OEDIPUS

1 *Oed. Tyr.*, 1014–65 (E. F. Watling)

2 *Il.* II, 505

3 Callinus *ap.* Paus. IX, 9, 5

4 *Ancient Near Eastern Texts*, p. 119, lines 5–9

5 Ath. X, 456b (J. T. Sheppard)

6 e.g. Paus. VIII, 29, 4

7 Ar. *Poet.*, XXV, 8

8 Ibid. XIII, 3

9 Soph. *Trach.*, 1136

10 Demosth., 1382, *C. Neaer.* LIX, 109; Lycurg. *C. Leocr.*, 146; Antiphon, *Tetral.* II, 8 f.

11 Soph. *Ajax*, 649 (J. Moore)

12 Soph. *Trach.*, 1276 f. (M. Jameson)

13 *Exultet* (Roman Missal)

14 Soph. *Philoct.*, 535–8

15 Soph., *fr.* 1129 Pearson

16 *Oed. Tyr.*, 1522–23

17 Ar. *Poet.* VI, 2

18 *Rep.*, 606b, c

19 *Oed. Tyr.*, 1184 ff.

20 *Oed. Col.* 1565–78 (R. Fitzgerald)

21 Hes. *WD.*, 110–200

22 Job X, 21–2

23 *Oed. Col.* 1656–66 (C. M. Bowra)

24 Ibid., 709–719 (R. Fitzgerald)

CHAPTER 8: ANTIGONE

1 *Antig.* 213–14, 218–20 (E. Wyckoff)

2 Ibid., 354–75 (D. Fitts & R. Fitzgerald)

3 Ibid., 773–7 (E. Wyckoff)

4 Ibid., 872–5 (E. Wyckoff)

5 Ibid., 1017–22, 1029 (E. Wyckoff)

6 Ibid., 1231–6 (E. Wyckoff)
7 Ibid., 141–7 (D. Fitts & R. Fitzgerald)
8 *Oed. Col.*, 1617 f., cf. 529 f.
9 Ibid., 254
10 Ibid., 1769 f., cf. 1405
11 Heraclit., *fr.* 23 B 114 Diels
12 *Antig.*, 745 f.
13 Ibid., 1113 f.

14 Xen. *Mem.* IV, 4, 5–25
15 Thuc. II, 35
16 Ar. *Rhet.* I, x, 3; I, xiii, 1
17 *Antig.* 453–68 (D. Fitts & R. Fitzgerald)
18 Ibid., 909–15
19 Ibid., 61–77 (D. Fitts & R. Fitzgerald)
20 Ibid., 471, 875

CHAPTER 9: HERACLES WHO CONQUERS DEATH

1 Eur. *Alc.*, 122–9 (R. Lattimore)
2 Ibid., 196–8 (R. Lattimore)
3 Ibid., 455–65 (R. Aldington)
4 Ibid., 1146–8 (R. Lattimore)
5 Ibid., 1156–7 (R. Lattimore)
6 Ibid., 280 f. (D. Fitts & R. Fitzgerald)
7 Ibid., 1061–9 (do.)
8 Eur. *El.*, 294–6 (E. T. Vermeule)
9 Eur. *Tro.*, 95–7 (G. Murray)
10 Eur. *Alc.*, 682 f. (D. Fitts & R. Fitzgerald)
11 Aristoph. *Frogs*, 1301 f.
12 Eur. *Hipp.*, 487
13 Eur. *Bacch.*, 200 f. (W. Arrowsmith)
14 Diog. Laert. VIII, 21
15 Xenophanes, *fr.* 10 Diehl (F. L. Lucas)
16 Ibid., *fr.* 13 (F. L. Lucas)
17 *Nem.* VII, 22–4 (C. M. Bowra)
18 *Ol.*, 1, 28–9

19 Herod. VII, 152, 3
20 Ibid. IV, 195, 2
21 Critias, *Sisyphus*, *fr.* 25 Diels, 1–15 (T. A. Sinclair)
22 Eur. *Herc. Fur.*, 1341–6 (F. L. Lucas)
23 Ibid., 1232
24 Eur. *Melanippe*, *fr.* 506 Nauck
25 Eur. *El.*, 743 f.
26 Eur. *Bellerophon*, fr. 288 Nauck (J. A. Symonds)
27 Eur. *Hec.*, 491; cf. *Cycl.*, 606 f.
28 e.g. Eur. *Hipp.*, 197
29 Eur. *Alc.*, 747–60 (R. Lattimore)
30 Ibid., 787–9 (D. Fitts & R. Fitzgerald)
31 *Il.* V, 395 f.
32 Eur. *Alc.*, 840–56 (D. Fitts & R. Fitzgerald)
33 *Isthm.* IV, 61–73 (R. Lattimore)
34 *Ol.* IX, 28–35 (R. Lattimore)

CHAPTER 10: DIONYSUS WHO GIVES ECSTASY

1 Eur. *Bacch.*, 126–147 (W. Arrowsmith)
2 Ibid., 233–41 (W. Arrowsmith)
3 Ibid., 378–85 (W. Arrowsmith)

4 Ibid., 430–2 (W. Arrowsmith)
5 Ibid., 734–70 (W. Arrowsmith)
6 Ibid., 1020–3 (W. Arrowsmith)
7 Ibid., 1122–36 (W. Arrowsmith)
8 Ibid., 1388–92 (W. Arrowsmith)
9 Ibid., 64–169 (W. Arrowsmith)

10 Diehl, *Anth. Lyr.* II, 252 f.,
    cf. Eur. *Bacch.*, 114-19
11 Mark XVI, 18
12 Herod. II, 49, IX, 34
13 Livy XXXIX, 9, 18

CHAPTER 11: THE QUEST FOR THE GOLDEN FLEECE

1 Apol. Rhod. *Argon.* I, 564 ff.
    (E. V. Rieu)
2 Ibid., 946–54 (E. V. Rieu)
3 Ibid., 1018–29 (E. V. Rieu)
4 Ibid., 1011–21 (E. V. Rieu)
5 Ibid. IV, 167–73 (E. V. Rieu)
6 Ibid., 596–616 (E. V. Rieu)
7 Ibid., 672–81 (E. V. Rieu)
8 *Od.* XII, 69–72

9 *Pyth.* IV, 69
10 *Il.* II, 511
11 *Pyth.* IV, 184–7 (H. T. Wade-
    Gery & C. M. Bowra)
12 Str. I, 2, 39; XI, 2, 19
13 Apol. Rhod. *Argon.* III, 967
    (G. Allen)
14 Ov. *Her.* VI, *passim*

CHAPTER 12: THE QUEST FOR A LOST WIFE

1 Virg. *Georg.* IV, 391–414 (C.
    Day Lewis)
2 Ibid., 489–503 (C. Day Lewis)
3 Ibid., 82 f. (C. Day Lewis)
4 Serv. Don. *ap.* Virg. *Georg.* I,
    14
5 Hes. *fr.* 70
6 *Pyth.* IX, 55 f.
7 Apol. Rhod. *Argon.* II, 500 f.
8 *Il.* XVIII, 35 f.
9 cf. *Judges* XIV, 8
10 *Od.* 384 f.
11 Virg. *Georg.* IV, 396
12 Pl. *Symp.*, 179d
13 *II Cor.* XII, 2–3
14 Pl. *Rep.* 364e

15 Virg. *Georg.* IV, 221 (C. Day
    Lewis)
16 Anacr., 44 Diehl (R. Lattimore)
17 Paus. X, 28 ff.
18 Pind. *Ol.* II, 61–72 (R. Latti-
    more)
19 Pind. *fr.* 129 (H. T. Wade-Gery
    & C. M. Bowra)
20 e.g. Aesch. *Ag.*, 1629; Pind.
    Pyth. IV, 176
21 Simon., *fr.* 27 Diehl II (J.
    Sterling)
22 *Phaedr.*, 245a
23 Ar. *Poet.* XXIV, 8
24 Ibid., 9, 3
25 Ov. *Met.* X, XI, XV

CHAPTER NOTES

CHAPTER 13: THE QUEST FOR A NEW HOME

1 Virg. *Aen.* II, 355 f. (R. Humphries)
2 Ibid. IV, 169 (R. Humphries)
3 Ibid. IV, 393 f. (R. Humphries)
4 Ibid. VI, 126–48 (R. Humphries)
5 Ibid. VI, 271 f. (W. F. Jackson Knight)
6 Ibid. VI, 295–314 (R. Humphries)
7 Ibid. VIII, 347–58 (R. Humphries)
8 Ibid. X, 501–9 (C. Day Lewis)
9 Ibid. XI, 843–9 (C. Day Lewis)
10 Ibid. IV, 447 f. (C. Day Lewis)
11 Ibid. XII, 1–9 (R. Humphries)
12 Ibid. XII, 926–44 (R. Humphries)
13 Hes. *Theog.*, 1013
14 Virg. *Aen.* VI, 791 f. (R. Humphries)
15 Str. V, 244
16 Heraclit., *fr.* 22 B 92 Diels
17 Virg. *Aen.* VI, 136 ff. (R. Humphries)
18 Ibid., 205
19 Plin. *NH.* XIII, 29
20 Virg. *Aen.* VI, 777 f. (R. Humphries)
21 Od. XIX, 562–9 (F. Fletcher)
22 Virg. *Aen.* VI, 893–6; for *insomnia* cf. *Aen.* IV, 9
23 Cic. *Rep.* VI, 26, 29
24 *I Kings* III, 1–15
25 Cleanth. *Hymn to Zeus, Collectanea Alexandrina, No. 1,* 4–13, J. V. Powell (M. Balkwill)
26 Virg. *Georg.* IV, 221–4 (C. Day Lewis)
27 Varro *ap.* Aug. *Civ.* IV, 31
28 Virg. *Aen.* VIII, 549
29 Ov. *Fast.* II, 641–2

CHAPTER 14: THE QUEST FOR A ROMAN PAST

1 Livy I, 1 f.
2 Ibid., 6 f. (A. de Selincourt)
3 Ibid., 9 f. (A. de Selincourt)
4 Ibid., 11 f. (A. de Selincourt)
5 *Exodus* II, 3
6 Dion. Hal. I, 79
7 Dio Cass. XLVIII, 43, LIV, 29
8 Vitruv. II, 1
9 Livy I, 13
10 Ibid. VII, 6
11 *BMC. Emp.* I, p. 6, No. 29
12 Caes. *BG.* VI, 17
13 Livy I, 48 f.; II, 8–11
14 Ibid., 54 f. (A. de Selincourt)
15 Cic. *Rep.* II, 30, 52
16 Livy I, 34
17 Tac. *Ann.* IV, 65
18 Livy I, 8
19 Ibid. I, 39
20 *ILS*, 212
21 Livy II, 1
22 *Diegeseis*, ed. Norsa-Vitelli, V, 26 f.
23 Livy II, 9
24 Polyb., VI, 55

CHAPTER 15: OVID

1 Ov. *Met.*, XV, 177 f.
2 Ov. *Ars Am.* III, 3
3 *Met.* IV, 55 f.
4 Ibid., 88 f. (A. E. Watts)
5 *Met.* III, 341 f.
6 Ibid., 407 f. (G. Highet)
7 Plot. *Enn.* I, vi, 8
8 *Met.* VIII, 183 f.; *Ars Am.* II, 21 f.
9 *Met.* VIII, 132 f., IX, 736 f.; *Ars Am.* I, 289 f.
10 *Met.* VIII, 152 f. (A. E. Watts)
11 Herod. II, 148
12 *Met.* VIII, 172 f.; *Ars Am.* I, 525 f; cf. *Her.* X.
13 Plut. *Thes.*, 19
14 *Met.* X, 560 f.
15 Ibid., 674 f. (A. E. Watts)
16 Ibid. VIII, 414
17 Theocr. III, 40–2
18 *Met.* IV, 610 f.
19 Ibid. IV, 724 f. (A. E. Watts)
20 Hes. *Theog.*, 270, *Scut.*, 216
21 Jos. *BJ.* III, 9, 2
22 *Met.* I, 318 f.
23 Ibid., 322 f. (A. E. Watts)
24 *Ol.* IX, 41–6
25 *Met.* VIII, 618 f.
26 Ibid., 637 f. (L. P. Wilkinson)
27 *Acts* XIV, 7 f.

CHAPTER 16: THE INVISIBLE LOVER

1 Apul. *Met.* V, 3–4 (R. Graves)
2 Ibid. V, 15, 16 (R. Graves)
3 Ibid. V, 27 (R. Graves)
4 Ibid. VI, 13 (R. Graves)
5 Ibid. VI, 18, 19 (R. Graves)
6 Eur. *Iph. Aul.*, 548 f.
7 *Il.*, XIX, 91 f.
8 *Rep.*, 514a
9 e.g. *Gal.* IV, 22–6
10 Apul. *Met.* VI, 8, 9
11 Ibid. V, 30
12 Ibid. VI, 24
13 Aug. *Civ. Dei* VIII, 12
14 Euseb. *Praepar. Evang.*

CHAPTER 17: HE DIED FOR LOVE

1 Mus. *Hero and Leander*, 263–73 (F. L. Lucas)
2 Ibid., 332–40 (M. Balkwill)
3 *Georg.* III, 258–63
4 Ov. *Her.* XVIII, 77–80 (L. P. Wilkinson)
5 Ibid. XIX, 161–4; cf. *Am.* II, xvi, 31–2
6 *Anth. Pal.* VII, 666 (F. L. Lucas)

INDEX